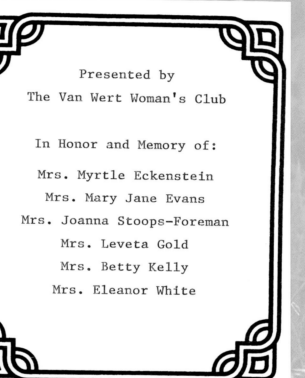

THE ILLUSTRATED ENCYCLOPEDIA OF
WILD FLOWERS
AND FLORA OF THE
AMERICAS

THE ILLUSTRATED ENCYCLOPEDIA OF
WILD FLOWERS
AND FLORA OF THE
AMERICAS

An authoritative guide to more than 750 wild flowers
of the USA, Canada, Central and South America,
beautifully illustrated with 1750 specially commissioned
watercolours, photographs and maps

MARTIN WALTERS & MICK LAVELLE

LORENZ BOOKS

This edition is published by Lorenz Books

Lorenz Books is an imprint of Anness Publishing Ltd
Hermes House, 88–89 Blackfriars Road, London SE1 8HA
tel. 020 7401 2077; fax 020 7633 9499
www.lorenzbooks.com; www.annesspublishing.com

If you like the images in this book and would like to investigate using them for
publishing, promotions or advertising, please visit our website
www.practicalpictures.com for more information.

© Anness Publishing Ltd 2007

UK agent: The Manning Partnership Ltd; tel. 01225 478444; fax 01225 478440;
sales@manning-partnership.co.uk

UK distributor: Grantham Book Services Ltd;
tel. 01476 541080; fax 01476 541061; orders@gbs.tbs-ltd.co.uk

North American agent/distributor: National Book Network; tel. 301 459 3366;
fax 301 429 5746; www.nbnbooks.com

Australian agent/distributor: Pan Macmillan Australia; tel. 1300 135 113;
fax 1300 135 103; customer.service@macmillan.com.au

New Zealand agent/distributor: David Bateman Ltd; tel. (09) 415 7664; fax (09) 415 8892

ETHICAL TRADING POLICY
Because of our ongoing ecological investment programme, you, as our customer, can
have the pleasure and reassurance of knowing that a tree is being cultivated on your
behalf to naturally replace the materials used to make the book you are holding. For
further information about this scheme, go to www.annesspublishing.com/trees

A CIP catalogue record for this book is available from the
British Library.

Publisher: Joanna Lorenz
Editorial Director: Helen Sudell
Editor: Rosie Gordon
Designer: Nigel Partridge
Production Controller: Lee Sargent
Illustrators: Mike Atkinson, Peter Barrett, Penny Brown, Martine Collings,
    Stuart Jackson-Carter, Paul Jones, Fiona Osbaldstone, Mike Saunders.
Photographers: Peter Anderson and Jerry Sires

ACKNOWLEDGEMENTS
The publishers would like to thank the following people and picture libraries for
permission to use their images: Alamy: 77, 148, 158, 168; Ardea: 26 br, 27tc;
DW Stock Picture Library: 150, 239; Garden Matters: 238, 174; OSF: 152; Photos
Horticultural: 26 bl, 72, 115, 101, 149, 176, 182; Jennifer Anderson @ USDA-NRCS
PLANTS Database: 6, 62; Antandrus: 38; Robert H. Mohlenbrock @ USDA-NRCS
PLANTS Database / USDA SCS: 23; Gary A Monroe @ National Plants Database:
160, 164; Ken Thomas: 39; Amadej Trnkoczy: 27, 60, 68, 112, 118, 149.

Previously published as part of a larger volume, *The Illustrated Encyclopedia of Wild
Flowers and Flora of the Americas.*

Page 1 Water lily, *Nymphaea.*
Page 2 Bachelor's button, *Centaurea cyanus.*
Page 3 Rocky Mountain iris, *Iris missouriensis;* Sulphur flower, *Erigonum umbellatum;*
    Mixed wild flowers in Wind River Mountains.
Page 4 Left: Yucca, *Yucca glauca.* Right: Plains prickly pear cactus, *Opuntia polyacantha.*
Page 5 Top: Whitestem sunflower, *Wyethia scabra.* Below top: Blue flax, *Linum lewisii.*
Centre: Yellow goatsbeard, *Tragopogon dubius.* Below centre: Skyrocket, *Ipomopsis
aggregata.* Bottom: Dame's violet, *Hesperis matronalis.*

NOTE
Please note that the maps in this book mark the areas where plants of a particular
species have usually been found. However, many species may be present in lesser
numbers outside of these areas.

CONTENTS

WHAT IS A WILD FLOWER?

The question of what a wild flower is seems to be controversial. Purists argue that they must be native to an area, and conservationists often condemn introduced species, despite them essentially "growing wild".

Flowers are generally considered to be "wild" if they grow without someone having planned where they should be planted. We think of wild flowers as growing in their natural state, with no interference from us, but if we consider the wild species that spring up in gardens, backyards, streets and fields the picture becomes more complex. These plants are indeed wild but thrive in habitats created by humans. In fact, despite every attempt to interfere with their growth, they may well continue to plague farmers, gardeners and city maintenance teams.

Wild flowers are plant species that are at home in a particular place, whether their habitat is natural or the result of human intervention. In any location, from high mountain pastures to great forests, some plants will prosper and others do less well. Each pretty wild flower is the result of countless generations of plants that have striven to exist against staggering odds to ensure that their evolutionary "line" will survive into the future. Some flowers have become highly adapted in order to grow in these places. They may be

Above: Traditional prairies are home to many showy species of wild flower, such as the Blue Flag Iris (Iris versicolor).

dependent not only upon their surroundings but upon other plants, for example by providing shelter from weather, or a stem to scramble through; and even dependent upon animals for their survival, for example, to help spread seed or promote root growth by grazing. Many strange and wonderful plant species have been shaped by their homes, their weather and other local inhabitants into the perfect form for the survival of the species.

It is the showiest flowers that we tend to spend most time looking at; we walk past myriad delicate wild flowers to gaze at one large bloom. Every time we walk across a grassy patch we may carelessly crush hundreds of flowering plants underfoot. They are

Left: Plants of deciduous woodland, like these Dutchman's Breeches (Dicentra cucullaria), flower and set seed before the leaf canopy hides the light in summer.

Above: Shady banks and overgrown roadsides often boast a rich variety of species that have disappeared from the surrounding area.

everywhere, and many deserve a closer look. A detailed inspection of even the most common wayside flower reveals an intricacy and beauty that the work of human hands can rarely approach. Wild flowers are among nature's loveliest gifts: carefree and simple, abundant and serendipitous, they provide an ever-changing panorama of colours, shapes, sizes and textures. It is precisely the informal spontaneity of wild flowers – the random mingling of colours and species, and the way that they change through the seasons – that delights us.

The natural floral jewellery that adorns so much of the Earth's surface has enraptured scientists, artists and writers throughout our history, yet it is easy to forget the true depth of this bounty. Its richness is what this book is all about. All flowering plants – even the tiniest ones – deserve our attention, and to understand them fully we must look both closely and carefully. Describing the wonders of just one flower could fill a whole book; to attempt to include here all the flowering plants in the Americas would be impossible. This book aims to present a selection: it could be

described as a "look through the keyhole" at a continent more beautiful than can easily be comprehended. Many plants have had to be omitted and perhaps some of your own favourites are missing. Hopefully, however, you will be inspired to go out and take a fresh look at wild flowers, perhaps travelling to regions you have never visited before, and marvel at the remarkable range and beauty of the plants growing all over the Americas.

Below: Even mown or grazed turf may harbour an abundance of small yet colourful wild flower species.

HOW FLOWERS LIVE

Flowering plants are the most diverse and widely studied group in the plant kingdom. They are found all across the Earth's surface, wherever plants have learned to live. From mountain tops and the high Arctic to lush tropical forests, flowers are a familiar feature of every landscape. This wide range of habitats has led to flowers assuming a huge diversity of form. In some cases, the flowers have become so reduced as to be insignificant when compared to the plant as a whole. In others, however, the plant itself may hardly be noticed until it produces a huge flower that seems to arrive from nowhere.

Flowers have even driven the process of evolution, harnessing an army of helpers that include almost every conceivable form of land- or air-living creature to help with each phase of their reproductive cycle. Many of the showiest flower types trade rich, nutritious, sugary nectar in return for the services of the "diner" in cross-fertilization. Flowers are the courtship vessels of plants and are often highly adapted to receive the attention of just a few creatures, some of which are adapted to exploit only their food source. Others use a variety of tricks and even entrapments to fulfil this need, and yet others have abandoned the need for animals, preferring the wind or water to do the job.

Once the seed is fertilized, the relationship of many species with animals does not end. There are a whole range of ingenious methods by which they recruit animals into spreading their seed for them, and by doing this they not only guarantee the survival of future generations but also spread the offspring far and wide from the parent plants.

Left: A scene in Wyoming. Wild flowers adorn all the habitats of the Americas. Their vivid colours are designed to attract pollinators, but have also long attracted the human eye.

HOW PLANTS ARE CLASSIFIED

In an attempt to understand the world, humans have become fascinated with the classification of every aspect of it. While such classifications are useful to us, they do not naturally occur in nature and are, at best, approximations of the true nature of diversity.

Classification helps us to recognize millions of individual species of plants. In pre-literate times plant recognition was a practical necessity, since eating the wrong plants could be fatal.

The earliest written record of a system of plant classification can be attributed to Theophrastus (*c*.372–287BC), a student of Plato and Aristotle, to whom even Alexander the Great sent plant material that he encountered on his expeditions. In his *Enquiry into Plants* and *On the Causes of Plants*, Theophrastus included the classification of species into trees, shrubs, subshrubs and herbs, listing about 500 different plants; he also made a distinction between flowering and non-flowering plants.

The binomial system

The shift toward modern systems of classification began at the time of the Renaissance in Europe (1300–1600). Improvements in navigation, which opened up the world and enabled plants to be collected from much further afield, coincided with the invention of the printing press, which meant information about the new

discoveries could be published widely. Interest in plants increased enormously, and by the 17th century the number of known species was becoming too high to manage without a classification system. The British naturalist John Ray is credited with revising the concept of naming and describing organisms. However, most were classified using a whole string of words that resembled a sentence rather than a name. During the 18th century, the Swedish botanist Carl von Linné (1707–78), who published his work under the Latinized form of his name, Carolus Linnaeus, created a referable system of nomenclature that became the foundation of the system used today. He is often cited as the "father" of modern taxonomy, or hierarchical classification.

Linnaeus chose to use Latin, then the international language of learned scholars, which enabled scientists speaking and writing different native languages to communicate clearly. His system is now known as binomial

Below: Primula vulgaris, *the primrose, gets its genus name* Primula *from the Latin* primus *referring to its early appearance in spring.*

Above: The rose has been highly bred, and many of the types now in cultivation bear little resemblance to wild types. The genus name Rosa *is the original Latin name for the plant.*

nomenclature (from *bi* meaning "two", *nomen* meaning "name" and *calatus* meaning "called"). Each species is given a generic name – something like a surname – and a specific name, the equivalent of a personal or first name. We still use this system, which has been standardized over the years, for naming and classifying organisms.

The generic (genus) name comes first, and always starts with a capital letter. It is followed by the specific (species) name, which is always in lower case. This combination of genus and species gives a name that is unique to a particular organism. For example, although there are many types of rose in the genus *Rosa*, there is only one called *R. palustris* – commonly known as the swamp rose. (These names are usually italicized in print.)

The names of plants sometimes change. Name changes usually indicate reclassification of plant species, often as a result of advances in molecular biology. For example, the

Chrysanthemum genus has recently been split into eight different genera, including *Dendranthemum*, *Tanacetum* and *Leucanthemum*. It may take the botanical literature years to reflect such changes, and in the meantime inconsistencies in the printed names of plants can appear.

Plant families

Another useful way of classifying plants is by family. Many families are distinctive in terms of their growth characteristics and preferences, while others are very large and diverse, including numerous different genera. There are 380 families of flowering plants, containing all the species known to science that have already been classified. The largest family is the Asteraceae (daisy family), which contains more than 1,500 genera and 22,000 species; these are a common sight in most habitats. In contrast, some plant families are very small: an example is the Cephalotaceae, or saxifrage family, which contains 35 genera and about 660 species. In the Americas, these prefer temperate areas.

As our understanding increases, and more species are discovered and classified, there is sure to be intense debate over the placement of new and existing species within families.

Below: Geranium (shown here) is often confused with the closely related genus Pelargonium *due to Linnaeus mistakenly classifying both as* Geranium *in 1753.*

Above: Ferns and mosses represent an ancient lineage of plants that do not produce flowers or seed and as such, are classified as lower plants.

Below: Salad burnet (Sanguisorba minor) is a small herbaceous plant in Rosaceae, yet at first glance it does not appear even remotely similar to the woody genus Rosa.

THE ORIGIN OF SPECIES

The earliest flowering plants appeared on Earth around 350 million years ago in the ancient carboniferous forests, although they really began their "takeover" of the planet 120 million years ago, when the dinosaurs roamed the world.

The first flowers were probably quite insignificant by current standards, but their appearance, coupled with their ability to produce a protective fruit around the seed, marked the beginning of a new era. Despite their rather low key entrance in the early Cretaceous period, by the time the dinosaurs met their end some 55 million years later, most of the major flowering plant groups had already appeared.

Two distinct ways of life emerged for flowering plants. Some continued to reproduce as they had always done – letting the wind control whether pollen from one flower met another flower of the same type. Others worked in harmony with insects and other animals, which they enticed with sweet nectar and large, colourful flowers. The relationship was very successful and led to the almost infinite variety of forms and colours that we see around us in plants today.

Below: 500 million years ago non-vascular plants such as hornworts, liverworts, lichens, and mosses grew on Earth.

The first living things

The Earth is around 4.5 billion years old, and life is estimated to have begun around 3.75 billion years ago: for around 750 million years the Earth was (as far as we know) lifeless. It was a hostile environment, with a surface hot enough to boil water and an atmosphere that would have been poisonous to us, yet life is likely to have begun as soon as the surface was cool enough for water to lie on its surface. It was not life as we know it – more a thick soup of chemicals than the miracle of creation – but it was life. This was the situation for 500 million years, until a strange twist of fate assured the rise of the plants.

Primitive single-celled bacteria, which we now know as cyanobacteria, evolved from the existing life forms. They probably appeared remarkably similar to their counterparts, but with one spectacular difference. These cells

Below: 425 million years ago seedless vascular plants such as club mosses, early ferns and horsetails became evident.

were able to take carbon dioxide (which was then very abundant in the Earth's atmosphere) and water and convert them into sugar (an energy-rich food) and oxygen. The effect would have been barely noticeable at first, but over a period of a few hundred million years it changed the atmosphere from one rich in carbon dioxide to one that was at one point almost one-third oxygen. Over this time many of the formerly dominant species died out, but the plant-like bacteria gained the ascendance.

Despite this, plants remained water-bound for another 2.5 billion years. It was not until 425–500 million years ago (the date is still hotly contested) that they made their first tentative appearance on land. The earliest forms were very simple in comparison to modern plants, but their descendants still exist and probably look similar in many respects – mosses and liverworts

Below: 200 million years ago seeded vascular plants such as the gymnosperms, seed ferns, conifers, cycads and ginkgoes thrived.

are the best examples. The first advance that we know of was marked by the appearance of a plant called *Cooksonia*, 430 million years ago. Within 70 million years, species had diversified and evolved to form lush tropical forests; despite being relatively new to the land, plants had made up for lost time in spectacular style.

The fossil record

Evidence of early plants has been found in the fossil record. As mud and other sediments were deposited, forming rocks, pieces of living organisms were deposited with them. Surviving as fossils, these give us an extraordinary picture of what the Earth was like at any one time. In addition, the chemistry of the atmosphere and hydrosphere (the oceans, rivers, lakes and clouds) of the time can be determined by analysis of the rock. These signs allow us to piece together the story and understand how plants have changed over time.

Darwin's theory of evolution

In 1859, the British naturalist Charles Darwin published *On the Origin of Species*. The work caused a stir at the

Below: 120 million years ago recognizable species of seeded vascular plants, such as magnolias and water lilies evolved.

time as it opposed conventional Church doctrine. Darwin argued that the Earth had been created not tens of thousands of years ago (as the Church claimed) but billions of years ago. The idea was seen as revolutionary or even heretical, but in fact it reflected a growing school of thought that recognized that animal and plant species could change over time. Darwin's grandfather had written on the topic, and Darwin himself acknowledged 20 predecessors who had added to the subject. His original contribution, however, was to sift through this increasing body of evidence and combine it with his own observations during his travels around the world from 1831 to 1836.

Darwin determined that single species, through environmental influence, were able to change over time to suit their surroundings. These changes happened not within the lifetime of an individual organism but through the inheritance of characteristics that were valuable in aiding survival and competing with other organisms for the essentials of life. Though he did not then understand the mechanism by which this happened, Darwin concluded that all modern species have evolved through the process of natural

Above: Though it is a modern species, this Magnolia *flower is very similar to the earliest flower forms of 120 million years ago.*

selection, or "survival of the fittest". The theory revolutionized the study of biology and his work remains a cornerstone of evolutionary science.

Since Darwin's time, the body of evidence for his theory has grown. There is still much that we do not know, but many evolutionary scientists believe that there are more species on the planet today than at any time in its entire history. We now mostly understand how changes are passed on to offspring and have been able to piece together an evolutionary hierarchy, where we can see when plants first appeared and how they have changed over time.

Below: Today there are more species of flowering plants in the world than there have been at any other time.

THE PARTS OF A PLANT

While plants have undergone many individual changes over millions of years, most of them still have features in common. Flowering plants generally possess roots, stems, leaves and, of course, flowers, all of which may be useful in identifying them.

Learning to recognize species is essentially a question of simple observation combined with knowledge of plant structure. This is because all modern flowering plants have evolved from a common ancestry – just as most mammals, birds and reptiles possess one head, four limbs, up to five toes per leg and sometimes a tail, because they are all variants of a prior design.

Even when plants have become highly specialized, the common features still persist, albeit in a modified form, and this often betrays a relationship between species that appear unrelated.

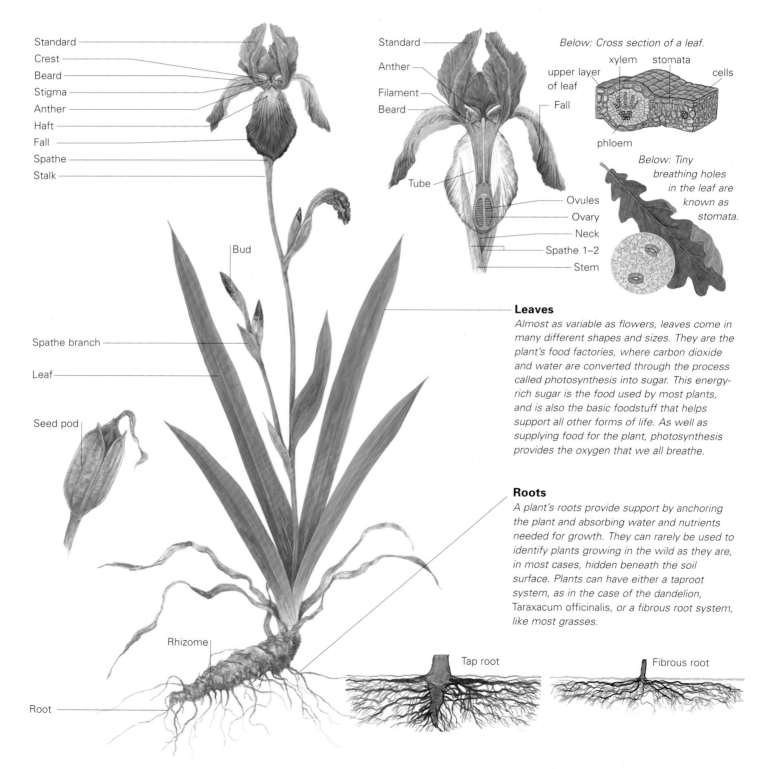

Standard
Crest
Beard
Stigma
Anther
Haft
Fall
Spathe
Stalk

Standard
Anther
Filament
Beard
Fall
Tube
Ovules
Ovary
Neck
Spathe 1–2
Stem

Below: Cross section of a leaf.

upper layer of leaf — xylem — stomata — cells — phloem

Below: Tiny breathing holes in the leaf are known as stomata.

Bud
Spathe branch
Leaf
Seed pod
Rhizome
Root

Leaves

Almost as variable as flowers, leaves come in many different shapes and sizes. They are the plant's food factories, where carbon dioxide and water are converted through the process called photosynthesis into sugar. This energy-rich sugar is the food used by most plants, and is also the basic foodstuff that helps support all other forms of life. As well as supplying food for the plant, photosynthesis provides the oxygen that we all breathe.

Roots

A plant's roots provide support by anchoring the plant and absorbing water and nutrients needed for growth. They can rarely be used to identify plants growing in the wild as they are, in most cases, hidden beneath the soil surface. Plants can have either a taproot system, as in the case of the dandelion, Taraxacum officinalis, or a fibrous root system, like most grasses.

Tap root
Fibrous root

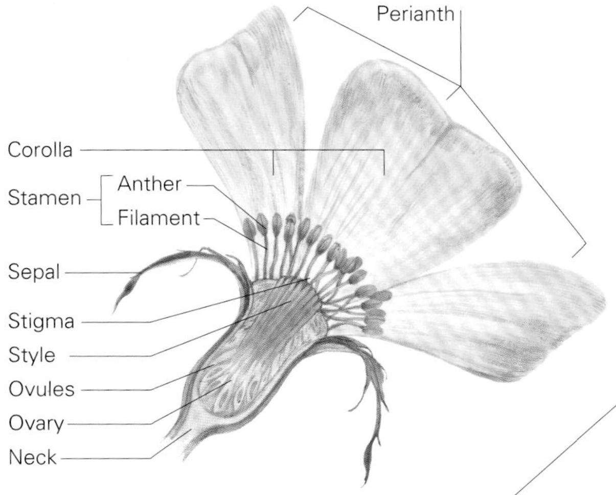

Perianth

Corolla

Stamen — Anther
          — Filament

Sepal

Stigma

Style

Ovules

Ovary

Neck

Petal

Pedicel
(flower stalk)

Leaf

Vein

Lamina
(leaf blade)

Midrib

Seedpod

Flowers

There are many flower types, differing in size, shape and colour, and flowers are possibly the most important part of a plant for identification. However, most flowers have the same basic parts. The arrangement of the female part (the pistil) and the male part (the stamen) is important in determining which family and genus the plant belongs to. Petals are also important in identification. Many plants have brightly coloured petals to attract pollinators, such as bees and butterflies. Behind the petals are smaller, green, leaf-like parts called sepals. These protect the flower when it is in the bud. In some species the petals are very small and insignificant, and the flowers are accentuated by showy, coloured modified leaves called bracts.

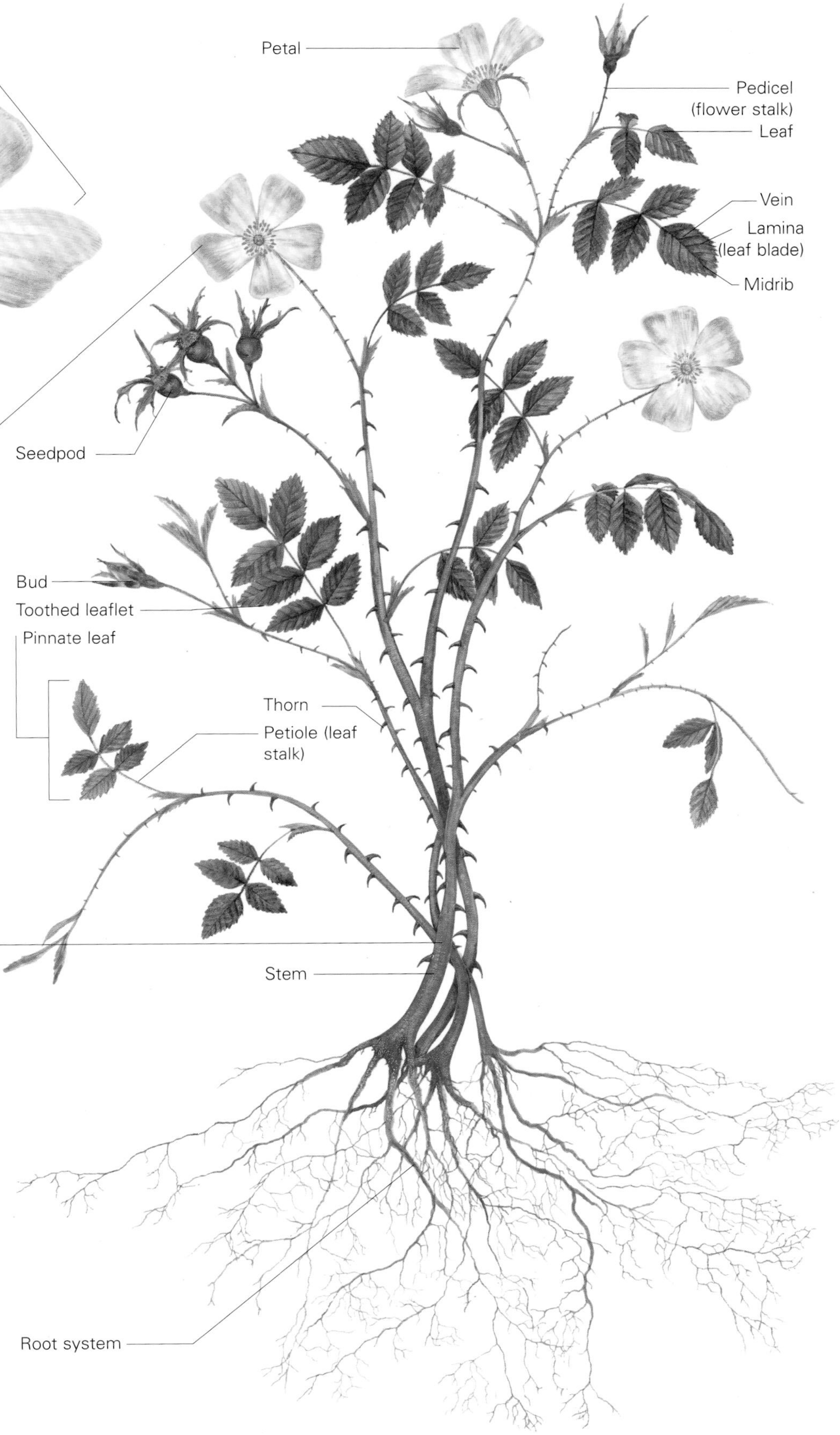

Bud

Toothed leaflet

Pinnate leaf

Thorn

Petiole (leaf
stalk)

Stems

Plant stems carry the water and nutrients taken up by the roots to the leaves; the food produced by the leaves then moves along the stems to other parts of the plant. Stems also provide support, allowing the leaves to reach the sunlight they need to produce food. Stems may be very distinctively shaped and are frequently helpful in identifying plants.

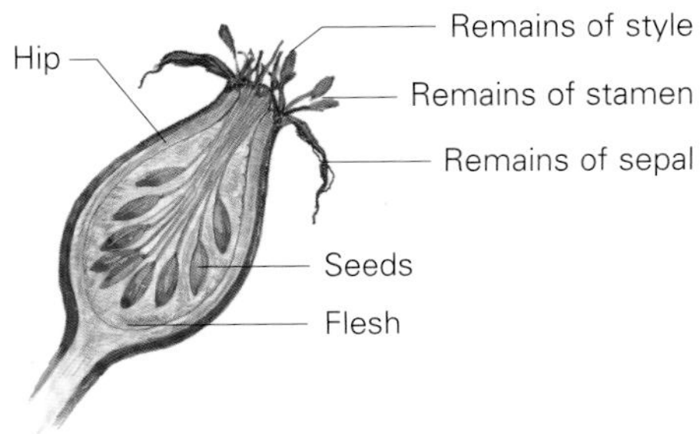

Stem

Hip

Remains of style

Remains of stamen

Remains of sepal

Seeds

Flesh

Root system

LEAF FORMS AND SHAPES

While leaves vary considerably in appearance, all are basically similar in terms of their internal anatomy. Leaves are the factories within which plants produce their own food, although in some plants, they have become highly adapted and may fulfil a variety of other roles.

Leaves are able to breathe: air passes freely in and out through specialized pores known as stomata, which are usually found on the lower leaf surface, or epidermis. The stomata can be opened and closed by the plant to regulate water evaporation. This is crucial as it allows the plant to cool down, preventing damage through overheating, though the leaves of some plants (those in dry climates) have few stomata in order to conserve water. Leaves also contain vascular tissue, which is responsible for transporting water to the leaves and food from the leaf to other parts of the plant. Veins are easily visible on both the surface and the underside of most leaves. The same types of tissue are present in the plant's stems and collectively they form a link from root tip to leaf tip.

Leaf fall
When leaves have finished their useful life the plant sheds them. Deciduous trees and shrubs shed all their leaves annually and enter a dormant phase, usually in the autumn in temperate areas or immediately preceding a dry season in warmer climates, to avoid seasonal stresses such as cold or excessive heat damage. Herbaceous plants (also known as herbs) and other

Above: Cacti live in very harsh dry conditions and have leaves that are reduced to small spiny pads.

non-woody plants normally lose all of their top growth, including the leaves, for similar reasons. Many plants of the arctic, temperate and dry regions fall into this category.

Plants that do not shed all their leaves at once are said to be evergreen. These plants ride out harsh conditions but may also enter a dormant phase where no new growth commences until conditions improve. Evergreen plants also shed leaves, but tend to do so all through the year, particularly during active growth periods. Many tropical plants fit into this category.

Leaf modifications
Leaves are arguably the most highly modified of all plant organs, and show a vast diversity of form and function. Flower petals are thought to have arisen from leaves. The adaptations in leaves often reflect ways in which plants have changed in order to cope

with specific environmental factors in their natural habitats.

Cactus spines are an example of an extreme leaf modification. The spines are part of a modified leaf called an areole. They are in fact modified leaf hairs, and the small furry base of the spine, or spine cluster, is all that remains of the leaf itself. Cacti and some other succulents have altered so that the stem is the main site of food production, and the leaves have adopted a defensive role.

Other leaf modifications include the development of tendrils to help plants climb, coloured bracts around flowers to attract potential pollinators, and even traps that attract and ensnare insects to supplement the plant's mineral requirements.

Leaf shape
Leaves grow in a tremendous variety of sizes and shapes, which are useful in helping to identify the plant:

• Leaf margins, or edges, occur in a variety of forms. The simplest is a smooth, continuous line, which is described as "entire". Often, however, the edge is broken up in a definite pattern, such as "serrated" or "lobed".
• The apex, or leaf tip, may vary in shape, even between closely related species. This may reflect environmental factors. The base of the leaf is also variable and is considered along with the way the leaf is attached to the stem.
• Venation may form an identifiable trait. Monocotyledonous plants have parallel veins that run the length of the leaf. Dicotyledonous plants have a netted arrangement that is complex.
• Leaves can be categorized as simple or compound. A simple leaf is one single leaf blade on a stalk. Compound leaves are made up of a group of leaflets, with a single stalk, attaching the group to the stem.

Leaf arrangements
How leaves are attached or arranged on a stem can be a useful tool in plant identification.

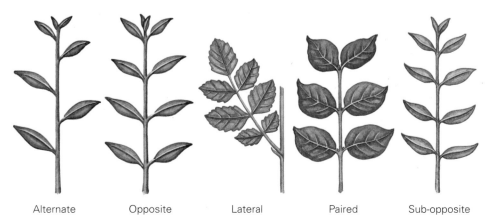

Alternate   Opposite   Lateral   Paired   Sub-opposite

Leaf shapes

Leaves are almost as varied as flowers in respect of their shapes, although they offer less of a clue as to the relationships *between even quite closely related species. Similar shapes, sizes and colours of leaf may occur on quite unrelated species and it is* *thought that this is mainly due to the original environmental circumstances that a plant evolved within.*

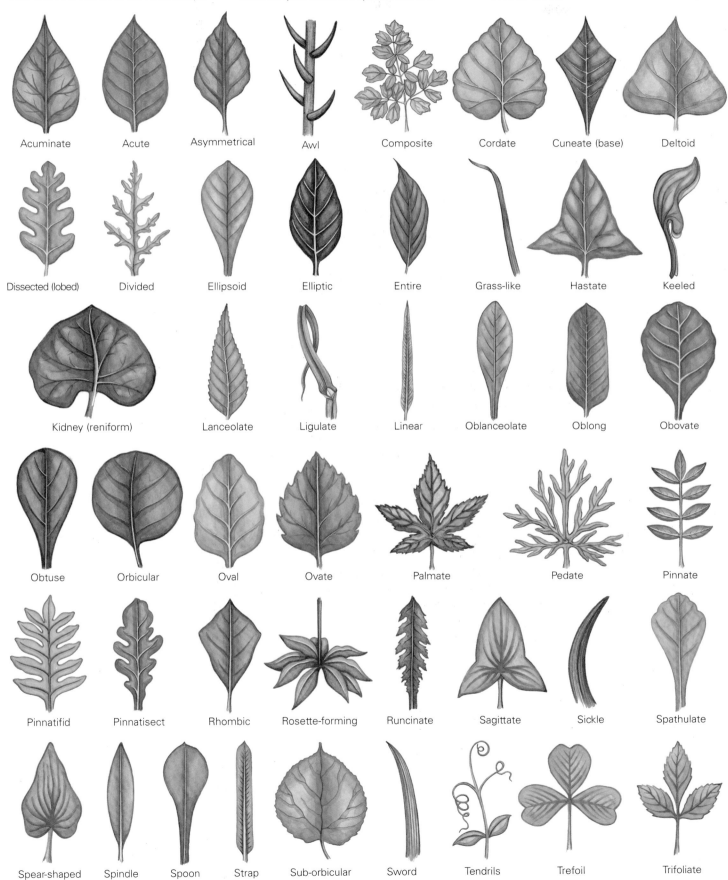

Acuminate   Acute   Asymmetrical   Awl   Composite   Cordate   Cuneate (base)   Deltoid

Dissected (lobed)   Divided   Ellipsoid   Elliptic   Entire   Grass-like   Hastate   Keeled

Kidney (reniform)   Lanceolate   Ligulate   Linear   Oblanceolate   Oblong   Obovate

Obtuse   Orbicular   Oval   Ovate   Palmate   Pedate   Pinnate

Pinnatifid   Pinnatisect   Rhombic   Rosette-forming   Runcinate   Sagittate   Sickle   Spathulate

Spear-shaped   Spindle   Spoon   Strap   Sub-orbicular   Sword   Tendrils   Trefoil   Trifoliate

FLOWERS AND FLOWER FORMS

A flower is the reproductive organ of plants classified as angiosperms – plants that flower and form fruits containing seeds. The function of a flower is to produce seeds through sexual reproduction. The seeds produce the next generation and are the means by which the species is able to spread.

It is generally thought that a flower is the product of a modified stem, with the petals being modified leaves. The flower stem, called a pedicel, bears on its end the part of the flower called the receptacle. The various other parts are arranged in whorls on the receptacle: four main whorls make up a flower.

• The outermost whorl, located nearest the base of the receptacle where it joins the pedicel, is the calyx. This is made up of sepals (modified leaves that typically enclose the closed flower bud), which are usually green but may appear very like petals in some flowers, such as narcissus.

• The next whorl is the corolla – more commonly known as the petals. These are usually thin, soft and coloured, and are used to attract pollinators such as insects.

• The androecium (from the Greek *andros* and *oikia*, meaning "man's house") contains the male flower parts, consisting of one or two whorls of stamens. Each stamen consists of a filament topped by an anther, where pollen is produced.

• The last and innermost whorl is the gynoecium (from the Greek *gynaikos*

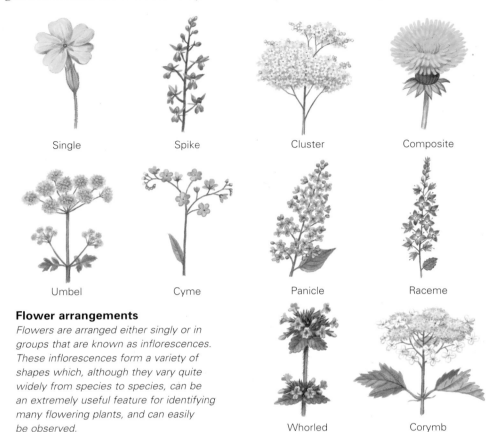

Single   Spike   Cluster   Composite

Umbel   Cyme   Panicle   Raceme

Whorled   Corymb

Flower arrangements

Flowers are arranged either singly or in groups that are known as inflorescences. These inflorescences form a variety of shapes which, although they vary quite widely from species to species, can be an extremely useful feature for identifying many flowering plants, and can easily be observed.

and *oikia*, meaning "woman's house"), which consists of a pistil with one or more carpels. The carpel is the female reproductive organ, containing an ovary with ovules. The sticky tip of the pistil – the stigma – is where pollen must be deposited in order to fertilize the seed. The stalk that supports this is known as the style.

This floral structure is considered typical, though many plant species show a wide variety of modifications from it. However, despite the differences between genera, most flowers are simply variations on a theme and a basic knowledge of their arrangement is all you really need to get started with their identification.

Flower shapes

Flowers display a wide variety of shapes that may be in the form of individual flowers or the close arrangement into a flower-like compound inflorescence.

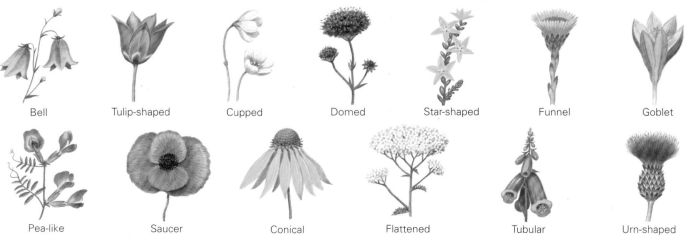

Bell   Tulip-shaped   Cupped   Domed   Star-shaped   Funnel   Goblet

Pea-like   Saucer   Conical   Flattened   Tubular   Urn-shaped

Monoecious and dioecious plants

In most species, the individual flowers have both a pistil and several stamens, and are described by botanists as "perfect" (bisexual or hermaphrodite). In some species, however, the flowers are "imperfect" (unisexual) and possess either male or female parts only. If each individual plant has either only male or only female flowers, the species is described as dioecious (from the Greek *di* and *oikia*, meaning "two houses"). If unisexual male and female flowers both appear on the same plant, the species is described as monoecious (from the Greek *mono* and *oikia*, meaning "one house").

Attracting pollinators

Many flowers have evolved specifically to attract animals that will pollinate them and aid seed formation. These commonly have nectaries – specialized glands that produce sugary nectar – in order to attract such animals. As many

Different growing habits

Plants exhibit a variety of growing habits, often reflecting the type of habitat or niche they have specifically evolved to occupy. These are often important features to note when identifying a plant as the flowers may not be present all year round. The growing habits shown below cover all of the flowers that are featured in this directory.

Above: Flowers that attract bees and other insects will often have a wide surface for landing and copious amounts of nectar.

pollinators have colour vision, brightly coloured flowers have evolved to attract them. Flowers may also attract pollinators by scent, which is often attractive to humans – though not always: the flower of the tropical rafflesia, for example, which is pollinated by flies, produces a smell like that of rotting flesh.

There are certain flowers whose form is so breathtaking as to render them almost unnatural to our eyes. Flowering plants such as orchids have developed a stunning array of forms and many have developed intricate relationships with their pollinators. Flowers that are pollinated by the wind have no need to attract animals and therefore tend not to be showy.

Above: Flowers whose petals form a protective cup or tube are especially attractive to butterflies or other insects with long mouthparts.

Types of inflorescence

Some plants bear only one flower per stem, called solitary flowers. Many other plants bear clusters of flowers, which are known as inflorescences. Most inflorescences may be classified into two groups, racemes and cymes.

In a raceme, the individual flowers making up the inflorescence bloom progressively from the bottom of the stem to the top. Racemose inflorescences include arrangements called spike, raceme, corymb, umbel and head. In the cyme group, the top floret opens first and the blooms continue to open downward along the peduncle, or inflorescence stalk. Cymes may be simple or compound.

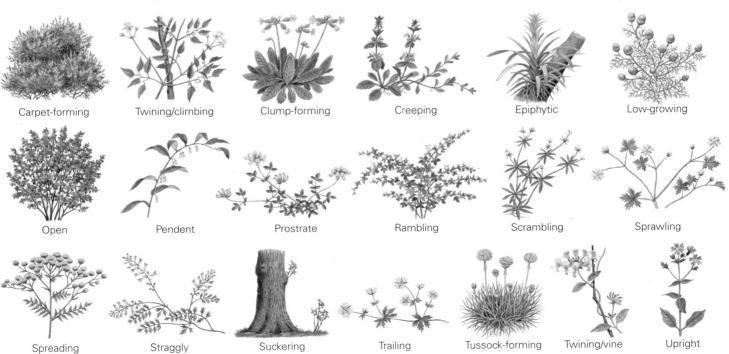

Carpet-forming   Twining/climbing   Clump-forming   Creeping   Epiphytic   Low-growing

Open   Pendent   Prostrate   Rambling   Scrambling   Sprawling

Spreading   Straggly   Suckering   Trailing   Tussock-forming   Twining/vine   Upright

THE LIFE CYCLE OF FLOWERING PLANTS

All flowering plants, from giant forest trees that live for thousands of years to the most ephemeral desert annuals that live for only a few weeks, follow the same pattern of life. Their lifespan, size, apparent durability and survival strategies vary considerably, but they have much in common.

Above: Field poppy, Papaver rhoeas, *is an annual that completes its life cycle in one season.*

Above: Wild carrot, Daucus carota, *is a biennial that grows one year and flowers the next.*

Above: Yellow flag, Iris pseudacorus, *is a perennial that lives and flowers for many years.*

All flowering plants begin life as seeds. These are in essence tiny, baby plants that have been left in a state of suspended animation with enough food to support them in the first few days of their new life. In order to grow, seed must be viable (alive). It is a misconception that seed is not living. It is and, like all living things, has a life-span. However, many types of seed can remain dormant for decades, waiting for the right opportunity to commence their cycle of growth and development.

Eventually, the seed will be triggered into germinating by the right combination of moisture, temperature and a suitable soil or growing medium.

Some seeds have specific needs; *Emmenanthe* and *Romneya* germinate promptly when exposed to smoke, and many berries, such as mistletoe, need to be exposed to the stomach acid of an animal. In most cases, the germinating plant is totally reliant on the energy stored in the seed until it pushes its growing tip above the soil.

The maturing plant

Once above ground the stem grows up toward the light and soon produces leaves that unfold and begin to harvest light energy. As the stems grow upward the plant also extends its roots down into the soil, providing

stability and allowing the plant to harvest both water and minerals that are vital to its growth.

Once the plant reaches its mature phase of growth, changes in its internal chemistry enable it to begin flowering. When this happens depends upon the species, but many plants – except those with the briefest life cycles – continue to grow while they produce flower buds. These buds develop into flowers, which are pollinated by the wind or by pollinators such as bees, moths or other animals.

Once a flower has been pollinated, it will usually fade quickly before turning into fruit, as the fertilized

Yearly life cycle of herbaceous plants

All flowering plants begin life as a seed. Some grow and flower within the first season, while others grow for several years before they flower. Herbaceous plants whether annual or perennial, grow and flower before dying back down at the end of the season.

ovary swells and the new seeds develop. The seeds will continue to develop within the fruit until the embryos are fully mature and the seeds are capable of growing into new plants. This may be very quick in the case of small herbs, but in some shrubs and trees it can take two or more seasons for the seeds to develop fully.

Plants may take just one season to reach flowering stage, or may live for many years before they flower. Once flowering begins, certain species flower repeatedly for many seasons, some lasting decades or even centuries. There is much variability between species, but most plants follow one of three main types of life cycle.

Annuals

Plants that live for a single growing season, or less in some cases, are called annuals. Their life cycle is completed within a year. In this time the plant will grow, flower, set fruit containing seeds, and die. Many common flowering plants adopt this strategy which has the advantage of allowing them to colonize areas quickly and take advantage of the available growing conditions.

Biennials

Plants that need two growing seasons to complete their life cycle are known as biennials. Generally, biennials germinate and grow foliage in the first growing season before resting over the winter. In the second growing season the plant enters a mature phase, in which it flowers, sets fruit and then dies. Like an annual, a biennial flowers only once before dying. A few plants may grow only foliage for several years before finally flowering and dying.

Perennials

All the remaining plant types live for longer: at least three or more years, and they may go on growing, flowering and producing fruit for many years. Some perennial species may take a number of years to grow to flowering size, but all of them are characterized by a more permanent existence than that of annuals and biennials.

Life cycle of a dandelion

Above: The flower begins life as a tight bud that opens from the tip to reveal the yellow petals of the tiny individual flowers.

Above: As the flower opens further, it widens and flattens in order to make a perch for the bumblebees, which are its pollinators.

Above: Once the flower has been pollinated, it closes up again and the plant commences the process of seed production.

Above: Once the seed is ripened, the flower bracts re-open, and the parachute-like seed appendages (achenes) spread to form a globe.

Above: As the ripened seed dries, it is easily dislodged and is carried away from the parent plant by even a light breeze.

Above: Once the seed has been dispersed, the flower stalk is redundant and quickly withers, leaving only the rosette of sepals.

WHAT IS POLLINATION?

Before a flower can develop seeds for reproduction it must be pollinated: pollen must be moved from the male anthers to the female stigma. Some flowers self-pollinate – pollen from their own anthers is deposited on the stigma – but most need some outside help.

Wind moves the pollen for some plants, such as grasses, but others require the assistance of an animal pollinator. These move pollen from the anthers to the stigma of a flower, and also often carry it between different flowers or plants of the same species. Animals that commonly perform this task include butterflies, bees, hummingbirds, moths, some flies, some wasps and nectar-feeding bats.

The benefits of pollination

Plants benefit from pollinators because the movement of pollen allows them to set seed and begin a new generation. For the pollinators this action is an incidental by-product of their efforts to collect nectar and/or pollen from flowers for themselves. In evolutionary terms it is an example of two unrelated species adapting to mutual dependence, where both benefit. Some plants have become so dependent on a particular pollinator that their flowers have adapted to favour them.

Flower forms and pollinators

Wind-pollinated plants often have small, numerous and inconspicuous flowers. They produce huge amounts of pollen, which saturates the air to ensure that some reaches nearby plants.

Below: Pollinators, such as this swallowtail butterfly, feed upon the energy- and protein-rich nectar while pollinating the plant.

Plants pollinated by bees may have fragrant yellow or blue flowers that produce sweet nectar. Some plants are pollinated by beetles. Their flowers are usually white or dull in colour, mostly with yeasty, spicy or fruity odours. Flowers that rely on fly pollination are usually dull red or brown and have foul odours. Butterflies mainly pollinate flowers that are long and tubular – although this can vary – while moths typically pollinate flowers that are yellow or white and fragrant as they visit them at night.

Some plants are pollinated by birds, though they are far fewer than those visited by insects. Plants that attract hummingbirds, for example, have brightly coloured flowers but very little fragrance, since the birds have no sense of smell. All bird-pollinated flowers are similar in structure to those pollinated by butterflies, in that they have a long tubular shape.

Self- and cross-pollination

While it is possible for some individual plants to pollinate their own flowers, this is not ideal. Many plants have developed some factor that promotes cross-pollination between different individuals of the same species.

Dioecious plants (those with separate male and female plants) easily achieve cross-pollination. Self-pollination is simply not possible.

Monoecious plants (those that produce both female and male flower parts on the same plant) avoid self-pollination by having their male or female parts mature at different times. In cases where the male and female structures mature at the same time, the physical separation of the stamens and stigma can help prevent self-pollination. However, self-pollination is the norm in some species and is advantageous in environments where there are few pollinators.

Fertilization

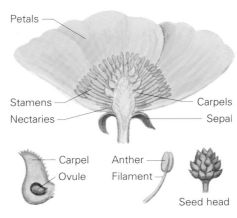

Petals
Stamens
Nectaries
Carpels
Sepal

Carpel
Ovule
Anther
Filament
Seed head

Above: In this buttercup the male flower parts (stamens, each comprised of an anther and a filament) are laden with pollen and surround ovule (egg) containing female parts (carpels).

Above and below: Bees tend to visit flowers whose petals form a wide enough surface for them to land upon. As they take the nectar the bees are dusted with pollen, which brushes on to the flowers they visit next.

Once a pollen grain has landed on the stigma, it must reach the ovaries of the flower in order to fuse with the female cell and begin to form a seed. It does this by germinating and growing a long thin tube that reaches down the style into the flower's ovaries. The pollen tube provides a pathway for the male chromosomes to reach the egg cell in the ovule. One pollen grain fertilizes one egg cell, and together they form the new seed.

SEEDS AND SEED DISPERSAL

For flowering plants, seed production is the main method of reproduction. Seeds have the advantage of providing the plants with a way to spread and grow in new places, which in some cases may be some distance from the parent plant. Their ability to do this is extremely important.

If seeds were not dispersed the result would be many germinating seedlings growing very close to the parent plant, leading to a crowded mass of the same species. Each would be in competition with the others, and with the parent plant, for nutrients, light, space and water. Few of the offspring (or the parent) would prosper.

Seeds are dispersed using a number of strategies. The majority are carried by wind, water or animals, though some plants have adopted the strategy of shooting seeds out explosively.

Wind dispersal

Seeds that depend upon wind dispersal are usually very light. Orchid seeds, for example, are as fine as dust. In addition, composite flowers such as the dandelion, *Taraxacum officinalis*, have hairy appendages on each seed that act like parachutes, carrying the seeds over long distances.

The small size of wind-dispersed seeds is reflected in the amount of food reserves stored in them. Larger seeds contain greater food reserves, allowing the young seedlings more time to grow before they must begin manufacturing their own food. The longer a seedling

Below: In some species such as the opium poppy, Papaver somniferum, *the wind sways the ripe fruits, shaking out the seeds like pepper from a pepper pot. The wind then carries the seeds away from the parent plant.*

has before it must become self-sufficient, the greater its chance of becoming successfully established. However, large seeds are disadvantaged by the fact that they are more difficult to disperse effectively.

Explosions

Some plants have pods that explode when ripe, shooting out the seeds. Many members of the pea family, Papilionaceae, scatter their seeds in this way. Once the seeds are ripe and the pod has dried, it bursts open and the seeds are scattered. In some of these plants, such as common gorse, *Ulex europaeus*, seed dispersal is further enhanced because the seeds possess a waxy cuticle that encourages ants to carry them around, moving them further from the parent plant.

Water dispersal

The fruit and seeds of many aquatic or waterside plants are able to float. Water lily seeds, for example, are easily dispersed to new locations when carried by moving water, and coconuts can travel huge distances across seas and oceans, which is why coconut palms grow on so many Pacific islands.

Below: Jewelweed, Impatiens capensis, *has seedpods that 'explode' when touched, dispersing seeds over several metres. The plant dies after one season, so seed dispersal needs to be efficient.*

Animal dispersal

The production of a nutritious, fleshy fruit that animals like to eat is another strategy that many plants have adopted. An animal eating the fruit digests only the fleshy outer part. The well-protected seeds – the stones or pips in the fruit – pass through the animal's digestive system and are excreted in droppings that provide a rich growing medium. The seeds are often deposited a long way from the parent plant by this means.

Many types of mistletoe have sticky fruits that are attractive to birds. The sticky berries create equally sticky droppings that the bird needs to "rub off" on the branches of trees. The seeds are deposited, with the droppings, on the bark to grow into new plants.

A few plants, such as common burdock, *Arctium pubens*, produce seeds with hooks that catch on the fur of animals and are carried away. The animal eventually removes the burrs through grooming or moulting, and the seeds are then deposited.

Fire

Some plants living in fire-prone areas have evolved traits that allow them to use this to their advantage when reproducing or regenerating. For most of these species, the intensity of the fire is crucial: it must be hot, but not so hot that it cooks the seed. In addition, fires should not occur too frequently, as the plant must have time to mature so that new seed can be produced.

Some fire-tolerant species have cones that open only after a fire. Many plants that grow in the Californian chaparral are reliant on fire. In many cases the heat triggers seed dispersal but it is the chemicals in the smoke that initiate seed germination. Many plants take advantage of the cleared ground after a fire to proliferate.

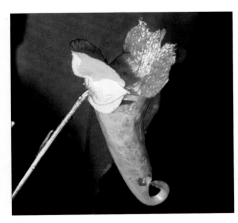

HERBACEOUS PLANTS

Looking at plants in the wild, it quickly becomes apparent that there are two basic types. Those that have permanent woody stems, whose shoots do not die back, are generally referred to as trees and shrubs. The remainder lack permanent stems and are often described as herbaceous plants, or herbs.

Herbaceous plants are those that die down to the ground each year and produce new stems in the following growing season. The word is used in a broader sense, however, to describe any plant with soft, non-woody tissues, whether it is an annual, perennial or bulb. To begin to understand how

Below: Grasslands are an ideal habitat for many herbaceous plants and provide a home for a rich diversity of species.

these plants live and grow, we can examine a seedling. Universally, in seedlings and small plants it is the water content of the cells in the leaves and stems that holds the plants erect. All young plants are similar in this respect. However, as they grow, woody plants begin to build up the strong layers of their characteristic structure. Non-woody plants, on the other hand, always retain soft stems.

Above: The water hyacinth, Eichhornia crassipes, *is a non-woody plant that has become adapted to an aquatic lifestyle.*

Stem structure

Soft stems remain upright because their cells have rigid walls, and water in the cells helps retain their shape. This has the obvious disadvantage that during a dry period water can be drawn out of the cells; the cells become limp and the plant droops or wilts. Many species have stems with a soft inner part – commonly called the pith – that is used to store food. Others, however, have hollow cylindrical stems. In these, the vascular bundles (the veins that transport water, nutrients and sugars around the plant) are arranged near the outside of the stem. This cylindrical formation gives the stem a much greater strength than a solid structure of the same weight.

The relatively short lifespan of non-woody plants (compared with that of many woody plants) and the lack of a strong, rigid structure generally limit the height to which they can grow. Despite this, plants such as the giant hogweed, *Heracleum mantegazzianum*, can easily reach heights of 3–4m/10–13ft; larger than many shrubs. Such giants are rare, however, and most herbaceous plants are no more than 1–2m/3–6½ft in height.

Survival strategies

Non-woody plants usually produce completely new stems each year, because cold or other adverse weather (such as drought) causes the stems to die back to the ground. The climate in which the plant grows greatly affects the survival strategy it adopts. Some species survive periods of cold by forming underground bulbs or tubers for food storage, while others – the annuals – complete their life cycles within one growing season, after which the whole plant dies.

Herbaceous plants are generally divided into those with broad leaves (called forbs) and grass-like plants with very narrow leaves (called graminoids). Some species have become herbaceous vines, which climb on other plants. Epiphytes have gone one step further: they germinate and live their whole life on other plants, never coming in contact with the soil. Many orchids and bromeliads are epiphytes. Other species have adapted to life largely submerged in water, becoming aquatic plants. Many of these are rooted in the sediment at the bottom of the water, but a few have adapted to be completely free floating.

Below: Open woodland and forest clearings are often rich in herbaceous plants that enjoy the shelter and light shady conditions.

Right: Bulbs such as this petticoat daffodil, Narcissus bulbocodium, flower in spring in alpine pasture before dying down to avoid the hot dry summer.

A few species have adapted to use the efforts of other plants to their own ends. Some are semi-parasites – green plants that grow attached to other living, green plants. These unusual plants still photosynthesize but also supplement their nutrients by "stealing" them directly from their unfortunate host plants. A few species, however, are wholly parasitic – totally dependent upon their host for nutrition. They do not possess any chlorophyll and are therefore classed as "non-green" plants. Many remain hidden, either inside the host plant or underground, appearing to the outside world only when they produce flowers.

Subshrubs

Some plants, while they are woody in nature, resemble non-woody plants because of their small size coupled with their ability to shoot strongly from ground level or from below ground. They are known as "subshrubs", a term borrowed from horticulture, where it is used to describe any plant that is treated as a herb in respect of its cultivation. In terms of wild plants it is used occasionally to describe low-growing, woody or herbaceous evergreen perennials whose shoots die back periodically.

Small plants

The world's smallest plant species is water meal, *Wolffia globosa*, a floating aquatic herb which, when mature, is not much larger than the full stop at the end of this sentence. Despite its small size, it is a flowering plant. The flowers occur only rarely and would be hard to see without the aid of a microscope. It mainly reproduces vegetatively and quickly forms a large floating colony on the surface of slow-flowing or still bodies of water.

WOODY PLANTS

Any vascular plant with a perennial woody stem that supports continued growth above ground from year to year is described as a woody plant. A true woody stem is mainly composed of structured cellulose and lignin.

Cellulose is the primary structural component of plants, and lignin is a chemical compound that is an integral part of the cell walls. Most of the tissue in the woody stem is non-living, and although it is capable of transporting water it is simply the remains of cells that have died. This is because most woody plants form new layers of tissue each year over the layer of the preceding year. They thus increase their stem diameter from year to year and, as each new layer forms, the underlying one dies. So big woody plants are merely a thin living skin stretched over a largely lifeless framework of branches. In effect, as a woody plant grows, the proportion of living material compared to the non-living parts steadily decreases.

Bamboos appear to be woody plants, and indeed do have permanent woody stems above the ground, but are more akin to the grasses, to which they are closely related, than to the more common woody species. They grow a dense stand of individual stems

Below: Bamboos are the only examples of the grass family to have evolved permanent stems above ground.

Above: All woody plants can be defined by their permanent, often long-lived growth.

that emerge from underground stems called rhizomes. In many ways the biology of bamboos is more like that of non-woody plants, despite their appearance.

Pros and cons of woody stems

There are more than 80,000 species of trees on earth and a considerably higher number of shrubby species. Although the exact number is not known, it is obvious even to a novice plant spotter that woody plants are an extremely successful group. This is because they are bigger than other plants, so they are able to gather more light and therefore produce more food. In areas where inclement weather induces plants to enter a seasonal dormant period, woody plants have the advantage of a head start when growth restarts. They do not have to compete with other emerging plants and can start producing food from the moment they recommence growth.

Despite their obvious success, however, woody plants have not managed to dominate the entire

land surface. Only the largest trees are fully immune to the effects of large plant-eating mammals, and in some areas, such as the tundra, weather patterns are so extreme that only low-growing woody plants can survive, and they must compete with the surrounding herbage.

Support strategies

As well as trees and large shrubs, there are woody species, many of them flowering plants, that exploit other woody plants around them. Lianas, for instance, germinate on the ground and maintain soil contact, but use another plant for support. Many common climbers or vines are lianas.

The hemi-epiphytes also use other plants for support, at least during part of their life: some species germinate on other plants and then establish soil contact, while others germinate on the ground but later lose contact with the soil. The strangler figs, *Ficus* species, are interesting examples: they begin life as epiphytes,

Below: Woody plants include the largest living plant species, the giant redwood Sequoiadendron giganteum, *among their ranks.*

Above: The permanent stems of woody plants are prone to disease, such as this canker, and older specimens contain much dead wood.

Above: Mistletoe is a shrubby plant that has adapted to be partially parasitic on other, larger woody plants such as trees.

Above: Cacti are highly specialized plants that are descended from woody ancestry and have spiny permanent stems.

growing on other trees, unlike other tree seedlings that have to start their struggle for survival on the forest floor. The young strangler fig grows slowly at first, as little water or food is available to it, but its leathery leaves reduce water loss. It then puts out long, cable-like roots that descend the trunk of the host tree and root into the soil at its foot. Now readily able to absorb nutrients and water, the young fig tree flourishes. The thin roots thicken and interlace tightly around the supporting tree trunk.

Below: The Bristlecone Pine, Pinus longaeva, is one of the oldest plants on earth. The oldest known specimen, known as 'Methuselah', is thought to be 4,838 years old.

The expanding leafy crown of the strangler shades the crown of the support tree and its roots start to strangle its host. The host tree eventually dies and slowly rots away, leaving an independent strangler fig, which may live for hundreds of years.

Other woody plants, such as the mistletoe, "plug" themselves into a branch of a living tree and harvest nutrients directly from it. Apart from a free supply of food and water they gain the added advantage of being high above competing plants and trees, so that they receive enough light to photosynthesize. Mistletoe is a partial parasite that retains its woody stems and green leaves.

The largest plants

The identity of the world's largest plant is debatable, not only because woody plants are only partly living tissue, but also because it has still not been fully researched. In practice, it is extremely difficult to measure how much of a tree is actually living tissue, although the usual candidate is the giant redwood, *Sequoiadendron giganteum*. The banyan tree, *Ficus benghalensi*s, can easily cover an area of 2 hectares/5 acres, and the related *Ficus religiosa* can allegedly cover even more. Whether any of these species are really the largest is a moot point, but it is certain that the title of largest flowering plant will always be held by a woody species.

The oldest plants

Among the oldest plants on Earth are the bristlecone pines, *Pinus longaeva*. Some individuals are known to be more than 4,000 years old and others are estimated to be nearer 5,000 years old. Some creosote plants, *Larrea divaricata* ssp. *tridentata*, are even older. The creosote plant sends up woody stems directly from ground level, so that all the stems in a dense stand are clones of the original plant. An ancient stand in California's Mojave Desert, known as the King's Clone, is estimated to be 11,700 years old, although the individual stems live for much shorter periods.

ECOLOGY AND HABITATS

The study of the ways in which plants, animals and their environment interact with one another is known as ecology. All evolutionary change takes place as a direct response to the ecological pressures that affect the plants and animals in a particular habitat.

Any given habitat will have a number of ecological pressures. Plants may be grazed by animals – or the plant species that thrive may be the result of changes in the wider environment, such as the changing seasons or the effect of flooding.

Interaction

To understand the complexities of even relatively small habitats, three basic principles must be remembered. First, living things do not exist as isolated individuals or groups of individuals. They are part of a continuum of life that stretches across the entire surface of the Earth. Second, all organisms interact with other members of their own species, with other species, and with their physical and chemical environments. Third, all organisms have an effect on each other and their surroundings, and as they interact with both they may actually change them over time: for example, trees gradually modify the soil they grow in by constantly dropping dead leaves that decompose and are incorporated into it.

Below: Plants such as the California poppy, Eschscholzia californica, *are vulnerable to habitat loss.*

Plant groups

The plants within an environment are grouped together in a number of ways.
• A "species" is a natural group that interbreeds, or has the potential to do so, and will not normally interbreed with other related groups.
• A "population" describes all the individuals of a given species in a defined area, such as all the dandelions in an area of grassland.
• A "community" refers to the grouping of all the different populations that occur together in a particular area.
• An "ecosystem" is the community, or series of communities, together with the surrounding environment. It includes the physical and chemical environment, such as the rocks, water and air.

In an ecosystem, all the organisms composing the populations and communities require energy for survival. In the case of the plants, that energy comes from the sun: plants use sunlight for photosynthesis, which converts the light energy into basic sugars, which the plant uses as its food and stores in the form of sugars, starches and other plant material. Any animals in the ecosystem derive their energy from this store, either by eating the plants or by eating other animals that feed on the plants.

Habitats

The location where a particular species is normally found is its "habitat". A single ecosystem may contain many different habitats in which organisms can live. Salt-marsh ecosystems, for example, include areas that are flooded twice daily by tides as well as areas that are inundated only by the highest tides of the month or the year. Different plants inhabit each of these areas, though there may be some overlap, but they are all considered inhabitants of the same ecosystem.

Above: Grazing animals may change or even destroy habitats where densities of animals become too high.

Some plants can thrive and reproduce in different habitats, as long as each provides the appropriate combination of environmental factors. The correct amount of light, water, the necessary temperature range, nutrients, and a substrate on which to grow – sand, clay, peat, water or even another plant – must be within the range of the plants' tolerance. Even a common plant will disappear from a habitat if an essential environmental factor shifts beyond its range of tolerance. For example, sun-loving plants, such as the common daisy, *Bellis perennis*, flourish in full sun but gradually disappear when surrounding trees and shrubs grow large enough to shade the area.

Common plants tend to be those that have adapted to withstand a range of conditions, whereas rare species survive where narrowly defined environmental conditions exist. It is due to their narrow range of tolerance that some plants become rare. Their lack of habitat may be due to gradual changes over thousands of years, such as climate change, that reduce suitable areas. Increasingly, loss of habitat is due to humans altering the landscape and atmosphere.

CONSERVING ENDANGERED SPECIES

Many plant species are now classified as endangered, because their long-term survival is under threat. There are many reasons for this, such as the erosion of a habitat, or the extinction of a key pollinator, and in some cases it is likely that the plant was never particularly numerous.

Extinction is a normal part of evolution, and without it there would be no room for new species, but scientists are becoming increasingly concerned that the rates of extinction are far above the rate at which species can easily be replaced. Attempts are now being made to prevent further loss of the world's rare plants.

Collecting wild plants

Though it may be tempting to pick wild plants, it is worth asking yourself why you want to do this. While it is true that some collections are undertaken as part of scientific research, some plants have been overpicked to the extent that they have become endangered. In the USA, for instance, the fairy slipper orchid, *Calypso bulbosa,* and violet wood sorrel, *Oxalis violacea,* have been so admired by enthusiasts and collectors that they have declined to a dangerous level. The impact of collecting one plant may seem insignificant, but the small actions of many collectors can lead to plant extinction.

Introduced alien plants

Many plants have become endangered because of competition from a new arrival. When plants are taken from their native environments and introduced elsewhere, they can often become highly invasive, ultimately displacing the native plants. There are numerous instances worldwide of whole native plant communities being threatened by introduced plant species.

Climate change

It is likely that climate change will have a considerable impact on most or all ecosystems in the 21st century, and that changing weather patterns will alter the natural distribution ranges of many species or communities. If no physical barriers exist, it may be possible for species or communities to migrate. Habitats such as forest or grassland, for instance, may move to higher latitudes or higher altitudes if average temperatures increase. There is nothing new about this: at the end of the last Ice Age (12,000–10,000 years ago) many plant communities moved north or south in response to the rapid global warming that followed.

In most cases, the real threats to habitats arise where natural or artificial barriers prevent or limit the normal movement of species or communities. Many national parks, nature reserves and protected areas are surrounded by urban or agricultural landscapes, which inhibit the migration of species.

Protected areas

In the Americas, as throughout the world, there are conservation areas to protect animals, plants and other natural and cultural features. Only conservation *in situ* allows the natural processes of evolution to operate on whole plant and animal communities. It permits every link in the web of life, including invertebrates, soil microbes and mycorrhiza (fungi associated with

Below: Over-collection of the large-flowered trillium, Trillium grandiflorum, *has resulted in it being endangered in some American states.*

plant roots), to function and interact fully within the ecosystem and is essential to allow the continued development of resistance to fungal and other diseases.

Plant collections

Living collections of rare and endangered plants are a necessary inclusion in many botanic gardens. Their role is often indirect in relation to conservation; they serve to inform visitors of the danger of extinction that faces many species. However, the expertise developed in growing these plants can be useful when growing stocks for reintroduction to the wild and may improve our understanding of the needs of threatened plant species.

Seed banks ensure that plants that are threatened with extinction can be preserved. The seed is gathered by licensed collectors and, after treatment, is stored at sub-zero temperatures. The seed bank works out the best method to grow the seed so that, if the wild plants vanish, the species can be successfully reintroduced.

Reintroduction of wild plants

When plants have become rare, endangered or even extinct, it is occasionally possible to reintroduce them to former habitats. This is rarely a simple matter, however. Its success depends on the removal of whatever pressure made the plant rare in the first place.

The café marron, *Ramosmania rodriguesii,* was thought to have been extinct for 40 years in Rodrigues in the Indian Ocean. However, in 1980 a student unearthed a small shrub half-eaten by goats. His teacher, who was keen on finding interesting plants, identified it as the café marron. Recent work has resulted in its producing seed for the first time, and it may yet be reintroduced to the wild.

WILD FLOWER HABITATS

Flowering plants live on every continent and can be found from the ocean shores to the mountains. They are the most successful group of plants on earth, but there are very few that can boast the ability to live anywhere. Even the most widespread species have their limits and, ultimately, their preferred habitats.

Wetlands

All plants need water to live, but many species are likely to suffer and die if they get too much. If there is excessive water in the soil it forces the air out, ultimately suffocating the roots. Some plants, however, are specially adapted to living in wetlands.

Wetland plants grow in seasonally permanently wet conditions. There are many types of wetlands in America, including swamps, bogs, salt marshes, estuaries, flood plains, lakeshores and riversides. Wetlands occasionally support trees: these areas, known as wet woodland or swamp forests, are filled with rare species that tolerate wet, shady conditions.

Wetlands are rich in flowers, demonstrating that where land and water meet a rich habitat usually

results. Until recently huge areas of wetland were being drained and turned into grassland or filled for development. While this continues apace in some places, wetlands are gaining a new stature in the 21st century. Many are now highly valued as natural sponges, in which water is retained on the land surface instead of flowing quickly to the sea, causing erosion and flooding as it goes.

As in all areas, wetland ecology relies upon wildflowers, which provide food for insects, which are food for frogs and birds, and so on.

Woodlands

Forest and woodland are extremely important habitats for many types of flowering plants, not least trees. Tree cover was once the natural vegetation

Below: A woodland and riverside scene showing different plants and habitats. The Americas are full of variation, from Alaskan ice to tropical rainforests, and the continent sustains a huge diversity of flora and fauna.

over much of the Earth's surface and great forests stretched across vast tracts of every continent except Antarctica. Over the last 10,000 years human activity has removed considerable amounts of this natural cover, particularly in Eurasia and South America, and over the last century the trend has become global.

Despite the loss of forest, many areas remain, and these are very important havens for forest-dwelling flowers. Such flowers need to cope with low light levels for much (or even all) of the year, and have often adapted by completing their life cycle when the trees are leafless and light can penetrate. Trees provide a rich growing medium, through their decomposing fallen leaves, and may also provide homes for flowering climbers and epiphytes (plants that grow on other plants, but are not parasites).

Above: Flora can survive in many seemingly inhospitable places, such as this Nutall's Larkspur on an arid plain.

Exposed habitats

Where tree cover is not the dominant vegetation – whether due to human intervention or through natural changes – conditions are much more favourable to those species that need a lot of light. Exposed areas are mainly either grassland or scrubland and many support a truly dazzling array of wild flowers.

In temperate zones, open spaces are among the most diverse wild flower habitats to be encountered. Even open areas that are the result of human intervention, such as traditional hay fields, are capable of supporting many flowering species. These rich habitats have become increasingly rare over the last 100 years, due mainly to agricultural improvement programmes, making those that remain precious.

Life in the extreme

In challenging locations from frozen mountain peaks to the hottest deserts, flowering plants have learned to eke out a living. Habitats of this kind are often referred to as fragile, and while the idea of a fragile desert or mountaintop may seem strange, it is entirely accurate. Extreme survival specialists are finely tuned to make the best of scarce resources. If the conditions change even slightly, plants do not always possess the right adaptations and may face extinction. Alpine plants, for instance, are much beloved by gardeners, but need specialist care, and treatment that mimics, as closely as possible, the conditions they enjoy in the wild, if they are to survive in cultivation.

In arid areas, many plants actually rely on regular fires to recover from the dominance of other plant species and clear the ground, allowing more light for germination. Fire also releases some fixed nitrogen from plants, which then goes back in the soil in the form of nitrate, an essential nutrient for plant growth.

Like certain animals, some plants have adapted to thrive in arid desert land. Cacti have tiny leaves to reduce transpiration, and are able to conserve water. Phreatophytes are plants with roots so long that they can reach beneath the arid desert soils to the water table, and so sustain life.

1 Oak and Hickory
2 Snow on the mountain
3 Blue sage
4 Butterfly milkweed
5 Golden rod
6 Black-eyed Susan and Prairie rose gentian
7 Petunia
8 Phlox
9 Thistle
10 Sunflower
11 Western wheatgrass
12 Bergamot
13 Cottonwood
14 Prairie coneflower
15 Columbine

DESERT HABITAT

Much of the Earth's surface is characterized by land that is dry for much of the year. The plants that live in dry areas are specifically adapted to deal with the harsh extremes of these environments and many have become highly distinctive in appearance.

Desert characteristics

While they occur on every continent, deserts vary greatly in the amount of annual rainfall they receive and their average temperature. In general, evaporation exceeds rainfall. Many deserts, such as the Sonoran in Arizona, California and New Mexico, are hot all year round, but others, such as the Chihuahuan, have cold winters.

Temperature extremes are a characteristic of most deserts. Searing daytime heat gives way to cold nights. Not surprisingly, the diversity of climatic conditions supports a rich array of habitats. Many are ephemeral in nature and often reflect the scarcity and seasonality of available water. Despite their harsh conditions, many deserts have extraordinarily rich floras that in some cases feature high numbers of species that are endemic.

Cacti are the plants that are most strongly associated with arid deserts. They have adapted to thrive, with thick stems that can both store water and contain all the chlorophyll the plants need for growth. The characteristic spikes shade the stem to reduce transpiration. Many species have leaves that last only for a short time, until the succulent stem has developed sufficiently. Other plants have roots that spread over a wide

Above: Woody-stemmed shrubs and plants tend to be more characteristic of desert regions than tender varieties.

area or reach extremely deep, thus increasing the plant's chance of finding sufficient water.

Below: The deserts of the Americas are well known for their cacti, but can host a surprising variety of flowering plants.

1 Saguaro
2 Agave
3 Cholla
4 Prickly pear
5 Threadleaf groundsel
6 Claret cup cactus
7 Lupin
8 Joshua tree
9 Sand verbena
10 *Orotius*
11 Snakeweed
12 Crimson sage
13 Mexican gold poppies
14 Desert lily

CONIFEROUS WOODLAND

Among the most ancient of flowering plants, conifers once dominated the whole of the Earth's surface. In modern times, however, they have become more restricted and broad-leaved flowering plants have now become the dominant group.

Boreal forest

Also known as taiga or northern coniferous forest, boreal forest is located south of tundra and north of temperate deciduous forests or grasslands. Vast tracts of this forest span northern North America. Boreal forests cover around 17 per cent of the Earth's surface. They are characterized by a cold, harsh climate, low rainfall or snowfall and a short growing season. They may be open woodlands with widely spaced trees or dense forests whose floor is in shade. The dominant ground cover is mosses and lichens, with a few specialized flowering plants.

Below: A conifer forest of north-western North America, with many familiar native plants in bloom.

Above: When sunlight penetrates the canopy, wild flowers thrive on the forest floor.

Tropical coniferous forest

Found predominantly in North and Central America, in tropical regions that experience low levels of rain and moderate variability in temperature, these forests feature a thick, closed canopy, which blocks light to the floor and allows little to grow beneath. The ground is covered with fungi and ferns and is usually relatively poor in flowering plants.

Temperate rainforest

In temperate regions, evergreen forests are found in areas with warm summers and cool winters. Conifers dominate some, while others are characterized by broadleaved evergreen trees.

Temperate evergreen forests are common in the coastal areas of regions that have mild winters and heavy rainfall, or in mountain areas. Temperate conifer forests sustain the highest levels of plant material in any land habitat and are notable for trees that often reach massive proportions.

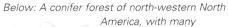

1 Dogwood
2 Fireweed
3 Meadow goldenrod
4 Tiger lily
5 Calypso
6 Bunchberry
7 Yellow fawn lilies
8 Wood nymph
9 Rocky mountain lilies
10 Spring beauty
11 Dwarf waterleaf

HEDGEROW HABITAT

Hedgerow, or fencerow, used to divide up North America's agricultural landscape, but disappeared as fields were enlarged to accommodate modern farming methods. The ecological importance of natural habitats is now recognized, and farmers are being encouraged to reintroduce hedgerows.

A diverse environment

At the heart of an old hedgerow is a dense shrub layer, and at intervals along it trees form a broken canopy. At ground level, a rich layer of herbs grows beneath the hedge and at the field's edge. The older the hedgerow, the greater diversity of animal and plant life it will support. The easiest way to age a hedge is to mark out a 30m/33yd length, then count the number of different species of trees and shrubs it contains. It is reckoned to take about 100 years for each woody plant to establish, so for each woody species add a century to the age of the hedge. In America, many hedgerows date back to the Euro-American settlement in the 1850s.

Hedgerows provide effective "corridors" for wildlife, allowing species to disperse and move from one habitat area to another. While it is difficult for most plants to spread across open fields, they can "travel" along the base of a hedge.

Vanishing hedgerows

The agricultural policies of recent decades have led to concern about the disappearance of hedgerows. Since the 1950s, more than half of America's hedgerows have disappeared. This loss occurs not only when hedges are deliberately removed to make larger fields, but also when they are left to become derelict: if they are not regularly cut and managed, they grow into open lines of bushes and trees.

Pesticide or fertilizer damage can be a particular problem on farmland, where weedkillers have often been applied to hedge bottoms to eliminate weeds. This has proved to be damaging for the natural wild

Above: The reinstatement of hedgerows has many ecological benefits, encouraging a wide diversity of flora and fauna.

flower population of hedgerows. Almost as damaging is fertilizer "drift" (unintentional leakage) into the hedge. Often, the species that will dominate are of very little conservation value.

Below: North American hedgerows can support many flowering plants.

1 Western red cedar	9 Red alder
2 Oregon white oak	10 Ceanothus
3 Vine maple	11 Big leaf maple
4 Blueberry	12 Redcurrant
5 Serviceberry	13 Nootka rose
6 Mountain ash	14 Oregon grape
7 Elderberry	15 Wild strawberry
8 Snowberry	16 White crowned sparrow

BROAD-LEAVED FOREST

Many types of forest can be classified as broad-leaved. The principal types are temperate lowland forests, tropical rainforests and cloud forests, and tropical and sub-tropical dry forests. All of these typically have large, broad-leaved trees as their dominant vegetation.

Temperate deciduous forest

In cool, rainy areas forests are characterized by trees that lose their leaves in the autumn. By shedding its leaves, a tree conserves energy, and once on the forest floor, the leaves decompose and provide a rich soil.

Many low-growing plants that live in these areas take advantage of the period when the trees are bare. During this time the absence of shade allows them to complete their life cycle in a few months while (for them) light levels are highest. The seeds of some species lie in the soil until trees fall, or are felled, before they germinate and grow. These plants may make a showy stand for a few years until the forest canopy closes and shades them out.

Temperate deciduous forests are found around the globe in the middle latitudes: in the Northern Hemisphere they grow in North America, Europe and eastern Asia, and in the Southern Hemisphere there are smaller areas, in South America, southern Africa, Australia and New Zealand. They have four distinct seasons.

Tropical rainforest

Very dense, warm and wet, rainforests are located in the tropics – a wide band around the equator, mostly in the area between the Tropic of Cancer and the Tropic of Capricorn. They grow in South America, West Africa, Australia, southern India and South-east Asia.

A fairly warm, even temperature, coupled with a high level of rainfall, characterizes tropical rainforests. They are dominated by semi-evergreen and evergreen trees. These contribute to the highest levels of species diversity of any terrestrial habitat.

Dry forest

Tropical and subtropical dry forests are found in Central and South America, Africa and Madagascar, India, Indochina, New Caledonia and the Caribbean. Though they occur in climates that are warm all year round and may receive heavy rain for part of the year, they also have long dry seasons that last several months. Deciduous trees are the dominant vegetation in these forests, and during the drought a leafless period occurs, allowing the trees to conserve water. Throughout this time, sunlight is able to reach ground level and plants utilize this period to grow, flower and seed beneath the trees.

Below: Oak and hickory forest in the eastern states of North America forms a patchwork with prairie lands in some areas. Many of the flowers have adapted to the seasonal shade.

1 Blue jay
2 Black cohosh
3 Dutchman's breeches
4 White ash
5 Oak
6 Shagbark hickory
7 Wood poppy
8 Bloodroot
9 American bellflower
10 Butternut hickory

GRASSLAND AND PRAIRIE

Windy and partly dry, grassland generally lacks woody vegetation, and the dominant plant type is, of course, grasses. Almost one quarter of the Earth's land surface is grassland, and in many areas grassland is the major habitat separating forests from deserts.

Temperate grassland

Grasslands, also known as savannah, pampas, campo, plain, steppe, prairie and veldt, can be divided into two types – temperate and tropical. Located north of the Tropic of Cancer and south of the Tropic of Capricorn, temperate grasslands are common. They experience a range of seasonal climatic variations typified by hot summers and cold winters. The combination of open, windy sites and dense stands of grasses mean that the evaporation rate is high, so little of the rain that falls reaches the rich soil.

The extraordinary floral communities of the North American plains have been largely destroyed due to the conversion of these lands to agriculture. In surviving areas of North American tall-grass prairie, as many as 300 different plant species may grow in 1 hectare/2.5 acres. The agricultural

Below: Plants of montane grasslands display characteristic features such as rosette structures and waxy leaf or stem surfaces.

plants that have been replaced are much more susceptible to the droughts or torrential rains that can afflict prairie areas, as they do not have the long roots of the native flora. The root structure of native plants helps to prevent the kind of top-soil erosion that led to the catastrophic "dust bowl" conditions of farmed prairie areas in the 1930s.

Tropical grassland

The annual temperature regime in tropical grassland is quite different to that of temperate grassland: in tropical regions it is hot all year, with wet seasons that bring torrential rains interspersed with drier seasons. Tropical grasslands are located between the Tropic of Cancer and the Tropic of Capricorn and are sometimes collectively called savannas. Many savannas do have scattered trees, and often occur between grassland and forest. They are predominantly located in the dry tropics and the subtropics, often bordering a rainforest. The plant

diversity of these regions is typically lower than that of other tropical habitats and of temperate grassland and prairie.

Montane grassland

At high levels in tropical, subtropical and temperate regions, Montane grasslands are found. The plants often display striking adaptations to cool, wet conditions and intense sunlight, including features such as rosette structures or waxy surfaces on their leaves or stems. In the tropics these habitats are very distinctive: examples are the puna of Bolivia and Peru and paramo of the northern Andes.

Flooded grassland

Large expanses of grassland flooded by either rain or river, usually as part of a seasonal cycle, can support numerous plants adapted to wet conditions. The Florida Everglades, for example, which contain the world's largest rain-fed flooded grassland, are home to some 11,000 species of flowering plants.

1 Iris
2 Feverfew
3 Anemone
4 Yellow asphodel

FIELD HABITATS

Farmland, fields or paddocks are essentially an environment constructed by humans, who have altered the natural landscape for the purposes of agriculture. The general term "pasture" describes grassland, rough grazing land and traditionally-managed hay fields.

Rough pasture

There are two types of pasture: permanent and rough. Permanent pasture is closed in, fertilized and sown with commercial grass species. It is often treated with herbicides that allow only a few species of grass to grow, so that it does not support a wide range of wildlife species. Rough pasture is usually much older and is typically land that is very difficult to plough so is left undisturbed.

Pasturelands owe their existence to farm livestock, and are very sensitive habitats that can easily be over- or undergrazed. They generally contain a single early stage of native vegetation, which is prevented from developing further by grazing; if the animals are removed, shrubs quickly establish and woodland develops soon afterwards. This is because many livestock animals graze very close to the ground and, while this does not damage grasses (which regrow from just above their roots), many taller plants cannot tolerate it. Grazing animals also

Above: California poppies and lupines form colourful swathes in North American pastures.

remove nutrients from the environment so many traditional grassland areas are fairly infertile.

The wild flowers of pasture grow low and so avoid being eaten by animals. They may creep or form low rosettes of leaves and, although small in general, they often have showy flowers that readily attract pollinators.

Below: Many governments are introducing agricultural policy to let areas of farmland "go wild", to conserve wild flowers.

Meadows

A true meadow is a field in which the grasses and other plants are allowed to grow in the summer and are then cut to make hay. The plants are cut while still green and then left in the field to dry. In many countries this has been the traditional method of providing feed for cattle during the winter. Hay fields can support a huge range of wild flowers, some of which have become extremely rare as traditional haymaking has been superseded by modern farming methods.

Crop fields

Many fields are used to grow crops other than grass, such as grains or vegetables. In these situations, weed species often find the conditions to their liking and thrive there. Many of these are annual flowers and some – such as poppies and daisies, introduced from Europe – are colourful additions to the agricultural landscape.

1 Poppy
2 Oxeye daisy
3 Hedge woundwort
4 Buttercup

CHAPARRAL HABITAT

Mediterranean scrubland, or chaparral, is rare; in the Americas it is found only in parts of Chile and, more notably, in southern California, yet it supports an extraordinary diversity of flora. Around 20 per cent of Earth's plant species live in these regions, which are highly prone to wildfire.

Mediterranean scrubland

Regions described as Mediterranean scrubland tend to have hot, dry summers followed by cool, moist winters. These conditions occur in the middle latitudes near continental west coasts: the Chilean matorral, and the chaparral of California, south-central and south-western Australia, the fynbos of southern Africa, and the Mediterranean itself. Most rainfall occurs from late autumn to early spring, and for many plants this is the prime growing and flowering season.

The word "chaparral" is dervied from the Spanish *chaparro*, meaning dwarf oak. Scrub oaks grow densely on chapparal, as do many other drought-hardy species.

Wildfires

Dense, woody scrub and the largely-arid climate make the area highly prone to wildfires. Although often perceived as a terrifying natural phenomenon that can devastate plant and animal habitats, wildfires are an essential part of the area's ecology. Many plants that grow on the chaparral are adapted to the regime of regular fires, and actually depend on this disturbance for their survival. For example, fireweed seeds will lie dormat in the soil until they are released by a deep burn. The ponderosa pine sheds its lower limbs as it matures, thus protecting the tender new growth on its higher branches from the flames.

Californian chaparral can sustain long periods without fire. Some chaparral plants' seeds require a build up of about 30 years' worth of humus before they can germinate, so would die out if fires occurred more frequently.

Above: This area of densely-packed scrub oaks in the Santa Ynez mountains has not had a wildfire since the 1960s. The eventual fire is likely to be fierce, with so much dry wood and scrub to fuel it.

Below: Chaparral can sustain a wide array of flowering plants, despite the arid conditions. Fire helps to prevent the domination of a species (as above) and promotes this great diversity.

1 Blue oak
2 Mahogany
3 Fireweed
4 Fiddleneck
5 Wild onion
6 Needlegrass
7 Saltmarsh bird's beak
8 French broom
9 King protea
10 Fairy duster
11 Pine

MOUNTAINS AND MOORLAND

Collectively, mountains and upland areas make up around 20 per cent of the world's landscape, and about 80 per cent of our fresh water originates in them. Upland heath, or moorland, occurs at altitudes above 300m/1,000ft in most temperate zones but may be found at much higher altitudes in the tropics.

Mountains

All mountain ranges feature rapid changes in altitude, climate, soil, and vegetation over very short distances. The temperature can change from extremely hot to below freezing in a matter of a few hours. Mountain habitats harbour some of the world's most unusual plants, and collectively they are home to a huge range of species. This diversity is due to their range of altitude, which results in distinct belts, or zones, of differing climates, soils and plantlife.

Vegetation on a mountain typically forms belts. This is because as the altitude increases the temperature steadily decreases – by about 2°C per 300m/3.5°F per 1,000ft. This, coupled with the thinning of the atmosphere, leads to unusually high levels of ultraviolet light and means that as plants grow higher on the

mountainside they need special adaptations to survive. Typically, as the altitude increases the plant species become increasingly distinct.

Moorland

The vegetation in moorland regions is similar in character to that of lowland heath, but it grows on deep layers of peaty or other organic soil. Moorland

Left: Mountain vegetation often forms distinct belts according to the altitude. This photograph taken from Mount Mitchel, the highest point in the Appalachian mountains (north-east America), shows a dense cover of pine trees.

characteristically occurs below the alpine belt and (usually) above the tree line. Natural moorlands (those which are largely unmanaged by people) are generally diverse habitats, containing stands of vegetation at different stages of growth. Animal grazing and burning may be the only factors preventing them from developing into scrub or woodland. Moorland, including those small areas of moorland in North America, is typically dominated by a few species – dwarf shrubs, such as heather – over an understorey of small herbs and mosses. At the southernmost tip of South America is the Magellanic subpolar forest ecoregion. There are an abundance of low-lying and cushion plants here that seem able to thrive on poor, rocky soil in unforgiving windy, rainy conditions.

Below: Mountains are often isolated habitats and may contain a unique diversity of species.

1 Fir
2 Bluets
3 Rhododendrons
4 Jack in the pulpit
5 Mountain laurel
6 Oak
7 Maple
8 Serviceberry
9 Jewelweed
10 Solomon's seal
11 Trillium

TUNDRA AND ALPINE HABITATS

In the areas nearest the poles, and in the high mountainous places of the world, the conditions for plant growth become extreme. These cold, often frozen, environments present plants with a real challenge that only the hardiest species can withstand.

Cold places

The predominant habitat in the outer polar regions and on mountaintops is known as tundra. Although arctic and alpine (mountain) tundra display differences, they often support plants with similar adaptations.

Tundra is a cold, treeless area, with very low temperatures, little rain or snow, a short growing season, few nutrients and low species diversity. It is the coldest habitat to support plantlife.

Arctic tundra

The frozen, windy, desert-like plains of the arctic tundra are found in the far north of Greenland, Alaska, Canada, Europe and Russia, and also in some sub-Antarctic islands. The long, dry winters of the polar regions feature months of total darkness and extreme cold, with temperatures dipping as low as -51°C/-60°F. The average annual temperature is -12 to -6°C/10 to 20°F.

The annual precipitation is very low, usually amounting to less than 25cm/10in. Most of this falls as snow during the winter and melts at the start of the brief summer growing season. However, a layer of permafrost (frozen subsoil), usually within 1m/3ft of the surface, means that there is very little drainage, so bogs and ponds dot the surface and provide moisture for plants. The short growing season, when the sun gains enough strength to melt the ice, lasts for only 50–60 days. Ironically, the surface snow that marks the end of the growing season acts as an insulating blanket, ensuring that the plants do not freeze solid in winter.

The tundra supports sedges and heaths as well as dwarf shrubs. Most of these plants are slow-growing and have a creeping habit, forming a low, springy mass. This adaptation helps against the icy winds, and lessens the chances of being grazed on by animals.

Above: Despite their harshness, tundra and alpine regions often support showy species.

Alpine tundra

Above the tree line and below the permanent snow line, alpine tundra is located high in mountains worldwide. In contrast to the arctic tundra, the soil of alpine tundra is very well drained and may become quite dry during the growing season, which lasts for about 180 days. Night time temperatures are usually below freezing.

Below: The tundra's short growing season often results in brief but dazzling displays of colour.

1 Cotton-grass
2 Arctic poppy
3 Arctic forget-me-not
4 Cinquefoil

CLIFFS AND ROCKY SHORES

Rocky coasts and cliffs occur where the underlying rocks are relatively resistant to the constant pounding of the sea, rain and wind. Often the landscape is one of grandeur, characterized by steep cliffs, rocky outcrops and small bays with deep, usually clear, offshore waters.

Coastlines

Rocky coasts are often quite exposed and the constant exposure to salt-laden winds, coupled with a shortage of soil in which plant roots can anchor themselves, reduces the range of plants to a few specialist species.

Cliffs

Coastal cliffs, especially those in exposed locations, are often drenched in salt spray as the sea is driven on to the shore. Plants that grow above the spray line, out of reach of the waves and regular salt spray, are likely to be salt-tolerant, whereas those on the beach at the bottom of a cliff, or in rock crevices that are sometimes washed by salt spray, must be tolerant of salt to survive. Plants rarely grow near the base of cliffs that rise directly from the sea because the waves prevent them from becoming established.

The exposure and lack of soil in all but the deeper rock crevices means that the plants that live on cliffs often face a similar challenge to those found in the higher rocky areas in mountain ranges. This is why they often show similar adaptations, such as deep roots, creeping or hummocky growth habit and the ability to withstand exposure and drought.

The rocky coast may include indentations known as fjords, formed by glaciers wearing away depressions that were subsequently flooded by the rising water following the end of the last Ice Age, 10,000 years ago. These fjords may have salt marshes at their head and may be surrounded by steep-sided wooded slopes, creating a rich and varied habitat.

Below: The high winds of coastal regions mean that plants growing there are often short and ground-hugging.

Above: Many coastal plants, such as sea pink, flower profusely despite their small size.

Rocky shores

Bedrock outcrops and boulders dominate rocky shores. The lower zones of the rocks are flooded and exposed daily by the tides and support only marine plants, whereas the upper zones are flooded during unusually high tides or in strong storms. In spite of being frequently washed by seawater, salt-tolerant land plants survive here by being well rooted in crevices in the lower-lying rocks.

1 Sea lavender
2 Thrift
3 Cornish heath
4 Sea aster

BEACHES AND SAND DUNES

Coastlines are often areas of extreme biological diversity. Areas where one habitat meets another always offer an array of flora and fauna, as animals and plants from both habitats merge. Beaches may seem like the exception where plants are concerned, as they often have limited vegetation.

Beaches

Generally, beaches are made up of sand, gravel, cobbles (shingle) and fragments of seashells, corals or other sea creatures. The proportions of all of these vary from beach to beach. Level areas of sand that are exposed only during low tide are called sandflats. Although an amazing variety of animals thrive in this habitat, very few flowering plants survive, mainly because of wave action and the saltiness of seawater. Those that do grow on them usually occur near the high tide line.

Sand dunes

Usually occurring immediately inland from sandy beaches, sand dunes are found in many parts of the world but are less well developed in tropical and subtropical coastal zones, due to lower wind speeds and damper sand. There

Above: The salty conditions and unstable sandy soil can be challenging for plants.

Above: The showy flowerheads of sea holly, Eryngium maritimum, *are common on dunes.*

are exceptions, however, such as the vast desert dune expanses of the Namib Desert in south-western Africa.

Sand is blown from the beach and initially accumulates in a characteristic steep windward face and more gently sloping leeward face. A change to dune meadow or dune heath eventually happens as grasses establish and stabilize the dune system, usually some

way inland. These dune slacks become dominated by low scrub, which rarely exceeds 90cm/3ft in height and is often much smaller. A few larger shrubby species are also capable of invading sand dunes to form scrub and can ultimately revert to woodland.

Below: Sand dunes are mobile, and may shift by several metres per year.

1 Searocket
2 Sea holly
3 Sea spurge
4 Seashore false bindweed
5 Yellow horned poppy
6 Burnet rose

RIVERSIDES AND WETLANDS

Wetlands are being lost at an alarming rate and many species that live in them are suffering. The habitats along rivers, waterholes and streams are critical landscapes: they help to maintain water quality and the shape and form of streams, as well as supporting species diversity in surrounding habitats.

Riversides

In their upper reaches, rivers are fast flowing with no vegetation in the water, although bankside vegetation is usually present. In the lower reaches, the water is calmer, and floating leaved and semi-aquatic plants can survive.

Riverside habitats are diverse. Grazed riverside pastures, flood meadows, marshes, reedbeds and riverine forest are common features beside many rivers, although the natural richness of the soil in the river flood plain has led people to cultivate and plant crops right to the edge of the

Below: Along the river banks of Central and South America many exotic species are found.

water in many regions. Rivers may also be altered, with their curves straightened and banks raised to create flood defences. All these factors mean that truly natural riverside habitats are scarce in areas of human occupation.

Wetlands

Marshes and flood meadows are low-lying wet areas that often flood on a seasonal basis. Reedbeds occur on land that is flooded for most of the year, often at the edges of lakes or in shallow lagoons, and often support a very diverse range of plants. Fens are areas where peat has been deposited over a long period and are often associated with extensive tracts of

Above: Reedbeds are often home to a rich diversity of plant and animal species.

marshes and reedbeds. They may contain large areas of open water and shallow, slow-flowing rivers, and are found on ground that is permanently, seasonally or just periodically waterlogged.

1 Coral plant
2 Bromeliads
3 Vriesea
4 Flowering tree
5 Vridia
6 Bromeliad
7 Red Passionflower
8 Heliconia
9 Orchid
10 Strelitzia
11 Orchid
12 Rosy orchid

ESTUARIES, SWAMPS AND COASTAL MARSHES

Rivers eventually end by flowing out into the sea. As the river slows, the material that it has carried in the water is deposited, and sedimentary deltas, wetlands, lagoons, salt marshes and swamps may be formed.

Deltas

A delta is formed where a river flows into a calm sea. As the river slows down it drops its sediment, which builds up over years to create a delta. Over time, the river splits into smaller channels called distributaries. Occasionally this can happen inland where a river flows into a low-lying basin. It forms an immense low-lying wetland, such as that of the Mississippi Delta on the Gulf Coast.

Marshes and swamps

Salt marshes are made up of plant communities that are tolerant of being

Above: Saltwater marshes are among the most productive habitats on earth.

Below: Tropical and subtropical marshlands are home to many beautiful plant species.

submerged for short periods by the tide. They can be 'transitional zones', which merge with nearby areas of reed swamp, sand dune, shingle, freshwater wetland or woodland, and are rich in a wide variety of plants. They are often brackish (less salty than the sea but saltier than the river) and may contain a mix of riverside and coastal plants.

The term 'swamp' is usually applied to warm, wet areas that are teeming with both animal and plant life. They are often (but by no means always) heavily forested, with trees that are highly adapted to waterlogged ground. Some of these areas may be very extensive and include both coastal and freshwater habitat, such as are found in the Florida Everglades.

Mangroves are marine tidal forests that are generally most luxuriant around the mouths of large rivers or sheltered bays, growing in both salt and freshwater. They are found mainly in the tropics where annual rainfall is fairly high.

River mouth habitats are usually extremely diverse and may include rare species.

1 Bald cypress
2 Floating hearts
3 Scarlet ladies tresses
4 *Thalia dealbata*
5 Sawgrass
6 Palmetto
7 Water spider orchid
8 Ghost flower orchid
9 Night fragrance orchid
10 Goldenclub
11 Water lettuce

OPEN WATER HABITATS

Flowering plants face possibly their biggest challenge in open water. Plants living in this environment must be able to survive either submerged beneath or floating on the surface of a body of water, and all are specially adapted to allow them to do this.

Lakes and ponds

A lake describes any large body of fresh water, ranging from small ponds to huge bodies of water. It can be an extremely variable habitat, ranging from almost lifeless, acidic mountain tarns to lowland lakes teeming with life. Lakes are closely associated with rivers, chiefly because some lakes are the source for rivers. A pond is a body of water shallow enough to support rooted plants, which, in time, may grow all the way across it.

Lakes and ponds are both fresh water and share similar characteristics, animals and plants.

Below: Although certain plant species have evolved to live in the water, the richest diversity occurs where land and water meet.

Above: Plants need to adapt to thrive in challenging open water habitats.

Slow-flowing rivers and streams

When rivers flow slowly they may support aquatic plants in a similar way to lakes. Plants in slow-flowing rivers will be species that are able to root into the bottom sediment, to stop them being washed away.

As the river runs more slowly it warms up, favouring plant growth, though in areas where the banks are tree-lined this can reduce plant growth in the water. Some river plants are only semi-aquatic, growing out of the water on the bank when the stream dries up, before being re-flooded during rainy seasons.

Obtaining sufficient oxygen is the greatest problem facing plants that live in a watery habitat. The muddy sediment at the water bottom has few air spaces, and therefore hardly any oxygen is available.

1 Great willow herb
2 Flowering rush
3 Branched bur-reed
4 Water crowfoot
5 White water lilies
6 Reed manna grass
7 Yellow flag iris
8 Marsh marigold
9 Water dropwort
10 Marsh thistle
11 Bulrush

HOW TO USE THE DIRECTORIES

The following directories of flowers found in the North-Central and Central-South areas of the Americas includes a diverse selection of the wild flowers that visitors may encounter.

The plant kingdom can be divided into two major groups: flowering plants that produce seeds (known as "higher plants") and those that do not flower, but instead produce spores (sometimes called "lower plants"). The latter group includes the mosses, liverworts, ferns and their allies. Though many of these plants are important components of American habitats, for reasons of space it has not been possible to feature them here. Among the flowering plants, the gymnosperms (conifers and cycads) have also been omitted. The selection made for this

Plant Family
The directory of flowers is mostly arranged according to plant family. Each family shares a group of common characteristics, though visually the plants may seem quite different.

book concentrates on the attractive specimens that are most likely to be encountered in the wild, but also aims to illustrate the vast range of flower forms on this continent.

The plants featured fall into two groups – the dicotyledonous plants are the large group, so-named because their seed has two distinct cotyledons, or embryonic leaves. The second group, the monocotyledons, contains plants that have only one seed leaf. The two groups differ evolutionarily, but both contain stunning examples of wild flower diversity.

How the directories work

The flowers are arranged according to their families, then genus and then species. Examples of major plants are

illustrated to aid identification in the field. The introduction to each family describes some common characteristics, and each main entry discusses the primary characteristics of the plant. Wherever possible, this includes information about the type of habitat that the plant may be found in. Many entries feature interesting facts about the species, as well as a detailed description. Maps show the plant's natural distribution – of course, there is overlap between the species in north, south and central areas, so these geographical groupings are for guidance only. A quick-glance box then describes other species of note within the family.

Any technical terms used in this description are found in the glossary.

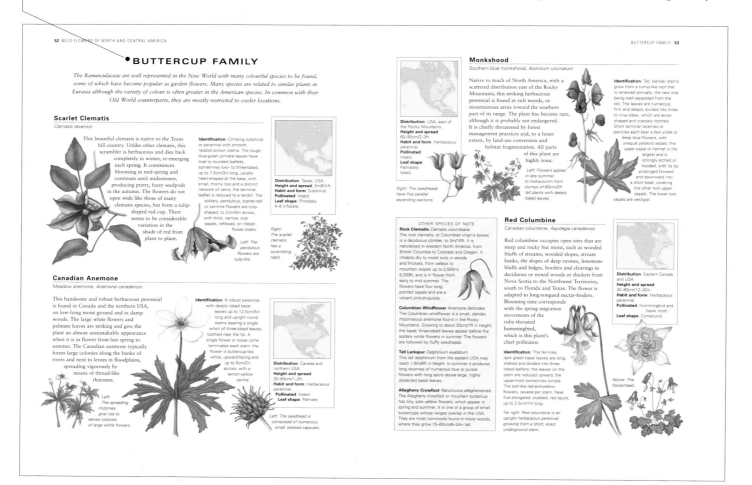

Other Common Name(s)
Some wild flowers have different common names in other regions and countries. These are listed underneath its primary common name.

Common Name
This is the most popular, non-scientific name for the wild flower entry.

Botanical Name
This is the internationally accepted botanical name for the wild flower entry. It is always in Latin.

Introduction
This provides a general introduction to the wild flower and may include information on usage, preferred conditions, and other information of general interest.

Identification
This description will enable the reader to properly identify the wild flower. It gives information on flower and leaf shape, size, colour and arrangement, and type of flower.

Canadian Anemone

Meadow anemone, *Anemone canadensis*

This handsome and robust herbaceous perennial is found in Canada and the northern USA, on low-lying moist ground and in damp woods. The large white flowers and palmate leaves are striking and give the plant an almost unmistakable appearance when it is in flower from late spring to summer. The Canadian anemone typically forms large colonies along the banks of rivers and next to levees in floodplains, spreading vigorously by means of thread-like rhizomes.

Left: The spreading rhizomes give rise to dense colonies of large white flowers.

Identification: A robust perennial, with deeply lobed basal leaves up to 12.5cm/5in long and upright round stems bearing a single whorl of three-lobed leaves, toothed near the tip. A single flower or loose cyme terminates each stem: the flower is buttercup-like, white, upward-facing and up to 5cm/2in across, with a lemon-yellow centre.

Distribution: Canada and northern USA.
Height and spread: 30–60cm/1–2ft.
Habit and form: Herbaceous perennial.
Leaf shape: Palmate.
Pollinated: Insect.

Left: The seedhead is composed of numerous, small, beaked capsules.

Habit
The habit is the way in which a plant grows. For example, it could have an upright, sprawling or rambling habit.

Profile
The profile is a botanically accurate illustration of the plant at its time of flowering.

Plant Detail
A small detail shows an important identifying feature of the plant.

Distribution: Canada and northern USA.
Height and spread: 30–60cm/12–24in.
Habit and form: Herbaceous perennial.
Leaf shape: Palmate.
Pollinated: Insect.

Map
The map shows the area of natural distribution of the featured plant. The relevant area is shaded in yellow. The natural distribution shows where in the world the plant originated. It does not mean that this is the only place where the plant now grows.

Distribution
This describes the plant's natural distribution throughout the world.

Height and spread
Describes the average dimensions the plant will grow to given optimal growing conditions.

Habit and form
Describes the plant type and shape.

Leaf shape
Describes the shape of the leaf.

Pollinated
Flora can be pollinated by many different animals and insects, as well as by the action of air.

Other species of note
The flora featured in this tinted box are usually less well-known species of the family. They are included because they have some outstanding features worthy of note.

Species names
The name by which the plant is most commonly known is presented first, followed by the Latin name and any other common name by which the plant is known.

Entries
The information given for each entry describes the plant's main characteristics and the specific features it has that distinguish it from better known species.

OTHER BUTTERCUP FAMILY SPECIES

Rock Clematis *Clematis columbiana*
The rock clematis, or Columbian virgin's bower, is a deciduous climber, to 3m/10ft. It is naturalized in western North America, from British Columbia to Colorado and Oregon. It inhabits dry to moist soils in woods and thickets, from valleys to mountain slopes up to 2,500m/8,200ft, and is in flower from early to midsummer. The flowers have four long, pointed sepals and are a vibrant pinkish-purple.

Columbian Windflower *Anemone deltoidea*
The Columbian windflower is a small, slender, rhizomatous anemone found in the Rocky Mountains. Growing to about 30cm/1ft in height, the basal, three-lobed leaves appear before the solitary white flowers in summer. The flowers are followed by fluffy seedheads.

Tall Larkspur *Delphinium exaltatum*
This tall delphinium from the eastern USA may reach 1.8m/6ft in height. In summer it produces long racemes of numerous blue or purple flowers with long spurs above large, highly dissected basal leaves.

Allegheny Crowfoot *Ranunculus allegheniensis*
The Allegheny crowfoot or mountain buttercup has tiny, pale yellow flowers, which appear in spring and summer. It is one of a group of small buttercups whose ranges overlap in the USA. They are most commonly found in moist woods, where they grow 15–60cm/6–24in tall.

WILD FLOWERS OF NORTH AND CENTRAL AMERICA

America was called the "New World" by Europeans when they began settling there five centuries ago. The land is anything but new, however, and contains many plants with ancient lineages. North America was attached to Asia until recently, in geological terms, and many of the plants that grow there resemble species found across Eurasia. Throughout North and Central America an abundance of habitats produces a wealth of wild flowers; there is always something in bloom, in the deserts and chaparrals, on the coast, in woodlands, on rocky mountain slopes, in hedgerows or on the prairies. Although many habitats are changing or threatened, conservancy preserves across the region offer an opportunity to see the diversity of American wild flowers, which includes some of the world's rarest, most familiar and most fascinating flora.

Above from left: Dark throat shooting star (Dodecatheon pulchellum); *Indian paintbrush* (Castillega angustifolium)*; Whitestem sunflower* (Wyethia scabra).

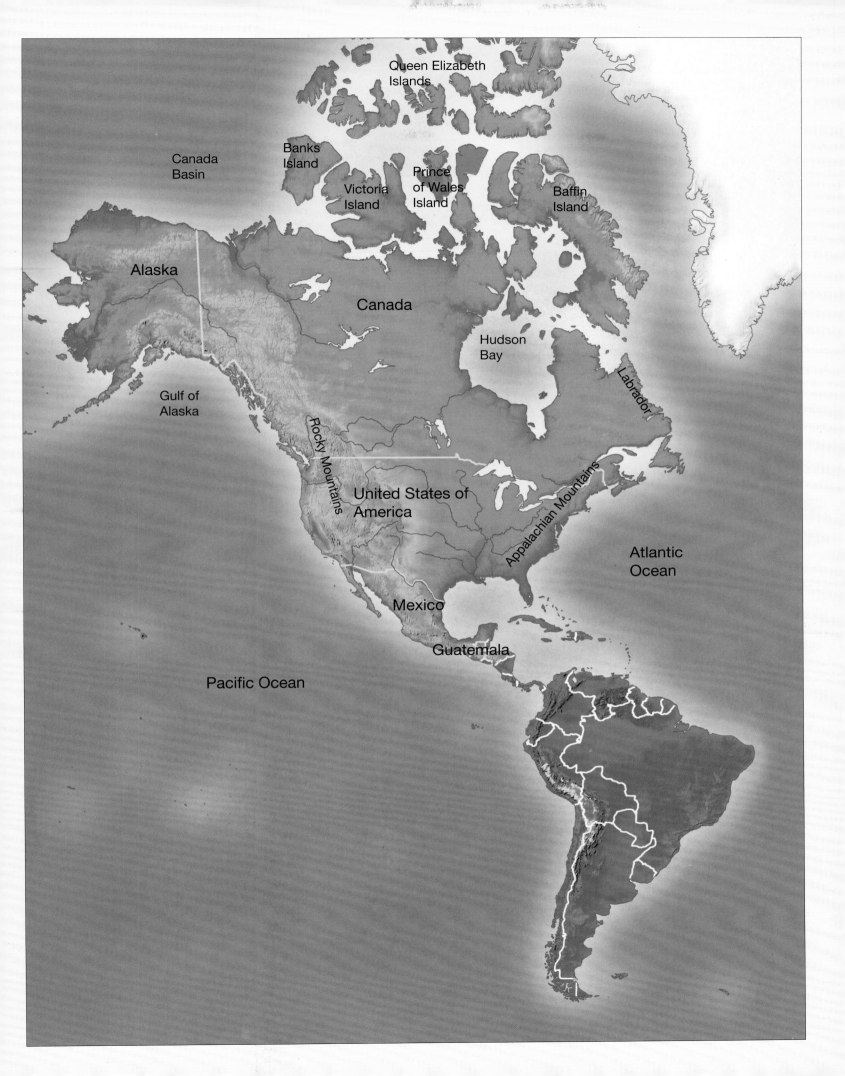

BIRTHWORT AND BARBERRY FAMILIES

The birthwort family (Aristolochiaceae) contains about 500 species of woody vines or herbs, often with heart-shaped leaves and quite large and showy flowers, frequently with a nasty aroma (like rotting flesh) to attract flies for pollination. The barberry family (Berberidaceae) consists of herbs and shrubs, typically with spiny stems, and mostly producing berry fruits. There are some 680 species.

Long-tailed Wild Ginger

Asarum caudatum

The flowers of this unusual plant are not easy to spot, as they grow very close to the ground and are shaded by the leaves. Like many other members of the family, the plant is aromatic. In fact the stems and roots were used in earlier times as a substitute for ginger. There are several other species of wild ginger, found in similar moist, shady habitats.

Left: The distinctive flowers tend to remain hidden beneath the large, heart-shaped leaves.

Identification: This creeping plant grows in moist woodland below about 1500m/5000ft, and produces purplish-brown or greenish-yellow flowers from April to July. The flower is partly hidden under the leaves and is up to 12cm/5in across, and has a bowl-shaped base, a rather slender tip and 12 stamens.

Below: The plant is commonly found in the woodlands of northwest America.

Distribution: British Columbia to northeast Oregon, south to central California.
Height and spread: To 15cm/6in.
Habit and form: Creeper.
Pollinated: Insect.
Leaf shape: Heart-shaped.

Northern Inside-out Flower

Vancouveria hexandra

This species takes its name from the unusual flowers which look as though they are opening the wrong way round, facing back towards their stems. The plant is found in shaded sites in coniferous forests in the Pacific northwest. This and other species in the genus such as Golden Inside-out Flower (*V. chrysantha*), which has yellow flowers, are useful in the garden because they provide good ground cover for shady areas.

Left and right: The plant has attractive flowers and leaves, and a ground-covering habit.

Identification: This flower grows in clusters and patches on the forest floor. The base leaves are pinnate and have a leathery texture. The flowers are most unusual, with the white sepals and petals bending backwards up the stems. The leaves are long and divided into lobes. The flowering period is May to July.

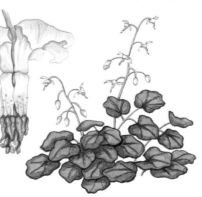

Distribution: Western Washington State to northwest California.
Height and spread: 15–50cm/6–20in.
Habit and form: Grows in patches.
Pollinated: Insect.
Leaf shape: Lobed.

Wild Ginger

Asarum canadense

Distribution: From Manitoba, North Dakota and New Brunswick, south to Florida.
Height and spread: 15–30cm/6–12in.
Habit and form: Low-growing.
Pollinated: Insect.
Leaf shape: Heart-shaped.

Despite its name, this plant is not related to the true gingers, but is so called because the rhizome has a strong spicy smell rather like ginger. Indeed it is edible when cooked and can be used as a flavouring. It grows in woods with a rich soil and flowers in April and May. A similar species, with the lovely name Little Brown Jugs (*A. arifolium*) has green-purple flowers and evergreen, triangular leaves.

Identification: The leaves are large and hairy, usually hiding the green-brown or red-brown flower which grows from between pairs of leaves. The flower is deep and cup-shaped with three sharply pointed lobes, and the fruit is a round capsule up to 30cm/12in across.

Left: The tiny flowers, with their three distinctive pointed lobes, nestle low to the ground beneath large, heart-shaped leaves. The flowers can be hard to spot.

Right: The white stems and fresh green leaves contrast pleasantly. These and the flowers are covered in fine 'hairs'.

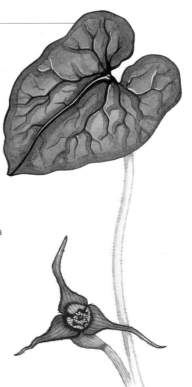

OTHER SPECIES OF NOTE

Common Barberry *Berberis vulgaris*
A spiny shrub, native to Europe, but widely naturalized in North America. It is useful as a protective hedge around fields. The clusters of yellow flowers produce bright red berries which can be turned into drinks and preserves.

Blue Cohosh
Caulophyllum thalictroides
This is a flower of damp woods, found mainly in the eastern states. The flowers are in loose clusters and are purplish-brown or yellow-green. The blue seeds are reported to have been used as a coffee substitute.

Twinleaf *Jeffersonia diphylla*
Each leaf is divided into two halves, hence the common name. The leaves are basal only. The plant loves rich, moist limestone woodland and the white flowers, with eight petals and four sepals appear in April and May. The genus name honours Thomas Jefferson who had an interest in botany.

Mayapple, Mandrake *Podophyllum peltatum*
The flower looks rather like that of an apple and opens in May, hence the common name, and the root resembles that of the (unrelated) true mandrake. The single white flower is fragrant, and the edible fruit is a large yellow, fleshy berry. It grows commonly in oak-hickory forests.

Dutchman's Pipe

Aristolochia macrophylla

The species name means 'large-leaved' and indeed this plant has distinctive big leaves. The common name comes from the shape of the flower, which resembles the old-fashioned tobacco pipes once particularly popular in the Netherlands. The usual habitat is damp woodland with rich soils, and the plant is also found alongside streams. The flowers open from April to June.

Identification: Tall-growing vine with striking brownish-purple S-shaped flowers. Each flower is 5cm/2in long, and the sepals open into three lobes. The long, untoothed leaves are bright green beneath. The fruit is a 10cm/4in long capsule, opening to reveal many winged seeds. The heart-shaped leaves are up to 25cm/10in long.

Above and right: The plant grows as a vine, producing large dark flowers, then a long fruit.

Distribution: From Michigan south to Alabama and Georgia.
Height and spread: To 20m/65in.
Habit and form: Climbing vine.
Pollinated: Insect.
Leaf shape: Heart-shaped.

BUTTERCUP FAMILY

The Ranunculaceae are well represented in the New World with many colourful species to be found, some of which have become popular as garden flowers. Many species are related to similar plants in Eurasia although the variety of colour is often greater in the American species. In common with their Old World counterparts, they are mostly restricted to cooler locations.

Scarlet Clematis

Clematis texensis

This beautiful clematis is native to the Texas hill country. Unlike other clematis, this scrambler is herbaceous and dies back completely in winter, re-emerging each spring. It commences blooming in mid-spring and continues until midsummer, producing pretty, fuzzy seedpods in the autumn. The flowers do not open wide like those of many clematis species, but form a tulip-shaped red cup. There seems to be considerable variation in the shade of red from plant to plant.

Identification: Climbing subshrub or perennial with smooth, reddish-brown stems. The tough, blue-green pinnate leaves have oval to rounded leaflets, sometimes two- to three-lobed, up to 7.5cm/3in long, usually heart-shaped at the base, with small, thorny tips and a distinct network of veins; the terminal leaflet is reduced to a tendril. The solitary, pendulous, scarlet-red or carmine flowers are tulip-shaped, to 2cm/¾in across, with thick, narrow, oval sepals, reflexed, on ribbed flower stalks.

Left: The pendulous flowers are tulip-like.

Distribution: Texas, USA.
Height and spread: 2m/6½ft.
Habit and form: Subshrub.
Pollinated: Insect.
Leaf shape: Pinnately 4–8 trifoliate.

Right: The scarlet clematis has a scrambling habit.

Canadian Anemone

Meadow anemone, *Anemone canadensis*

This handsome and robust herbaceous perennial is found in Canada and the northern USA, on low-lying moist ground and in damp woods. The large white flowers and palmate leaves are striking and give the plant an almost unmistakable appearance when it is in flower from late spring to summer. The Canadian anemone typically forms large colonies along the banks of rivers and next to levees in floodplains, spreading vigorously by means of thread-like rhizomes.

Identification: A robust perennial, with deeply lobed basal leaves up to 12.5cm/5in long and upright round stems bearing a single whorl of three-lobed leaves, toothed near the tip. A single flower or loose cyme terminates each stem: the flower is buttercup-like, white, upward-facing and up to 5cm/2in across, with a lemon-yellow centre.

Distribution: Canada and northern USA.
Height and spread: 30–60cm/1–2ft.
Habit and form: Herbaceous perennial.
Pollinated: Insect.
Leaf shape: Palmate.

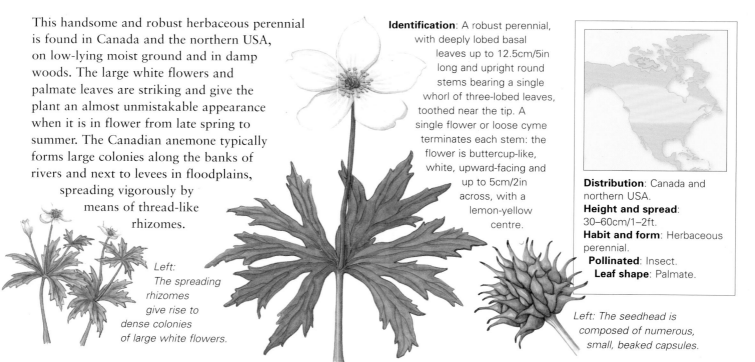

Left: The spreading rhizomes give rise to dense colonies of large white flowers.

Left: The seedhead is composed of numerous, small, beaked capsules.

Monkshood

Southern blue monkshood, *Aconitum uncinatum*

Native to much of North America, with a scattered distribution east of the Rocky Mountains, this striking herbaceous perennial is found in rich woods, or mountainous areas toward the southern part of its range. The plant has become rare, although it is probably not endangered. It is chiefly threatened by forest management practices and, to a lesser extent, by land-use conversion and habitat fragmentation. All parts of this plant are highly toxic.

Distribution: USA, east of the Rocky Mountains.
Height and spread: 60–90cm/2–3ft.
Habit and form: Herbaceous perennial.
Pollinated: Insect.
Leaf shape: Palmately lobed.

Right: The seedheads have five parallel ascending sections.

Left: Flowers appear in late summer to mid-autumn from clumps of 60cm/2ft tall plants with deeply lobed leaves.

Identification: Tall, slender stems grow from a turnip-like root that is renewed annually, the new one being well separated from the old. The leaves are numerous, firm and deeply divided into three to nine lobes, which are lance-shaped and coarsely toothed. Short terminal racemes or panicles each bear a few violet or deep blue flowers, with unequal petaloid sepals: the upper sepal or helmet is the largest and is strongly arched or hooded, with its tip prolonged forward and downward into a short beak, covering the other two upper sepals. The lower two sepals are vestigial.

OTHER SPECIES OF NOTE

Rock Clematis *Clematis columbiana*
The rock clematis, or Columbian virgin's bower, is a deciduous climber, to 3m/10ft. It is naturalized in western North America, from British Columbia to Colorado and Oregon. It inhabits dry to moist soils in woods and thickets, from valleys to mountain slopes up to 2,500m/8,200ft, and is in flower from early to mid summer. The flowers have four long, pointed sepals and are a vibrant pinkish-purple.

Columbian Windflower *Anemone deltoidea*
The Columbian windflower is a small, slender, rhizomatous anemone found in the Rocky Mountains. Growing to about 30cm/1ft in height, the basal, three-lobed leaves appear before the solitary white flowers in summer. The flowers are followed by fluffy seedheads.

Tall Larkspur *Delphinium exaltatum*
This tall delphinium from the eastern USA may reach 1.8m/6ft in height. In summer it produces long racemes of numerous blue or purple flowers with long spurs above large, highly dissected basal leaves.

Allegheny Crowfoot *Ranunculus allegheniensis*
The Allegheny crowfoot or mountain buttercup has tiny, pale yellow flowers, which appear in spring and summer. It is one of a group of small buttercups whose ranges overlap in the USA. They are most commonly found in moist woods, where they grow 15–60cm/6–24in tall.

Red Columbine

Canadian columbine, *Aquilegia canadensis*

Red columbine occupies open sites that are steep and rocky but moist, such as wooded bluffs of streams, wooded slopes, stream banks, the slopes of deep ravines, limestone bluffs and ledges, borders and clearings in deciduous or mixed woods or thickets from Nova Scotia to the Northwest Territories, south to Florida and Texas. The flower is adapted to long-tongued nectar-feeders. Blooming time corresponds with the spring migration movements of the ruby-throated hummingbird, which is this plant's chief pollinator.

Distribution: Eastern Canada and USA.
Height and spread: 30–80cm/12–30in.
Habit and form: Herbaceous perennial.
Pollinated: Hummingbird and hawk moth.
Leaf shape: Compound.

Identification: The fern-like, dark green basal leaves are long, stalked and divided into three lobed leaflets; the leaves on the stem are reduced upward, the uppermost sometimes simple. The bell-like red-and-yellow flowers, several per stem, have five elongated, clubbed, red spurs, up to 2.5cm/1in long.

Far right: Red columbine is an upright herbaceous perennial growing from a short, erect underground stem.

Above: The flowerhead.

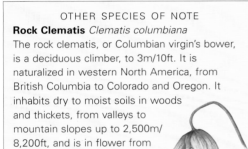

Western Monkshood

Aconitum columbianum

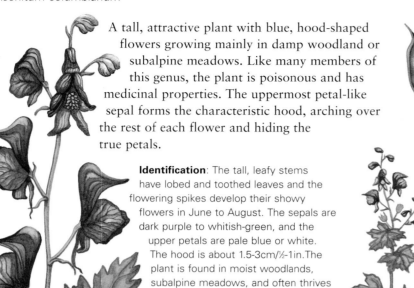

A tall, attractive plant with blue, hood-shaped flowers growing mainly in damp woodland or subalpine meadows. Like many members of this genus, the plant is poisonous and has medicinal properties. The uppermost petal-like sepal forms the characteristic hood, arching over the rest of each flower and hiding the true petals.

Identification: The tall, leafy stems have lobed and toothed leaves and the flowering spikes develop their showy flowers in June to August. The sepals are dark purple to whitish-green, and the upper petals are pale blue or white. The hood is about 1.5-3cm/½-1in. The plant is found in moist woodlands, subalpine meadows, and often thrives beside streams.

Above: The seeds in the pod are black, shiny and triangular.

Left: Leaves are dark green and deeply divided, and larger at the base.

Distribution: From New Mexico and Colorado, the southern Sierra Nevada, South Dakota and Montana, north to Alaska.
Height and spread: 30–210cm/1–7ft.
Habit and form: Herbaceous perennial.
Pollinated: Insect.
Leaf shape: Palmately lobed.

Left: All parts of the plant, which is also known as wolf bane, are poisonous.

Baneberry

Actaea rubra

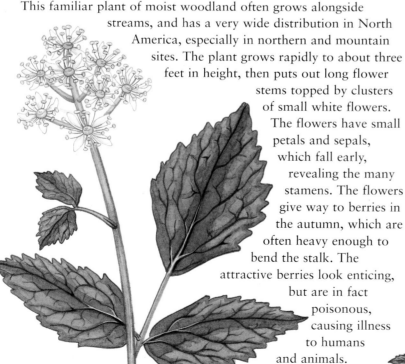

This familiar plant of moist woodland often grows alongside streams, and has a very wide distribution in North America, especially in northern and mountain sites. The plant grows rapidly to about three feet in height, then puts out long flower stems topped by clusters of small white flowers. The flowers have small petals and sepals, which fall early, revealing the many stamens. The flowers give way to berries in the autumn, which are often heavy enough to bend the stalk. The attractive berries look enticing, but are in fact poisonous, causing illness to humans and animals.

Left: Baneberry is a common sight in North America.

Above: Baneberry is one of the north's abundant woodland plants. The common name serves as a reminder to avoid the poisonous berries.

Below: The plant forms in clumps.

Distribution: Through the west and north and north-east, and south to Nebraska.
Height and spread: 30–90cm/1–3ft.
Habit and form: Herbaceous perennial.
Pollinated: Insect.
Leaf shape: Pinnately divided.

Identification: A branching plant with large, divided leaves and racemes of small white flowers, arising from the axils or terminally.

Round-lobed Hepatica

Anemone americana

This is a pretty plant, with bright open flowers that can be white, lavender blue or pink, with five to nine (often six) petal-like sepals, and many stamens. What seem to be sepals are in fact green sepal-like bracts. The flowers appear in early spring and the leaves persist throughout the following winter. The closely-related sharp-leaved hepatica (*A. acutiloba*) has more pointed leaf lobes. The main habitat of this flower is dry woodland.

Distribution: From Manitoba to Nova Scotia, and south to Florida.
Height and spread: 10–15cm/2–2.5in.
Habit and form: Herbaceous perennial.
Pollinated: Insect.
Leaf shape: Basal leaves have three rounded lobes.

Identification: Small herb with round-lobed leaves, and hairy flower-stalks.

Above, right and left: The delicate flowers of round-lobed hepatica balance on fine hairy stalks.

OTHER SPECIES OF NOTE

Blue Anemone *Anemone oregana*
This anemone grows in woodland and scrubby hillsides from northern California to Washington State. Its flowers are usually lavender-blue, but can vary from white to pale pink, and appear from March to June. The flower stalks grow up from a whorl of basal leaves. The plant spreads by sending out underground stems.

Desert Anemone *Anemone tuberosa*
This is mainly found in rocky deserts in Texas, New Mexico, Utah and California. In addition to the basal leaves there is a whorl mid way up the tall stem. The pink-purple or white flowers are clustered around the flowering stems. The beaked seeds are in a woolly seed-head.

Wood Anemone *Anemone quinquefolia*
This pretty, rather delicate woodland flower grows mainly in open woods and clearings across much of eastern North America. From the whorl of three divided leaves arises a central flower stalk. The flowers are white or pinkish, with four to nine petal-like sepals.

Thimbleweed *Anemone virginiana*
This tall, hairy anemone is a woodland flower, usually favouring rocky sites. It is mainly found from Alberta to Newfoundland, south to Georgia. The flowers are white or greenish-white and the name comes from the thimble-shaped pistils.

Scarlet Larkspur

Cardinal larkspur, *Delphinium cardinale*

One of North America's most attractive wild flowers, with brilliant red flowers on tall stalks. It is all the more impressive as it often grows in groups on sites such as scrub and rocky slopes, or woodland clearings. The rather similar red larkspur (*D. nudicaule*) has somewhat less showy, orange-red flowers, and is less tall and prominent.

Identification: The loose tall flower spikes open from May to July. The basal leaves are palmately lobed, and about 5–20cm/2–8in wide. Each individual flower is 2–3cm/¾–1¼in across, with five scarlet sepals, the upper sepal with a characteristic back-projecting spur. The four slim petals are yellow, often tipped scarlet.

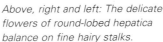

Distribution: Mainly along the coastal ranges from central California, south to northern Baja California.
Height and spread: 30–250cm/1–8ft.
Habit and form: Herbaceous perennial.
Pollinated: Hummingbirds, insects.
Leaf shape: Broad, divided, with 5-7 deeply toothed lobes.

Left: Showy larkspur flowers brighten up chaparral and scrubby coastal areas.

Right: Inside the scarlet sepals are four yellow petals with red tips.

Golden Columbine

Aquilegia chrysantha

A beautiful wild flower growing mainly in moist habitats, across the south west of the region. From a distance the flowers are rather daffodil-like. Not surprisingly this species is popular in gardens. It is easy to cultivate and is also the parent of many garden hybrids. In the wild it is thought to be retreating in the face of global warming. Columbines take their name from the Latin for dove, the flowers fancifully thought to resemble a group of doves. The similar Yellow Columbine (*A. flavescens*) is a mountain plant, with bent tips to the petal spurs.

Left: The plants form clumps, and reach a height of about 90cm/3ft. The striking colour and spurs make the flowers distinctive and easy to identify in the wild.

Identification: A tall species, with large leaves repeatedly divided into leaflets, about 4cm/1¼in long and with rounded tips. The showy flowers have many stamens and five protruding styles. The bushy plant has several stems bearing bright golden yellow flowers in July and August, each 4–7.5cm/1½–3in across. Each flower has five sepals and five petals, the latter with backward-projecting spurs.

Distribution: West Texas, Colorado and New Mexico, west to Utah and Arizona.
Height and spread: 30–90cm/1–3ft.
Habit and form: Herbaceous perennial.
Pollinated: Insect.
Leaf shape: Large and divided.

Far left: Aquilegia comes from the Latin word for eagle, referring to the flower's spurs which supposedly resemble an eagle's talons.

Plains Larkspur

Prairie Larkspur, *Delphinium carolinianum*

This widespread species has several subspecies and related species, with varying flower colour (mostly white or blue), and the group is difficult to classify, especially as hybrids are common. Most blue-flowered species have white variants. The flowers open from May to July and the favoured habitats are open fields, prairies and hill slopes. When it first blooms, the flowers can carpet acres of prairie before the grasses take over. Stems are fuzzy, and usually simple, but on a vigorous plant will branch.

Identification: Erect and felty plant with a raceme of flowers that may be white, or pale (sometimes dark) blue. Each flower is about 2.5cm/1in across with five crinkled sepals, the upper sepal with a long backward-projecting spur. The four petals are in the centre of the flower.

Right and left: The plant is covered in tiny hairs. It forms clumps, and flowers appear in various shades, from white to blue.

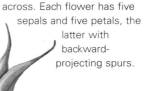

Above: Larkspur growing among prairie grasses.

Distribution: Manitoba, North Dakota, Minnesota, Wisconsin, south to Texas, Missouri and Colorado.
Height and spread: 1.5m/5ft.
Habit and form: Herbaceous perennial.
Pollinated: Insect.
Leaf shape: Large and pinnately divided.

Right: Developing fruits, which eventually dry and split open.

Marsh Marigold

Elk's Lip, *Caltha leptosepala*

Distribution: Mountains, from New Mexico and eastern Arizona north to Alaska.
Height and spread: 2.5–20cm/1–8in.
Habit and form: Herbaceous perennial.
Pollinated: Insect.
Leaf shape: Long, oblong, with scalloped margins.

These bright, shining flowers appear in the eastern mountain range between May and August. Marsh Marigolds, as their name suggests, grow in wet flushes and marshy sites high in the mountains. A typical habitat is around melting snowdrifts. The prominent flowers attract passing insects. The alternative name, Elk's Lip, comes from the shape of the leaves, which are somewhat curled. The related species Twin-flowered Marsh Marigold (*C. biflora*) nearly always has two flowers on each stalk.

Identification: A leafless stem grows up from a basal rosette of leaves and produces a cup-shaped white flower at its tip. Each flower is 1.5–3cm/½–1¼in across, and comprises five to ten petal-like sepals containing many stamens. The petals are absent.

Left and far right: Flowers appear above the basal leaves on pink stalks.

Right: The seed pod.

OTHER SPECIES OF NOTE

White Baneberry, Doll's Eyes
Actaea pachypoda
Found in woods and thickets from Ontario and Nova Scotia south to Florida, the small white flowers appear in May and June. The names come from the white (sometimes red) poisonous berries that resemble the china eyes of old-fashioned dolls.

Nuttall's Larkspur *Delphinium nuttallianum*
This is a low-growing species with blue or violet flowers, appearing from March to July. Mainly a western species, from British Columbia south to northern California, the plant is found on dry soils, sagebrush deserts and open pine woods.

Sagebrush Buttercup *Ranunculus glaberrimus*
A small plant with rather fleshy stems, this is one of the first spring flowers to appear. Another western species found in open pine woods and sagebrush, and very often next to juniper trees, it has shiny yellow flowers from March to June. The leaves sometimes have rounded teeth.

Marsh Marigold, Cowslip *Caltha palustris*
A familiar, showy species, also known as the king cup, inhabits marshes, swamps and stream sides. The large, bright and shiny yellow flowers are like those of a large buttercup and appear from April to June. The leaves are glossy, dark green and heart-shaped, with blunt, serrated edges. The stems are hollow.

White Virgin's Bower

Pipestems, Pepper Vine, Traveller's Joy, *Clematis ligusticifolia*

Like many members of this genus, this is a woody vine, clambering over other shrubs and trees, in a wide range of soils and habitats, from deserts to pine woods, though more typically in river valleys and gullys. The plant was used by Native Americans, who chewed the stems and leaves as a remedy against sore throats. This traditional use is reflected in the name Pepper Vine.

Identification:
From May to September it produces hundreds of small cream-coloured flowers, each about 2cm/¾in across, with five petal-like sepals. The fruit heads are also rather attractive, composed of feathery plumed seeds.

Right: A showy seed head.

Distribution: Western species, from British Columbia to southern California, Arizona and New Mexico; also introduced to Pennsylvania.
Height and spread: 3m/10ft.
Habit and form: Semi-woody perennial.
Pollinated: Insect.
Leaf shape: Opposite, pinnately compound.

Below: White virgin's bower has a clambering habit.

Blue Columbine

Aquilegia caerulea

Blue Columbine is a popular garden plant, in addition to being the state flower of Colorado. It has attractive large flowers, usually blue and white. In its various cultivated forms there are several colour variants ranging from pale blue to white, pale yellow and pinkish. Often the flowers are bicoloured and some forms have doubled flowers. It has been successfully hybridised with other aquilegias. In the wild it prefers mountain sites, such as montane aspen woods. The related Alpine Blue Columbine (*A. saximontana*) is a much shorter plant found at higher altitudes only in Colorado.

Identification: A tall, bushy plant, growing to approximately 20-60cm/6in-2ft tall, with several stems, attractive divided leaves and beautiful flowers. The blooms are each up to 7.5cm/3in across, with five spreading blue sepals and five petals, and backward projecting spurs to 5cm/2in long. The sepals are often blue, but can be pale yellow or pink. The flowers open between June and August.

Distribution: New Mexico and Arizona, north to west Montana.
Height and spread: 90cm/3ft.
Habit and form: Herbaceous perennial.
Pollinated: Insect.
Leaf shape: Divided and lobed.

Left: The sepals of most columbine forms are a different shade to the petals.

Crimson Columbine

Red Columbine, Sitka Columbine, *Aquilegia formosa*

One of a number of red-flowered species that attract hummingbirds as pollinators, this is one of the most beautiful members of this genus. The spreading deep crimson and yellow flowers appear in May to August and are suspended from the branch tips. Crimson Columbine readily adapts to many zones and conditions from rocky mountain slopes to sea level. Its sweet nectar attracts not only hummingbirds, but bees and butterflies and its flowers can be used as an edible salad garnish. Native Americans used the leaves and roots medicinally for a wide range of ailments.

Identification: The leaflets of the deeply divided leaves are about 4cm/1.5in in length, and lobed and indented at the tips. The individual flowers are 5cm/2in across, each with five bright red petal-like sepals. The five yellow petals each have a backward pointing spur.

Distribution: From Baja California north to southern Alaska, and east to Idaho, Utah and Wyoming.
Height and spread: 15–90cm/6–36in.
Habit and form: Herbaceous perennial.
Pollinated: Hummingbird and insect.
Leaf shape: Divided and lobed.

Left: The tall, delicate flower stems rise over a leafy clump.

Left: The flowers are vibrant and showy.

Vase Flower

Sugar Bowls, Leather Flower, Lion's Beard *Clematis hirsutissima*

Distribution: Mainly western, from British Columbia to northern Arizona and New Mexico, but east to Montana and Wyoming.
Height and spread: 20–60cm/8–24in.
Habit and form: Semi-woody perennial.
Pollinated: Insect.
Leaf shape: Long, opposite, finely divided.

Unusually for a clematis, this species is not a climbing vine, but grows as a clump producing several stems from a woody branched base. Each flowering stem has a single rather dull coloured red or purplish-brown flower, dangling down like an upside-down cup. The flowers open from April to July. It grows mainly in open pine forests, sagebrush and grassland. The rounded seedheads have long silvery plumes, giving this species its folk name Lion's Beard. The seed floss is traditionally used as tinder for starting fires.

Right: In contrast to their dull exterior, the flowers are richly coloured inside.

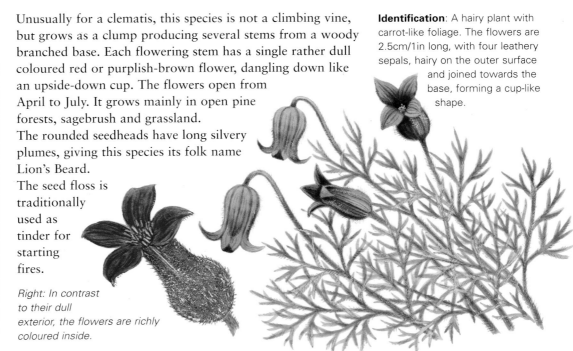

Identification: A hairy plant with carrot-like foliage. The flowers are 2.5cm/1in long, with four leathery sepals, hairy on the outer surface and joined towards the base, forming a cup-like shape.

OTHER SPECIES OF NOTE
Spring Larkspur, Dwarf Larkspur
Delphinium tricorne
This is a pretty woodland flower with a rather eastern distribution. It takes its species name from the horn-like fruit pods, three in number. The blue flowers are borne in a loose cluster. The plant is toxic, and it was apparently used by soldiers in the American Civil War to treat lice.

Pasque Flower
Pulsatilla patens
A widespread grassland plant with blue, purple or white flowers. The common name comes from the Easter flowering time. The fruiting head is highly distinctive, being covered in silky hairs.

Common Buttercup *Ranunculus acris*
This highly familiar flower of fields and meadows is found throughout North America, having spread vigorously after being introduced from Europe. Its bright yellow shiny flowers enliven many a meadow. There are five overlapping petals above five green sepals, which turn yellow as the flower matures.

Lesser Celandine, Pilewort *Ranunculus ficaria*
A plant of shady and moist sites, forming an attractive carpet of dark foliage and deep yellow flowers. It has glossy, heart-shaped basal leaves and blooms from March to April atop slender stalks. It was once used as a treatment for piles.

Virgin's Bower

C. virginiana

Virgin's Bower is a common species, often seen clambering and trailing over shrubs, trees or fences, especially in moist riverside locations, and along woodland edges. It is sometimes grown in gardens deliberately as the female plant produces attractive displays of feathery plumed fruits in late summer and autumn.

Identification: The leaves have sharp-toothed lobes, with leaflets about 5cm/2in long. The flowers are white, in clusters from the leaf axils. Each flower is about 2.5cm/1in across with four or five white, petal-like sepals and no petals. Male and female flowers are borne on separate plants (the plant is dioecious). The female flowers have many pistils and the male flowers many stamens.

Distribution: Nova Scotia and Manitoba, south to Florida and west to Texas.
Height and spread: Stems to 3m/10ft.
Habit and form: Semi-woody perennial.
Pollinated: Insect.
Leaf shape: Compound.

Above: The female plant's feathery fruits.

POPPY FAMILY

The poppy family (Papaveraceae) consists of annuals, herbaceous perennials and low shrubs that are mainly restricted to the Northern Hemisphere and the New World is not an exception to this. North America is especially rich in members of the poppy family, providing a concentration of species not found anywhere else in the world.

California Poppy

Eschscholzia californica

California poppy is a well-known and highly variable plant: it exists as a long-lived prostrate perennial along the coast, an erect perennial in inland valleys, and an annual in the interior. As the name suggests, it is a native of California, extending from the Columbia River valley in south-western Washington into the Baja California peninsula and sporadically on to the Cape Region, west to the Pacific Ocean, and east to western Texas. It grows in grassy and open areas to 2,000m/6,560ft.

Identification: Erect or spreading, glaucous stems arise from a heavy taproot in the perennial forms. The blue-green leaves, basal and on the stem, are deeply dissected, with blunt or pointed tips. Large cup-shaped flowers, solitary or in small clusters, open from erect buds; the four petals, 2.5–5cm/1–2in long, are yellow, usually with an orange spot at the base, although the flower colour can range from a uniform orange to various orange spots and shadings at the base of deep yellow or golden petals.

Left: The large flowers often form extensive showy drifts.

Distribution: Western USA.
Height and spread: 5–60cm/2–24in.
Habit and form: Herbaceous perennial herb or annual.
Leaf shape: Deeply dissected.
Pollinated: Insect.

Celandine

Greater Celandine, *Chelidonium majus*

This erect, leafy herb is confusingly named as it is a member of the poppy family and not a true celandine (the latter is in the buttercup family). It has pretty deep yellow flowers, and also bright yellow, poisonous sap, which can cause skin irritation, and was used at one time for treating warts. Greater Celandine has a long history of medicinal use and is still employed in herbal medicine today for a wide variety of ailments.

Identification: The flowers each have four yellow petals and are about 2.5cm/1in across, and borne in branching umbels. The long leaves are alternate, pale green and deeply divided.

Right: Inside the pods, the small black seeds have fleshy elaiosomes which attract ants to disperse the seeds.

Above: Greater Celandine grows as a spreading weed in rough ground, around houses and at woodland edges.

Distribution: Native to Europe and W Asia; introduced to eastern North America, where it is found from Newfoundland, south to Georgia, and west to Nebraska and Ontario.
Height and spread: 30–60cm/1–2ft.
Habit and form: Biennial/perennial herb.
Pollinated: Insect.
Leaf shape: Finely lobed.

Matilija Poppy

Tree Poppy, *Romneya coulteri*

This beautiful perennial has large, white, yellow-centred, scented, solitary flowers, which look like fried eggs and are the largest of any plant native to California. Found in southern California and northern Mexico, this suckering perennial is a fire-follower: it may occur in areas of sage scrub, or more typically in chaparral, or along rocky watercourses away from the immediate coast, up to 1,200m/4,000ft. Open or mildly disturbed terrain is usually favoured and mature chaparral or sage scrub limits its spread. It is popular in cultivation and can be found as a localised garden escapee.

Distribution: Southern California and northern Mexico.
Height and spread: 90cm–2.5m/3–8ft.
Habit and form: Shrubby perennial.
Pollinated: Insect.
Leaf shape: Pinnately divided.

Left: The strong upright growth and large, showy flowers make this a spectacular wild flower.

Identification: This tall, leaning, heavily branched, shrubby perennial is woody at the base. The leaves are 5–20cm/2–8in long, grey-green, pinnately divided into three or five main divisions, which may have a few teeth or again be divided. The leafy, branched stems grow in patches. Each bears five to eight large, fragrant, white flowers in late spring to midsummer. The flowers are 10–18cm/4–7in across, with six fan-shaped petals; the three sepals are smooth and differentiate this plant from other *Romneya* species. Its many stamens are yellow, forming a ball in the centre with a bristle-haired ovary.

Far left: The large, fragrant, white-petalled flower with its yellow centre has become a favourite of gardeners everywhere, leading to its widespread cultivation.

OTHER SPECIES OF NOTE

Cream Cups *Platystemon californicus*
This annual native of California and the surrounding desert regions was once common in open fields, especially following fires, but in recent years it has become scarce across much of its range. The dainty, spreading, grey-green foliage is smothered with flowers of creamy-yellow to white in spring.

Wind Poppy *Stylomecon heterophylla*
This beautiful and rare, red-flowered wild poppy is native to California. Along with their striking appearance, the flowers have a fragrance like lily-of-the-valley, which is quite a rarity for a poppy. Naturally found in grasslands and mountain foothills, the flowers appear off and on throughout spring and summer.

Bloodroot *Sanguinaria canadensis*
This herbaceous perennial is found through most of the eastern USA. It can reach 25cm/10in tall, but is only about half that height at the time of flowering. The flowers are up to 5cm/2in wide, with about 12 strap-like, satiny, white petals and yellow centres. The first blooms appear in late winter and continue into early spring.

White Bearpoppy

Arctomecon merriamii

The white bearpoppy is a perennial found in flat desert scrub habitats such as the Mojave Desert. It prefers shallow, gravel, limestone soils, usually on rocky slopes between 900–1,400m/2,950–4,600ft; it is also, less frequently, encountered on valley bottoms. It is a distinctive plant, with blue-green basal leaves. From this, several long, blue-green stems arise, each bearing a single, showy white or pale yellow flower with a golden centre in the late spring.

Distribution: Mojave Desert and southern Nevada, south-western USA.
Height and spread: 35cm/14in.
Habit and form: Herbaceous perennial.
Pollinated: Insect.
Leaf shape: Obovate or wedge-shaped.

Identification: The plant has glaucous, densely hairy stems and mainly basal leaves, which are egg- or wedge-shaped, 25–75cm/10–30in long, with rounded teeth and dense shaggy white hairs. The white or yellow flowers are solitary, terminal, opening from nodding buds, with two or three long, hairy sepals. They have four or six free, oval petals, 2.5–4cm/1–1½in long, which generally persist after pollination. The fruits are oval to oblong, opening at the tip and containing a few oblong, wrinkled, black seeds.

Above: The flowers are held high above the foliage.

FUMITORY FAMILY

This family (Fumariaceae) contains about 530 species, mainly in northern temperate regions, with a few in African mountains. Most of them are leafy herbs, with swollen underground parts. They tend to have rather succulent stems and the flowers are borne in racemes. The fruit is a single-chambered capsule. A number of species of Corydalis *and* Dicentra *are popular garden plants.*

Golden Smoke

Scrambled Eggs, *Corydalis aurea*

This weak-stemmed plant has clusters of bright yellow flowers, lending it its common name Scrambled Eggs. The flowers appear from February to September and are pale to bright yellow, growing in groups of four to twelve. It prefers light sandy soil and its favoured habitat is rough, rocky hillslopes and scrub; it is also found under trees and along creek bottoms. It often invades disturbed sites such as roadsides, clearings and recently burned areas, although its survival in these locations appears to be short lived. Like many of its relatives, it is rather poisonous to livestock if consumed in large quantities. The Navajo Native American Indians are said to have used the plant for some medicinal treatments, but ingesting it should be avoided.

Identification: The dense leafy rosette produces rather weak stems with pinnate leaves and racemes of yellow, spurred flowers. Each flower is about 2cm/¾in long, and has tiny sepals, and four petals. The upper petal forms a hollow spur, and a hood. The flower encloses six stamens. The leaves are a bluish green, and divided.

Above: Corydalis derives its name from the Greek for "crested lark" after the shape of the flower, which resembles the bird's spur.

Distribution: Widespread in the west, east of the Cascades and Sierra Nevada, and to Arkansas, Illinois and Pennsylvania.
Height and spread: 10–60cm/4–24in.
Habit and form: Annual or biennial.
Pollinated: Insect.
Leaf shape: Twice-pinnate.

Golden Ear-drops

Dicentra chrysantha

This pretty flower often appears in abundance following scrub fires, the fire scarification causing the seeds to germinate. It also appears in disturbed waste ground. The flowering period is from April to September, and the flowers have a strange, pungent aroma. This toxic plant is particularly dangerous to animals after a burn, when it is at its most prolific.

Identification: The yellow flowers are an odd shape in that the outer petals extend out sideways. The blue-green foliage is feathery and fern-like, with pinnate leaves up to 30cm/1ft long, with finely divided leaflets. The individual flower has four petals, the inner pair enclosing the six stamens.

Left: The dramatic flower spikes can grow up to 150cm/5ft tall.

Above: The plants are a common sight across California and the Sierra Nevada.

Left: The bright sulphur-yellow flowers bring vivid patches of colour to areas scorched by fire.

Distribution: Mainly southern California.
Height and spread: 45–150cm/1½–5ft.
Habit and form: Annual/perennial.
Pollinated: Insect.
Leaf shape: Pinnate.

Tall Corydalis

Roman Wormwood, Rock Harlequin, *Corydalis sempervirens*

Distribution: North-east USA and Canada.
Height and spread: 12.5–60cm/5–24in.
Habit and form: Annual/biennial.
Pollinated: Insect.
Leaf shape: Pinnate.

Tall corydalis is of the most attractive of the genus, and often grown in gardens, in a number of cultivated forms. The wild form has pale pink or purple tubular flowers, tipped yellow, and there are garden forms with white or pink flowers. The multi-lobed leaves are a pale blue-green providing a pleasing contrast to the flowers. The main flowering time is May to September. It grows mainly in rocky clearings and disturbed areas, and does very well in full sunlight. Like others in its family, this plant thrives in fire-scorched zones and it is thought that the seeds require heat for germination.

Identification: Each flower is about 10cm/4in long and consists of four petals, the outer two with a rounded, upwardly projecting spur. The fruit is a slender and rather smooth capsule.

Above: The pale-to-dark pink and yellow blossoms dangle from slender branching stems through the summer months.

OTHER SPECIES OF NOTE

Case's Fitweed *Corydalis caseana*
A tall, succulent species with hollow stems and fern-like foliage. The flowers are pale pink in dense racemes, each with a long, straight spur. It flowers in June to August in moist mountain soils from Oregon south to the central Sierra Nevada, and east to Colorado and Idaho.

Western Bleeding Heart
Dicentra formosa
The heart-shaped pink flowers over fern-like blue-green foliage are extremely striking. Its habitat is damp shady sites from southern British Columbia to central California. This is another popular garden plant.

Steer's Head *Dicentra uniflora*
Although this is a common western species, it is often overlooked as it is so small, growing to about 10cm/4in. It prefers well-drained sites in open woodland or sagebrush. The pink or white flowers are a peculiar shape – like a cow's head, hence the common name. The plant blooms from early spring to late summer.

Wild Bleeding Heart *Dicentra eximia*
A pretty perennial, common in mountain woods in the eastern USA. It produces pink or red drooping, heart-shaped flowers, the inner petals resembling a drop of blood. It is also called Staggerweed, and has been said to have an intoxicating effect on cattle. This is another popular garden species.

Dutchman's Breeches

Dicentra cucullaria

This delicate nodding spring flower favours shade and is found on north-facing mountain slopes and in shady ravines, preferring long-undisturbed sites. It is pollinated mainly by bumblebees, which can reach the pollen with their long probosces. The short flowering season is April to May.

Identification: The flowers are white or pink, with a yellow tip, and are about 2cm/¾in long. The flowers are sometimes damaged by bees biting through the sides of the petals to get at the nectar and pollen inside. The plant grows from a short root with many small bulblets. The basal leaves are finely divided.

Left: The seed pod contains shiny black seeds.

Distribution: Nova Scotia south to Georgia and west to Oklahoma and Mississippi; also in the Pacific north-west.
Height and spread: 10–30cm/4–12in.
Habit and form: Annual/perennial.
Pollinated: Insect.
Leaf shape: Compound.

Left: The amusing name of this species comes from the fancied resemblance of its flowers to old-fashioned pantaloons (upside down).

WATER LILY FAMILY

Nymphaeaceae, the water lily family, are aquatic plants of five genera and 50 species. They have showy flowers on long stalks, and are often considered the most primitive of the flowering plants. In the New World there are some remarkable examples of these plants: the family reaches its zenith in the huge plants of the tropical Victoria genus, with their giant leaf pads and curious night-blooming flowers.

Spatterdock

Yellow cow lily, yellow pond lily, *Nuphar polysepala*

This perennial, water-lily-like plant from western North America can form extensive stands in the shallow waters of lakes, ponds, sluggish streams and canals. Mature plants have large "elephant's ear" leaves and yellow flowers. Unlike the showy, many-petalled fragrant water lily flowers, spatterdock blossoms are simple yellow globes that partially open to reveal reddish poppy-like centres from early to late summer, standing just above the water surface. The leaves float on, or stand above, the water, on thick, fleshy stalks.

Identification: Fibrous roots anchor the scaly, log-like rhizomes to the sediment; the rhizomes are up to 20cm/8in in diameter and 5m/16ft long. The leaves are 10–45cm/4–18in long and 7.5–30cm/3–12in wide, green, heart-shaped, with a notched base, a blunt tip, a prominent mid-vein and a leathery surface; they rise directly from the rhizome, floating on or extending above the water. In early summer, large, delicate underwater leaves resembling lettuce precede the floating leaves. The flowers arise directly from the rhizome in summer. They are waxy, bright yellow, cup-shaped globes, 5–10cm/2–4in across, rising above the water; they usually have nine sepals, but can have up to 17; the stamens are reddish. The flowers are sweetly scented on the first day after opening, malodorous later.

Distribution: Western North America.
Height and spread: 5m/16ft or more.
Habit and form: Floating, aquatic perennial.
Leaf shape: Cordate.
Pollinated: Insect, especially flies.

Left: The fruits are urn-shaped.

Below: The leaves float.

American Lotus

Yellow lotus, water chinquapin, *Nelumbo lutea* syn. *N. pentapetala*

This deciduous, perennial water plant occurs in quiet waters in ponds, lakes and the edges of slow-moving streams and rivers of eastern North America, the West Indies, Central America and south to Colombia. Its large, spongy rhizomes penetrate the mud beneath the water by as much as 2.5m/8ft, and the showy pale yellow flowers appear in late spring and summer. They are as magnificent as those of its Asian relative, *N. nucifera*, but it is less cultivated for ornament. It was probably originally confined to the floodplains of major rivers and their tributaries in the east-central United States, and was carried northward and eastward by Native Americans.

Identification: The stems arise directly from the rhizomes, reaching 2m/6½ft or more. The leaves may be 60cm/2ft or more across, with the stalk attached to the underside of the leaf at its centre, without the cleft seen in *Nymphaea* species. The leaves float on the surface, flattened, in deep water, or stand above it in shallow pools; the margins tend to rise above the centre, creating a "funnel" effect. The leaves are dull-satiny blue-green on top and pale green with prominent veins underneath. The large flowers, 25cm/10in across, have numerous pale yellow tepals, and anthers to 2cm/¾in long. Each bloom is borne singly on a long, stiff stalk, standing above the leaves. The woody rounded seedpods have a distinctive, flattened, pierced top like a showerhead.

Distribution: Eastern North America, West Indies, Central and South America.
Height and spread: Forms extensive colonies.
Habit and form: Aquatic perennial.
Leaf shape: Orbicular.
Pollinated: Insects.

Above left: Native Americans used the seeds and tubers for food.

Left: The blooms are held on long stems.

Indian Pond Lily

Spatterdock, Yellow Water Lily, *Nuphar lutea*

Distribution: Southern California, north to Alaska and east to Colorado.
Height and spread: Floating leaves and flowers, to 7.5cm/3in above surface.
Habit and form: Aquatic.
Pollinated: Insect.
Leaf shape: Heart-shaped.

Right: Floating leaves are attached at the stem, whereas submerged leaves are attached to the rhizome.

With its bright yellow flowers and shiny floating leaves, this aquatic plant adds welcome colour to slow rivers and ponds in the west of the region. The flowers open from April to September and float either just at the water surface, or raised slightly above the water. The plant is anchored in the mud and soil, and the shoots grow up through the water, producing the flat floating leaves and flowers at the surface. Native Americans used the seeds – either roasted, or ground into flour.

Identification: The submerged stalks may be 90cm/3ft or more long, and the cup-shaped flowers each about 10cm/4in across. There are normally nine sepals, the outer ones greenish, and the inner ones forming the yellow flower. The petals are small and narrow, and about the same length as the stamens.

Right: The seed head.

OTHER SPECIES OF NOTE

Fragrant Water Lily *Nymphaea odorata*
These are exceptionally beautiful water plants native to the eastern USA, with floating leaves and large, many-petalled white, or less frequently pink, fragrant blossoms. The nearly circular floating leaves are deeply cleft, glossy green above, with red or purple undersides.

Yellow Pond Lily, Bullhead Lily
Nuphar variegata
North America's commonest water lily is found in ponds and streams from much of Canada to Newfoundland and south to Pennsylvania. It has the typical yellow cup-shaped flowers, and the leaves have a V-shaped notch at the base.

Common Spatterdock *Nuphar advena*
This species is very similar to Yellow Pond Lily, and occurs mainly in the southern states, and north to New England, Ohio and Michigan.It is also found in Cuba, inhabiting slow-moving bodies of water. The heart-shaped leaves tend to float just beneath the water's surface.

Pygmy Water Lily *Nymphaea tetragona*
Although this has a wide distribution across North America, it is rather rare in the west, in Washington State and Idaho. Its white flowers are rather small, about 6cm/2in across. It is popular in gardens because of its size and the beauty of the inflorescence. The blooming period is July to August.

Banana Water Lily

Yellow water lily, Mexican water lily, *Nymphaea mexicana*

This aquatic perennial was identified from specimens collected in Mexico, although it is also found in east and south Texas and in Florida. It grows in standing water, where its round floating foliage acts as a foil for the showy, fragrant, multi-petalled yellow flowers. It grows from a stout, tuberous rhizome and spreads by runners, typically inhabiting water 45cm/18in deep. It was abundant throughout Florida until the introduction of *Eichhornia crassipes*, which has crowded it out from former strongholds.

Distribution: South-east USA and Mexico.
Height and spread: Forms extensive colonies.
Habit and form: Deciduous or evergreen aquatic perennial.
Leaf shape: Ovate to orbicular.
Pollinated: Insect, probably beetles.

Below: The leaves and flowers can stand above the water.

Identification: Stems arising directly from the submerged rhizome bear oval to circular leaves, floating or emergent, with smooth to toothed or wavy margins; they are shiny deep green, blotched brown above, reddish-purple below, 10–20cm/4–8in across, split from one edge to the stalk, with pointed or rounded lobes, sometimes overlapping. The flowers appear from spring to autumn, with a musty fragrance.

Right: The flowers are fragrant.

CARNATION FAMILY

The carnation family (Caryophyllaceae) contains many familiar garden plants, such as sweet williams and pinks as well as carnations. There are about 2,300 species, mostly in the northern hemisphere, and many in the cooler regions. The herb members of the family often have characteristically swollen nodes. Many species have thrived in America, after being introduced from Europe.

Moss Pink

Moss Campion, *Silene acaulis*

This attractive alpine is found throughout the northern hemisphere, and is a popular garden species. It is cushion-forming, creating mossy mats and pretty pink flowers on short stalks. A number of garden forms exist with white, double or golden flowers. The mat-growing habit is an adaptation to avoid excessive desiccation caused by strong winds in exposed habitats such as rocky cliffs and mountain slopes. This species thrives well in rock gardens which resemble the rocky crevices of its natural sites.

Left: The showy flowers make moss pink a popular choice for gardens.

Identification: The leaves are long and narrow, and the plant grows in the form of a moss-like mound. The deep pink flowers are each about 1.5cm/½in across and the five petals are notched at the tips. The blooms open between June and August and nestle very low against the foliage, adding to the cushion-like appearance of the plant.

Distribution: From Alaska to Greenland, and on mountains further south.
Height and spread: To 6.5cm/2½in tall, to 30cm/1ft across.
Habit and form: Perennial.
Pollinated: Insect.
Leaf shape: Opposite.

Left: The plant grows low to avoid disturbance from bitter mountain winds.

Indian Pink

Silene californica

Open, rocky woodland is the main habitat of the Indian Pink, one of the prettiest wild flowers of the region. However, unfortunately it is not very common anywhere. The flowers open from May to July and are very striking, with a circle of bright crimson notched petals, clustered towards the tips of long, leafy stems. The stems are rather weak and sometimes collapse to trail on the ground.

Left: The ragged-looking flower attracts humming birds.

Identification: The flowers are in a loose inflorescence. Each is about 4cm/1½in across, and has a long tubular calyx, with five teeth. The five petals are broad and notched towards the tip.

Distribution: Northern California and southern Oregon.
Height and spread: To 40cm/16in.
Habit and form: Perennial.
Pollinated: Insect and humming birds.
Leaf shape: Opposite.

Right: The weak stems often collapse and trail on the ground.

Stringflower *Silene hookeri*
The ragged looking flowers give the common name – each petal is divided and 'frayed'. Flowers may be white, pink or purple. The habitat is rocky ground in open coniferous forest or scrub, and it is found in southern Oregon and northern California.

White Campion *Silene latifolia*
Another introduction from Europe that has spread through most of North America, in fields and waste ground. It is a branching plant, with white (or pink), sweet-scented flowers that open in the evening to attract moths.

Bladder Campion *Silene vulgaris*
This pretty plant, with its clusters of white flowers and a bladder-like swollen calyx (the latter with obvious veins), is another European introduction, now a widespread weed.

Royal Catchfly *Silene regia*
Perhaps the most splendid of the genus, with its heads of bright red, five-petalled flowers born on tall herbaceous stalks, and leaves of a striking green, Royal Catchfly is endangered over much of its range, with a patchy distribution in the south east of the USA. It blooms from May through October.

Fire Pink

Silene virginica

This eastern species has sticky glandular hairs covering the stems. This feature is typical of many members of this genus, which are sometimes given the name 'catchfly' – the sticky hairs trapping small insects. The habitat is open woods, and also rocky slopes, often on sandy soils, as well as thickets. The common name is well chosen, as the flowers are a bright vivid red, in loose clusters on slender, often arching stems.

Identification: The sepals form a long sticky tube, above which the five, notched petals spread out impressively. The flowering period is from April to June. The fruit is a capsule containing many small seeds.

Above and right: Sticky hairs on the stem may trap undesirable crawling insects to allow more welcome pollinators access to the flowers.

Distribution: New York west to Minnesota, Louisiana and Oklahoma.
Height and spread: 15–60cm/6–24in.
Habit and form: Perennial.
Pollinated: Insect.
Leaf shape: Base leaves spoon-shaped; upper leaves opposite.

Corn Cockle

Agrostemma githago

The common name refers to one of the favoured habitats of this species – namely fields of cereal crops, notably wheat (often called corn in Europe). Formerly much commoner, when it could cause problems as its seeds are poisonous and used to get into flour. But it is a very pretty plant, with large pink-purple or white flowers. It grows in waste ground, such as fields and roadsides, and sometimes in grain crops. Some garden forms have deep red flowers.

Identification: Tall plant covered in dense hairs, with single large flowers at the tips of long stalks. The flowers open between June and September, and each flower has five petals and five sepals, the latter extending beyond the petals. The flowers are large – to 5cm/2in across, and the fruit is a many-seeded capsule.

Right: The Corn Cockle is one of many plants that have been successfully introduced to America from across the Atlantic.

Distribution: Introduced from Europe, but now found throughout most of the USA and southern Canada.
Height and spread: 30–90cm/1–3ft.
Habit and form: Annual.
Pollinated: Insect.
Leaf shape: Opposite.

Above: Corn Cockle is easy to grow in a sunny area of the garden.

Grass Pink

Deptford Pink, *Dianthus armeria*

The alternative name for this introduced flower refers to Deptford, in London, where this species was formerly abundant. It is a striking plant, with deep pink flowers in clusters atop rather stiff stalks. In many ways it resembles a miniature carnation. This is yet another introduced species that has thrived in dry fields and along roads, across many parts of North America.

Distribution: Mainly eastern states, but also in parts of the west.
Height and spread: 15–60cm/6–24in.
Habit and form: Biennial or annual.
Pollinated: Insect.
Leaf shape: Simple and narrow.

Right: A normal plant will produce about 400 seeds, which leads to an abundance of carnation-like, attractive plants growing in swathes in North America, particularly in the East.

Left and top right: The grass pink's cheerful blooms are a welcome sight in fairly open ground and the species' decline in Britain is due to urbanization or loss of pasture to arable land.

Identification: The cerise pink flowers, which open from May to October, are about 1.5cm/½in across, with five jagged-edged petals and leafy bracts below. The petals have white speckles towards the centre. The leaves are long, hairy, narrow and a pale green. The stem is simple, branching towards the top, and softly hairy. The fruit is a four-toothed capsule containing many tiny, dark brown seeds.

Ragged Robin

Lychnis flos-cuculi

Widely naturalised in the north east of the United States, this introduced species is well-named for its rather scruffy looking flowers – the deeply divided petals give it a distinctly ragged appearance. It is found mainly on waste ground and in meadows, with a preference for moist soils.

Identification: The leaves are opposite and increasingly small higher up the stem. The flowers are usually deep pink, but sometimes white and in clusters. Each flower is about 1.5cm/½in across and the five large petals are each divided into four thin lobes. The fruit is a many-seeded capsule.

Above: The flower is often found with other meadow favourites, such as buttercups.

Distribution: From Newfoundland south to Maryland and west to Ontario and Ohio.
Height and spread: 30–90cm/1–3ft.
Habit and form: Perennial.
Pollinated: Insect.
Leaf shape: Lanceolate.

Left: The leaves are rough-textured. They form opposite pairs higher up the stem.

Left: The flowers appear from May to August.

Soapwort

Bouncing Bet, *Saponaria officinalis*

Distribution: Throughout the region.
Height and spread: 30–75cm/2–3in.
Habit and form: Perennial.
Pollinated: Insect.
Leaf shape: Oval.

The strange common names reflect its use in earlier times as an aid in washing. The sap contains saponins which can create a soapy lather when the leaves are crushed. Bouncing Bet is an old-fashioned term for a washerwoman. Soapwort spreads and forms colonies by means of underground stems. Double flowered cultivars are widely available.

Identification: This robust species has smooth stems and clusters of white or pink scented flowers. Each flower is 2.5cm/1in across, and the fragrance attracts many insects, including moths. The leaves have three prominent veins. The fruit is the typical capsule, with many seeds.

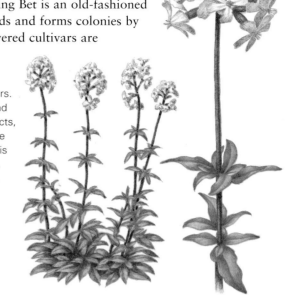

Left: Soapwort has delicate pink flowers.

Right: The plant blooms from May to September.

OTHER SPECIES OF NOTE

Beautiful Sandwort *Arenaria capillaris*
This is a dainty little flower of sagebrush plains and mountain slopes, found from Alaska south to Oregon, Nevada and Montana. The small white, star-like flowers grow on long stalks from a leafy mat-like base.

Fendler's Sandwort *Arenaria fendleri*
Common on rocky ledges in the southern Rocky Mountains, Fendler's Sandwort ranges south from Wyoming to Arizona, New Mexico and Texas. It has very narrow leaves that form a grass-like clump, up to a foot in diameter, and many small white flowers with prominent white stamen upon fairly long, brownish stalks.

Meadow Chickweed *Cerastium arvense*
A plant with a very wide distribution throughout the northern hemisphere. It has weak stems that often trail on the ground. The white petals of the bright flowers are deeply notched. It is often mistaken for Mouse-ear Chickweed (*Cerastium vulgatum*), but that species has rounder, hairier leaves (hence the name).

Maltese Cross *Lychnis chalcedonica*
A now-common garden plant that was introduced from Asia. The flowers are scarlet and the petal arrangement resembles a Maltese cross. Garden varieties with pink, white and double flowers are available.

Star Chickweed

Stellaria pubera

This chickweed is well-named as its pretty pure white flowers are indeed star-shaped. They stand out brightly against the dark green foliage of the woodland floor. It is found mainly in rich woods and also on rocky slopes, and the flowers open between March and May. The common name is supposedly due to chickens liking to eat the plant.

Identification: The very long petals are divided into narrow lobes. It resembles the European/Asian Stitchwort (*Stellaria holostea*), which is naturalised in North America, but has broader leaves. Each flower is 1.5cm/½in across and the five petals are so deeply divided that there appear to be ten.

Distribution: New York, west to Illinois and Louisiana; south to Florida.
Height and spread: 15–40cm/6–16in.
Habit and form: Perennial.
Pollinated: Insect.
Leaf shape: Elliptical, unstalked.

Below: The plant has reportedly been used for soothing minor skin irritations.

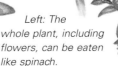

Left: The whole plant, including flowers, can be eaten like spinach.

CACTUS FAMILY

The Cactaceae are mostly spiny succulents with photosynthetic stems, comprising about 130 genera and 1,650 species. Their leaves are rarely well developed and fleshy, but generally reduced, absent altogether or associated with highly modified axillary buds called areoles, which bear spines. Most are native to the Americas, and found as far north as Canada and as far south as Patagonia.

Plains Prickly Pear

Opuntia polyacantha

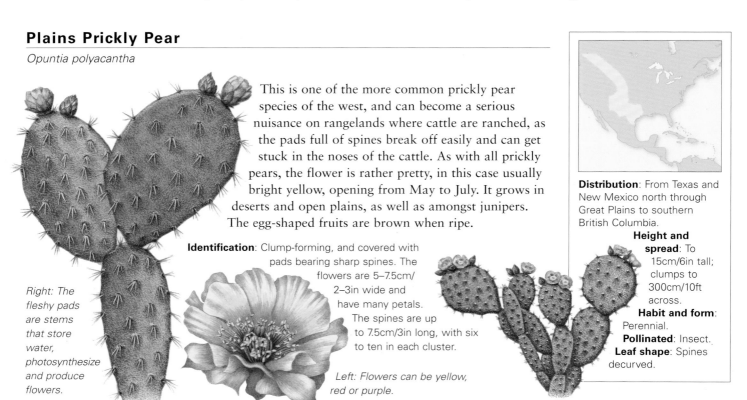

This is one of the more common prickly pear species of the west, and can become a serious nuisance on rangelands where cattle are ranched, as the pads full of spines break off easily and can get stuck in the noses of the cattle. As with all prickly pears, the flower is rather pretty, in this case usually bright yellow, opening from May to July. It grows in deserts and open plains, as well as amongst junipers. The egg-shaped fruits are brown when ripe.

Identification: Clump-forming, and covered with pads bearing sharp spines. The flowers are 5–7.5cm/2–3in wide and have many petals. The spines are up to 7.5cm/3in long, with six to ten in each cluster.

Right: The fleshy pads are stems that store water, photosynthesize and produce flowers.

Left: Flowers can be yellow, red or purple.

Distribution: From Texas and New Mexico north through Great Plains to southern British Columbia.
Height and spread: To 15cm/6in tall; clumps to 300cm/10ft across.
Habit and form: Perennial.
Pollinated: Insect.
Leaf shape: Spines decurved.

Pin-cushion Cactus

Coryphantha vivipara

This small, barrel-shaped cactus is sometimes found singly, but more often as a group. It has flowers varying in colour – yellow-green, pink, red or lavender. The fruit is green and smooth with brown seeds. It grows mainly in rocky deserts and on dry sandy soils in juniper, oak or pinewoods.

Identification: Each flower has many petals and is up to 5cm/2in across. The spines are in clusters of three to ten and are long and straight, with a ring of shorter white spines surrounding them.

Distribution: From Mexico north to central Canada.
Height and spread: 4–15cm/1½–6in.
Habit and form: Perennial.
Pollinated: Insect.
Leaf shape: Spines about 2cm/0.75in long.

Left: Once the flowers have finished, tasty berries develop.

Beavertail Cactus

Opuntia basilaris

Distribution: Northern Mexico, to southern California, western Arizona and south-west Utah.
Height and spread: 15–30cm/6–12in; clumps to 1.8m/6ft across.
Habit and form: Perennial.
Pollinated: Insect.
Leaf shape: Tiny bristles.

The imaginative name refers to the flat, paddle-shaped stems of this well-known cactus. Although lacking long spines, it is protected by hundreds of sharp bristles. In the wild it is found in deserts and other dry rocky sites, and is also a popular garden species; it has attractive red or pink flowers on the edges of the joints often almost covering the plant. Like other *Opuntia* species it can be easily propagated by breaking off a joint and planting it.

Identification: The individual flowers are 5–7.5cm/2–3in across, with many petals. The stem joints are up to about 30cm/1ft long. The ripe fruit is egg-shaped and grey-brown and contains many seeds.

Left and above: The striking flowers are followed by a brown-grey oval fruit containing many seeds.

OTHER SPECIES OF NOTE

Plains Prickly Pear *Opuntia macrorhiza*
This low-growing cactus from the USA forms clumps up to 1.8m (6ft) in diameter in mountainous, arid areas between 800 and 2,200m (2,600 and 7,000ft) elevation. The bluish-green stems, become wrinkled under very dry or cold conditions and the large yellow flowers with their vivid red centres appear in early summer.

Saguaro *Carnegia gigantea*
This giant, fluted cactus, is slow-growing but can reach heights up to 12m/40ft and may live up to 200 years or more. It grows in mountains, desert slopes and rocky and flat areas of southwest USA and northwest Mexico. In May and June it bears creamy-white, bell-shaped flowers with yellow centres.

Rainbow Cactus Comb Hedgehog
Echinocereus pectinatus
A low-growing cactus found in Arizona, Texas and Mexico, with bands of colourful spines – hence the name – and very large flowers to 14cm/5½in across that may be pink, yellow or lavender.

Claret Cup Cactus, King's Cup (Strawberry) Cactus *Echinocereus triglochidiatus*
This is one of the most beautiful of all cacti, with deep, cup-shaped, bright scarlet flowers covering the plant during the spring.

Teddybear Cholla

Opuntia bigelovii

Looking furry and cuddly from a distance (hence the common name), but actually covered with sharp, barbed spines, this cactus grows in hot deserts. It is a tall species, often the height of a small tree. The spines are not easily removed, so this is quite a dangerous species.

Identification: The joints are cylindrical and up to 25cm/10in long, covered in a fur-like mass of pale golden spines. The flowers are green or yellow, the petals often streaked lavender.

Distribution: Northwest Mexico, central Arizona and south-east California.
Height and spread: 90–270cm/3–9ft.
Habit and form: Perennial.
Pollinated: Insect.
Leaf shape: Spines, about 2.5cm/1in long.

Below: A dense covering of spines protects the stem from sunlight.

Above: The plant produces flowers but the fruits are usually sterile. It spreads when its branches fall and take root.

PURSLANE FAMILY

This family (Portulacaceae) consists of about 400 species, with the majority in warm or tropical regions, and from small trees and shrubs to herbs, many of which are succulent. A few, such as some Portulaca species, are edible, and many are grown as garden plants. The flowers are radially symmetrical, and they usually have four to six petals.

Western Spring Beauty

Claytonia lanceolata

This delicate plant is one of the earliest flowers to appear in the spring, often as the snow melts, growing quickly using reserves stored in its underground stem. The latter apparently tastes a little like radish. The Western Spring Beauty is a slender plant with narrow leaves, and occurs in small to large patches. It grows on moist soils, mainly on highland sites – a typical location is around snow patches. It is also found on the woodland floor.

Identification: The leaves are succulent and the pink or white flowers grow in a slender, drooping raceme. Each flower is 6–20mm/½–¾in across with two sepals and five petals. Often the petals have streaks of dark pink. The main flowering period is March.

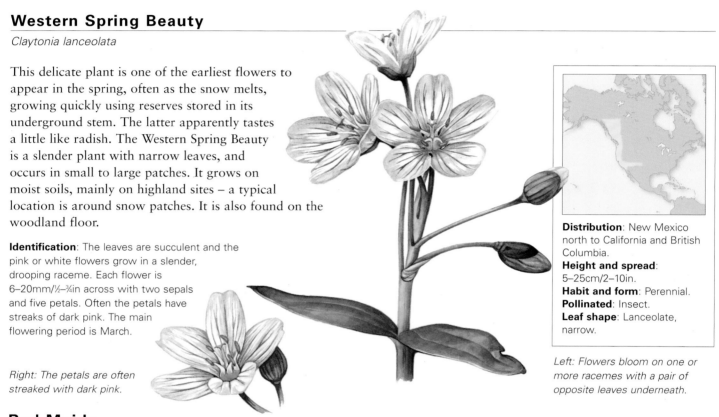

Right: The petals are often streaked with dark pink.

Distribution: New Mexico north to California and British Columbia.
Height and spread: 5–25cm/2–10in.
Habit and form: Perennial.
Pollinated: Insect.
Leaf shape: Lanceolate, narrow.

Left: Flowers bloom on one or more racemes with a pair of opposite leaves underneath.

Red Maids

Calandrinia ciliata

This is a large genus, with about 150 species. They are low-growing trailing herbs, and are mainly found in the tropics and subtropics. This species produces masses of very pretty bright red or pink flowers (rarely white). The flowers are borne on short stalks from the axils of the upper leaves. The habitat is open sites and waste ground, usually on moist soils.

Identification: Each flower is about 1.5cm/½in across, with two sepals and five petals, and they open in April and May.

Right: The cheerful flowers open on sunny afternoons.

Left: The plant is low-lying, and blooms among the grasses.

Distribution: Washington State south to California and New Mexico.
Height and spread: 5–40cm/2–16in.
Habit and form: Annual.
Pollinated: Insect.
Leaf shape: Long, narrow.

Flame Flower

Talinum aurantiacum

This species is well-named for its orange or red flowers. It grows on rocky slopes and desert canyons in western Texas and southern Arizona. The swollen roots were cooked and eaten by Native Americans. It has rather an extended flowering season, from June through October. The flowers are sometimes strikingly streaked with red.

Identification: A single orange-red flower, about 2.5cm/1in across, grows in each upper axil. The stems are sturdy and the leaves are narrow and succulent.

Distribution: West Texas and south Arizona.
Height and spread: 15–35cm/6–14in.
Habit and form: Perennial.
Pollinated: Insect.
Leaf shape: Long and narrow.

Right: This species has an unusually long flowering period, bearing colourful blooms from June to October.

Left and right: One orange flower apppears on each leaf axil.

OTHER SPECIES OF NOTE

Pussy Paws *Calyptridium umbellatum*
Pink flowers grow in dense clusters at the ends of the often trailing stems and resemble the soft pads on the underside of a cat's foot. Coniferous forests in the western states are the main habitat for this unusual plant, and the flowers appear from May to August.

Spring Beauty *Claytonia virginica*
A low-growing plant with clusters of pink or white flowers, each with darker pink stripes, opening in March to May. As it often grows in large patches, it makes a pretty show in the spring in moist woodland, and also in lawns. Mainly in the east of the region.

Rose Moss, Rose Purslane, *Portulaca pilosa*
Pink or purple flowers appear from June to October. Rose Moss grows on sandy soils from North Carolina to Florida, and in parts of the south west.

Tweedy's Lewisia *Lewisia tweedyi*
A large-flowered alpine species found in certain mountains in Washington State – notably Mount Stuart, between 1,800-2,000m/5,900-6,500ft, and sometimes grown as a garden alpine. It is an evergreen perennial that favours sites with full sun, and produces beautiful blooms, white tinged with rose pink, with vivid yellow stamens.

Common Purslane

Verdolaga, Portulaca oleracea

This is a common species, often encountered as a weed in disturbed ground, and also in gardens. However, it does have pretty yellow flowers, opening between June and September. An interesting feature of the species is that it is edible and has a long history of culinary and medicinal uses. The leaves and stems can be cooked and eaten, and it is also known as Little Hogweed.

Identification: Often grows as a low creeper. The leaves are long and rather fleshy, and the five-petalled yellow flowers about 6mm/¼in across.

Distribution: Southern Canada and much of the USA.
Height and spread: To 15cm/6in.
Habit and form: Annual.
Pollinated: Insect.
Leaf shape: Spoon-shaped, long.

Below: Purslane leaves are quite commonly used in salads or for other culinary purposes.

SORREL FAMILY

The sorrel family (Polygonaceae) is found mainly in the temperate regions. There are some 50 genera and about 1,150 species, including trees, shrubs, lianas and herbs. They have small flowers, usually radially symmetrical, borne in racemes. The fruits are hard and seed-like. Sorrels include edible species such as rhubarb (Rheum rhabarbarum), and some crops, such as buckwheat (Fagopyrum esculentum).

Northern Buckwheat

Eriogonum compositum

Several members of this genus are known as wild buckwheats. This species occurs on rocky open ground and flowers from May to July. It is a perennial that grows from a woody taproot. The seeds are eaten by many small animals, including ants, which may thus help in dispersal. The flowers are whitish or yellow and clustered tightly together in rounded heads. They provide an important source of food for butterflies.

Identification: The leaves are varied in shape – some being triangular, others heart-shaped or oval. The individual flowers are very small, about 3mm/⅛in across with six segments.

Right: The leaves may be triangular, heart-shaped or oval.

Above: The petals are creamy-white to lemon yellow.

Below: The flowering stem is stout and leafless.

Distribution: Northern California, north to Washington State and east to Idaho.
Height and spread: 10–50cm/4–20in.
Habit and form: Perennial.
Pollinated: Insect.
Leaf shape: Heart-shaped or ovate.

Sulfur Flower

Eriogonum umbellatum

The creamy yellow clusters of tiny flowers give this wild buckwheat its common name. This flower grows wild on dry ridges, in sagebrush deserts and is tolerant to cold, dry mountain conditions. Wild buckwheats are a difficult group to distinguish and this species is also very variable, which adds to problems of identification. The plant's habit is low growing and carpet-forming.

Identification: The flowerheads are 5–10cm/2–4in across, and consist of many tiny cups each with several tiny flowers, each just 6mm/¼in long and with six segments. The leaves are hairy beneath and grow close together at the ends of the branches.

Left: The leaves are fuzzy underneath.

Above: A ball-like cluster of flowers.

Distribution: Eastern slopes of Rockies from Colorado to Montana, and from southern California to British Columbia.
Height and spread: 10–30cm/4–12in.
Habit and form: Perennial.
Pollinated: Insect.
Leaf shape: Ovate.

Left: Flowers fade in colour as the seeds form.

Water (Swamp) Smartweed

Water Lady's Thumb, *Polygonum amphibium*

This is a widespread species that also occurs in Europe and Asia. It grows quite happily in water or in mud around lakes and ponds, adapting to the prevailing conditions. The pink flowers are in dense clusters and produced from June to September. It grows quickly and can become a nuisance as an aggressive weed.

Distribution: Much of North America.
Height and spread: Terrestrial 60–90cm/2–3ft; aquatic stems to 2m/6ft.
Habit and form: Perennial; semi-aquatic.
Pollinated: Insect.
Leaf shape: Lanceolate-ovate.

Identification: The flowers are very small – only about 4mm/⅛in, and the tight flower clusters vary from 1.5–17.5cm/½–7in. The seeds are dark brown to black and are an important source of nourishment for many water birds.

Right: Flowers open from July to August.

Right: This is the terrestrial form. In the water-based form, the leaves float.

OTHER SPECIES OF NOTE
Desert Trumpet Indianpipe Weed, Bladder Stem, *Eriogonum inflatum*
This is a common desert species in Arizona, California and southern Utah. It has swollen grey-green stems that go red, then white with age; and tiny yellow flowers. These are only really noticeable after heavy rainfall. The dried stems were used by Native Americans as tobacco pipes.

Cushion Buckwheat
Eriogonum ovalifolium
A variable species of sagebrush plains, woodland and rocky slopes, widespread in the west. It has distinctive, round, puff-ball like heads of purple, reddish or cream flowers and the leaves are distinctive; a lovely sage green, and oval, as the name suggests.

Winged Dock *Rumex venosus*
Sometimes known as Wild Begonia (though not related to true begonias), Winged Dock produces orange-red flowers in dense clusters and has reddish stems. It flowers from April to June on sandy grassland and in sagebrush deserts.

Sheep's Sorrel *Rumex acetosella*
Originally from Europe, now well established throughout North America. The arrow-shaped leaves have a sharp flavour, and the clusters of tiny red or green flowers attract many insects.

Japanese Knotweed

Polygonum cuspidatum (=P. japonicum)

This freely-suckering bushy plant has become notorious in recent years as a highly aggressive weed. It is an introduction from Asia and has spread rapidly. The young shoots can grow up even through asphalt and it is difficult to eradicate once established. The fresh young shoots are said to taste rather like asparagus, and the seeds are eaten by birds.

Identification: The flowers, produced in the autumn, are greenish-white and borne in open clusters about 7.5cm/3in long, arising from the leaf axils. The stems are hollow and jointed and have a mottled surface pattern.

Distribution: Widespread.
Height and spread: 90–210cm/3–7ft.
Habit and form: Perennial.
Pollinated: Insect.
Leaf shape: Rounded or ovate, tapering.

Above: The flowers are tiny and inconspicuous.

Left: The blooms are borne on panicles that tend to droop.

VIOLET AND PEONY FAMILIES

The violet family (Violaceae) comprises over 800 species, widely distributed in temperate and tropical regions of the world: the northern species are herbaceous, while others, natives of tropical areas, are trees and shrubs. Members of the peony family (Paeoniaceae) are mostly shrubby herbs with large, often showy, flowers. There are only two genera: Paeonia (33 species) and Glaucidium (one species).

Western Pansy Violet

Beckwith Violet, Great Basin Violet, *Viola beckwithii*

This large-flowered violet is very attractive and has pansy-like reddish-purple flowers. It is native to open pinewoods and sagebrush habitats in the west and flowers from March to May. The Sagebrush Violet (Desert Pansy) is very similar but has less divided leaves. This and many other violets are favourite garden plants with their cheerful, face-like colourful flowers.

Right: The leaves are mid-green and narrow.

Right: Tiny clumps form, with flower heads about thumbnail size.

Identification: The bilaterally symmetrical flowers face outwards and are brightly coloured. The upper two petals are red-purple, the lower three mauve, with yellow patches and reddish lines, the central one pouched. The long-stalked leaves are grey-green and divided into three narrow segments. It is commonly found among sagebrush.

Distribution: South east California to north east Oregon; east to Utah and Idaho.
Height and spread: 5–12.5cm/2–5in.
Habit and form: Perennial.
Pollinated: Insect.
Leaf shape: Divided.

Bog White Violet

Long leaf violet, *Viola lanceolata*

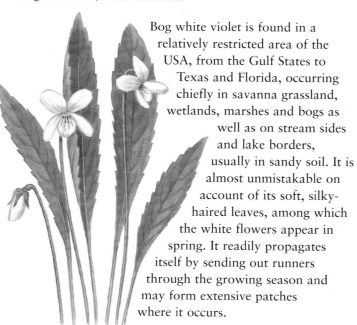

Bog white violet is found in a relatively restricted area of the USA, from the Gulf States to Texas and Florida, occurring chiefly in savanna grassland, wetlands, marshes and bogs as well as on stream sides and lake borders, usually in sandy soil. It is almost unmistakable on account of its soft, silky-haired leaves, among which the white flowers appear in spring. It readily propagates itself by sending out runners through the growing season and may form extensive patches where it occurs.

Identification: The leaves are basal, narrow or lance-shaped, 5–10cm/2–4in long, usually at least three times the width, somewhat irregularly toothed along the margin, tapering to the base, pinnately veined. The flowers are few, five-petalled, irregular in shape, white or light violet with purple markings on the three lower petals, beardless. They appear in late spring and continue into early summer. Self-pollinating flowers are also produced at the same time, lower in the leaf mass. The fruit that follows is a capsule. Sometimes confused with the similar and closely related *V. primulifolia*, which has more ovate leaves, although both species vary considerably.

Distribution: Gulf States to Texas and Florida, USA.
Height and spread: 15–20cm/6–8in.
Habit and form: Herbaceous perennial.
Pollinated: Insect.
Leaf shape: Linear or lanceolate.

OTHER SPECIES OF NOTE

Oregon Violet *Viola hallii*
Sometimes called Hall's violet, this rare plant from the western USA favours open woodland at altitudes of 300–1,850m/1,000–6,000ft. The dissected leaves make a graceful foil for the tricoloured flowers, which have creamy-white lower petals and two deep violet upper petals.

Evergreen Violet Redwood Violet, *Viola sempervirens*
Mats of thick leaves persist through the winter and the plant produces pretty yellow flowers from March to June. It is found form British Columbia south to southern Oregon (west of the Cascades) and to central California in redwood forests.

Woolly Blue Violet *Viola sororia*
A pretty plant, with blue, purple or white flowers. It is found throughout the east of the region in damp woods, roadsides, meadows and also lawns. The flowering period is March to June. Garden forms with pure white and freckled flowers are available.

Canada Violet Tall White Violet, *Viola canadensis*
Widespread, mainly in southern Canada and northern USA, and in mountains elsewhere, this is a relatively tall plant with attractive flowers appearing from April to June.The petals have a yellow tint towards the base and a purplish tinge on the back. In some states (e.g. Connecticut) this violet is now listed as endangered.

Stream Violet

Pioneer violet, Viola glabella

This violet occurs in woodland and near watercourses. Large colonies form bright green carpets, starred with yellow, under the trees in early spring. The plant occurs from Monterey County, California, northward into Alaska, at altitudes of up to 2,500m/8,200ft, with particularly fine stands around Portland and in Oregon. The species is also present in Japan. The heart-shaped leaves are often softly hairy all over and these emerge in spring, together with the bright yellow, neatly veined flowers.

Identification:
Knobbly green rhizomes range on, or just under, the surface, with true roots extending down into the soil. The leaves, on 5–10cm/2–4in stalks, are kidney- to heart-shaped and toothed. The flowers, up to 2cm/¾in across, are fresh yellow with purple veins, held above the leaves on leafy stems. They are followed by brownish capsules, which explode to disperse the seed.

Right: The small yellow flowers have veined petals and resemble tiny faces.

Distribution: California north to Alaska, Japan.
Height and spread: 5–30cm/2–12in.
Habit and form: Herbaceous perennial.
Pollinated: Insect.
Leaf shape: Reniform.

Western Peony

Paeonia brownii

Distribution: California and east Washington State, east to Utah, Idaho and western Wyoming.
Height and spread: 20–60cm/8–24in.
Habit and form: Perennial.
Pollinated: Insect.
Leaf shape: Divided.

This is one of only two species of peony in the American west, the other being *P. californica* which is found only in southern California. Western peony is a succulent leafy plant with rounded flowers dangling down at the ends of stalks. Its natural habitats are pine forests, sagebrush and chaparral, and it has a fairly wide distribution. It flowers from April to June. Native Americans used the roots to prepare a tea, used to treat lung problems.

Identification: Each flower is up to 4cm/1½in across with five to six greenish spoon-shaped sepals and five maroon, green-edged petals. The leaves have three main segments, each segment divided further into three parts.

Right: The plant avoids drought damage by dropping its leaves.

Above: The bowl shaped flowers are green, gold and maroon.

MALLOW FAMILY

The Malvaceae are herbs, shrubs or trees of about 75 genera and perhaps as many as 1,500 species. It includes well-known plants such as hollyhock (Althea rosea), cotton (Gossypium) and the edible okra (Hibiscus esculentus). Other members of the family are used as sources of fibre. Most mallows have showy petals, which makes them popular as ornamental plants.

Scarlet Globemallow

Red False Mallow, *Sphaeralcea coccinea*

There are about 60 species of globemallows in the western mountains and many of these have orange-red flowers. This species, which is most commonly found in the Great Plains area, has bright brick-red flowers that are saucer-like in shape and arranged in clusters in the axils of the upper leaves. The globemallow grows in open sites such as dry grassland and pine and juniper open forests. Other common species include scaly globemallow (*S. leptophylla*) and desert globemallow (*S. ambigua*).

Right: The flowering time is June to July. Each flower has leaf-like bracts underneath.

Identification: The plant has a woody base and rather arching foliage with short flower clusters. The individual flowers are about 3cm/1¼in across and have five petals. They open from April through August.

Right: The alternate leaves are deeply cut palmately and hairy underneath.

Distribution: Central Canada south to Montana, Idaho, Utah, to Arizona, Texas and New Mexico.
Height and spread: 50cm/20in.
Habit and form: Herbaceous perennial.
Pollinated: Insect.
Leaf shape: Divided, toothed.

Scarlet Rose Mallow

Scarlet hibiscus, Swamp hibiscus, *Hibiscus coccineus*

The scarlet rose mallow is a narrow, upright, herbaceous perennial with somewhat hemp-like leaves and extremely showy, deep red flowers that appear in mid- to late summer. Each flower lasts only a day, but new ones continue to open over a long period. It is attractive to many species of butterflies and hummingbirds. It occurs naturally in swamps, marshes and ditches, from southern Georgia and Alabama to central Florida, and is frequently encountered along southern rivers and streams, where it towers above the other aquatic plants, hence its other common name of swamp hibiscus.

Identification: A tall, vigorous, sturdy, erect, woody-based, herbaceous perennial, with smooth, blue-green stems. The leaves are deep green, 7.5–12.5cm/3–5in across, palmately three-, five- or seven-parted, or compound, the divisions narrow and sparsely toothed. The flowers are solitary and hollyhock-like, five-petalled, with a prominent and showy staminal column, borne on long stalks from the upper leaf axils. The deep red petals are up to 8cm/3¼in long, horizontally spreading.

Distribution: South-eastern USA.
Height and spread: Up to 3m/10ft.
Habit and form: Herbaceous perennial.
Pollinated: Insect.
Leaf shape: Palmate.

Left: The tall, rangy habit means that the deep red flowers are held well above the surrounding vegetation.

OTHER SPECIES OF NOTE

Mountain Hollyhock *Iliamna rivularis*
Similar in appearance to *I. grandiflora*, mountain hollyhock grows to around 2m/6½ft, with a showy spike of large white or pink flowers in summer. It is widely distributed in mountains from British Columbia south to California.

Desert Globemallow *Sphaeralcea ambigua*
Also known as the desert hollyhock, this is a loose, shrubby, herbaceous perennial of dry woodland, mountains and high desert regions in the south-west USA. Its orange, pink, white or red flowers are produced for much of the year.

Checkermallow, *Sidalcea neomexicana*
Clusters of deep pink flowers appear from June to September. Checkermallow prefers moist soils near ponds and streams or in mountain sites. It is found from Oregon south to California, New Mexico and Mexico, and east to Wyoming.

Halberdleaf Rose Mallow *Hibiscus laevis*
The halberdleaf rose mallow is found in large colonies in marshy areas throughout the eastern USA, mainly from Minnesota to Pennsylvania and further south. It blooms from midsummer to early autumn. It often grows where mud has

deposited along the banks of rivers and in swamps. The pale pink, to mauve, to near white flowers are showy and very attractive. The flowers are up to 15cm/6in in diameter.

Wild Hollyhock

Iliamna grandiflora

This handsome plant bears large pink "mallow" flowers on tall spikes in the summer. It is a plant of damp montane meadows and stream courses, and occurs through New Mexico, Arizona, Colorado, and Utah, at altitudes between 2,200–3,350m/7,000–11,000ft. Despite its wide distribution across these states, the plant occurs in sporadic locations and where it does grow it often has very low population numbers. The reason for its scarcity remains a mystery, although changes in land management practices could be partially responsible.

Identification: The tall stems and leaves are sparsely hairy; the leaves are palmate and deeply lobed, 5–10cm/2–4in long, and coarsely toothed. The coarsely hairy flower spike appears in summer. The bell-shaped flowers, intermittently distributed up the stem and opening from round buds, have petals 2.5cm/1in long, pink maturing to purplish or lavender, with densely hairy margins at the base. The staminal column is basally hairy and about 15mm/⅝in long. The fruits are flattened spheres.

Distribution: New Mexico, Arizona, Colorado, and Utah, USA.
Height and spread: 1–2m/3–6½ft.
Habit and form: Herbaceous perennial.
Pollinated: Insect.
Leaf shape: Palmate.

Desert Rosemallow

Hibiscus coulteri

Distribution: Northern Mexico, west Texas, southern Arizona.
Height and spread: To 1.2m/4ft.
Habit and form: Herbaceous perennial.
Pollinated: Insect.
Leaf shape: Divided, toothed.

This shrubby plant is covered in rough hairs and grows in hills and canyons in desert areas. It produces large pale yellow or whitish cup-shaped flowers, often with a red tinge. The closely related rock hibiscus *(H. denudatus)* has smaller pinkish-lavender or white flowers. Hibiscus species are commonly grown in gardens and many garden varieties have been bred from certain members of the genus, which contains some 220 species.

Identification: The individual flowers are 2.5–5cm/1–2in across with five petals and many stamens, the latter joined at the base, forming a tube. The flowers open in succession from the bottom of the stem upwards. They open between April and August and can be white or creamy yellow in colour. The lower leaves are oval, but those further up the stems have three narrow lobes.

Far right: The plant is a shrubby perennial; herbaceous but with a woody base. It is highly tolerant of drought.

CUCUMBER FAMILY

The Cucurbitaceae are a medium-sized plant family of some 120 genera and 775 species, primarily found in the warmer regions of the world. It is a major family for edible fruits, representing some of the earliest cultivated plants in both the old and new worlds. It includes Cucumis *(melons, muskmelons and cucumbers);* Cucurbita *(squashes, marrows, and pumpkins) and* Citrullus *(watermelons).*

Buffalo Gourd

Cucurbita foetidissima

This perennial, trailing vine occurs in dry, sandy areas, beside roads and railway tracks, predominantly in disturbed soils, throughout the south-west USA and into Mexico. It is often recognizable by its foetid odour before it is even seen, but despite this disagreeable characteristic various Native American and Mexican tribes used it for at least 9,000 years as a food, cosmetic, detergent, insecticide and ritualistic rattle. The deep yellow flowers appear during spring and early summer before the fruit.

Right: The melon-like fruits have a strong, disagreeable odour.

Identification: A prostrate or trailing vine with an extremely large taproot, which may attain a weight of more than 40kg/88lb in three or four years. The grey-green leaves are stiff, leathery and rough-textured, usually triangular in outline, tending to fold upward parallel to the midvein. The large, yellow flowers, 7.5–10cm/3–4in long and 2.5–5cm/1–2in wide, open in the mornings from late spring to early autumn; male and female flowers are borne on the same plant. The fruit is gourd-like but not as hard as other wild cucurbit species, spherical to elliptic, 5–7.5cm/2–3in in diameter, green with light green or yellow stripes, the whole fruit turning yellow or tan with age.

Distribution: South-west USA and Mexico.
Height and spread: 6m/20ft.
Habit and form: Perennial low-growing vine.
Pollinated: Insect.
Leaf shape: Deltoid.

Above: Buffalo gourd is a trailing vine.

Balsam-apple

Wild cucumber, *Echinocystis lobata*

This perennial, prostrate or climbing vine is found primarily in the north-eastern United States and adjacent to Canada, although it is widespread elsewhere in forests, particularly those on floodplains or wetlands; it is occasionally found on agricultural land. It is strong-growing, with a large, tuberous root and long stems. The separate male and female blooms appear at the end of long flowering stems from early summer to mid-autumn. The spiny fruits split from the tip as they gradually dry out, revealing the seeds within.

Right: The spiny green fruit dries to a papery consistency when ripe.

Identification: This tuberous perennial herb climbs by means of double or triple corkscrew-like tendrils. The large leaves are alternate, circular to palmate, with three to five pointed lobes and serrated margins. The male flowers are borne in panicles from the leaf axils, the female flowers are solitary or paired, borne at the same axils. The calyx has six bristly lobes and the corolla is green-white with six slender petals up to 6mm/¼in long. The fruit is an oval or round, spiny pod, 5cm/2in in diameter, containing four seeds.

Right: The plant spreads quickly from an underground tuber.

Distribution: North-eastern North America.
Height and spread: 6m/20ft.
Habit and form: Climbing vine.
Pollinated: Insect.
Leaf shape: Orbicular to palmate.

CUCUMBER FAMILY 81

Globe Berry

Ibervillea lindheimeri

Distribution: South-west USA.
Height and spread: 2–4m/6–13ft.
Habit and form: Climbing or trailing herbaceous perennial.
Pollinated: Insect.
Leaf shape: Cuneate to rhombic-ovate.

Right: The stems climb by means of long, corkscrew-like tendrils.

This native of North America is fairly limited in its range, which includes the south-west states of Texas, Oklahoma, New Mexico, Arizona and California. The small, elegant leaves can be unlobed or deeply three- or five-lobed and range from narrowly triangular to fan-shaped. The species is dioecious with flowers carried on slender branching stems, and the most ornamental aspect of this plant is the round fruit. The plants are usually found in open dry woodlands and open areas with rocky soil.

Below: The fruit turns vibrant red when ripe.

Identification: The leaves, up to 12.5cm/5in long on 4cm/1½in stalks, have three to five wedge- to diamond-shaped segments, with 12mm/½in teeth or lobes. The male flowers, borne five to eight per raceme, are yellow and tubular, with three stamens and five yellow or greenish-yellow petals that are not ornate; the solitary female flowers have three stigmas. The calyx is cylindrical and slightly downy. The globular fruits, 2.5–3cm/1–1¼in in diameter, are pale green, turning orange and then vibrant red, and containing around ten swollen, round seeds.

OTHER SPECIES OF NOTE

Star Cucumber *Sicyos angulatus*
The star or burr cucumber is a vine that produces white flowers in summer, in small clusters at the end of long flowering stalks. It is found in thickets and along the banks of streams and rivers throughout eastern and central North America. The flowers are followed by clusters of small, red, spiny, oval fruits.

Cucamonga Manroot *Marah macrocarpus*
This manroot is a common plant of dry areas of chaparral, washes, roadsides, coastal sage scrub and foothill woodland in south-west North America. It is most notable for its large, fleshy root, which may weigh as much as 45kg/100lb. The greenish-white flowers that appear in winter are quite insignificant, and the fruit that follows is egg-shaped and densely covered with stiff, flattened prickles.

Creeping Cucumber *Melothria pendula*
This perennial vine has a very scattered distribution, from the southern United States down as far as Bolivia, being most commonly found in thin woods, thickets and at swamp edges, and often occurring in large numbers on disturbed ground. The yellow flowers appear in late spring and are followed by fruits that resemble tiny watermelons.

California Manroot

Marah fabaceus

This perennial climbing or creeping vine can be found beside streams and washes, in shrubby and open areas up to around 1,600m/5,200ft. It is limited to California, principally the Mojave Desert and Baja California. Its common name refers to its surprisingly large tubers, which some claim look like a dead body when dug up, but which help it to survive the dry Californian summers. The prickly fruits look like cucumbers, although they are not edible. The plant dies to the ground after fruiting.

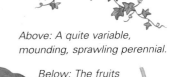

Distribution: California, USA.
Height and spread: 5–6m/16–20ft.
Habit and form: Trailing or climbing herbaceous perennial.
Pollinated: Insect.
Leaf shape: Cordate.

Identification: A large perennial with branched, coiling tendrils, the plant usually winds over and through other vegetation. The leaves are round or heart-shaped, with five to seven lobes. The male flowers appear in racemes or panicles while the female flowers are solitary, usually borne in the same leaf axil; the flowers are cup-shaped, up to 1.5cm/⅝in across, yellowish green, cream or white, appearing in spring. The fruit is a spiny, round capsule containing four seeds.

Above: A quite variable, mounding, sprawling perennial.

Below: The fruits appear from late spring onward.

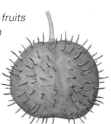

GERANIUM FAMILY

The Geraniaceae is a varied family of 11 genera and 700 species that usually feature five-petalled flowers and a beaked fruit that often disperses the seed explosively. They are primarily temperate annual and perennial herbs, frequently covered in glandular hairs. Most contain aromatic oils. The family contains both the true geraniums (Geranium) and gardeners' 'geraniums' (Pelargonium).

Filaree Storksbill

Clocks, *Erodium cicutarium*

This pretty little flower grows in many sites and has a wide distribution. It is a successful weed, colonizing waste ground and disturbed soils, especially on light, sandy substrates. It grows either as a small low-growing herb, or may be sprawling and many-branched. The leaves are fern-like, and up to 20cm/4in long. The name 'storksbill' refers to the fruit which is long, narrow and pointed.

Left: The flowers are among the first to appear in spring. Although pretty, it is considered a noxious weed that can damage crops and other native species.

Far left: Ripening seedpods twist into spirals.

Identification: The fern-like leaves (to 10cm/4in), are divided, with each segment further divided. The stems are often tinted red and the flowers are a pretty purple-pink, in loose clusters. Each flower is about 1.5cm/½in across with five petals, and the characteristic fruit is long and slender.

Distribution: Scattered throughout the region; introduced from Europe.
Height and spread: 2.5 to 30cm (1–12in).
Habit and form: Annual or biennial.
Pollinated: Insect.
Leaf shape: Pinnately divided.

Richardson's Crane's-bill/Geranium

Geranium richardsonii

This attractive woodland flower is one of the commonest wild geraniums of the west of the region. It grows mainly under partial shade, for example in woods, at a range of altitudes from lowland to the mountains. The name 'crane's-bill' refers to the elongate pointed fruit.

Above: The streaked petals.

Identification: Produces several stems with leaves about 15cm/6in across and with five to seven segments, and pointed lobes. The flowers are 2.5cm/1in across with five pale pink petals, veined purple. The fruit is about 2.5cm/1in long and pointed. In dry conditions the plant has few stems, flowers or leaves, but in moist soil it can become lush with many blooms.

Left: The pointed fruit contains seeds with coiled 'tails', which help them penetrate the ground.

Distribution: Western states, from New Mexico and California north to Oregon, Washington State and British Columbia; also in South Dakota and Saskatchewan.
Height and spread: 20–80cm/8–30in.
Habit and form: Perennial.
Pollinated: Insect.
Leaf shape: Palmately lobed.

Wild Crane's-bill

Geranium maculatum

This geranium flowers from April to June and grows in meadows, woods and scrub. The pink or white flowers grow in loose clusters, with between two and five flowers in each cluster.

Identification: Each flower has five sepals and five petals, measures about 4cm/1½in across, and contains ten stamens. The palmately lobed leaves, measuring 10–12.5cm/4–5in, are grey-green and the lobes are deeply toothed. Like other geraniums, this species has the typical long, narrow fruit capsule, that splits when ripe into five curved segments to release the seeds.

Distribution: Rather eastern distribution, from Georgia north to South Dakota, Minnesota, Ontario and Maine; west to Louisiana and Oklahoma.
Height and spread: 30–60cm/1–2ft.
Habit and form: Perennial.
Pollinated: Insect.
Leaf shape: Palmate.

Above: The flowers have five petals and are pink to purple.

Far right: Leaves have five palmate lobes.

OTHER SPECIES OF NOTE

California Stork's Bill
Erodium macrophyllum var. *californicum*
Also known as filaree, this annual, or occasionally biennial, herb is often encountered in valley grassland and woodlands in low mountain reaches in western North America. It is rare across much of its range. It has mainly basal leaves and white flowers, sometimes tinged with red-purple, which appear in summer.

Herb Robert
Geranium robertianum
This is an introduced species from Europe, now widely naturalised in North America, where it prefers rocky habitats and woodland. It is rather tall (to 60cm/2ft) and has pairs of pretty pink flowers, reddish stems and divided leaves which smell unpleasant when crushed.

Carolina Geranium *Geranium carolinianum*
A southern annual that is closely related to Geranium maculatum and has a wide distribution in eastern North America. The flower clusters are more compact than those of its relatives.

Sticky Geranium *Geranium viscosissimum*
Found in woods and meadows mainly in the western states, sticky geranium flowers from May to August and the flower clusters have sticky hairs on the stalks – hence the common name. The five-petalled flowers are pink or purplish.

Woolly Geranium

Northern geranium *Geranium erianthum*

This herbaceous perennial from the Arctic is distributed across north-west North America and north-east Asia, and is most commonly found in woods and sub-alpine meadows and scrub, from low to fairly high elevations in the mountains, and also on grassy slopes near the sea. It is slender-stemmed and branched, with bright blue flowers and, although common, it is scattered in its distribution. It is easily seen when flowering in early summer, and often has later flushes of flowers, though the extent to which this happens varies considerably between locations.

Identification: The basal leaves are 5–20cm/2–8in wide, with seven or nine deeply divided, acutely lobed and freely toothed divisions; the upper leaves are stalkless, with five or seven narrower divisions and hairy veins on the undersides. The leaves colour in autumn. Dense, umbel-like clusters of flowers appear in summer, occasionally with a later flush; the flowers are flat, not nodding, 2.5cm/1in across, with almost triangular petals, pale to dark blue-violet, with dark veins at the base and a dark centre. They are followed by explosive seedpods.

Distribution: North-west North America and north-east Asia.
Height and spread: 50cm/20in.
Habit and form: Herbaceous perennial.
Pollinated: Insect.
Leaf shape: Palmate.

SPURGE FAMILY

Euphorbiaceae has over 300 genera and more than 8,000 species, found mainly in warm regions. Most exude a white, noxious sap if broken. The name 'spurge' refers to the use of some species to purge the body as a laxative, although large doses can be poisonous. Some spurge are grown as ornamentals; others include the important crop rubber (Hevea) *and the edible cassava or tapioca* (Manihot esculenta).

Rattlesnake Weed

Chamaesyce albomarginata

A low-growing spurge with small, bright flowers found in the west of the region, in deserts, dry grassland and also in pine/juniper woodland. It creeps close to the ground, sending out long stems with small, roundish opposite leaves. The common name comes from the fact that it was formerly thought to be useful in treating snakebites, but this quality has not been conclusively proven. The blooming period is from April to November.

Identification: The tiny white flowers are not quite what they seem – the four–five small white appendages giving the impression of petals, each with a purple pad at the base. The fruit is a small triangular capsule that splits into three on ripening, each section with a single seed.

Above: The plant is low-growing with small flowers.

Above: The plant is also known as White-Margined Spurge, for its flowers.

Distribution: Mexico, southeast California, south Utah, east to Oklahoma.
Height and spread: Stems 5–25cm/2–10in; creeping.
Habit and form: Perennial.
Pollinated: Insect.
Leaf shape: Round or oblong.

Leafy Spurge

Euphorbia esula

This spurge was introduced to North America from Europe, and has, like many alien introductions, become a successful weed, spreading rapidly into open, disturbed habitats, partly as a result of its underground runners. It is toxic to livestock if they eat large quantities, on account of its poisonous, milky sap.

Identification: The flowers are tiny, associated in clusters with paired green bracts. The stem leaves are very narrow, while those near the flowerheads are heart-shaped and about 2cm/¾in long. The fruit is a round capsule.

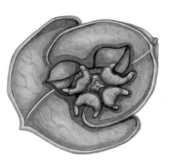

Left: The plant has smooth stems and showy flower bracts.

Above: The leafy bracts appear before the tiny true flowers, which bloom in June. The seed capsules will eventually explode, dispersing the contents up to 4.5m/15ft from the parent plant.

Distribution: Northern USA and southern Canada.
Height and spread: 20–90cm/8–36in.
Habit and form: Perennial.
Pollinated: Insect.
Leaf shape: Long, narrow.

Left: Due to the sap in the hollow stems, the plant is also known as Wolf's Milk.

Flowering Spurge

Tramp's Spurge, *Euphorbia corollata*

As its name implies, this spurge is rather more attractive than many, with somewhat more showy, bright white 'flowers', with a green centre. They open between June and October and this species occurs mainly in open woods, fields and alongside roads and tracks.

Distribution: Ontario and Maine, south to Minnesota, South Dakota and Florida; west to Texas.
Height and spread: 25–90cm/10–36in.
Habit and form: Perennial.
Pollinated: Insect.
Leaf shape: Long, oblong.

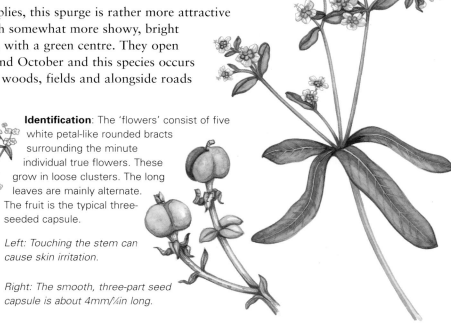

Identification: The 'flowers' consist of five white petal-like rounded bracts surrounding the minute individual true flowers. These grow in loose clusters. The long leaves are mainly alternate. The fruit is the typical three-seeded capsule.

Left: Touching the stem can cause skin irritation.

Right: The smooth, three-part seed capsule is about 4mm/¼in long.

OTHER SPECIES OF NOTE

Wild Poinsettia, *Euphorbia cyathophora*
White, red or yellow leaves surround a cluster of tiny flowers. The plant flowers in August and September in open woodland and disturbed sites, often on sandy soils, and is found in Texas, Georgia and Florida, north to South Dakota and Minnesota. It looks a little like the true poinsettia *(Poinsettia pulcherrima)* popular at Christmas.

Cypress Spurge, *Euphorbia cyparissias*
This came from Europe and has spread throughout much of North America. It is found mainly on disturbed ground such as along roadsides and wasteland, and quickly forms large patches as it spreads rapidly from underground roots.

Toothed Spurge, *Euphorbia dentata*
Similar to wild poinsettia, but this has hairier stems and its leafy bracts are normally green or white at the base. It's a fairly indistinct plant as the flowers are small and greenish-white. It produces a milky sap that can cause irritation.

Snow-on-the-mountain, Ghost Weed, *Euphorbia marginata*
This Midwest native is a softly hairy annual, growing to 1m/39in tall, with oblong, pale green leaves edged with white. A number of garden forms exist, notably 'White Top', an attractive, variegated cultivar.

Spurge Nettle

Tread Softly, *Cnidoscolus stimulosus*

As if belonging to the generally poisonous spurge family were not enough to discourage browsers, spurge nettle is further protected by its covering of stinging hairs (like a true nettle). Contact often produces a painful rash like a nettle-sting. There are about 75 species in this genus, found mainly in tropical and subtropical America. This species has large white, trumpet-shaped flowers.

Distribution: Florida and Louisiana, north to Virginia and Kentucky.
Height and spread: 15–90cm/6–36in.
Habit and form: Perennial.
Pollinated: Insect.
Leaf shape: Palmately lobed.

Identification: Flowers in terminal clusters, each male flower about 2.5cm/1in across, with five spreading calyx lobes.

Below: The entire plant is covered in hairs or spines.

Above: The flower is actually the calyx of the male plant.

PRIMROSE FAMILY

The Primulaceae include 22 genera and around 825 species, occurring mainly in temperate and mountainous regions of the northern hemisphere. Only one species of Primula *naturally occurs south of the equator in South America. The family also includes cyclamens and the aquatic water violet (Hottonia).*

Dark-throat Shooting Star

Dodecatheon pulchellum

The dark-throat shooting star is commonly found in damp meadows and adjacent edges from Alaska to Mexico and eastward to the western edge of the Great Plains, mostly at elevations below 2,750m/9,000ft. It has intensely coloured flowers and a long flowering period from mid-spring to late summer, depending on location. The genus name *Dodecatheon* is translated from Greek and means 12 gods, and alludes to the usual number of flowers in the inflorescences of these plants.

Identification: The erect, smooth stems arise from a slender rhizome with white, fleshy, fibrous roots. The light greyish-green leaves are basal, forming a rosette; they are strap-like to oval, 5–20cm/2–8in long, with pointed or rounded tips, occasionally with rounded teeth or wavy margins, mostly narrowing gradually to the leaf stalk. The flowers are borne in terminal umbellate inflorescences of two to twelve, on slender stalks. The sepals are green and persistent, and the petals are basally united with a short tube, a dilated throat and strongly reflexed lobes; the corolla tube is maroon, yellow above.

Distribution: Alaska south to Mexico.
Height and spread: 10–40cm/4–16in.
Habit and form: Herbaceous perennial.
Pollinated: Insect.
Leaf shape: Oblanceolate.

Far left: The nodding magenta or lavender flowers have strongly reflexed petals that give the plant its "shooting-star" look.

White Shooting Star

Dodecatheon dentatum

This pretty primula relative, also known as Ellis' shooting star, has attractive flowers, which grow up in an umbel from its basal bed of leaves. It flowers from May to July and is the only shooting star to have consistently white flowers, although the petals do vary slightly in colour. It grows well near waterfalls and streams where there is plenty of shade and moist soil.

Above and left: From bud to full bloom the flowers seem to turn themselves inside-out.

Identification: Small, dart-like flowers growing from a basal rosette of leaves. The stamens are maroon or yellow forming the 'point' of the dart. The petals are usually white or cream, but sometimes pink or pale violet (e.g. in Utah). The leaves are 3–10cm/1–4in long with toothed edges and a tapering base to a slender stalk.

Left: The leaves are an attractive bright, fresh green.

Distribution: Southern British Columbia south to northern Oregon and east to central Idaho and northern Utah; also in Arizona and New Mexico.
Height and spread: 15–40cm/6–16in.
Habit and form: Perennial herb.
Pollinated: Insect.
Leaf shape: Toothed.

Left: The stalks and flowers are delicate.

Parry's Primrose

Primula parryi

The bright colour of this primrose's attractive and soft-looking flowers makes it a favourite despite its unpleasant odour of rotting flesh. It is often found alongside streams and on wet ground. Genetic variation is insured by the fact that it is heterostylous – some plants have long styles and short anthers, while others have the opposite arrangement, thus encouraging outbreeding.

Identification: The attractive flowers emerge from a bed of oblong leaves. The stalk is relatively stout and leafless; flowers are 1.5-3cm/⅗–1in wide, and have five round petals, which spread out from a slender tube. The calyx and flower stalks are covered in tiny, glandular hairs. The leaves are 5–30cm/2–12in long, and fleshy.

Distribution: Idaho and Montana south to Navada, northern Arizona, and northern New Mexico.
Height and spread: 7.5–40cm/3–16in.
Habit and form: Perennial herb.
Pollinated: Insect.
Leaf shape: Oblong.

Left: The blooms' colour is intense in contrast to the bright green foliage.

Below: The flower has a deep, slender tube, ideal for the insect pollinators to crawl into.

Right: Just a light touch will bring out the plant's unpleasant smell.

OTHER SPECIES OF NOTE

Androsace chamaejasme
This small perennial herb has a wide Northern Hemisphere distribution along streams in poor dry soils. The hairy flowering stems bear umbels or, more rarely, solitary blooms that are creamy-white, yellow-centred, turning pink with age, or pink with contrasting markings.

Jewelled Shooting Star
Dodecatheon amethystinum
Found primarily in south-western Wisconsin and Minnesota, with scattered populations in Illinois, Missouri and Pennsylvania, this flower grows on north-facing cliffs and bluffs lining waterways, typically in thin alkaline soil. Its dark pink flowers are very noticeable when in bloom in late spring.

Sea Milkwort
Glaux maritima
This saltmarsh plant has oval leaves and tiny white, pink, purple or reddish, stalkless flowers that arise from thick leaf axils in June to July. It is widely distributed in North America.

Scarlet Pimpernel, Poor Man's Weatherglass
Anagallis arvensis
The latter nickname comes because it closes its flowers in cloudy weather, as well as in the late afternoon. It is a sprawling, low-branched plant with 6mm/⅛in wide, star-like flowers with five stunning orange to scarlet petals. It is fairly widespread from Canada to Texas.

Sierra Primrose

Primula suffrutescens

This unusual-looking primrose flowers from July-August. Its beautifully bright, slender flowers grow high above the leaves and flare outwards from a yellow tube with a yellow opening. The favoured habitat is rocky ground at high elevations. It grows in the treeless Arctic zone, 3,200m/ 10,500ft above sea level, so only determined hikers are likely to catch a glimpse of it. The colours are extremely vivid and distinctive.

Identification: The tall, leafless stalks rise above beds of basal rosettes of wedge-shaped leaves. They are topped with deep purple/pink flowers with five heart-shaped petals each, and vivid, orange-yellow centre tubes. The leaves are thick, with even teeth. In favourable conditions, swathes of the plant may form.

Distribution: Mountains of northern California south to Sierra Nevada.
Height and spread: Flower stalks reach 7.5–15cm/3–6in.
Habit and form: Perennial herb.
Pollinated: Insect.
Leaf shape: Wedge-shaped.

Right: Clusters of flowers form on a tall stem.

Far right: The plant forms a low-growing mat.

HEATHER FAMILY

The Ericaceae is a large family, mostly shrubby, comprising over 100 genera and some 3,400 species of mostly calcifuge (lime-hating) plants. The family includes shrubs, trees and herbs from mostly temperate, boreal, and montane tropical zones. Some have edible fruits – for example blueberries and cranberries. Rhododendrons and azaleas have very showy flowers and are popular garden plants.

Dusty Zenobia

Honeycup, *Zenobia pulverulenta*

This distinctive, extremely slow-growing, small deciduous shrub is a native of the coastal plain of the eastern USA, where it can be found in bogs and wet areas. It is the only species in its genus, and gets its common name from the dusty appearance of the bluish-green leaves. The small white flowers appear in the spring and are much more open than the pinched bells of *Vaccinium* and other related ericaceous species found in the same areas, adding to its distinctive appearance.

Identification: An open shrub with graceful, arching branches. The leaves are oval to oblong, pale green to grey-green with a waxy bloom and serrated margin, 2.5–5cm/1–2in long; they turn yellow-orange in autumn with a purplish-red tinge. Small bell-shaped, cream flowers with pale turquoise stems appear in early summer from the old wood. The pendent, white bells are rather plump and wide open and have a light citrus or anise scent.

Distribution: Eastern USA.
Height and spread: 60–180cm/2–6ft.
Habit and form: Deciduous shrub.
Pollinated: Insect.
Leaf shape: Ovate to oblong.

Far left: Although it eventually forms an open shrub, it is very slow growing.

Mountain Laurel

Calico bush, spoonwood, *Kalmia latifolia*

This large spreading shrub, native to eastern North America, is typically found around woodland edges, particularly by watersides or where light filters through the forest canopy. It is an evergreen with leaves clustered at the branch tips. Its star-shaped flowers range from red to pink or white, and occur in showy clusters. It is also known as spoonwood because native Americans used to make spoons from it.

Identification: This rounded, evergreen shrub may be dense and compact or open, depending on how much light it receives, with an irregular branching habit. The brown-tan bark is lightly ridged and furrowed, the trunks gnarled and twisted. The leaves are alternate, clustered toward the shoot tips, elliptic, 5–12.5cm/2–5in long, with pointed tips and smooth margins; they are dark green and glossy above, yellow-green in full sun. The lateral buds are hidden behind the bases of the leaf stalks. The flowers are pink, fading to white, up to 2.5cm/1in across; they appear in late spring in showy clusters at the branch tips, opening from star-shaped buds. The fruits are small, upright, dry, brown-tan capsules.

Right: The star-shaped flowers can be pink or white and appear in showy clusters in late spring.

Distribution: Eastern North America.
Height and spread: 1.5–3.5m/5–12ft.
Habit and form: Evergreen shrub.
Pollinated: Insect.
Leaf shape: Elliptic.

Mayflower

Trailing arbutus, *Epigaea repens*

Distribution: North America.
Height and spread:
10cm/4in or more.
Habit and form: Creeping
evergreen shrub.
Pollinated: Insect.
Leaf shape: Ovate.

The delicate pink flowers of this small, evergreen, flowering shrub are among the first to appear on sandy soils across many parts of North America, mostly under the shade of trees in northern or mountainous areas. It is very low-growing and forms dense, slowly spreading mats, the creeping branches rooting along their length to form a shrubby thicket. It is widespread but by no means common: its growing sites are easily destroyed when disturbed by people or livestock and seldom recover.

Identification: The yellow-orange, trailing stems of this evergreen shrub root along their length at the nodes. The leaves, on hairy stalks, are alternate and broadly oval with a short point at the tip, 2.5–4cm/1–1½in long, rough and leathery with wavy margins and hairy undersides; they are often spotted with dead patches. The flowers, which are very fragrant, are produced at the end of the branches in dense clusters, sometimes in late winter but mainly in spring. They are white, to 1.5cm/⅝in across, with a reddish tinge, divided at the top into five segments that spread open in the form of a star. This low creeping, evergreen shrub has numerous trailing twiggy, yellow-orange stems, all of which have a tendency to root along their length at the nodes.

OTHER SPECIES OF NOTE

Ground Pine Heather *Cassiope lycopodioides*
This small, low-growing, evergreen shrub is found across the upper Pacific rim, from Japan through Alaska and British Columbia, down as far as Washington State, occurring at altitude in southern locations. The small white bells, with a red calyx, grow toward the top of the branches.

Large-fruited Cranberry
Vaccinium macrocarpon
This is the familiar cranberry grown commercially and used in cooking. It occurs naturally in eastern North America in acid boggy ground, forming a low-growing, creeping mat.

Alabama Azalea
Rhododendron alabamense
The flower of the Alabama azalea is typically white with a bright yellow blotch, but can sometimes be flushed with pink. Blooms appear in mid-spring, and their attractive lemon fragrance is most distinctive. It grows naturally in north-central Alabama, western to central Georgia and South Carolina, and is widely cultivated.

Flame Azalea
Rhododendron calendulaceum
This is found in dry open woods and also on treeless mountain slopes, for example in the southern Appalachians, and ranges from Georgia and Alabama north to New York and Ohio. It has beautiful large orange red or yellow flowers and is widely cultivated as an ornamental in gardens and parks.

Salal

Gaultheria shallon

This evergreen plant is one of the most common understorey shrubs in some coastal forests in Alaska, British Columbia, California, Oregon and Washington. In drier coniferous forests it can form an almost continuous shrub layer. It is also common in some wet or boggy coniferous forests, and in areas near the coast the shrub layer can be impenetrable. The small, white urn-shaped flowers appear at midsummer in clusters around the branch tips.

Identification: A creeping to erect shrub of variable height, it spreads by layering or suckering, with hairy, branched stems that arch and root at the nodes. The leaves are thick and leathery, shiny, oval, 5–10cm/2–4in long and finely toothed, pointed at the tip and rounded at the base. The flowers, white to pink, pendent bells, five-lobed, are borne singly along the axis of the stem tip, in groups of 5–15, the reddish flower stalks bending so that the flowers are oriented in one direction; they appear from late spring to midsummer. They are followed by berries that mature by late summer.

Distribution: North-west North America.
Height and spread:
20cm–5m/8in–16ft.
Habit and form: Evergreen shrub.
Pollinated: Insect.
Leaf shape: Ovate.

Left: Growth is largely upright.

Right: The edible purple to black berries are often sweet.

CABBAGE FAMILY

The Cruciferae (Brassicaceae) are herbs or, rarely, subshrubs comprising about 365 genera and 3,250 species. The family includes familiar food plants such as cabbage, cauliflower, broccoli, Brussels sprouts, kohlrabi, and kale, which have all been derived from a single wild plant through human selection. Members of the cabbage family are found throughout temperate parts of the world.

Pennsylvania Bittercress

Cardamine pensylvanica

This perennial plant grows throughout much of North America. It is usually found in moist or wet soils, in wet woods, beside streams and along roadsides near woods. The flowering period varies according to its location, but is usually between early spring and midsummer. It can be confused with many similar species; the best way of identifying it is by its terminal leaflets, which are as large as, or larger than, the lateral leaflets.

Identification: The stems are erect, smooth or slightly hairy near the base, sometimes branched, up to 38cm/15in long, arising from a thickened rootstock. The leaves are alternate, pinnately compound with 5–13 smooth leaflets. The terminal leaflet is as large as, or larger than, the lateral leaflets, being up to 12mm/½in long and nearly as broad. All leaflets are oblong to oval, without teeth, toothed, or sometimes shallowly lobed. The tiny flowers, occurring in small groups on terminal racemes, are white, up to 6mm/¼in across, with four green, smooth sepals and four white petals, free from each other. The fruits are slender, cylindrical pods, ascending, up to 3cm/1¼in long, with a sterile beak. The seeds are pale brown.

Left: The fruit pods are long and slender.

Right: The plant is a biennial or herbaceous perennial.

Distribution: North America, from Newfoundland to Minnesota and Montana, south to Florida, Tennessee and Kansas.
Height and spread: 23–60cm/9–24in.
Habit and form: Herbaceous perennial.
Pollinated: Insect.
Leaf shape: Pinnately compound.

Waldo Rock Cress

Arabis aculeolata

Waldo rock cress is similar to the related McDonald's rock cress (*A. mcdonaldiana*), except that it is generally hairier and taller, with slightly smaller flowers. Its rosettes of glossy green, almost warty leaves send up short stems of bright pink flowers in summer. Restricted to the south-west USA, it occurs mainly on barren or shrub-covered shallow dry ridges, rocky outcrops and pine woodland at around 1,200m/4,000ft.

Right: The tall, thin flower stems are held high over the leaves.

Below: The showy flowers arise from reddish, tubular calyces.

Identification: The plant forms flattened rosettes of dark green oval-oblong to spoon-shaped leaves, with uneven to toothed margins. The basal leaves and lower parts of the stems are densely hairy, the upper parts are largely smooth. The flowers are almost 2.5cm/1in across, bright pink with spoon-shaped petals, borne in clusters at the top of 15–20cm/6–8in stems.

Distribution: South-west USA.
Height and spread: 10–20cm/4–8in.
Habit and form: Herbaceous perennial.
Pollinated: Insect.
Leaf shape: Obovate-oblong.

Beach Wallflower

Coast wallflower, *Erysimum ammophilum*

The beach wallflower is a short-lived perennial with bright yellow flowers, native to sandy coastal bluffs and old, eroded, inner dunes. It will grow only in full sun, and is found principally in Californian sagebush habitat, with a very sandy substrate seemingly a prerequisite for this species. Where it occurs it provides bright patches of colour among the sagebushes. Its habitats are increasingly threatened by development, and the plant is less common than it was.

Distribution: California, USA.
Height and spread: 5–60cm/2–24in.
Habit and form: Biennial or short-lived perennial.
Pollinated: Insect.
Leaf shape: Narrowly oblanceolate.

Far right: The flowers appear from early spring to early summer on a raceme.

Identification: The plant usually has several stems 5–60cm/2–24in long. The basal leaves are narrowly lance-shaped, smooth or slightly toothed on the edge, 4–15cm/1½–6in long; the stem leaves are wider, especially near the flowers. The yellow flowers are four-petalled, with each petal 12–25mm/½–1in long. The fruits are spreading to ascending, 2–12.5cm/¾–5in long.

Below: The fruits are long and slender.

OTHER SPECIES OF NOTE

Desert Prince's Plume
Stanleya pinnata var. *pinnata*
The desert prince's plume is a subshrub growing to 1.8m/6ft, with leathery blue-green leaves and yellow flowers. It is found in the high plains areas of the USA, from California to North Dakota, Kansas and Texas. The dense inflorescence appears in the autumn.

Smelowskia calycina
Close mats of silver fern-like foliage act as the perfect foil for the loose umbels of snowy flowers and tiny, upright, burgundy seedpods of this arctic plant. It is mostly found in high alpine or cold sites, typically those poor in nutrients such as scree and alluvial gravel, across Alaska and eastern Asia.

Gordon's Bladderpod
Lesquerella gordonii
This pretty plant from south-western USA and northern Mexico is a cool-season annual or short-lived perennial. It is more or less prostrate, and gives rise to a dense terminal raceme of yellow to orange flowers. The seedpods that follow are smooth and rounded, typically S-shaped, although sometimes may be straight.

Heartleaf Twistflower

Streptanthus cordatus

The twistflower's heart-shaped, blue-green leaves, with a white, powdery film, are commonly seen in early spring in the desert mountains of western USA. The plant is wide-ranging in rocky or sandy sagebrush scrub, pinyon/juniper woodland and ponderosa pine forest between 1,200–3,100m/ 4,000–10,000ft. Its long, slender, leaning stalk is topped by dark purple buds; as the flower stalk elongates, the lower buds open to yellow-and-purple twisted flowers. In moist springs the flower spikes may grow especially tall, with several dozen flowers arranged evenly up the stems.

Distribution: Western USA.
Height and spread: 20cm–1m/8–40in.
Habit and form: Herbaceous perennial.
Pollinated: Insect.
Leaf shape: Obovate.

Identification: The stem, which has a woody base, may grow from 20cm–1m/8–40in tall, and is generally smooth. The basal leaves are widely oval, with teeth, often bristly, around the upper margins. The upper leaves are lance-shaped to oblong, pointed and wrapped around the stem. The flowers are yellowish-green in bud, becoming purple in flower. The tips are generally bristly, the petals projecting to 12mm/½in long, linear, purple. They are followed by upward-curving, flattened seedpods, 5–10cm/2–4in long.

Above: An unusual twisted flower gives this plant its name.

Right: The distinctive blue-grey, leaves are covered in white powdery film.

Dame's Violet

Sweet Rocket, Dame's Rocket, *Hesperis matronalis*

This plant has long been grown in European gardens, sometimes as a double-flowered form. The pink, purple or white flowers appear from April to August, and are fragrant, especially towards dusk, attracting moths. It has been successfully introduced to America and can be found throughout the north in open woods, wasteland and roadsides.

Identification: A tall branching species, with terminal clusters of stalked flowers, each about 2cm/¾in long with four sepals and four petals. The leaves are 5–15cm/2–6in long and weakly toothed. The fruit develops as a long, slender pod about 5–10cm/2–4in long containing many seeds.

Left: The plant tends to grow along fences, ditches and roadsides. It is not widely cultivated in America.

Below: Hesperis is from the Greek for evening, which is when the fragrance of the flowers is at its best.

Right: The flowers are very symmetrical with four petals and four sepals. They are an attractive pink.

Distribution: Native to Europe; now scattered throughout much of North America.
Height and spread: 30–120cm/1–4ft.
Habit and form: Herbaceous perennial/biennial.
Pollinated: Insect.
Leaf shape: Lanceolate.

Spectacle Pod

Dimorphocarpa wislizenii

The common name of this annual of weedy sites comes from the fruit pod, which has two, rounded lobes, looking rather like miniature spectacles. The genus *Dithyrea* is closely related and is referred to by the same common name. This particular species has greyish hairy foliage and produces pretty, four-petalled white flowers in thick clusters from February to May. The blooms are delicately fragrant. The plant's favoured habitats are dry grasslands and deserts, on sandy soils.

Identification: The stalks are usually branching, with pinnately lobed leaves to 15cm/6in long. The flowers are white, and each about 1.5cm/½ in long with four petals. The fruit is a flattened pod with two rounded lobes, often darker-coloured around the edges. Flowers will keep appearing on the plant as the seed pods come to maturity.

Left: The foliage, stems, buds and seeds are covered in fuzzy grey hairs.

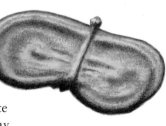

Above: The pods look like tiny pairs of spectacles, and make the plant easy to identify.

Distribution: Arizona and Utah east to Texas and Oklahoma, south to Mexico.
Height and spread: 60cm/2ft.
Habit and form: Annual herb.
Pollinated: Insect.
Leaf shape: Pinnately lobed.

Left: The spectacle pod has an open, weedy habit. It grows to 20-25cm/8-20in tall, and is often found along roadsides and in sandy areas from northern Chihuahua, Southwest and West Texas, New Mexico, Utah and Nevada.

Western Wallflower

Erysimum capitatum

Distribution: Mainly western, from British Columbia south to California and New Mexico.
Height and spread: 15–90cm/6–36in.
Habit and form: Biennial herb.
Pollinated: Insect.
Leaf shape: Narrow and lanceolate (upper leaves).

This is a highly variable species with erect stems and dense clusters of attractive colourful flowers – orange-purple, orange or yellow, from March to July. It grows generally on dry soils, for example in sagebrush, but also (in the alpine form *E. capitatum* var. *purshii*) at high altitudes in mountain tundra. These alpine forms have short stems and are low-growing to protect them from cold, drying winds.

Identification: The four-petalled flowers are about 2cm/¾in across, ripening to produce very slender pods 5–10cm/2–4in long. Lower leaves in a basal rosette, upper stem leaves narrow, with shallowly-toothed margins.

Left: The flowers have a sweetish aroma with a hint of ammonia.

Right: Western Wallflower plants grow singly or in large patches.

OTHER SPECIES OF NOTE

Flatpod *Idahoa scapigera*
A tiny annual and rather uncommon plant of open grassland and sagebrush habitats, especially those that are damp early in the year, this is also found in some pine and fir forests, and sometimes on mossy rocks.

Shepherd's Purse *Capsella bursa-pastoris*
A very familiar sight in its native Europe, shepherd's purse has spread throughout the world as a successful weed. It grows throughout North America. The flat, triangular fruit pods resemble simple purses, and the plant produces tiny white flowers.

American Sea Rocket *Cakile edentula*
This fleshy and low-growing plant has pretty, four-petalled, pale lavender flowers. It is a common annual growing on unstable sands along the coast and around the Great Lakes. The leaves have a sharp flavour like horseradish.

Peppergrass *Lepidium virginicum*
A common weed whose seeds can be used as a flavouring and have a sharp taste like pepper. The leaves are also eaten as greens or in salads. Like many crucifers, it produces clusters of tiny white flowers. The little fruits are green, rounded and flat, and have a winged structure around them that helps with dispersal.

Double Bladderpod

Rydberg Twinpod, *Physaria acutifolia*

The most distinctive feature of this genus of downy perennial herbs is the bladder-like inflated fruit pod. This species has silvery foliage and grows up from a basal rosette of leaves. The flowering stems bear dense clusters of yellow flowers from June to August. Double Bladderpod grows in coniferous forest, arid shrublands and gravelly or rocky dry soils.

Identification: The leaves are on long stalks and up to 4in/10cm long, with a rounded blade. The four-petalled flowers are each about 6cm/1½in across, and the inflated fruit pod has two papery lobes, with a bristle-like style between them.

Below: The plant looks silvery due to the abundance of short hairs.

Distribution: Colorado, Utah and Wyoming.
Height and spread: 3–20cm/1–8in
Habit and form: Perennial herb.
Pollinated: Insect
Leaf shape: Rounded, toothed.

Below: Plants are usually under 15cm/ 6in tall.

CURRANT FAMILY

The Grossulariaceae are mainly shrubs, and have a fairly cosmopolitan range, although they are most common in the northern hemisphere. There are approximately 24 genera and 340 species. Their leaves are usually simple and spirally arranged, and the fruit is a capsule or berry. Some have edible berries, such as gooseberry and some currants (Ribes).

Flowering Currant

Winter currant, *Ribes sanguineum*

The flowering currant is a deciduous woody bush from North America with pink flowers in pendent bunches, which are very attractive to bees and birds, appearing in spring, followed by inedible blue berries. It is most commonly encountered in open to wooded areas, moist to dry valleys and lower mountains, and ranges from British Columbia to northern California, from the coast to the east slope of the Cascades in Washington and northern Oregon, although it is widely naturalized elsewhere.

Right: The white-bloomed, blue-black berries appear in late summer.

Identification: The branches are softly downy, glandular, and red-brown. The leaves are 5–10cm/2–4in across, rounded with three to five lobes, heart-shaped at the base, dark green and slightly downy above, white felted beneath, irregularly toothed and finely serrated, pungently aromatic; the leaf stalk is glandular and downy. Dense, erect or pendent racemes, generally with 10–20 flowers per raceme, bear small tubular red or rosy pink flowers. They are followed by slightly hairy, blue-black fruits with a white bloom, which unlike other species of this genus are rather unpalatable.

Distribution: North America.
Height and spread: Up to 4m/13ft.
Habit and form: Deciduous shrub.
Pollinated: Insect.
Leaf shape: Rounded.

Left: The bush becomes laden with pendent bunches of pink flowers in the spring.

Fuchsia-flowered Gooseberry

Californian Fuchsia, *Ribes speciosum*

This is an attractive, normally evergreen shrub which produces red fuchsia-like flowers from January to May. These look impressive set against the glossy dark green foliage. In dry conditions it may lose its leaves during the summer. The native habitat is chaparral along the Californian coastal ranges. This is quite a popular garden shrub which is particularly useful as a hedge – its sharp spines providing a useful barrier.

Identification: The flowers droop from the branches and the very long stamens hang vertically downwards. The leaves are rather leathery and lobed and grow on short stalks close to the stems. The latter are covered in many sharp spines.

Distribution: California
Height and spread: To 4m/13ft.
Habit and form: Evergreen shrub.
Pollinated: Hummingbirds and insects.
Leaf shape: Lobed.

Left: The spiny shrub grows to 1.8m/6ft tall.

Centre: The stamens are very prominent.

OTHER SPECIES OF NOTE
False Mitrewort, Foam Flower, Lace Flower,
Tiarella trifoliata
This species is usually found along streambanks and
damp woods found from central California north to
Alaska and east to Montana and Idaho. The leafy
stems bear clusters of tiny white flowers, with a
lacy appearance from a distance, which open
between May and August.

Brookfoam
Boykinia aconitifolia
This pretty perennial with
palmate leaves has delicate
flower spikes with reddish
stems and many small, white
bells, each with a yellow centre.
They appear in summer. A native
of the Appalachian Mountains, it
has mounds of bright green, leathery foliage
produced in basal rosettes.

Island Alum Root *Heuchera maxima*
A perennial with a thick, fleshy rootstock and spikes
of small, pinkish flowers in spring, held above
rounded green leaves. It is rare, being found on
canyon walls and cliffs, chaparral and coastal sage
scrub below 450m/1,500ft, in only a few locations on
the north Channel Islands, California.

Grass-of-Parnassus *Parnassia californica*
This is found in montane to subalpine stream banks
and wet meadows from California to Oregon. It has
solitary, conspicuous, cream flowers that look like
pale buttercups. The leaves look very like those of
the plantain.

Umbrella Plant
Darmera peltata

The large, spreading leaves, held upright
on their centrally inserted stalks, give
this plant its common name. The small
pink flowers grow in large, branched and
rather rounded clusters, and open from
April to June. Look for the umbrella
plant alongside cold mountain streams
where it grows in clumps amongst wet
rocks, spreading by means of its thick,
creeping rhizomes.

Identification: Each flower
consists of five pink or
white petals, each about
6mm/¼in long and there
are ten stamens. The
leaves can grow up to
60cm/2ft in diameter, the
toothed leafblades are almost
round and the leaf stalk is
distinctly hairy.

Distribution: California
and Oregon.
Height and spread:
60–180cm/2–6ft.
Habit and form: Perennial
herb.
Pollinated: Insect.
Leaf shape: Round,
toothed.

*Below: The leaves turn red
in autumn.*

*Left: It forms
large, leafy
clumps and is
also known
as Indian
Rhubarb.*

False Goatsbeard
Astilbe biternata

This woodland plant is the only species of
Astilbe native to North America, found from
Maryland southward to Georgia and
Tennessee. Its large, bold foliage is quite
distinctive, and the large, creamy-white,
drooping, spike-like racemes of flowers are
covered with tiny, cream-coloured blooms in
midsummer. Unlike many in this
genus, it is relatively rare in
cultivation, and therefore hardly
ever occurs outside its natural
range.

Distribution: Maryland to
Georgia and Tennessee.
Height and spread: 90cm/3ft
or more.
Habit and form:
Herbaceous perennial.
Pollinated: Insect.
Leaf shape: Pinnately
compound.

*Far right: The distinctive glossy
green leaves are topped with
large, white, feathery
flowerheads in midsummer.*

Identification: A clump-forming
perennial with rhizomes branching
below ground and leaves to
75cm/30in long, conspicuously
jointed at the base and junctions
of the leaf stalks, glossy, red-
green, sparsely hairy. The leaf
blades are compound with three
to five leaflets, each up to
12.5cm/5in long, with a toothed
outer margin, sometimes partially
cut, oval, heart-shaped at the
base. The flowers are held on
large, much-branched, feathery,
spike-like racemes, appearing
very profusely in early summer;
the individual flowers are creamy-
white to yellow, generally much
reduced, consisting of a small,
cup-like base with 10 elongated
stamens, the petals minute
or absent.

ROSE FAMILY

The rose family (Rosaceae) includes trees, shrubs and herbs and comprises about 100 genera and about 3,100 species. Most members of the family have flowers with five petals and numerous stamens, but fruiting arrangements vary. The rose family includes some of our best-known wild flowers, important fruits and garden plants. There are more than 2,000 cultivated varieties of apple and 5,000 of roses.

Swamp Rose

Rosa palustris

The densely shrubby swamp rose grows in swamps and marshes, and along stream banks in eastern North America. Growing to a height of 1.8m/6ft, it blooms in early summer and is very fragrant. It is insect-pollinated, and birds that eat the fleshy hips help spread the seed.

Identification: A many-branched, deciduous shrub with stout, curved thorns, approximately 6mm/¼in long, with a flattened base. The leaves are pinnately compound, with narrow stipules at the base of the leaf stalk, barely extending out from the stalk until they flare at the end; the leaflets (usually seven) are oval to lance-shaped, with finely toothed edges. They are smooth on the upper surface and slightly hairy along the midrib underneath. The solitary flowers are pink and very fragrant. The hips are red, up to 12mm/½in thick, and may be either smooth or covered with minute hairs.

Right: The bright red hips appear from late summer onward.

Distribution: From Nova Scotia west to Minnesota, south to the Gulf of Mexico and east to Florida.
Height and spread: 1.8m/6ft.
Habit and form: Deciduous shrub.
Leaf shape: Pinnately compound.
Pollinated: Insect.

Right: Swamp rose forms a small hummocky bush in wet areas. It has many arching branches.

Dwarf Serviceberry

Amelanchier alnifolia var. *pumila*

The dwarf serviceberry is a very variable and highly adaptable, fire-tolerant species, occurring throughout western and central North America. *Amelanchier alnifolia* is a multi-stemmed, deciduous shrub or small tree growing to 5.5m/18ft high. It is mainly found in thickets, at woodland edges and on the banks of streams in moist, well-drained soils, with the small bushy forms growing on fairly dry hillsides and the larger forms growing in more sheltered locations. The variety *pumila* is a naturally occurring dwarf alpine form native to mountainous areas of the West. The fruits are attractive to birds.

Identification: Five-petalled, white flowers, up to 2cm/¾in in diameter, appear in abundant, compact clusters in early spring before the leaves. The leaves are finely toothed, oval to rounded, pale to dark green, turning variable shades of yellow in autumn. In midsummer the flowers give way to small, round, edible berries, which ripen to dark purplish-black and are covered in a light, white bloom. They resemble blueberries in size, colour and taste.

Distribution: Western and central North America, from Saskatchewan south to Colorado and Idaho.
Height and spread: 90cm/3ft.
Habit and form: Deciduous shrub.
Leaf shape: Oval.
Pollinated: Bee.

Left: White flowers appear in mid-spring, before the leaves, and are followed by edible fruits.

Prairie Rose *Rosa setigera*
This rose, which grows in open woodland in eastern and central North America, can climb to a height of 4m/13ft, and has large pink blooms that appear in late spring. The stem is usually lightly armed with curved thorns. The alternate leaves are divided into three or sometimes five-toothed leaflets. The flowers are followed by small red hips in autumn.

Meadowsweet *Spiraea alba*
This multi-stemmed woody shrub grows in damp meadows in the USA and bears white or pale pink flowers, 6mm/¼in across, in narrow upright terminal clusters 10–15cm/4–6in long from midsummer to mid-autumn. The narrow, lance-shaped leaves are green above, but paler below. The bark is smooth, greyish to reddish-brown, eventually peeling off in fine strips.

Appalachian Barren Strawberry
Waldsteinia fragarioides
The Appalachian barren strawberry is native to woods and clearings, mostly in the Appalachians, but also in scattered locations from South Carolina north to Canada and west as far as Arkansas and Minnesota. The large yellow flowers appear from mid-spring to early summer and these, along with the basal leaves on long stalks, resemble those of a strawberry, although the fruit does not.

Indian Plum

Oso berry, *Oemleria cerasiformis*

The Indian plum is a shrub or small tree with smooth, purplish-brown bark and is one of the first woody plants to bloom in the spring. The foliage emerges very early, and the fresh leaves taste of cucumber. The genus contains only this one species, which has a native range along the Pacific coast in moist to moderately dry locations, especially in white oak woodlands and open forests of Douglas fir. It is most common at elevations below 250m/800ft but occurs up to 1,700m/5,700ft in the southern part of its range. The ripening fruits are highly attractive to many birds and mammals.

Identification: An erect, loosely branched, large, deciduous shrub or small tree, it has slender twigs, green turning to reddish-brown with conspicuous orange lenticels. The leaves are simple, alternate and generally elliptic or oblong to broadly lance-shaped, 5–12.5cm/2–5in long, light green and smooth above and paler below; the margins are entire to wavy. The bell-shaped, greenish to white flowers, 12mm/½in across, appear in early to mid-spring, in small clusters. The fruits are egg-shaped drupes up to 12mm/½in long, pink to blue-purple, borne on a red stem and edible but bitter.

Distribution: Pacific Coast, USA.
Height and spread: 5m/16ft.
Habit and form: Deciduous shrub.
Leaf shape: Elliptical or oblong.
Pollinated: Insect.

Below: The berries attract wildlife.

Below: The bush is covered in white flowers in spring.

Arctic Bramble

Arctic blackberry, plumboy, *Rubus arcticus* subsp. *acaulis*

The arctic bramble (like many arctic species) has a circumpolar distribution, being native to northern parts of North America, Europe and Asia. Where it occurs in America it is fairly common in swamps and lakeside meadows, especially in peaty depressions rather than rocky limestone areas. The flowers appear in early summer, and are followed in late summer by sweet, shiny, red edible fruits like miniature raspberries. In full sun, the leaves often have a bronzy sheen.

Distribution: Circumboreal: northern North America, northern Europe and northern Asia.
Height and spread: 5–10cm/2–4in.
Habit and form: Dwarf shrub with herbaceous stems.
Leaf shape: Compound-trifoliate.
Pollinated: Insect.

Far right: The red berries often appear alongside the pink flowers from late summer onward.

Right: The small red fruits resemble raspberries and are sweet tasting.

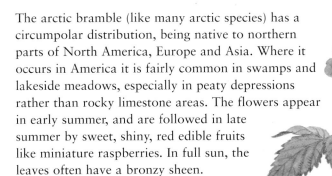

Identification: Alternate, leathery, trifoliate leaves have oval leaflets, 12–35mm/½–2¼in long. The two lateral leaflets are stalkless and often deeply divided while the terminal leaflet has a short stalk; the tips are pointed to rounded, the margins smooth near the base, toothed near the tip. Solitary, bright pink to reddish-purple flowers, with five to eight petals 12–15mm/½–⅝in long and numerous stamens, appear in midsummer and are followed by deep red to dark purple, raspberry-like fruits, 12mm/½in across, in late summer.

Cockspur Thorn

Hog-apple, *Crataegus crus-galli*

This shrub or small tree has a short trunk and spreading, spiny branches and twigs. It is found on moist soils in valleys and low hill country across a wide range, up to about 600m/2,000ft altitude. It has also been commonly planted, both for ornament and as a protective hedge. The leaves turn bright orange and scarlet in the autumn. Clusters of white flowers are followed by red fruits that stay into the new year.

Identification: The leaves are leathery, shiny above, paler beneath and the twigs carry long, slender spines. The flowers have five white petals and are borne in large clusters in late spring and early summer. The fruits are small greenish or dull red haws in drooping clusters, and remain on the tree often through the winter.

Left: The leaves are spoon-shaped, dark and glossy.

Far left: The flowers have an unpleasant odour.

Right: The tree's height is about 7m/25 ft when the tree reaches maturity, at about 25 years.

Distribution: South Ontario and Quebec to north Florida, and west to eastern Texas
Height and spread: To 9m/30ft.
Habit and form: Shrub or small tree.
Pollinated: Insect.
Leaf shape: Spoon-shaped, tapering at the base.

Downy Serviceberry

Shadbush, Juneberry, Shadblow *Amelanchier arborea*

This plant's native habitat is moist soils in deciduous forests, but it is widely planted as an ornamental in parks and gardens, mainly for its attractive flower clusters. The strange names Shadbush and Shadblow apparently derive from the fact that the flowering coincides with the ascent of shad (fish) up the rivers to spawn in early spring.

Identification: A narrow-crowned tree or shrub with white, star-shaped flowers. The twigs are slender and reddish-brown, often with white hairs when young. The flowers have five narrow white petals, borne in terminal clusters, and open before the leaves in spring. The edible fruit resembles a small apple, and is purple when ripe.

Above: Young leaves are fresh green, and downy on the underside. They have a rounded oval shape and are finely toothed at the edges. The berries turn an attractive shade of purple when they are ripe.

Right: The attractive white blooms look like apple blossoms, and have a similar fragrance. They smother the plant in June and July. The plant is usually spotted alongside streams, in bogs, or other similarly wet habitats.

Distribution: Widespread in central and eastern North America, south to northern Florida.
Height and spread: To 12m/ 40ft.
Habit and form: Shrub or small tree.
Pollinated: Insect.
Leaf shape: Ovate, elliptical, finely toothed.

Left: The shrub or tree (here shown covered in blossom) is usually 5–12m/16-40ft tall with a trunk of about 15cm/6in diameter.

White Mountain Avens

Dryas octopetala

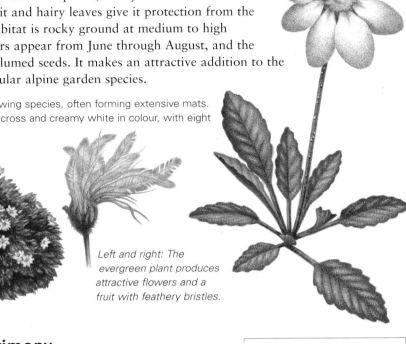

Distribution: Much of northern North America (also Europe and Asia).
Height and spread: 5–25cm/2–10in.
Habit and form: Shrublet.
Pollinated: Insect.
Leaf shape: Lanceolate, with scalloped margins.

This pretty flower is found in exposed, windy locations where its prostrate growth habit and hairy leaves give it protection from the elements. Its usual habitat is rocky ground at medium to high elevations. The flowers appear from June through August, and the fruits contain silver-plumed seeds. It makes an attractive addition to the rockery, and is a popular alpine garden species.

Identification: A low-growing species, often forming extensive mats. The flower is 2.5cm/1in across and creamy white in colour, with eight to ten broad petals.

Left and right: The evergreen plant produces attractive flowers and a fruit with feathery bristles.

OTHER SPECIES OF NOTE

Beach Strawberry *Fragaria chiloensis*
This a low-growing plant sending out runners, growing on dunes along the Pacific coast, from Alaska to mid California. The small white flowers produce small strawberries about 2cm across.

Bigleaf Avens Large-leaved Geum *Geum macrophyllum*
A widespread species of damp woods and meadows, with small yellow flowers appear from April to August. The large leaves are pinnately compound and grow up to 30cm/1ft in length.

False Violet, Robin-run-away *Dalibarda repens*
This is a low-growing, creeping plant of damp woodland and boggy sites. It has a northern distribution and grows well in bog gardens. It superficially resembles a violet, though the flower has typical rose symmetry.

Purple-flowering Raspberry *Rubus odoratus*
Unlike many of its genus, this lacks prickles. The rose-like flowers grow in loose clusters, and the fruits resemble raspberries. They have a pleasant flavour, but are full of seeds. The leaves are unusual in being shaped like those of a maple tree.

Agrimony

Agrimonia gryposepala

This is one of several rather similar members of this genus. The stem of this species has a characteristic strong spicy smell when crushed. The flowering stalk grows up tall between the leaves and carries a cluster of rather small yellow flowers.

Identification: The compound leaves are pinnately divided. The larger leaflets are between five and ten cm long are bright green and toothed, with many obvious veins on the surface. In between these large leaflets are much smaller leaflets. The individual flowers are only about 6mm/¼in across and have five petals. The fruit has hooked bristles at the tip.

Distribution: Mainly eastern North America.
Height and spread: To about 1.5m/5ft.
Habit and form: Herbaceous perennial.
Pollinated: Insect.
Leaf shape: Pinnate.

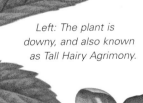

Left: The plant is downy, and also known as Tall Hairy Agrimony.

Above: Blooms lower down the raceme open first.

Common Silverweed

Potentilla anserina

This species has a wide distribution, being found also in Europe and Asia. It grows low, forming patches, and has characteristically silvery leaves and yellow flowers from through the summer. It prefers moist soils such as meadows and stream banks. It was once used in medicine and the cooked roots were eaten, and a root extract was used to tan leather. An infusion of the leaves is said to make a good skin cleanser, while a sprig left in a shoe will reportedly help prevent blisters.

Below: Flowers are hermaphrodite and pollinated by flying insects.

Identification: Each flower is about 2cm/¾in across, with five sepals and five petals, and many stamens. Flowers appear from May to August. The compound leaves have many rounded toothed leaflets.

Distribution: Western North America, across Canada and north east USA.
Height and spread: Stalks to 30cm/12in; runners 90–180cm/3–6in.
Habit and form: Creeping perennial herb.
Pollinated: Insect.
Leaf shape: Pinnate.

Below: The stems rise from clumps or tufts.

Shrubby Cinquefoil

Potentilla fruticosa

This species is also found in Europe and Asia. It is an attractive shrub growing in a range of habitats, from mountain slopes, open forests, and plains. It grows well in cultivation, and there are several garden varieties available, some with larger more colourful flowers. The wild form flowers mainly between June and August.

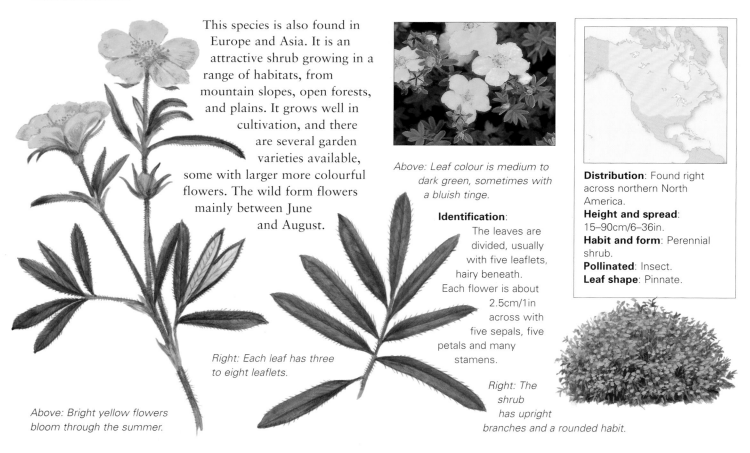

Above: Leaf colour is medium to dark green, sometimes with a bluish tinge.

Identification: The leaves are divided, usually with five leaflets, hairy beneath. Each flower is about 2.5cm/1in across with five sepals, five petals and many stamens.

Distribution: Found right across northern North America.
Height and spread: 15–90cm/6–36in.
Habit and form: Perennial shrub.
Pollinated: Insect.
Leaf shape: Pinnate.

Right: Each leaf has three to eight leaflets.

Above: Bright yellow flowers bloom through the summer.

Right: The shrub has upright branches and a rounded habit.

Sticky Cinquefoil

Potentilla glandulosa

Distribution: Alberta and British Columbia south to California; east to South Dakota and Wyoming.
Height and spread: To 50cm/20in.
Habit and form: Perennial herb.
Pollinated: Insect.
Leaf shape: Pinnate.

This cinquefoil is common in the west of the region, where it grows mainly in open exposed sites. It has rather bushy growth with several leafy, reddish, slightly sticky stems. The yellow flowers grow in loose branching clusters and open from May to July. The name 'cinquefoil' refers to the fact that the leaves of this and other species often have five leaflets, though in this species there can be more.

Identification: Each flower is 1.5–2cm/¾in across with five pointed sepals and five broad petals; the stamens number 25–40. The pinnate leaves have from five to nine ovate toothed leaflets.

Right: Petals vary from yellow-white to deep yellow.

OTHER SPECIES OF NOTE

Red Cinquefoil *Potentilla thurberi*
This species has pretty, intense, raspberry-red flowers with deeper red centres, opening from July to October. It grows in damp meadows and also in coniferous forests, from north Mexico to New Mexico and Arizona.

Canadian Dwarf Cinquefoil
Potentilla canadenis
Found from Canada, south to Texas and Georgia, in rocky, open woodland and sandstone soils, this is low-growing and spreading in growth, has pretty silvery stems, and yellow flowers that appear in the early spring.

Rough-fruited Cinquefoil
Potentilla recta
Pale yellow flowers with many stamens are borne in rather flat clusters from May to August. The stems are up to 50cm tall and hairy. Introduced from Europe, it is now found in dry fields, roadsides and waste ground in North America.

Dwarf Cinquefoil Robbins' Potentilla
Potentilla robbinsiana
An extremely small, hairy alpine plant growing at high altitudes in the White Mountains of New Hampshire. It is a rare species (and found in no other states), but coming back now that it has been protected from trampling by hikers and over-collection. It has pretty yellow flowers – up to 50 on any one plant – that bloom soon after the snow melts in May.

Canadian Burnet

Sanguisorba canadensis

This is a plant of swampy and boggy habitats. The many stamens give the flower clusters a distinctly hazy appearance. Each flowerhead consists of many tiny individual flowers all tightly packed together in a cylindrical structure. The genus name comes from the Latin words for blood and drink – the sap was once believed to stem bleeding.

Distribution: Newfoundland west to Quebec and Manitoba, south to Michigan, Illinois and Georgia; also in parts of the north-west.
Height and spread: 30–150cm/1–5ft.
Habit and form: Perennial herb or shrub.
Pollinated: Insect.
Leaf shape: Pinnate.

Left: The flowering time is June to October. Stalks are up to 150cm/5ft in height. The plant is known in some areas as caribou feed, Indian tobacco or marsh lily.

Identification: The tiny flowers are only about 6mm/¼in across, and the long stamens extend beyond the four small sepals (petals are absent). The pinnate basal leaves each have seven to 15 stalked leaflets with toothed edges. The flowering period lasts from August to September.

Multiflora Rose

Rosa multiflora

This is an introduced species of rose, native to east Asia. It has rather small flowers, opening in May and June. It is very invasive and has become something of a nuisance weed in some parts of North America. It is however a useful garden plant as it forms dense spiny hedges and provides cover for birds and other wildlife.

Identification: The small white flowers are clustered together, each flower to about 4cm/1½in across, with five sepals and five petals. The fruit is a typical small rose-hip, with many seeds.

Above: Berries attract birds, which spread the seeds. The plant also spreads vegetatively.

Left: Leaves are serrated and pinnately divided. The flowers are small and white, with many yellow stamens. The stems are thorny.

Distribution: Ontario and New Brunswick, and scattered elsewhere, south to Florida.
Height and spread: 1.8–4.5m/6–15ft.
Habit and form: Perennial shrub.
Pollinated: Insect.
Leaf shape: Pinnately divided.

Left: The rose was introduced in the 1860s, but unfortunately it crowds out native species.

Rugosa Rose

Wrinkled Rose *Rosa rugosa*

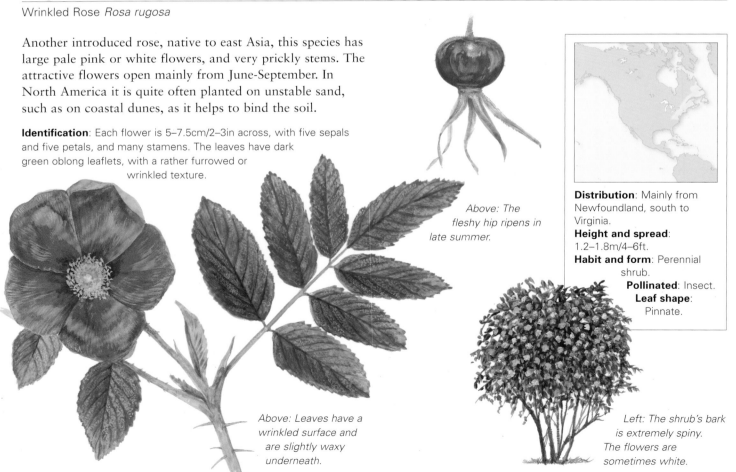

Another introduced rose, native to east Asia, this species has large pale pink or white flowers, and very prickly stems. The attractive flowers open mainly from June–September. In North America it is quite often planted on unstable sand, such as on coastal dunes, as it helps to bind the soil.

Identification: Each flower is 5–7.5cm/2–3in across, with five sepals and five petals, and many stamens. The leaves have dark green oblong leaflets, with a rather furrowed or wrinkled texture.

Above: The fleshy hip ripens in late summer.

Distribution: Mainly from Newfoundland, south to Virginia.
Height and spread: 1.2–1.8m/4–6ft.
Habit and form: Perennial shrub.
Pollinated: Insect.
Leaf shape: Pinnate.

Above: Leaves have a wrinkled surface and are slightly waxy underneath.

Left: The shrub's bark is extremely spiny. The flowers are sometimes white.

Virginia Rose

Rosa virginiana

As indicated by its name, this is a native species. It grows mainly in woodland clearings and also on the coast. It forms a dense shrub and has pink flowers from June to August. There are many rose species found in the region, several introduced from Europe, and they are often hard to identify. Many can be grown in gardens. The plant is thought to have some medicinal uses. However, its hairs are known to cause irritation in some people.

Distribution: From Newfoundland south to Georgia and Alabama.
Height and spread: 30–180cm/1–6ft.
Habit and form: Perennial shrub.
Pollinated: Insect.
Leaf shape: Divided.

Identification: Flowers are 5–7.5cm/2–3in across and the leaves have shiny toothed leaflets. The fruit is the typical bright red rose hip.

Left: The plant can form dense thickets.

Far right: The vibrant hip.

Above: The pink flowers have a lovely scent.

OTHER SPECIES OF NOTE

Prairie Rose
Rosa arkansana
An attractive native rose with clusters of pink or white flowers and very prickly stems. Its leaves are softly hairy beneath, the buds pink and the fruit a bright red hip. It is usually found on dry ground; on prairies or in thickets.

Nootka Rose *Rosa nutkana*
A thorny rose. It is an arching shrub with pale to bright pink flattish flowers from May to July and grows in wooded areas, mainly in upland and mountain sites from Alaska south to California.

Dwarf Bramble *Rubus lasiococcus*
This trailing shrub produces flowering shoots with one or two white flowers from June to August. Another western species, found from British Columbia to California, it grows mainly in woods. The name 'Lasiococcus' roughly translates as 'woolly-fruited'.

Red Chokeberry *Pyrus arbutifolia*
This is a native shrub related to pear. It produces clusters of attractive white or pink flowers from April to July. The fruit is more like a berry than a pear, and is dull red in colour. It grows wild in woods and clearings, but has also been adapted successfully to the garden.

Swamp Dewberry

Bristly Dewberry *Rubus hispidus*

The dewberries are closely related to brambles (blackberry) and are placed in the same genus. This species likes swampy or moist soils and is typically found in damp clearings and open woodland. The flowering stalks grow up from trailing stems and carry loose clusters of white flowers. The edible fruits are enjoyed by many wild animals, including small mammals and birds.

Identification: Flowers are about 2cm/¾in across, and there are five sepals and five petals. The leaves have mainly three large toothed leaflets, and the fruit is like a blackberry, ripening red or blackish.

Right: The fruit looks very like a blackberry.

Right: The vine stays in leaf all year.

Distribution: From Nova Scotia south to South Carolina.
Height and spread: 10–30cm/4–12in.
Habit and form: Creeping perennial shrub.
Pollinated: Insect.
Leaf shape: Three leaflets.

PEA FAMILY

In the Americas, the pea family (Fabaceae or Leguminosae) have many similar forms to those encountered in Eurasia. Several American species are extremely important economic plants, such as the groundnut (peanut) and the lupines, which are widely used in horticulture. The group includes plants that are variously trees, shrubs, herbaceous or annual.

Groundnut

Bog potato, *Apios americana*

Groundnut is a North American species, found mainly in moist areas near streams or bodies of water where it can get full sunlight at least for part of the day. The very aromatic, pink or brownish-red flowers appear in early summer, but this varies according to the location. It is a nitrogen-fixing, perennial vine, which climbs by twining up shrubs and other herbs in an anti-clockwise fashion. It is herbaceous in the north of its range, but the brown-skinned, white-fleshed tubers, on underground rhizomes, survive the winter.

Identification: A twining vine with alternate leaves, pinnately compound, usually with five to seven broadly pointed leaflets. The flowers, usually pink, maroon or brownish-red, have a typical pea-like structure, with a relatively large concave standard with a small hood at its apex into which the narrow, sickle-shaped keel is hooked; they are about 12mm/½in long, occurring in compact racemes 7.5–12.5cm/3–5in long. The fruits are pods 5–12.5cm/2–5in long, containing six–thirteen wrinkled, brown seeds.

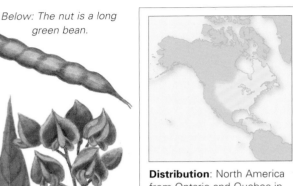

Below: The nut is a long green bean.

Distribution: North America from Ontario and Quebec in the north to the Gulf of Mexico and from the prairies to the Atlantic coast.
Height and spread: 90cm–6m/3–20ft.
Habit and form: Vine.
Leaf shape: Pinnately compound.
Pollinated: Insect.

Lady Lupine

Hairy lupine, *Lupinus villosus*

The lady lupine is a hairy plant whose lavender-blue flowers have a red-purple spot on the standard, or upper petal. The plant gets its common and botanical names from the Latin *lupus*, meaning "wolf", as it was once thought to deplete or "wolf" the mineral content of the soil. It is native to the USA and occurs in dry sandy habitats of the south-eastern states.

Identification: The plant has a soft-woody base and a shrubby appearance, with silvery, upright or spreading stems up to 90cm/3ft tall. The leaves, 2.5–7.5cm/1–3in long, are simple and lance-shaped, the lower ones clustered, the upper leaves alternate. They have a rounded base and pointed tip, and are covered with short, silver, densely shaggy hairs. The bracts at the base of each leaf are conspicuous. The flowers, which vary in colour from white, through rose to purple, are pea-like with a maroon-red spot on the upper petal and a two-lipped, silky calyx. They grow in erect clusters and are followed by woolly seedpods.

Left: Striking spikes of purple flowers are seen from spring to early summer, mainly in dry, open woodland.

Below: The spreading stems and long, hairy leaves form a dense, slightly shrubby mass through which the flower spikes emerge.

Distribution: North Carolina to Florida and west to Louisiana, USA.
Height and spread: 90cm/3ft.
Habit and form: Herbaceous perennial.
Pollinated: Insect.
Leaf shape: Lanceolate.

American Hog Peanut

Amphicarpaea bracteata

Distribution: Eastern and central North America.
Height and spread: Up to 90cm/3ft.
Habit and form: Annual vine.
Leaf shape: Trifoliate.
Pollinated: Insect.

There is only one species of *Amphicarpaea* in the Americas, although others exist in Asia and North Africa. The hog peanut is found in wet woods and thickets throughout eastern and central North America and is a twining annual, or occasionally perennial, vine. The flowers appear in late summer and early autumn and are unusual in occurring in two types. The visible flowers are violet and pea-like; flowers of the second type, which are cleistogamous (self-pollinating without opening) and without petals, are located near the base of the plant; they produce fleshy pods containing a single seed.

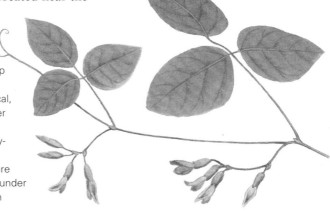

Identification: Thin, slightly hairy stems bear alternate leaves, each divided into three leaflets up to 7.5cm/3in long, but often much smaller, and somewhat oval. The lateral leaves are asymmetrical, tending to be slightly diamond-shaped on the outer edge. The flowers are irregular in shape, up to 2cm/¾in long, tinged purple to completely creamy-white, closely spaced in drooping racemes. Cleistogamous flowers with only vestigial petals are located low on the lateral branches, resting on or under the ground. The upper flowers form flat pods with several seeds.

OTHER SPECIES OF NOTE

Scarlet Milk Vetch *Astragalus coccineus*
This low-growing perennial bears racemes of vibrant red, pea-like flowers in late spring. Scarlet Milk Vetch is endemic to the canyons and ridges of the desert mountains of south-west USA, being widespread and locally abundant from Colorado to California.

Blunt Lobe *Lupinus ornatus*
The blunt lobe or silvery lupine is so named because of its silvery, flattened leaves. It grows at elevations of 1,200–3,200m/4,000–10,500ft on dry flats and slopes in Washington, Idaho and California. It blooms from late spring to autumn, bearing spikes of flowers that are blue with a lilac spot at the base of the upper petal.

Campo Pea *Lathyrus splendens*
Pride of California, or campo pea, is a 60–120cm/2–4ft, deciduous, perennial vine or shrub with large crimson-red flowers. It climbs over chaparral shrubs and thrives in partial sun and the protection provided by other shrubs. The showy flowers attract hummingbirds and butterflies.

Goldenbanner *Thermopsis gracilis*
The slender goldenbanner has tall, erect spikes of bright yellow flowers, carried on loosely branched stems above the foliage, which is silky when young, becoming smooth with age. It is chiefly distributed in the west and north-west of North America in open, grassy places.

Canadian Milk Vetch

Astragalus canadensis

Canadian milk vetch is fairly common throughout most of eastern North America, at least as far south as Georgia. It prefers rich to moist soil and the creamy-white flowers appear in the summer. It is an important food source for birds, as it retains its seed late into the autumn and early winter. The plant is easy to identify while in flower, but vegetatively it can be mistaken for many other plants.

Distribution: Eastern North America.
Height and spread: 90cm/3ft.
Habit and form: Herbaceous perennial.
Pollinated: Insect.
Leaf shape: Pinnate.

Identification: The multiple stems are erect, branching, reddish in strong sun. The leaves are alternate and pinnate, each with 13–20 pairs of leaflets, elliptic to oblong, abruptly pointed, with smooth margins. Axillary racemes up to 15cm/6in long, bearing 30–70 flowers, appear from late spring to late summer. The flowers are pea-like but elongated, up to 2cm/¾in long, creamy-white to greenish-white or with a tinge of lilac. The fruits are inflated, to 12mm/½in long, smooth, beaked with a persistent style, containing around 10 seeds.

Above: The strong, upright flowering stems arise from underground rhizomes and are divided near their bases.

Butterfly Pea

Clitoria mariana

This striking plant displays its dramatic, butterfly-like flowers from June to August. These are inverted, with the keel upwards and the standard petal pointing towards the ground. It enjoys dry soil, thickets and open woodland. The upside-down flowers mean that it is easily confused with the Spurred Butterfly Pea *(Centrosema virginianum)*. It has a shorter calyx tube than its calyx lobes, however, of which the opposite is true in the Spurred Butterfly Pea.

Identification: A beautiful vine with large, showy lavender to pink pea flowers, which are usually solitary in axils of compound leaves, although they occasionally appear in groups of twos or threes. The leaves divide into groups of three ovate little leaves, each 2.5–6.5cm/1–2½in long.

Above and below: The plant trails but rarely climbs.

Distribution: Minnesota east to New York, south to Florida, west to Texas, and north to Nebraska.
Height and spread: 30–90cm/1–3ft.
Habit and form: Perennial climber.
Pollinated: Insect.
Leaf shape: Three leaflets.

Left: The flower has a large, rounded standard with a small notch at the tip.

Blue Palo Verde

Cercidium floridum (=Parkinsonia florida)

The Spanish name meaning 'green tree' is appropriate for this tree whose bark is a blue/green colour all year round. This is largely due to photosynthesis, which occurs primarily within the bark rather than in the leaves (the tree is leafless for most of the year), therefore conserving water through a reduction in surface area. Its bright yellow flowers appear in loose clusters from March to May. They are an important source of nectar and pollen for insects in the dry habitat. The plant's favoured habitat is a low sandy site.

Identification: A round tree covered loosely with yellow flowers (when in bloom) and with an unusual green/blue coloured bark. Each flower is about 2cm/¾in across, with five petals. There are few leaves, each about 1.5–2 cm/⅔–¾in long, with a pair of ovate leaflets.

Right: Flowers are bright yellow with five petals.

Below: In mature specimens blooms cover the canopy, creating an outstanding display.

Distribution: Southern California, southern Arizona, and northwestern Mexico.
Height and spread: Up to 10m/33ft tall.
Habit and form: Shrub or tree.
Pollinated: Insect.
Leaf shape: Paired leaflets.

Right: The mounding habit reduces water evaporation from under the tree.

Western Redbud

Cercis occidentalis

Distribution: Most of California east to southern Utah and central Arizona.
Height and spread: 1.8–5.1m/6–16.7ft.
Habit and form: Shrub or small tree.
Pollinated: Insect.
Leaf shape: Round.

Western Redbud is one of the most attractive shrubs of the western foothills. Native Americans used extracts from the bark for medicinal purposes and its shredded bark was also used for baskets. It thrives on dry slopes, the rosy pink flowers appearing in all their glory from February to April.

Identification: This shrub is leafless when in bloom, with many erect stems and covered with rosy-pink bilaterally symmetrical flowers, forming in clusters along branches. The leaves are rounded and kidney-shaped, smooth and glossy, 3–9cm/1–3½in wide.

Above and right: The pink flowers and pods are edible.

White Priarie Clover *Dalea candida*
A clover that thrives on plains and at roadsides, flowering from May to September. The bilaterally symmetrical flowers consist of dense, white spikes. It has bright green leaves and several branched stems.

Feather Peabush Feather Plume
Dalea formosa
The Feather peabush is a low, scraggy shrub with tiny leaves, dark bark and attractive bright yellow and purple flowers. It ranges from Central Arizona east to western Oklahoma and south to northern Mexico, living in high plains and deserts among other vegetation.

Purple Prairie Clover *Dalea purpurea*
This slender plant prefers the dry or moist soil of meadows and forest openings. The leaves have five narrow leaflets; its thick flowers have dense, crimson-purple hairy spikes, which appear in all their splendour from May to August.

Wild Indigo *Baptisia tinctoria*
A plant that prefers dry fields, this is widely distributed from Ontario and Maine south to Georgia and northwest to Tennessee, Indiana, Wisconsin, and Minnesota. It has numerous clusters of bright yellow pea-like flowers. Some species are used to produce an indigo dye.

Hog Potato

Camote de Raton, Pig Nut *Hoffmannseggia glauca*

This plant's Spanish name means "mouse's sweet potato"; all the names refer to the many animals that get their nourishment from the plant's edible swellings on its roots. It is common along roadsides and as an agricultural weed, enjoying alkaline areas and growing in patches.

Identification: A low plant with yellow/orange flowers and pinnately compound leaves. The leaves have 5–11 pairs of oblong leaflets (3–9 mm long), which are further divided.

Below: The plant has green, fern-like leaves and erect flower stalks.

Distribution: Southern California east to southern Colorado and Texas, and south to Mexico.
Height and spread: 10–30cm/4–12in.
Habit and form: Perennial herb or small shrub.
Pollinated: Insect.
Leaf shape: Pinnate.

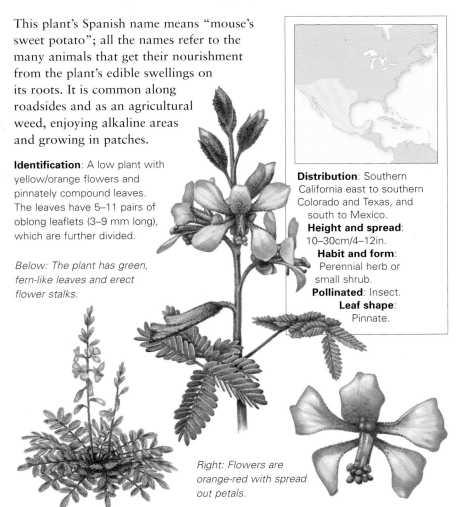

Right: Flowers are orange-red with spread out petals.

Deer Weed

California Broom, *Lotus scoparius*

Like most other members of the pea family, this species can enrich soil with nitrogen, via its root nodules. Like many other flowering plants, it thrives after fire has ravaged chaparral-covered slopes. Its flowering season is between March and August. It grows quickly and is therefore very useful for stabilising eroded slopes, securing the soil and preventing slippage.

Identification: The plant has tough, erect green stems with compound leaves and red-yellow flowers, which appear in the upper leaf axils and go red with age. Each flower is about 9mm/⅜in long, with five petals. The fruit is a curved, rather slender, beaked pod containing two seeds. The leaflets are 6–13mm/¼–⅜in long.

Distribution: Most of California south to northern Baja California.
Height and spread: 30–90 cm/1-3ft.
Habit and form: Perennial herb.
Pollinated: Insect.
Leaf shape: Three oblong leaflets.

Above: Blooms are clustered. The yellow petals turn reddish with maturity.

Left: The bushy shrub provides food for deer as well as birds and insects.

American Vetch

Vicia americana

This slender climbing plant clings to other vegetation and structures by means of its coiling tendrils. Its showy pink-purple or reddish-lavender flowers are unusually big for the genus, looking more like those of a species of *Lathyrus*. They are clustered in loose racemes of 3–10 flowers, and open from May through July. Look for this flower in woodland clearings, banks and hedgerows.

Identification: On stalks from leaf axils, the deep pink flowers are 1.5–3cm/½–1½in long. The petals become bluer with age. Each leaf consists of 8–12 leaflets.

Above: The attractive flowers can vary in colour. Some blooms are blue with red near the base.

Below: The flowers are tubular, about 1.5–3 cm/½–1½ in in length.

Distribution: Throughout the West; also in eastern Canada and the northeastern United States.
Height and spread: 60–120 cm/2–4 ft.
Habit and form: Perennial herb/climber.
Pollinated: Insect.
Leaf shape: Pinnately compound.

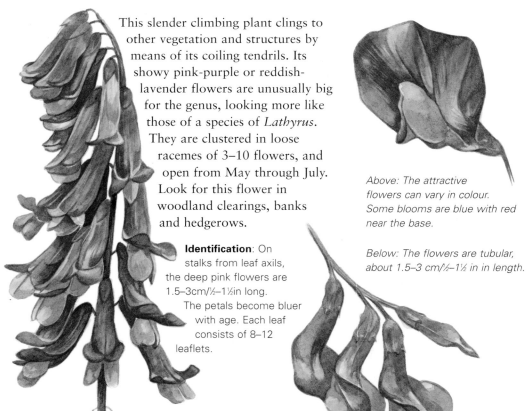

Left: After producing its many blooms, the plant bears pods, about 3cm/1in long with five–seven seeds each. These tender seeds have been eaten by Native American Indians.

Spurred Butterfly Pea

Centrosema virginianum

The flowers of this showy but delicate vine are characterised by their upside-down position, and the spreading petals have a distinctly butterfly-like appearance. Vines reach up to 120cm/4ft long and flower from July until August. This species prefers acid soils, as for example in sandy woods or fields.

Identification: A trailing or twining vine with violet pea flowers that are solitary or in groups of two to four and in axils of compound leaves. The flowers are 2–4cm/¾–1½in long and the keel has a small spur at its base. Three ovate lanceolate leaflets (2.6–6.5 cm/1–2¾ long).

Distribution: Maryland south to Florida, west to Texas and Oklahoma, and northeast to Missouri, Illinois, and Kentucky.
Height and spread: 60–120 cm/ 2–4 ft long.
Habit and form: Perennial herb.
Pollinated: Insect.
Leaf shape: Divided, lanceolate.

Left: Blooms are thumbnail-sized and violet or blue.

OTHER SPECIES OF NOTE

Hill Lotus *Lotus humistratus*
The hill lotus is a common weed in California. It is very attractive with its hundreds of yellow pea-like flowers that nestle in attractive clusters of green compound leaflets. It grows at roadsides, riverbanks, gullies and in old fields, preferring disturbed ground. It flowers from March to June.

Wright's Deer Vetch
Lotus wrightii
A plant that prefers rocky slopes. The plant is dark green with several erect stems bearing stalkless leaves. Its deep yellow flowers turn red with age. Ranging from Southern Utah and Colorado south to Arizona and New Mexico, Wright's Deer Vetch is a favoured by deer and domestic livestock.

Prairie Mimosa *Desmanthus illinoensis*
This erect plant has bell-like groups of white or greenish flowers on tall stalks, which arise from compound leaves. It grows on plains, prairies, and riverbanks and flowers mainly between June and August.

Illinois Tick Trefoil *Desmodium illinoense*
This plant lives on dry prairies in South Dakota east to Wisconsin and south to Arkansas and Oklahoma. It is showy when in flower, displaying beautiful white, purple or pink pea flowers and producing long fruits with segments that stick to fur or clothing, thus dispersing the seeds.

Showy Tick Trefoil

Desmodium canadense

An erect, bushy plant with elongated clusters of pink or purple pea flowers. This is the showiest of the tick trefoils, distinguished by its leaf and fruit shape: the jointed fruits facilitate seed dispersal by breaking into segments that stick to clothes and animal fur. It thrives in moist open woods and at the edges of fields. Stalks bearing flowers grow horizontally from the tall upright stem, above the leaves.

Identification: The flowers are stalked and about 1.5cm/½in long. The fruit is a hairy, jointed pod with three to five segments. The compound leaves have three oblong, un-toothed leaflets with stipules at the base of the stalk.

Distribution: Manitoba east to Nova Scotia, south to Virginia, west to Missouri and Texas, and north to North Dakota.
Height and spread: 60–180cm/2–6ft.
Habit and form: Perennial herb.
Pollinated: Insect.
Leaf shape: Pinnately compound.

Left: The plant has large pink or purple pea-like flowers.

Left: The stems are pubescent, as are the leaves.

DOGWOOD AND GARRYACEAE FAMILIES

The Cornaceae, or dogwood family, comprises about 15 genera, widespread in North America but largely absent from South America. They are mainly woody shrubs and treees. The Garryaceae family has two genera; Garrya, which is found in North America, contains only 16–18 species. Garrya are small evergreen shrubs or trees.

Pacific Dogwood

Western dogwood, *Cornus nuttallii*

This variable, long-lived tree is found at low elevations in moist, open woods, extending from southern British Columbia to southern California, where it prefers the shade and humidity found under a canopy of conifers. The large white bracts stand out brilliantly and are often mistaken for flowers, although the true flowers are tiny and clustered in a centrally positioned head between the bracts.

Identification: The crown is rounded when growing in the open, irregular in the understorey. The bark is thin, grey, smooth when young, breaking into rectangular scales and blocks with age. The leaf buds are small and pointed; the flower buds are larger. The leaves are opposite, undivided, oval to elliptic, 7.5–12.5cm/3–5in long, with smooth to wavy margins, with distinctively curved veins, turning brilliant red in autumn. The tiny, greenish-white flowers, without petals, are borne in a dense, rounded head, surrounded by four or six large, showy, white to creamy-white bracts. The fruits are flattened, red drupes, borne in a tight cluster.

Above: The berry-like fruit.

Right: The tree has a straight main trunk and many branches.

Distribution: Pacific north-west.
Height and spread: 6–20m/20–65ft.
Habit and form: Deciduous flowering tree.
Pollinated: Insect.
Leaf shape: Ovate to obovate.

Bunchberry

Cornus canadensis

The bunchberry is widely distributed, stretching from southern Greenland to Alaska and Maryland to South Dakota, occurring across boreal forests in a broad range of stand types and soil/site conditions. It has a distinctive, four-petalled flower-like bract and six-leaf combination that makes it easy to distinguish from other low-growing forest plants. The white bracts attract flying insects, which pollinate the minuscule true flowers. When an insect alights, its touch induces the flowers to catapult pollen at it.

Identification: Stems 10–15cm/4–6in tall and woody at the base arise from a spreading rhizome, often forming large colonies. The evergreen leaves are opposite, with four to six leaves in a whorl at the top of the stem, often with one or two pairs of smaller, leaf-like scales on the stem below; they are elliptic or oval, 2.5–5cm/1–2in long, with margins tapering to a point at both ends and curving veins parallel to the margins. In early summer, dense clusters of small, greenish-white to purplish flowers appear above the leaf whorl, surrounded by four showy, white to purple-tinged, petal-like bracts, 1.5cm/⅝in long. The fruits are bright red, fleshy and berry-like in a terminal cluster, ripening by midsummer.

Above: The bright red berries appear in the branch tips by midsummer.

Right: The short upright stems arise from a spreading rhizome.

Distribution: Southern Greenland to Alaska, and Maryland to South Dakota.
Height and spread: 10–15 x 30cm/4–6 x 12in.
Habit and form: Herbaceous perennial.
Pollinated: Insect.
Leaf shape: Elliptic or ovate.

Silk Tassel Bush

Garrya elliptica

Distribution: Oregon and California.
Height and spread: To 4m/12ft.
Habit and form: Large shrub.
Pollinated: Wind.
Leaf shape: Wavy, rounded.

This popular garden plant grows wild on dry soils, mainly in Oregon and California. It is named in honour of Nicholas Garry of the Hudson's Bay Trading Company. Its main feature is the long (male) and shorter (female) catkins, produced in winter and spring. These hang down in a most decorative manner. It is frost hardy, but does best in a sheltered sunny position. The shrub can develop into a tree of about 9m/30ft in height. It is evergreen.

Identification: A large evergreen shrub, with rather rounded leaves that are grey and woolly underneath. The individual flowers are tiny and are clustered together in the dangling catkins. The fruits are purple-green with deep purple juice.

Left: The catkins are an atttractive feature in the winter months. The male catkins are showier, and about 30cm/1ft in length, while the female catkins are followed by berries.

OTHER SPECIES OF NOTE

Flowering Dogwood *Cornus florida*
This large shrub or small tree from the eastern USA has a short trunk and a full, rounded crown, spreading wider than its height. It blooms in the spring, as its new leaves are unfolding, with four showy, petal-like bracts, usually snow-white or pink, surrounding a cluster of tiny, inconspicuous, yellowish flowers.

American Dogwood *Cornus stolonifera*
The American or red-stem dogwood is an elegant open shrub producing creamy-white flower clusters in spring and very attractive red stems in winter. It can be found in moist areas, in sun or shade, often along the banks of streams or slow-running water. The fruit of this dogwood is very attractive to woodland birds.

Roughleaf Dogwood *Cornus drummondii*
This tough, thicket-forming deciduous shrub has soft, furry leaves and blooms in mid-spring, with white clusters of "true" flowers. In early autumn, the white fruit attracts forest birds, with the leaves turning to red, orange and purple.

Silky Dogwood, Swamp Dogwood
Cornus amomum
This is a medium-sized shrub with clusters of white flowers, found mainly along streams and in wet soils, in the east of North America. It has slightly hairy red twigs and clusters of blue, berry-like fruit, maturing in late summer.

Pagoda Dogwood

Cornus alternifolia

The species is shade-tolerant and is the dominant understorey shrub in aspen forests. It is often found along forest margins, on stream and swamp borders and near deep canyon bottoms. It is widely distributed from Newfoundland through New England to the Florida Panhandle, and west to Arkansas and Mississippi, where it often occurs alongside the commoner flowering dogwood, *C. florida*. It has tiered, horizontal branches. The light green summer foliage turns rich red and orange in autumn.

Identification: The slender branches of this large shrub or small tree are often horizontal and it develops a flat-topped crown. The smooth bark is dark green, streaky, eventually developing shallow fissures. The leaves are alternate, elliptic to ovate-lanceolate, with wavy margins, and often crowded at the end of the twig, appearing before the white, flat-topped or hemispheric, open flower cymes. Blue fruits ripen in late summer.

Distribution: Eastern North America.
Height and spread: Up to 9m/30ft.
Habit and form: Large shrub or small tree.
Pollinated: Insect.
Leaf shape: Elliptic to ovate-lanceolate.

Below: Pagoda dogwood is a small tree.

Above right: Blue-black berries appear in August.

CARROT FAMILY

A large family with about 450 genera and 3,500 species, Umbelliferae consists mostly of aromatic herbs with hollow stems and flat- or round-topped clusters (umbels) of small flowers. Many have finely divided fern-like leaves. They generally grow in northern regions. Many species yield food or seasonings: for example carrot, parsnip, celery, coriander, caraway, parsley and dill.

Cow Parsnip

Heracleum lanatum

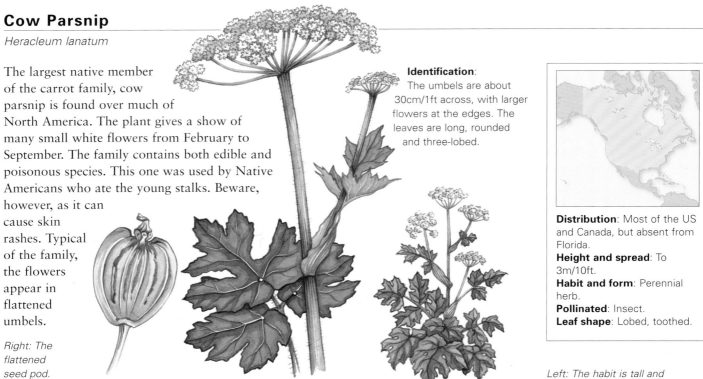

The largest native member of the carrot family, cow parsnip is found over much of North America. The plant gives a show of many small white flowers from February to September. The family contains both edible and poisonous species. This one was used by Native Americans who ate the young stalks. Beware, however, as it can cause skin rashes. Typical of the family, the flowers appear in flattened umbels.

Right: The flattened seed pod.

Identification: The umbels are about 30cm/1ft across, with larger flowers at the edges. The leaves are long, rounded and three-lobed.

Distribution: Most of the US and Canada, but absent from Florida.
Height and spread: To 3m/10ft.
Habit and form: Perennial herb.
Pollinated: Insect.
Leaf shape: Lobed, toothed.

Left: The habit is tall and spreading.

Mexican Thistle

Wright's Coyote Thistle *Eryngium heterophyllum*

Although definitely thistle-like and spiny, this is not a true thistle, althought both of this plant's common names – Mexican Thistle and Wright's Coyote Thistle – would lead to that assumption. It has the typical carrot family umbels of flowers. In this species the umbels are domed and surrounded by prickly bracts. It flowers from July to October and grows mainly on sandy soils in grassland, open woods and along streams.

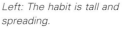

Identification: The tiny flowers that make up the umbels are a delicate pale blue. The umbels are about 1.5cm/⅝in tall, and 1cm/⅜in across and nestle within the protective spiny bracts.

Distribution: Mexico, north to west Texas and Arizona.
Height and spread: 20–60cm/8in–2ft.
Habit and form: Perennial herb.
Pollinated: Insect.
Leaf shape: Divided and spiny.

Left: Flowerheads rise from spiny whorls.

Right: The flowers perch on leafy branched stems.

Poison Hemlock

Conium maculatum

Distribution: Scattered throughout, except the far north.
Height and spread: To 3m/10ft.
Habit and form: Biennial herb.
Pollinated: Insect.
Leaf shape: Divided with lobed leaflets.

This species is one of the most notorious of all the poisonous members of this family, and all the parts of the plant contain the toxic alkaloid coniine. Its effects were known to the Ancient Greeks who used it to kill people, possibly including the philosopher Socrates. It is native to Europe but has spread to many other countries, and is scattered throughout North America. It typically grows in colonies, for instance alongside roads and on waste ground.

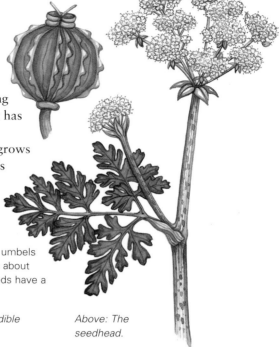

Identification: It has beautiful delicate fern-like foliage, purple blotches on the stem, and small umbels of white flowers. The umbels are about 5cm/2in across, and the long seeds have a rough surface.

Left: The plant grows from an inedible parsnip-like root.

Above: The seedhead.

OTHER SPECIES OF NOTE

Wild Carrot *Daucus carota*
The ancestor of cultivated carrots. Originally from Europe it has spread over most of North America. The umbels of white or pink flowers bend inwards to form a basket-like structure when mature. The root of the wild carrot is much smaller than the cultivated forms.

Water Hemlock *Cicuta douglasii*
This is another example of a deadly poisonous species, and proves the need for accurate identification in this family! It has swollen stem bases that help aerate the tissues in its wetland habitat, mainly in the Pacific coastal regions. The toxins are concentrated in the root stock, but also present in the stem and leaves. One bite ingested is enough to kill a human.

Spotted Water Hemlock *Cicuta maculata*
Another member of the family that looks very similar and is equally deadly. It is distinguished from water hemlock by its purple-streaked stems, but is otherwise very similar. It is highly poisonous to people and livestock alike.

Rattlesnake Master
Eryngium yuccifolium
Native Americans used the plant as an antidote to rattlesnake bites – hence the common name. It grows on prairie, and in open woods, and has greenish white (later bluish), rather thistle-like flowerheads, and very spiny foliage. The leaves resemble those of the yucca.

Sweet Fennel

Foeniculum vulgare

This is another introduction from Europe, where it is widely used as a flavouring in cooking. The young shoots are edible, and the leaves and seeds are used to add a mild aniseed flavour to salads and other dishes.

Above: The capsule contains the seed-like fruits.

Identification: Tall, with feathery leaves and umbels of yellow flowers. Umbels are about 15cm/6in across, and the pinnately divided leaves are 30–40cm/12–16in long and roughly triangular in outline.

Right: The foliage is fine and feathery. To be sure it is fennel and not the similar-looking Poison Hemlock, crush the foliage and check for an aniseed smell.

Distribution: Mainly Cascade Range and Sierra Nevada.
Height and spread: 90–210cm/3–7ft.
Habit and form: Biennial or perennial herb.
Pollinated: Insect.
Leaf shape: Pinnate, triangular.

GENTIAN FAMILY

Worldwide, the Gentianaceae comprise around 75 genera and 1,225 species, mainly herbs but also including a few shrubs or small trees. They are particularly well represented in mountain areas. Many have showy, bell-shaped flowers and are justly popular as garden plants. Some yield bitter compounds used medicinally and for flavouring drinks.

Explorer's Gentian

Gentiana calycosa

This leafy gentian species has pretty, funnel-shaped blue flowers that open mainly between July and October. The plant looks delicate but thrives in mountain conditions, tolerating cold winters and long summer days. It grows along streams and in meadows in the mountains and is one of the most attractive North American alpine flowers. Like many gentians it is suitable for growing in rock gardens.

Identification: The leaves are rather long, to about 3cm/1⅛in. The bell-shaped calyx has five lobes, as has the corolla, and the latter is bright blue, although sometimes can be tinged yellow or green.

Left: Leaves are a soft green, smooth, ovate and opposite. The flower's corolla measures about 2.5-4cm/¾–1¾in length.

Distribution: Sierra Nevada and Rocky Mountains.
Height and spread: 5–30cm/2in–2ft.
Habit and form: Perennial herb.
Pollinated: Insect.
Leaf shape: Ovate, oppposite.

Left: The plants form tufts of colour. The habit is sometimes rather sprawling.

Closed Gentian

Bottle Gentian *Gentiana andrewsii*

The common names reflect the flower shape of this attractive gentian. The flowers are shaped a little like a bottle and are almost closed at the tip. They grow in compact groups in the axils of the upper leaves, from August to October. This is one of the most common gentians in the east of the region and also one of the easiest to grow in gardens, where it prefers damp soil. In the wild its habitats are moist scrub and meadows. The flowers are different shades of blue depending on their stage of maturity.

Identification: The flowers are up to 4cm/1in long and the five-lobed corolla has a whitish base. The leaves are up to 10cm/4in long, and grow in whorls below the flowers.

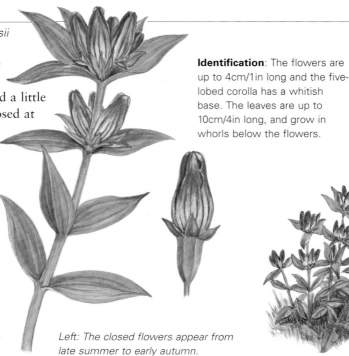

Left: The closed flowers appear from late summer to early autumn.

Distribution: Quebec and North Dakota, south to Virginia.
Height and spread: 30–60cm/1–2ft.
Habit and form: Perennial herb.
Pollinated: Insect.
Leaf shape: Ovate or lanceolate.

Left: Multiple stems without branches grow from the taproot.

Prairie Gentian

Tulip Gentian, Bluebell *Eustoma grandiflorum*

Distribution: Texas and New Mexico north to Nebraska and Colorado.
Height and spread: 25–70cm/10–28in.
Habit and form: Annual or perennial herb.
Pollinated: Insect.
Leaf shape: Ovate, opposite.

One of the finest flowers of the prairie, the prairie gentian has large, prominent bluish or purple flowers (sometimes pink or whitish), opening from June to September. It grows up tall amongst the prairie grasses, and the bell-shaped flowers open in small clusters at the top of the plants where they are obvious to passing insects. The plant tends to grow in damp sites in prairie, fields and meadows.

Identification: The long ovate leaves have three prominent veins. Each flower is about 8cm/3in across with five broad corolla lobes.

Right: In the cut flower market, Prairie Gentian is common and usually known as Lisianthus.

OTHER SPECIES OF NOTE

Northern Gentian *Gentiana affinis*
This decumbent or occasionally erect gentian from the western USA blooms in late summer, with sky-blue, tubular flowers, 2–3cm/¾–1¼in long, near the ends of the stems. The top edges of the flower petals have white spots on them. It is found in moist meadows and on the edges of aspen groves. It grows to 20–30cm/8–12in in height.

Centaury Rosita
Centaurium calycosum
This has clusters of pink trumpet-shaped flowers from April to June. It grows in damp meadows and streamsides in the west, from northern Mexico to Texas, Utah and California.

Northern Gentian *Gentianella amarella*
This familiar European biennial is also widespread in damp mountain meadows from Alaska south as far as New Mexico, but listed as endangered or threatened in Maine and Vermont. It is also known as the Autumn Dwarf Gentian. The trumpet-shaped flowers are purple, blue or pinkish.

Stiff Gentian *Gentianella quinquefolia*
Also called Small Agueweed, this is a pretty annual gentian with blue or lilac flowers and a rectangular stem. It has a mainly eastern distribution, but is endangered, partly due to over-collection, in many eastern states, and feared extirpated in Maine.

Catchfly Gentian

Seaside Gentian *Eustoma exaltatum*

This is a close relative of the prairie gentian, with a more southerly and western distribution. It grows on the sandy coasts of California, as well as on inland salt and freshwater marshes of the Great Plains. It has very pretty, purple or white, rather crocus-like flowers, borne singly or in clusters, usually from May to October. The plant sometimes blooms nearly all year round.

Identification: The petals are fused at the base, and open out into five lobes, about 4cm/1in across. The leaves are opposite, about 7.5cm/3in long and covered in a whitish bloom.

Distribution: California, Montana, and South Dakota, to Florida.
Height and spread: 30–90cm/1–3ft.
Habit and form: Annual or short-lived perennial herb.
Pollinated: Insect.
Leaf shape: Oblong, opposite.

Below: Blooms are solitary or in few-flowered clusters.

Left: The plant grows to about 90cm/3ft tall.

Felwort

Star Swertia *Swertia perennis*

This pretty mountain species has pale blue or purplish star-shaped flowers, spotted green or white, opening from July to September. The stem is thick and glabrous. Sometimes the flowers are very dark – almost black. Felwort grows mainly in damp meadows at high altitudes in the mountains and the north. It is also found in Europe, especially in northern European fens. It prefers moist ground.

Identification: Each flower is about 2cm/¾in across, with four or five petals and sepals. They are various shades of blue, with darker veins and light-coloured spots. The flowering period is July to August. The basal leaves are spoon-shaped or oblong, with rounded tips. The higher leaves are elliptic.

Right: Flowers have either four or five petals and sepals each and have a very regular, star-like form.

Above: The leaves are narrow and fairly fleshy.

Distribution: Alaska south to the Sierra Nevada; north to Canada through Rockies.
Height and spread: 5–50cm/2–20in.
Habit and form: Perennial herb.
Pollinated: Insect.
Leaf shape: Lanceolate.

Left: Plants grow to 10–13cm/ 4–5in tall on thick stems. There may be one or more rosettes of basal leaves. These are rather spoon-shaped and may have a blunt or pointed tip.

Monument Plant

Deer's Ears *Swertia radiata* (= *Frasera speciosa*)

This extremely tall, stately and somewhat conical plant has flowers clustered tightly to the stem. It may live for several years, but flower only once, after which it dies. The flowering season is May to August, and the plants are generally found in mixed conifer forests. The genus name *Swertia* is in honour of the Dutch botanist Emanual Sweert (1552–1612), while *Frasera* is named after the Scottish nurseryman John Fraser (1750–1811). The plant's root has been used to make poisons as well as medicines.

Identification: The stem leaves are evenly spaced in whorls around the stem and the flowers are yellow-green, spotted purple.

Right: Leaves and flowers whorl evenly around the stem.

Above: The flower has four purple speckled petals, each with a line of stiff hairs down the centre. Narrow green sepals add to the spectacular effect. The blooms are 2.5–4cm/1–1½in wide with four stamens.

Distribution: Washington State, south to central California, Texas, Montana and northern Mexico.
Height and spread: 1–2m/4–7ft.
Habit and form: Biennial or perennial herb.
Pollinated: Insect.
Leaf shape: Lanceolate.

Left: The flower spike is only seen once before the plant dies.

Left: The leaves of the huge basal rosette are long, narrow, smooth and a pale green. The flowering period is May to August.

Fringed Gentian

Gentianopsis crinita

The pretty blue trumpet-shaped flowers of this gentian develop at the top of separate stems. The name refers to the fact that the open edge of each petal has a distinct ragged fringe. It is a late-flowering species – August to November – and grows in damp meadows and wet thickets. One of the most beautiful of all gentians, it is also endangered.

Distribution: Manitoba east to Quebec, south to Georgia.
Height and spread: 30–90cm/1–3ft.
Habit and form: Biennial herb.
Pollinated: Insect.
Leaf shape: Ovate to lanceolate, opposite.

Identification: Each flower is about 5cm/2in long and tubular. The calyx has four, unequal pointed lobes topped by the intense blue corolla. Fruits develop from November to January.

Left: One plant can yield up to 175 startling blue flowers in its two-year lifetime. In the first year there are no flowers and the plant remains very small.

Above: The fringed flowers remain closed on cloudy days.

OTHER SPECIES OF NOTE

Pennywort *Obolaria virginica*
This low-growing fleshy plant has purplish or white flowers and whorls of dark, thick stem leaves that seem to support them. It is found in damp woods and thickets from New Jersey and Pennsylvania south to Florida and Texas. The flowers open from March to May.

Large Marsh Pink *Sabatia dodecandra*
Similar to saltmarsh pink, but with larger flowers and reaching 60cm/2ft, this is found from Florida and Louisiana north to Connecticut, although it is considered a threatened species in some parts. It is commonly known as the Marsh Rose Gentian. The blooms are deep pink with a yellow centre, and have an attractive fragrance.

Slender Marsh Pink *Sabatia campanulata*
Another close relative to the above, growing on damp peat or sand along the coasts, from Massachusetts south to Florida, and also in the southern Appalachians. It is another plant that is decreasing in numbers, largely due to habitat loss or disturbance.

Lesser Fringed Gentian
Gentianopsis procera
(= *G. virgata*)
This is yet another endangered gentian, found on the prairie and in lowland forests in the mid-west. It flowers mainly from August to October. It looks very similar to the fringed gentian (top right).

Saltmarsh Pink

Sea Pink *Sabatia stellaris*

This gentian relative, also known as The Rose of Plymouth, inhabits brackish coastal marshes and salty meadows. It likes open sandy soils, for example at the upper edges of saltmarshes and amongst sand dunes. Pink flowers appear from July to October, each with a bright yellow, star-shaped centre. Some plants produce white flowers. The plant is widespread along the Atlantic and Gulf coasts, becoming commoner in the south. In New York and New England this plant is rare.

Distribution: Coastal, from Massachusetts and New York south to Florida and Louisiana.
Height and spread: 15–45cm/6–18in.
Habit and form: Annual or biennial herb.
Pollinated: Insect.
Leaf shape: Linear to lanceolate.

Identification: The flowers are about 4cm/1in across, and the red-edged sepals are shorter than the petals. The leaves are long and light green.

Below: Each plant has one stem with branches. The stem and leaves are delicate.

Left: White flowers are sometimes seen on this plant, but the blooms are usually pale pink.

NETTLE AND DOGBANE FAMILIES

Urticaceae, the nettle family contains about 48 genera and 1,050 species. Most are herbs but a few are shrubs or small trees, mainly tropical, though several occur widely in temperate climates. The some 200 genera and 2,000 species of the Apocynaceae, dogbane, are primarily found in the tropics, subtropics and neotropics. Plants of the Apocynaceae are rich in alkaloids or glycosides and are often poisonous.

Blue Dogbane

Amsonia tabernaemontana

A pretty flower of damp or wet woodland and streamsides, blue dogbane has light blue, star-shaped flowers borne in branching clusters, opening from April to July. Several plants have this specific name, which is in honour of the 16th century German herbalist Jakobus Tabernaemontanus. As its common name suggests, it is poisonous, and not just to dogs. It is usually found in clumps with numerous stems and few branches.

Identification: The flowers are a pretty light blue to purple, with five long, narrow petals joined at the centre into a funnel-shaped tube. The fruits develop as paired slender pods that open along one side. The stem exudes a milky sap if damaged.

Distribution: New York and Massachusetts south to Florida.
Height and spread: 30–90cm/1–3ft.
Habit and form: Perennial herb.
Pollinated: Insect (and sometimes hummingbird).
Leaf shape: Lanceolate.

Right: Leaves are alternate and lanceolate. The stems are about 4-5mm/⅙in thick and slightly hairy, rising from woody roots.

Left: The slender corolla tube expands into five pointed and narrow lobes.

Spreading Dogbane

Apocynum androsaemifolium

This widespread flower grows in fields, roadsides and woodland margins. It forms a bushy plant with small pink flowers that droop. Opening from June to August, they are pink with darker pink stripes inside, and fragrant. They attract a huge number of butterflies. The leaves are opposite. Pods are 10–15cm/4–6in in length, and slender. The plant is toxic and exudes a milky sap when broken. In some places it is a serious weed.

Identification: The bell-shaped, sweetly scented flowers are in clusters at stem tips and leaf axils. The sepals are tinged pink at the tips.The fruit develops in August and September, is cylindrical and contains many cottony seeds.The leaves are smooth on top and slightly hairy underneath.

Distribution: Scattered throughout, except the Arctic; commoner in the east.
Height and spread: 30–120cm/1–4ft.
Habit and form: Perennial herb.
Pollinated: Insect.
Leaf shape: Ovate, opposite.

Right: The plant is large and bushy. It prefers sunny hillsides, where the soil is well drained.

Left: The plant is reported to cause serious poisoning to livestock. Also, when entered by insects, scales in the throats of the flowers spring inwards, trapping intruders.

Clearweed

Pilea pumila

Distribution: Throughout much of the east.
Height and spread: 10–50cm/4–20in.
Habit and form: Annual.
Pollinated: Insect.
Leaf shape: Ovate, opposite, toothed.

This nettle relative is an annual with translucent stems and small greenish-yellow flowers in the leaf axils. It grows in moist, rich soil, in shady sites, often forming large colonies. The leaves are nettle-like but lack stinging hairs. They are dark green above, whitish below. The plant is an important food plant for the larvae of several kinds of butterfly. Small flowers cluster on racemes in August.

Identification: The small flowers develop in narrow, slightly curved racemes. The flowers lack petals and are about 4mm/⅛in long. The tiny seed-like fruits are green, and are dispersed by the wind. In young plants, the stem looks translucent.

Right: Petal-less flowers on a raceme. The plant blooms in August, but the glossy leaves are its most attractive feature.

Left: The dark green leaves have no stinging hairs.

OTHER SPECIES OF NOTE
Periwinkle *Vinca minor*
Once introduced this became widespread, especially in the east. It is also commonly grown in gardens. An evergreen trailing plant, it has blue or purple (sometimes white) flowers that contrast well with its dark green foliage.

Lesser Clearweed *Pilea fontana*
This plant is very similar to clearweed but has dull black seed-like fruits. It is found from Quebec south to Florida, in shady habitats on moist soil.

Bog Hemp
Boehmeria cylindrica
Bog hemp or false nettle grows in swampy meadows, along streams and spring branches and in low wet woods in the eastern USA. The plant resembles a stinging nettle but has opposite leaves and no stinging hairs and is therefore harmless. Small greenish flowers cluster around the stem in mid- to late summer.

Wood Nettle *Laportea canadensis*
The Canada nettle or wood nettle has sharp hairs along the stem which, when touched, can give a painful sting to exposed skin. It is found infrequently in wet woods in much of the eastern USA. Tiny feathery clusters of flowers appear from midsummer to early autumn.

Stinging Nettle

Urtica dioica

This familiar widespread plant grows in damp rich forest soils and on waste ground. It deserves respect as the stems and leaf veins have tiny hollow hairs that release formic acid when brushed against. This causes 'nettle-rash' (urticaria) on the skin and can be quite painful. This probably evolved as a deterrent to grazing animals. Young shoots can be eaten like spinach and a tea made from an infusion of dried leaves.

Identification: The individual flowers are inconspicuous, very small and greenish, each about 2mm/¹⁄₁₆in long. The leaves are coarsely toothed.

Distribution: Throughout the region; also in Europe and Asia.
Height and spread: 60–120cm/2–4ft.
Habit and form: Perennial.
Pollinated: Insect.
Leaf shape: Ovate, opposite, toothed.

Above: Nettles form in familiar 'beds' or clumps.

BINDWEED FAMILY

The Convolvulaceae are mostly twining herbs or shrubs, sometimes with milky sap, comprising about 58 genera and 1,650 species. Many have heart-shaped leaves and funnel-shaped solitary or paired flowers. They are found in both temperate and tropical regions. The genus Ipomoea *contains both morning glories with their showy flowers and also the sweet potato* (I. batatas), *grown for its edible roots.*

Field Bindweed

Possession Vine *Convolvulus arvensis*

This European native grows from rootstock and seed, and spreads rapidly as an aggressive weed, therefore it is not always welcome in the garden. Yet it has beautiful flowers and often brightens up waste ground and roadsides. The large, funnel-shaped flowers are prettily patterned in white and pink, with yellow centres. The flowering period is long – from May to October. The flowers open each morning and close into a narrow twist in the evening.

Identification: Each flower opens to about 2.5cm/1in across and is a beacon to passing insects. Two long bracts sit below the calyx. Leaves that grow from seed are square with a notch at the tip. Plants from rhizomes lack these and have the more familiar heart-shaped leaves.

Distribution: Throughout, mainly in the west.
Height and spread: 30–90cm/1–3ft.
Habit and form: Perennial herb.
Pollinated: Insect.
Leaf shape: Triangular, arrow-shaped or ovate.

Arizona Blue-eyes

False Flax *Evolvulus arizonicus*

The imaginative common name refers to the bright blue or purplish flowers that open from April to October. The colour varies from region to region, those in the drier desert habitats being a less pure blue; in other regions the flowers are as clear blue as those of the true flax *(Linum)*, hence the alternative common name. It grows in dry pinyon pine and juniper woodland, and in deserts.

Identification: The five-lobed corolla is to 2cm/¾in across and the flowers grow on narrow stalks. The upright stems have a covering of grey hairs. The leaves are green-grey and lanceolate.

Left: The stems are slender and sprawling.

Below: The spread is usually to just 30cm/1ft. The plant is also known as the Wild Dwarf Morning Glory.

Distribution: Northern Mexico, New Mexico and southern Arizona.
Height and spread: To 30cm/1ft.
Habit and form: Perennial herb.
Pollinated: Insect.
Leaf shape: Lanceolate.

Common Morning Glory

Ipomoea purpurea

Native to tropical America, this pretty climber is a popular garden plant, and also grows as a weed on waste ground. It grows quickly, clambering and attaching itself by tendrils, and produces large numbers of showy, funnel-shaped flowers, usually purple, but red and white forms are also found. Each flower opens in the morning but wilts by evening – hence the common name.

Distribution: Widespread, especially in warmer regions.
Height and spread: Stems to 3m/10ft.
Habit and form: Annual climber.
Pollinated: Insect (and sometimes hummingbird).
Leaf shape: Heart-shaped or three-lobed.

Identification: Each flower is up to 6.5cm/2½in across, with a trumpet-shaped corolla. The five sepals are fused at the base, and hairy. The leaves are usually heart-shaped.

Left: The vines extend to 1.2–3m/4–10 feet in length.

Right: Attractive, round flowers appear from July to October.

OTHER SPECIES OF NOTE

Railroad Vine *Ipomoea pes-caprae*
Despite its name, this native to the West Indies is now found typically on coastal sand dunes and beaches (rather then railways), mainly from South Carolina to Florida and Texas. Its purple or pink flowers open throughout the year.

Scarlet Creeper Star Glory *Ipomoea cristulata*
This climber found mainly in Arizona and Texas, in dry brushland, has scarlet flowers with pointed lobes, opening from May to October.

Bush Morning Glory *Ipomoea leptophylla*
As its name implies, this is not a clambering vine like most of the other species, but grows as a leafy bush. It has dark centred pinkish purple flowers from May to July, and grows on sandy soils, mainly in the west.

Beach Morning Glory *Calystegia soldanella*
This is a bindweed rather than a true morning glory. It grows worldwide on sandy beaches and has pretty streaked pink flowers and thick kidney-shaped leaves.

Small Red Morning Glory

Ipomoea coccinea

Another native of tropical America, this is also grown commonly in gardens and has escaped into the wild, where it turns up on waste ground such as roadsides. The flowers are small and bright red, funnel-shaped and distinctly five-lobed. They open from July to October. The plant is also known as Red Star, possibly because each flower has five regular parts.

Identification: The flowers are rather small, only about 2cm/¾in across, red, with a yellow centre and with protruding stamens and stigma.

Distribution: Michigan and Massachusetts, south to Florida and Texas.
Height and spread: Vine, to 2.7m/9ft long.
Habit and form: Annual climber.
Pollinated: Insect and hummingbird.
Leaf shape: Long, heart-shaped.

Right: Flowers are up to 2.5cm/1in long.

Right: This attractive vine likes to clamber through undisturbed field borders.

MINT FAMILY

The Labiatae are mostly herbs or shrubs, comprising about 250 genera and 6,700 species distributed all over the world. They include many well-known herbs, ornamental plants and weeds, usually with square stems and clustered flowers. Familiar aromatic members include mint (Mentha), marjoram (Origanum), thyme (Thymus), sage (Salvia) and lavender (Lavandula).

Bee Balm

Bergamot, Oswego tea, *Monarda didyma*

Bee balm is a native of the eastern USA. It originally occurred from New York, west to Michigan and south in the Appalachian Mountains to Tennessee and northern Georgia, though it is now much more widely distributed, probably due to its popularity as a garden ornamental, resulting in its escaping and becoming established as far north as Quebec. It occurs along wooded stream banks and in moist hardwood forests.
The scarlet blooms first appear in early summer and continue into late summer. Its aromatic leaves have traditionally been used to make infusions.

Identification: A tall, upright-growing, spreading, clump-forming perennial, arising from short underground stolons in spring. The square stems carry leaves in opposite pairs. The leaves are toothed on the margins, lance-shaped to oval near the base, elongating to a pointed tip, 5–15cm/2–6in long and about a third to a half as wide, fragrant when bruised. The inflorescences are whorled clusters of scarlet-red flowers, borne singly or (rarely) in pairs. The flowers are irregular in shape and up to 4cm/1½in long, tubular, terminating in two lips; the upper lip erect and hood-like, the lower lip with three spreading lobes. Directly beneath each inflorescence is a whorl of reddish bracts, some leafy and some bristly.

Distribution: Eastern USA.
Height and spread: 120 x 60cm/4 x 2ft.
Habit and form: Herbaceous perennial.
Leaf shape: Lanceolate to ovate-acuminate.
Pollinated: Insect, especially bee.

Left: The spreading underground stems eventually result in a large clump.

Ground Ivy

Glechoma hederacea

This pretty flower was introduced from Europe and is now found throughout the region as a rampant weed, especially in and around damp woodland. It also turns up frequently in lawns where, though quite pretty, it is not always welcome. The flowering period is March though June and the flowers are a delicate shade of blue-violet.

Identification: Each flower is to about 2.5cm/1in long with a lipped and hooded corolla, which is internally beared and spotted. Flowers produced four nutlets each. The leaves are hairy and rounded, about 3cm/1in long, with scalloped margins and long slender stalks.

Above: The flowers range in colour from pink to blue.

Distribution: Throughout.
Height and spread: Creeping stems to 40cm/16in.
Habit and form: Perennial herb.
Pollinated: Insect.
Leaf shape: Rounded or kidney-shaped.

Above: Flowers are funnel-shaped and blue to lavender. The plant has a creeping habit and is aromatic.

Below: The size and shape of the leaf earns Ground Ivy the common name 'catsfoot'.

Small-leaf Giant Hyssop *Agastache parvifolia*
An erect, rhizomatous, perennial subshrub native
to the USA. Small-leaf giant hyssop is a drought-
tolerant species, reaching a height of 60cm/2ft
at maturity. It sports spikes of mauve blooms
in late spring.

Eastern Bee Balm *Monarda bradburiana*
Eastern or Bradbury bee balm can be found in
woods and on slopes in the mid-western USA.
The square, erect stems are covered with
opposite, toothed, greyish-green, aromatic
leaves, with pink to white flowers in terminal
heads in late spring and early summer.

Nettleleaf Horsemint *Agastache urticifolia*
This is a woodland mint with tight spikes of pale
pink flowers, and typical mint foliage of toothed
leaves. Its habitat is open glades in woodland,
from British Columbia south to California.

Yerba Buena
Satureja douglasii
Another western mint of
shady woodland. The
Spanish name
meaning 'good
herb' refers to its
medicinal use; it
also makes a
pleasant, mild
tea. It spreads
across the ground,
often rooting.
Flowers are tubular and may be white to a pretty
shade of blue. They appear in July.

Purple Giant Hyssop

Agastache scrophulariifolia

A perennial plant native to eastern North
America, naturally inhabiting the edges of
the upper limits of floodplains associated
with steep rivers and streams, and favouring
areas where competition from other plants
is limited. It is a species that is dependent on
soil disturbance and often grows in areas
close to human settlements, although it
rarely persists for long. The branching
stems bear spikes of pinkish-purple
flowers from midsummer to early
autumn, and the whole plant is
highly fragrant, smelling strongly
of anise. Historically, it ranged
from New England south to
Georgia, west to Kansas and
north into Ontario, although its
range appears to have been
shrinking in recent years.

*Below: This erect, tall, late-
flowering, mostly herbaceous
perennial is little
branched in
its lower
parts, more
so above,
with hairless
square
stems,
usually tinged
with purple.*

Distribution: Eastern North
America.
Height and spread: Up to
2m/6½ft.
Habit and form: Herbaceous
perennial.
Leaf shape: Ovate to ovate-
lanceolate.
Pollinated: Insect.

Identification: The leaves are
opposite, paired, oval to lance-
shaped, rounded to heart-shaped
at the base with pointed tips, up
to 12.5cm/5in long, conspicuously
hairy and coarsely serrated. The
inflorescence, which grows up to
15cm/6in long, is composed
of small flowers compacted
into terminal, cylindrical or
tapering whorled clusters
1.5–2cm/⅝–¾in across.
Hairless, inconspicuous bracts,
often with coloured margins,
subtend the inflorescence.
The flowers range from pale
pink to purple, projecting
significantly beyond the white or
purplish calyces.

Vinegar Weed

Common Blue Curls, *Trichostema lanceolatum*

Distribution: Northwest
Oregon south through
California.
Height and spread:
60–150cm/2–5ft.
Habit and form: Annual
herb.
Pollinated: Insect.
Leaf shape: Long and
narrow.

This is a tall-growing plant with a rather unpleasant smell, hence one
of its common names. The flowers are pale blue or purple and borne
in long clusters, opening from July to October. It grows mainly on
open dry fields. A closely related species, woolly blue curls (*T.
lanatum*), has a pleasant smell and woolly flower clusters. American
Indians of northern California used the plant as a cold and fever
remedy and a flea repellent.

Identification: Each flower is 1.5cm/⅔in long
with a tubular corolla opening into five narrow
lobes. The stamens
and style
are very
prominent.

*Right: The
habit is loose and
rosemary-like.
It is also known as
Wild Rosemary.*

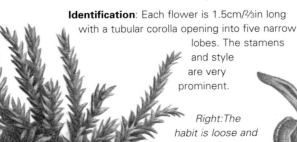

Field Mint

Mentha arvensis

This widespread species also occurs in Europe and Asia. Unlike most mints, its flower clusters grow along the stem rather than towards the top of the stems. The foliage has a pleasant mint aroma and the compact whorls of small pink flowers, opening from July to September, are almost hidden by the leaves. It prefers damp soil, such as in marshy ground or alongside streams. This the only species of mint native to the USA.

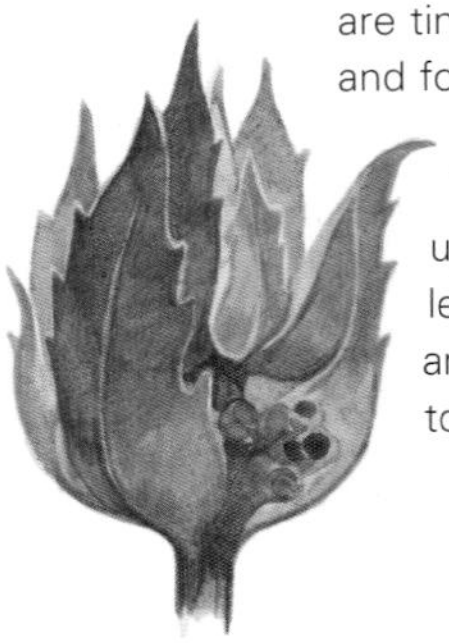

Identification: The individual flowers are tiny – only about 6mm/¼in long, and found at the base of the leaves. The leaves are sharply toothed. The stem is hairy, square and upright with pairs of opposite leaves, which have a short stalk, are serrate, and slender towards the tip.

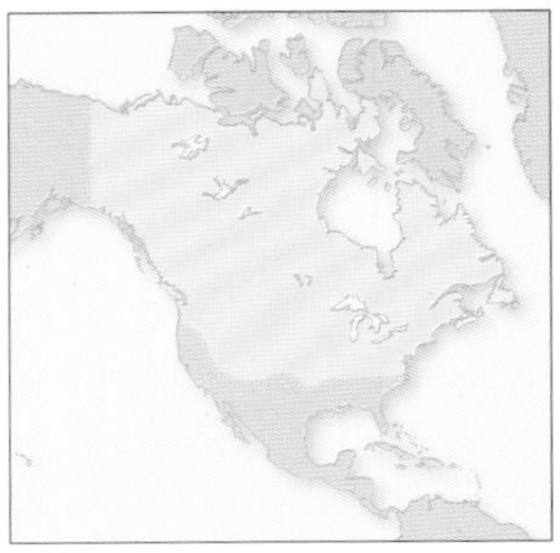

Distribution: Throughout, except the warm south.
Height and spread: 20–80cm/8–30in.
Habit and form: Perennial herb.
Pollinated: Insect.
Leaf shape: Lanceolate, toothed.

Left and above: Leaves are in opposite pairs, broad, with conspicuous veins and characteristic serrated edges. The leaves are used as a culinary herb.

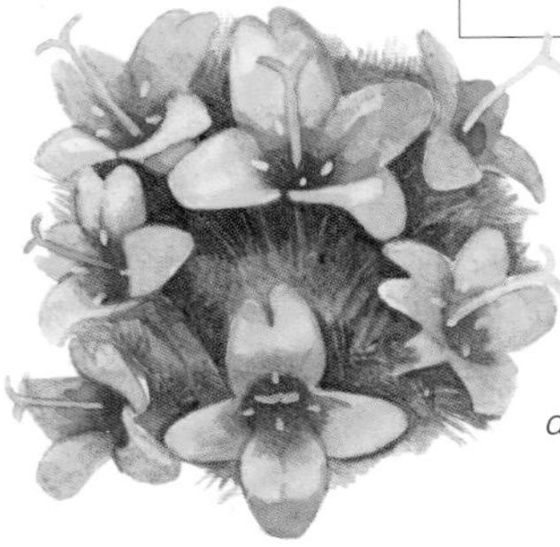

Left: Pink, white or purple flowers cluster on the stem. The prominent stamens give the clusters a fluffy look from a distance.

Red Monardella

Monardella macrantha

This low-growing plant is relatively insignificant until it flowers, from June to August. The flowers are a brilliant red and long and tubular in shape, evolved perfectly for pollination by hummingbirds. These agile birds hover close to each flower, inserting their narrow bill and reaching the nectar with their tongues. Red Monardella grows in chaparral and dry pine forests. Large colonies form, thanks to the creeping rootstock. Coniferous forests and chaparral are highly favoured by this plant, which is also known as Red Mountainbalm.

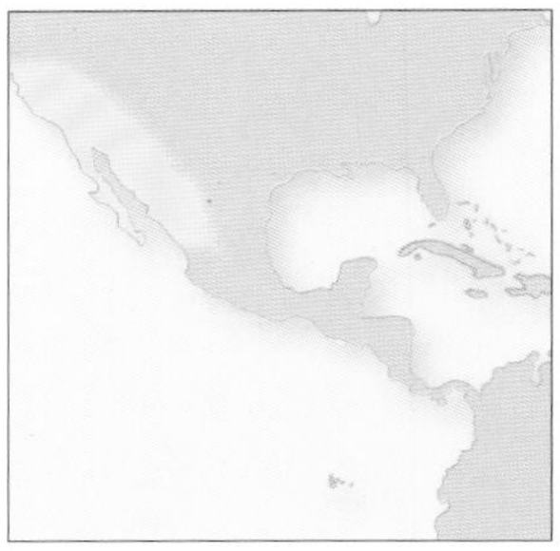

Left: The red and green make a vivid contrast.

Distribution: Southern California.
Height and spread: 10–50cm/4–20in.
Habit and form: Perennial sub-shrub.
Pollinated: Hummingbird and insect.
Leaf shape: Ovate.

Identification: Each flower is about 2in/5cm long with a pointed, five-lobed corolla and four stamens. The leaves are opposite and ovate, and aromatic.

Above: The large flowers are attractive to bees and hummingbirds.

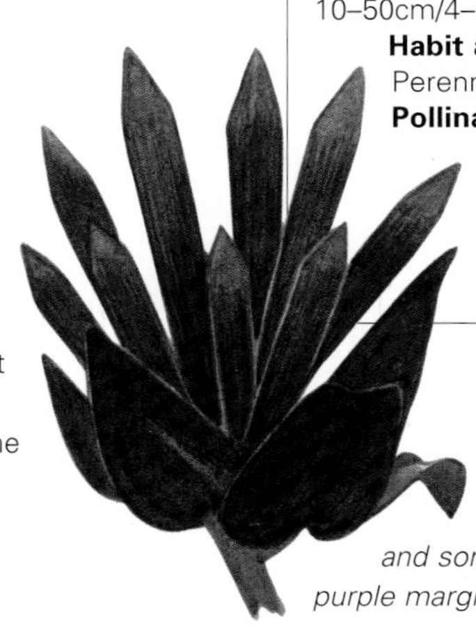

Left: Leaves are dark and shiny, and sometimes have purple margins.

Obedient Plant

False Dragonhead *Physostegia virginiana*

Distribution: Mainly eastern Canada and US, south to Texas and Florida.
Height and spread: 30–120cm/1–4ft.
Habit and form: Perennial herb.
Pollinated: Insect and hummingbird.
Leaf shape: Lanceolate, pointed.

The pink flowers of this species look a little like those of a snapdragon. The unusual common name comes from the fact that the flowers tend to remain for a while in their new position if bent. This is a popular garden plant and several cultivars are available, with white-flowered and variegated forms. The native habitats are swamps, damp thickets and prairies. The stiffly erect flower spikes grow from a basal rosette of narrow leaves.

Identification: Each flower is to 2.5cm/1in long with a two-lipped tubular corolla and four stamens. The leaves are to 10cm/4in, opposite, narrow, toothed and pointed.

Right: The flowers are arranged in vertical columns on the spike.

Far right: The flowers are reminiscent of those of the snapdragon.

Left: The leaves have toothed edges.

OTHER SPECIES OF NOTE

Coyote Mint *Monardella odoratissima*
This is an aromatic mint with grey foliage and dense heads of whitish or pale pink flowers. In has a western distribution and grows on dry slopes and rocky sites.

Hoary Mountain Mint
Pycnanthemum incarnum
Mainly found in eastern North America, hoary mountain mint grows in woods and thickets and has dense rounded clusters of pale lavender flowers. It can get to 2m/7ft tall, but is usually half that height.

Motherwort *Leonurus cardiaca*
This is a perennial introduced from Europe, but now found throughout most of North America as a weed. It has clusters of pale lavender flowers and lobed, opposite leaves that are hirsute along the veins underneath.

Wild Basil
Clinopodium vulgare
An aromatic herb that grows in fields and along roadsides, and produces its small, rather woolly pinkish purple flowers from June to September. A tea can be made from leaves. It is pollinated by bees, moths and butterflies. It grows to 25–45cm/10-18in tall.

Water Horehound

Lycopus americanus

This is a mint of wet habitats, one of about ten rather similar species. It has clusters of tiny white flowers in the leaf axils, and the squarish stem typical of the mint family. The main flowering period is from June through September. The leaves are unusual for this family, in that they are not aromatic.

Distribution: Throughout except the far north.
Height and spread: 15–60cm/6–24in.
Habit and form: Perennial herb.
Pollinated: Insect.
Leaf shape: Lanceolate.

Above: The white flowers are about 3mm/⅛ inch long.

Below: Flowers cluster at the base of the long leaves.

Identification: Each flower is only 2mm/⅛in long, with two stamens. The long leaves are toothed, especially the lower leaves.

Thistle Sage

Salvia carduacea

The prickly, round flower clusters give this sage its common name. The flowers are a rather attractive shade of lavender and the clusters develop at the top of leafless stems. It flowers from March to June and grows on sand or gravel soils in open sites. It is one of the prettiest of the sages, with bright lavender flowers and bright red anthers.

Identification: Each flower is about 2.5cm/1in long and the lips of the colourful corolla are fringed in a rather lace-like fashion. The bracts extend beyond the petals and are woolly. The lavender-to-blue corolla has deep red anthers. Leaves are narrow and lanceolate, giving the thistle-like appearance, and the seed heads and leaves are spiny. The stem is erect and either simple or few-branched with woolly herbage. Flowering period is March to June.

Distribution: California.
Height and spread: 10–50cm/4–20in.
Habit and form: Annual or perennial herb.
Pollinated: Insect.
Leaf shape: Lanceolate.

Left: The seed heads are covered in spines. These spines are not as sharp as they appear.

Above: There are several flowers borne on each stem. Gardeners often grow the plant as a patio-tub annual for its colourful blooms.

Left: Sometimes the flowers can cover acres of land. Thistle Sage is one of the most glamorous native Californian plants.

Blood Sage

Salvia coccinea

This species is commonly grown in gardens, and there are several varieties with different shades of red, white, and bi-coloured flowers, opening from May onwards in a loose spike. It is found growing wild in sandy sites or on wasteland in southern and eastern regions, and is perennial in warm places and annual where temperatures drop below freezing for more than a couple of hours at a time. This salvia, like all mints, has opposite leaves. Nutlets form after flowering, enclosed by the calyx.

Above: Blooms appear from early summer to first frost. The stamens are very prominent.

Distribution: South Carolina to Florida and west to Texas.
Height and spread: 30–60cm/1–2ft.
Habit and form: Annual herb.
Pollinated: Insect and hummingbird.

Identification: The flowers are each about 2.5cm/1in long, with a two-lipped corolla and two stamens. The upper lip of the corolla has two lobes, the lower is three-lipped. Reaches 60–90m/2–3ft tall, with 2.5–5cm/1–2in opposite, triangular leaves on long petioles (leaf stems).

Right: The flower spike tapers towards the tip, and the flowers open from the bottom to the top.

Chia

Salvia columbariae

Distribution: Mainly California, Arizona and New Mexico.
Height and spread: 10–50cm/4–20in.
Habit and form: Annual or perennial herb.
Pollinated: Insect.
Leaf shape: Oblong, divided.

This, and a number of other *Salvia* species were used by Native Americans to make a thick drink and also a flour from the seeds, called pinole. The flowers are a deep blue-purple in dense, rounded clusters near the top of the stems. It grows in dry sites, such as coastal-sage scrub and chaparral, under 1,200m/3,900ft above sea level.

Identification: Flowers each about 1.5cm/⅔in long with upper and lower lips, two stamens and spiny bracts below the flower clusters.

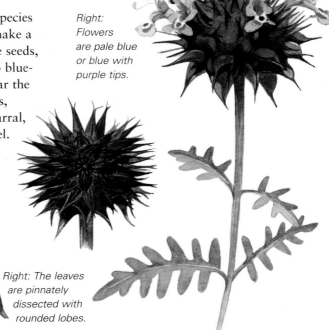

Right: Flowers are pale blue or blue with purple tips.

Right: The lower lip is twice the size of the upper lip.

Right: The leaves are pinnately dissected with rounded lobes.

OTHER SPECIES OF NOTE
Blue Salvia *Salvia azurea*
A perennial sage of open prairie and pastures, mainly in the east. It grows tall and sports large blue or violet flowers in a spike-like cluster. It is most attractive to insects.

Lyre-leaved Sage
Salvia lyrata
Rising from the rosette of basal elongated leaves, the squarish stem has whorls of lavender flowers, each about 2.5cm/1in long, appearing from April to June in abundance, although flowering can continue through the year. It grows mainly in open woods in the east.

Desert Sage Grey-ball Sage *Salvia dorii*
A western sage of dry flats and sagebrush habitats. It is a bushy plant with very aromatic silvery leaves, spiny branches and striking, pale blue to purple flowers.

Wood Sage *Teucrium canadense*
This tough perennial has spikes of lavender-pink flowers and long, toothed leaves. It grows in woods and shorelines from Saskatchewan and Newfoundland south to Florida, and scattered in the west. It flowers from June to September and is found on prairies and on wet ground, as well as alongside railtracks.

Crimson Sage

Salvia henryi

This rather slender sage has grey, softly hairy foliage and bright red flowers borne horizontally in pairs near the tops of the stems. It flowers from April to September and grows mainly amongst rocks, frequently in pinyon or juniper communities. Insects and hummingbirds are attracted to the conspicuous flowers.

Distribution: Mexico and west Texas to southern Arizona.
Height and spread: To 50cm/20in.
Habit and form: Perennial herb.
Pollinated: Insect and hummingbird.
Leaf shape: Pinnate, opposite.

Above: Dark green and slightly hairy buds open to reveal the striking red flowers.

Identification: The three-lobed crimson corolla is 2.5–6.5cm/1–2½in long and has two stamens. Foliage is greyish-green and hirsute. Stems are delicate.

Left: Leaves are pinnate and opposite.

FIGWORT FAMILY

The Scrophulariaceae consist mostly of herbs but also a few small shrubs, with more than 260 genera and 5,100 predominately temperate species. They include many that are partial root parasites and a few that are without chlorophyll and are wholly parasitic. They have a cosmopolitan distribution, with the majority found in temperate areas, including tropical mountains.

Shrubby Penstemon

Penstemon fruticosus

With more than 250 species, the penstemons constitute the largest genus of flowering plants endemic to North America. Shrubby penstemon inhabits rocky slopes stretching from the foothills into alpine areas, ranging from British Columbia, south through the Washington Cascades, and eastward to the Idaho panhandle. It is a low, dense shrub with abundant lavender flowers appearing between late spring and late summer.

Identification: A low, dense, woody, mat-forming perennial with numerous flowering and sterile stems ascending or erect above mats of leaves. The flowering stems reach a height of 40cm/16in, branching freely; new stems are slightly hairy, older stems hairless. The leaves are evergreen, leathery, shiny green, opposite, elliptic, generally pointed, entire or toothed, both basal and on the stems, with the latter being smaller. The funnel-shaped, lavender-blue flowers are borne in pairs in short clusters, densely hairy inside, about 2.5–5cm/1–2in long and 12mm/½in wide at the mouth. The fruit is a capsule, 8–12mm/⅜–½in long appearing in autumn.

Right: The flowers are funnel-shaped.

Left: The beautiful purple flowers and attractive leaves make this a spectacular shrub when in bloom.

Distribution: North-western North America.
Height and spread: 40cm/16in.
Habit and form: Woody, mat-forming perennial.
Pollinated: Insect.
Leaf shape: Elliptic.

Scarlet Monkey Flower

Mimulus cardinalis

This spreading perennial plant, native to western North America, stretches from Oregon south as far as northern Mexico. It generally inhabits shady, wet places from streamside to seepages and spreads by rhizomes, often forming good-sized colonies. Its brilliant scarlet to orange-red (sometimes yellowish) flowers are short-lived but appear prolifically from spring to autumn. While most *Mimulus* species are bee-pollinated, *M. cardinalis* is pollinated by hummingbird.

Identification: Scarlet monkey flower has hairy stems and lime-green, oval to oblong-elliptic, toothed leaves 7.5–10cm/3–4in long, with longitudinal veins. The brilliant scarlet, tubular, lipped flowers are 5cm/2in long, the upper lip arched and ascending, the lower lips flared and curved back. The narrow throat is tinged yellow; the stamens are hairy and protruding. The fruit is a capsule that opens to shed the seeds.

Left: A freely-branched, erect to lax herbaceous perennial.

Distribution: Western North America, Oregon to northern Mexico.
Height and spread: 30–120cm/1–4ft.
Habit and form: Herbaceous perennial.
Pollinated: Hummingbird.
Leaf shape: Ovate to oblong-elliptic.

Purple Chinese Houses

Innocence *Collinsia heterophylla (= Collinsia bicolor)*

Distribution: Southern California.
Height and spread: 30–60cm/1–2ft.
Habit and form: Annual herb.
Pollinated: Insect.
Leaf shape: Lanceolate.

This is one of California's most impressive wild flowers, with its separated whorls of striking purple and pink flowers, rather reminiscent of a Chinese pagoda – hence one of its common names. The individual flowers are like those of members of the pea family, and have variable colours. The plant grows on sandy soils and the flowers open from March to June. The flowers are particularly attractive to the Checkerspot Butterfly.

Below: Purple Chinese Houses spreads fast and is quite commonly seen in large groups on hillsides.

Right: Leaves are lanceolate with a slightly serrated edge.

Identification: The corolla is about 2cm/⅔in long with a two-lobed upper lip and a three-lobed lower lip, the middle lobe distinctly folded, enclosing the style and four stamens.

OTHER SPECIES OF NOTE

Large Beardtongue *Penstemon bradburii*
Found over a wide range in central North America, chiefly in prairie and plain habitats. Large beardtongue has terminal clusters of slender, tubular, dark lilac flowers that bloom on open stems, which reach 60cm/2ft. The attractive, glossy, light green leaves below provide a perfect foil for the flowers.

Low Beardtongue
Penstemon humilis
This native of the Rocky Mountains is a variable species, from 15–30cm/6–12in in height. It flowers between late spring and midsummer, with erect stems ending in panicles of azure to blue-violet inflated tubular flowers, borne in three or more whorls.

Purple Gerardia *Agalinis purpurea*
This annual of damp soils is found mainly in the east. It has pretty, delicate pink-purple bell-shaped flowers, speckled within, opening from July to September. There are about 15 species in this region. The leaves and stems, which are slender, are often tinged purple.

Lyon's Turtlehead *Chelone glabra*
Each flower looks a bit like the head of a turtle peeping from under its shell – hence the common name. Clusters of pink-tinged white flowers Grow atop tall stems. It grows in damp, rich woods or on stream banks, and flowers from July to September.

Desert Paintbrush

Castilleja angustifolia

The flaring bright red flowers of this dry country species stand out like paintbrushes dipped in fresh red paint, in contrast to the rather drab and dull foliage. It is one of the commoner paintbrush species of the west. Dry open soil such as sagebrush is its habitat. The flowers open from April through August and attract hummingbirds as well as insects.

Identification: The red-orange calyx is deeply cleft with four lobes and the corolla is pointed and slender, pale orange with red edges. The flower clusters have reddish-orange bracts. The leaves are narrow, the upper leaves lobed.

Below: The plant is a grey-green, branched perennial that likes a dry, open habitat.

Distribution: Eastern Oregon north to Alberta, east to Utah, Wyoming and Montana, and south to California.
Height and spread: 10–40cm/4–16in.
Habit and form: Perennial herb.
Pollinated: Insect and hummingbird.
Leaf shape: Narrow.

Below and left: The calyx and leaf bracts have scarlet tips, as if they have been dipped in red paint.

CARNIVOROUS PLANTS

Strictly, carnivorous plants are those that attract, capture, kill and digest animals and absorb the nutrients from them. The Droseraceae either trap their victims in sticky hairs (e.g. Drosera), or in active traps (e.g. Dionaea); the Lentibulariaceae include aquatic bladderworts (Utricularia) which use bladder-traps and terrestrial butterworts (Pinguicula) with sticky glandular leaves, and the Sarraceniaceae have pitcher-traps.

Venus Flytrap

Dionaea muscipula

This is possibly the best known of all carnivorous plants. It famously traps insects with its specially adapted leaves. As soon as an insect, or anything else, touches any of the three sensitive hairs on its surface the trap rapidly closes and then extracts nutrients from the unfortunate victim. This added nutrition enables the plant to survive in poor soils that few other plants could tolerate. Despite its being so well known, the Venus flytrap is actually endangered in the wild, being restricted to wet sandy areas, bogs and savannas mainly on the coastal plain of North and South Carolina.

Identification: The basal leaves are semi-erect or held close to the ground in a rosette, each consisting of two hinged, round, glandular lobes, which become glossy red with exposure to sunlight, with spines on their margins and three sensitive hairs on the upper surface that cause the leaf to fold when stimulated twice in quick succession. Once folded the spines mesh, trapping insects. Each leaf is on a winged, flat, spatula-shaped stalk that looks more leaf-like than the trap itself. The flowers are white shot with green veins, five-petalled, up to 2.5cm/1in across, widening from the base; they are clustered at the end of leafless stalks in umbel-like cymes, appearing in mid-spring into early summer.

Distribution: North and South Carolina, USA.
Height and spread: 30–45cm/12–18in.
Habit and form: Low-growing herbaceous perennial.
Pollinated: Insect.
Leaf shape: Two-hinged, orbicular traps.

Yellow Pitcher Plant

Huntsman's horn, *Sarracenia flava*

This carnivorous plant traps wasps, bees and flies in long, upright modified leaves. The leaves form tubes, which fill with water and drown the victims inside. It is found along the south-eastern coastal plain of the USA, from Alabama to a few sites in Virginia, and like many carnivorous plants it is threatened, primarily by habitat destruction. Its flowers are yellow, borne on stalks that clear the foliage and appear in spring before the pitchers, to prevent the trapping of pollinating species. The species is quite variable and is usually divided into seven varieties, distinguished mostly by pitcher pigmentation.

Identification: This large, carnivorous plant is rhizomatous, with thin wiry roots. The pitcher, 30–120cm/1–4ft tall with a rounded lid raised above the wide mouth, is yellow-green, often heavily veined red on the lid, especially at the base, sometimes totally red or maroon externally. The winter leaves are straight or slightly curved, and glaucous. The flowers, borne on leafless, unbranched stems up to 60cm/2ft tall, are up to 10cm/4in across, yellow and pendulous, with oval- to lance-shaped petals slightly constricted at the middle; the calyx, subtended by persistent bracts, has five overlapping, persistent sepals; the style is dilated at the end into an umbrella-like structure, with five ribs ending in hook-like stigmas.

Right: The yellowish, red-veined pitchers are topped with a heart-shaped lid.

Distribution: South-eastern USA coastal plain, from Alabama to Virginia.
Height and spread: 30–120cm/1–4ft.
Habit and form: Herbaceous perennial.
Pollinated: Insect.
Leaf shape: Pitcher-shaped traps.

Thread-leaved Sundew

Drosera filiformis

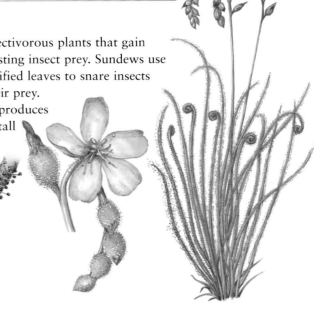

This is one of a fascinating genus of insectivorous plants that gain extra nourishment by trapping and digesting insect prey. Sundews use the sticky secretions of their highly modified leaves to snare insects and slowly extract the proteins from their prey. This sundew has long sticky leaves and produces pink flowers in a lop-sided cluster on a tall leafless stem, from June to September. The favoured habitat is wet sandy soil in coastal areas.

Identification: Each flower is about 1.5cm/½in wide with five petals.

Right: The narrow green leaves are covered in sticky red 'hairs'.

Distribution: Nova Scotia south to North Carolina and Florida.
Height and spread: 10–30cm/4–12in.
Habit and form: Perennial herb.
Pollinated: Insect.
Leaf shape: Long, with sticky hairs.

OTHER SPECIES OF NOTE

Huntsman's Cap *Sarracenia purpurea*
This low-growing carnivorous species is widespread in the eastern USA and Canada, extending from New Jersey to the Arctic. The pitchers are slender at the basal rosette, rapidly becoming swollen higher up. They are usually green with purple tints and the lids stand erect. The flowers, which appear in spring, are purple or greenish.

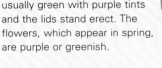

White-topped Pitcher Plant
Sarracenia leucophylla
This plant has pitchers up to around 90cm/3ft tall, and sports large red flowers in the spring. The lower part of the pitcher is green while around the mouth and lid it is white with red or sometimes green veining. It is native to boggy and marshy areas in the south-eastern USA.

Swollen Bladderwort *Utricularia inflata*
This common aquatic bladderwort is found over much of the south-eastern USA and is identified by its large radial floats on the flowering stems, which keep the showy yellow flowers erect and above water. Looking something like green wagon wheels floating on the water, they can reach up to 23cm/9in in diameter.

Cobra Lily *Darlingtonia californica*
This plant looks like a snake ready to strike, and is closely related to the genus *Sarracenia*. The trap is a twisted upright tube with nectar glands that attract insects toward the mouth or opening, which is under the dome. It grows in the north-eastern states of California and Oregon on ground permeated by running water.

Hooded Pitcher Plant

Sarracenia minor

This is the commonest pitcher plant in Florida; its method of trapping insect prey is remarkable. The hood prevents rainwater entering the pitcher, but the base of the pitcher has digestive juices. The winged pitcher-leaves have a trail of nectar, eagerly followed by insects, some of which enter the hood. The walls of the hood have translucent 'windows' through which the insects try to climb, eventually falling exhausted into the digestive broth below, where the plant extracts nutrients.

Identification: The yellow flowers are about 5cm/2in across with many stamens. The modified leaves grow taller than the flower stalks.

Distribution: Florida to North Carolina.
Height and spread: 15–60cm/6–24in.
Habit and form: Perennial herb.
Pollinated: Insect.
Leaf shape: Long, winged at one edge.

Below: Flowers appear in springtime.

Left: The plant grows to 15–60cm/6–24in tall.

ACANTHUS FAMILY

The Acanthaceae are mostly herbs or shrubs comprising about 230 genera and 3,450 species. Most are tropical herbs, shrubs or twining vines, while others are spiny. Only a few species are distributed in temperate regions. Typically there is a colourful bract subtending each flower; in some species the bract is large and showy. The family is closely allied to the Scrophulariaceae.

Water Willow

Justicia americana

This is a colonial aquatic that grows in large patches in shallow water and along wet shores. Its common name comes from the narrow willow-like leaves. The flowers, opening from June to October, are quite striking, rather large and white, with purple spots. The leaves are also distinctive, with a prominent white mid rib.

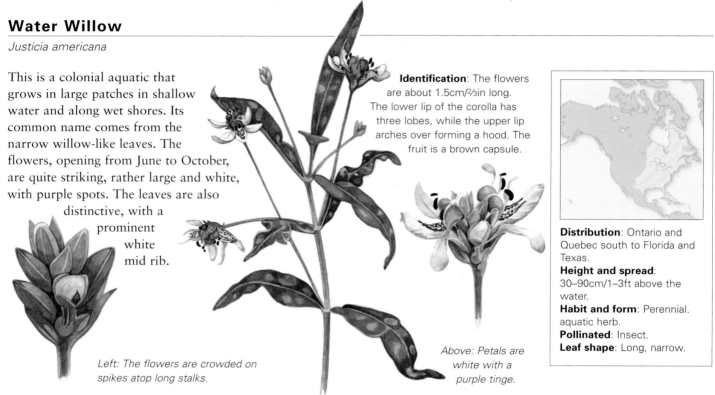

Identification: The flowers are about 1.5cm/⅔in long. The lower lip of the corolla has three lobes, while the upper lip arches over forming a hood. The fruit is a brown capsule.

Left: The flowers are crowded on spikes atop long stalks.

Above: Petals are white with a purple tinge.

Distribution: Ontario and Quebec south to Florida and Texas.
Height and spread: 30–90cm/1–3ft above the water.
Habit and form: Perennial. aquatic herb.
Pollinated: Insect.
Leaf shape: Long, narrow.

Chuparosa

Beleperone *Justicia californica*

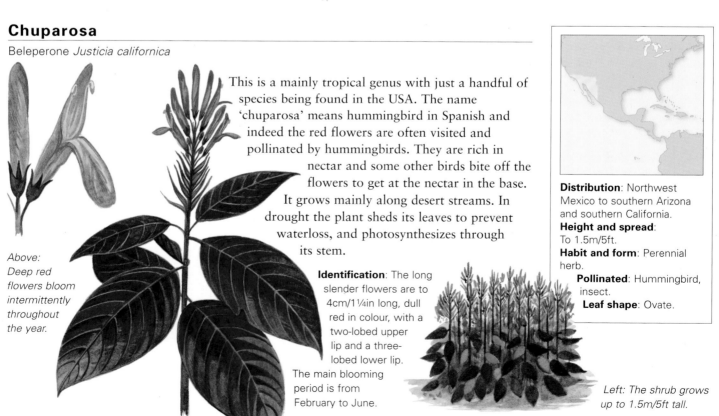

This is a mainly tropical genus with just a handful of species being found in the USA. The name 'chuparosa' means hummingbird in Spanish and indeed the red flowers are often visited and pollinated by hummingbirds. They are rich in nectar and some other birds bite off the flowers to get at the nectar in the base. It grows mainly along desert streams. In drought the plant sheds its leaves to prevent waterloss, and photosynthesizes through its stem.

Above: Deep red flowers bloom intermittently throughout the year.

Identification: The long slender flowers are to 4cm/1¼in long, dull red in colour, with a two-lobed upper lip and a three-lobed lower lip. The main blooming period is from February to June.

Distribution: Northwest Mexico to southern Arizona and southern California.
Height and spread: To 1.5m/5ft.
Habit and form: Perennial herb.
Pollinated: Hummingbird, insect.
Leaf shape: Ovate.

Left: The shrub grows up to 1.5m/5ft tall.

Shaggy Tuft

Stenandrium barbatum

Distribution: Mexico, New Mexico and west Texas.
Height and spread: To 6.5cm/2½in.
Habit and form: Perennial herb.
Pollinated: Insect.
Leaf shape: Narrow, lanceolate.

Also known as Shaggy Narrowman, this is a tiny, pretty plant found on stony and rocky banks and on limestone. It has a dwarf growth form with grey, hairy foliage. The flowers are an attractive rose-pink, clustered in short spikes and opening from March to June. It is one of the earliest spring flowers to appear. It hosts the caterpillars of the Definite Patch butterfly.

Identification: The corolla is about 1.5cm/½in wide, tubular, and opening into five lobes, streaked pink and white. The foliage is silver grey in colour.

Left: Shaggy Tuft buds about to open.

Right: The upper two lobes are often slightly darker than the lower three.

Above and right: The flower has five lobes that flare from a tube. The leaves are lanceolate and covered in grey hairs.

OTHER SPECIES OF NOTE

Loose-flowered Water Willow *Justicia ovata*
This is a perennial herb resembles water willow, but has looser flowering spikes. It is an aquatic found from Alabama and Florida north to Virginia. The very pretty flowers are bi-coloured, and the plant forms colonies thanks to a network of underground stems.

Branched Foldwing, *Dicliptera brachiata*
This purple-flowered herb is found mainly in the southern states of the USA. It is loosely branching and the flowers are usually in groups of three. It grows well as a garden plant, reaching a height of about two feet.

Carolina Scalystem, *Elytraria caroliniensis*
This is a perennial native to South Carolina, Georgia and Florida. Its favoured habitats are lime-rich soils in wet woodland, lake shores and damp slopes. Flowers are pure white, with five rather irregular-oblong petals and a deep corolla.

Carolina Wild Petunia, *Ruellia caroliniensis*
This endangered species is native to the eastern and southern USA. It is a perennial herb with attractive pale purple flowers and long, dark green leaves. It is very attractive to hummingbirds and butterflies. This plant does well in the garden, and can be grown from seed.

Wild Petunia

Stalked Ruellia *Ruellia pedunculata*

The pretty violet flowers of this woodland species open from June to September. They are trumpet-shaped opening into five lobes. In shape the flowers are a little like those of garden petunias, hence one of the common names. It prefers rich woodland soils, especially on limestone, but is commonly found along roadside and in waste areas.

Distribution: Mainly South Carolina south to Florida.
Height and spread: 30–60cm/1–2ft.
Habit and form: Perennial herb.
Pollinated: Insect.
Leaf shape: Elliptical, opposite.

Identification: Each flower is about 5cm/2in long, with a long-lobed calyx and leafy bracts below. The leaves have short stalks and are downy.

Below: The delicate flowers appear in May.

Left: Stems are erect and branching, with hairs that are longer at the nodes.

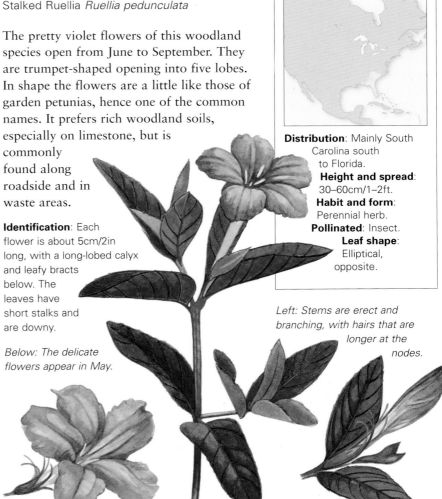

LOBELIA FAMILY

The Bellflower or Lobelia family, Campanulaceae, are herbs, shrubs, or rarely small trees, usually with milky sap, comprising about 80 genera and 2,000 species. Many of the species are highly ornamental and have become familiar plants in cultivation. Flowers are bisexual, bell-shaped, and often blue. The fruits are usually berries. The best-known genera are Campanula *and* Lobelia, *each with about 300 species.*

Cardinal Flower

Lobelia cardinalis

This extremely showy, short-lived herbaceous perennial grows in moist meadows, bogs and along stream banks in eastern North America. In some areas it is very abundant, forming mats of floating vegetation and even clogging waterways. This is one of the most striking species of the genus found anywhere. The deep red flowers are easily noticed above the purplish leaves, and it is the only *Lobelia* species in the USA with such coloration.

Identification: The dark green, lance-shaped to oblong leaves are arranged alternately, stalked below and stalkless and smaller above; they are generally smooth or sparsely hairy, serrated to toothed, up to 20cm/8in long, tapered at both ends, often with undulating margins. The flowers appear from midsummer to mid-autumn on terminal racemes around 70cm/28in in height, each subtended by a single leafy bract; they are brilliant red, up to 5cm/2in long, tubular, five-lobed, with the three promiment lobes joined to form a lower lip and two narrower lobes above. The five stamens, with red filaments, are united into a tube surrounding the style. The fruits are two-celled pods with numerous seeds.

Distribution: Eastern North America, from New Brunswick west to Minnesota, and south to central Florida and eastern Texas.
Height and spread: 60–90 x 45cm/24–36 x 18in.
Habit and form: Herbaceous perennial.
Pollinated: Hummingbird.
Leaf shape: Lanceolate to oblanceolate.

Left: This tall, stout plant has extremely striking red flowers set above the mass of purplish leaves.

Southwestern Blue Lobelia

Lobelia anatina

A small lobelia with pretty blue flowers, this western species is found in marshy areas, along streams and in damp meadows, and opens its flowers between July and October. The slender flowering stems carry loose racemes of flowers. Native Americans are said to have used lobelia to treat respiratory and muscular disorders.

Identification: A spike of blue flowers forms in the summer. The flowers have a corolla of about 2.5cm/1in long, tubular and two-lipped, an upper lip with two lobes and a lower lip with three lobes. The long leaves often have blunt teeth.

Below: Buds forming at the tip of the stem.

Distribution: Northern Mexico, New Mexico and Arizona.
Height and spread: To about 70cm/28in.
Habit and form: Perennial herb.
Pollinated: Insect.
Leaf shape: Lanceolate.

Above: This attractive plant has vivid violet-blue flowers.

Bluebell, Harebell

Campanula rotundifolia

Distribution: Scattered, especially in western mountains.
Height and spread: 10-100cm/4-40in.
Habit and form: Perennial herb.
Pollinated: Insect.
Leaf shape: Long, narrow; rounded.

This is also a familiar flower in Europe and Asia. The blue flowers are indeed bell-shaped and hang down nodding from the stems. The typical habitats are meadows and rocky slopes, and it flowers from June to September. This species is also known as bluebell in Scotland, but the European bluebell is unrelated.

Identification: The corolla is to about 2.5cm/1in long and has five pointed lobes. The stem leaves are very narrow, while those at the base have rounded blades, hence the name 'rotundifolia'.

Left: The thin wiry stems support nodding pale blue flowers.

Right: The thimble-sized flowers grow in loose clusters.

OTHER SPECIES OF NOTE

Indian Tobacco *Lobelia inflata*
Also known as bladder pod, this is a native of Canada and the eastern USA. From a rosette of soft, green, finely hairy elliptic leaves, the upright flower stems, with tiny, two-lipped, pale blue flowers, appear in early summer. The seed capsules that follow look like round pouches, reflected in the species name *inflata*.

Great Blue Lobelia *Lobelia syphilitica*
This herbaceous perennial from the east grows along streams and in swampy areas, reaching 60–90cm/2–3ft tall. The tall leafy stems produce terminal racemes that are densely covered with blue flowers from late summer to mid-autumn.

Spiked Lobelia *Lobelia spicata*
This is a variable eastern species of fields, woods and meadows. The small lavender or purplish-blue flowers open from June to August in a slender spike. The leafy stem is often reddish and hairy at the base.

Venus's Looking Glass
Triodanis perfoliata
This eye-catching bellflower has blue-purple flowers, each sitting above a clasping leaf on a wand-like stem. A few flowers are open at any one time from late spring to late summer. It is usually found in dry fields and open woods, in infertile soil, and reaches 15–60cm/6–24in in height.

Tall Bellflower

Campanulastrum americanum

Although known as a bellflower, the flowers of this eastern species are open and star-like rather than bell-shaped. They are pale blue to violet and grow in small groups or singly in an open spike, showing from June to August. The plant grows very tall and is an impressive sight when in bloom. Rich damp woods are the usual habitat and it is often found along woodland paths.

Identification: The corolla is about 2.5cm/1in across, with five lobes and a long, protruding style, and leafy bracts beneath. The broadly lanceolate leaves are distinctly toothed at the margins.

Distribution: Ontario, south to Florida.
Height and spread: 60–80cm/2–6ft.
Habit and form: Annual herb.
Pollinated: Insect.
Leaf shape: Ovate to lanceolate.

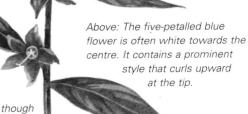

Left: The stem is usually unbranched, though lower side stems may develop.

Above: The five-petalled blue flower is often white towards the centre. It contains a prominent style that curls upward at the tip.

DAISY FAMILY

The Asteraceae (Compositae) is the largest of all the plant families, with over 1,500 genera and about 22,750 species, including herbs, shrubs or, less commonly, trees. The family is characterized by the flowers, organized into a composite cluster of tiny individual flowers called a 'capitulum', which superficially resembles a single bloom. The family includes many familiar garden flowers and vegetables.

Stokes Aster

Stokesia laevis

Stokes aster is a low-growing herbaceous perennial, native to wetlands, including pine flatwoods, savannas and bogs, on the coastal plain from North Carolina to Louisiana. The rosette clump of strap-like leathery leaves may persist through the winter, and the flowers, which appear over several weeks between late spring and early autumn, have many narrow light blue or lilac petals. *Stokesia* is a monotypic genus (it has only one species), named after Jonathan Stokes, a 19th-century British botanist.

Identification: Several erect stems, with small, clasping leaves, arise from the basal leaf rosette in late spring, bearing the flowers terminally. The strap-like, pointed, leathery leaves are 15–20cm/6–8in long, dark green, with the stems and leaf veins tinged with purple. Each inflorescence comprises one to four shaggy, cornflower-like flowerheads 7.5–10cm/3–4in across. The ray florets are fringed, blue, lavender, pink or white, in two concentric rows; the disc florets are in darker shades of the same colours.

Distribution: Coastal plain from North Carolina to Louisiana, USA.
Height and spread: 30–60cm/1–2ft.
Habit and form: Herbaceous perennial.
Pollinated: Insect.
Leaf shape: Lanceolate.

Left: The strap-like leaves often form a dense rosette from which the flowers emerge.

Clasping Coneflower

Rudbeckia amplexicaulis

This annual coneflower, native to Georgia and Texas and north as far as Missouri and Kansas, gets its name because of the way that its cauline leaves clasp the stems (*amplexicaulis* means "stem-clasping"). It is typically found along roadsides, in waste areas and along streams, where it often forms dense colonies. The flowers that appear from early summer onward resemble the larger "Mexican hat", *Ratibida* species, with the yellow outer ray florets, which droop as the flowers mature, surrounding an elongated, conical, brown centre. The plant is sometimes listed in the monotypic genus *Dracopis*, chiefly due to the presence of chaff subtending the ray flowers.

Identification: The plant is erect and loosely branched, with alternate glaucous, elongated oval or oblong leaves, with margins that are smooth to wavy or toothed and a clasping, heart-shaped base. The flowerheads appear over a long period during the summer and are long-stemmed, up to 5cm/2in across, with five to ten yellow (sometimes partly orange or purple) drooping rays, which are orange or brownish at the bases, and a cone-shaped or columnar, dark brown central disc.

Distribution: South-eastern USA.
Height and spread: 30–60cm/1–2ft.
Habit and form: Annual.
Pollinated: Insect.
Leaf shape: Ovate or oblong.

Left: The outer ray florets are bright in colour.

Right: The "Mexican hat" blooms are held high on branched stems.

Large-leaved Aster

Aster macrophyllus

This widespread rhizomatous perennial from north-eastern North America, seen from Canada to Ohio, is common in woods except those on wetlands, favouring dry or moist sites in pine woods. It often forms dense groundcover in large colonies. It is most easily distinguished by its very large, soft, thick, heart-shaped leaves, which are much more noticeable than the sparsely borne lavender or sometimes white flowers that appear in late summer.

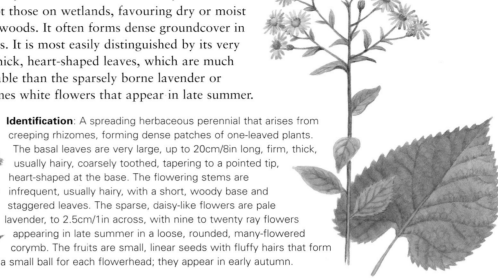

Distribution: North-eastern North America.
Height and spread: 90cm/3ft or more.
Habit and form: Herbaceous perennial.
Leaf shape: Cordate.
Pollinated: Bumblebee.

Right: The flowering stems are borne sparsely among the dense mat of leaves.

Identification: A spreading herbaceous perennial that arises from creeping rhizomes, forming dense patches of one-leaved plants. The basal leaves are very large, up to 20cm/8in long, firm, thick, usually hairy, coarsely toothed, tapering to a pointed tip, heart-shaped at the base. The flowering stems are infrequent, usually hairy, with a short, woody base and staggered leaves. The sparse, daisy-like flowers are pale lavender, to 2.5cm/1in across, with nine to twenty ray flowers appearing in late summer in a loose, rounded, many-flowered corymb. The fruits are small, linear seeds with fluffy hairs that form a small ball for each flowerhead; they appear in early autumn.

OTHER SPECIES OF NOTE

Texas Yellow Star *Lindheimera texana*
The Texas yellow star is a hairy, upright annual with tapered leaves and yellow, star-like flowerheads consisting of five rays with two or three times as many disc flowers. It blooms in spring and can be found in full sun in the sandy or rocky soils of the Edwards Plateau region.

Indian Blanket
Gaillardia pulchella
This annual or short-lived perennial is found from Virginia to Florida and westward to Colorado and New Mexico, extending south into Mexico. It is noted for its brilliant, daisy-like flowers, which appear in summer. They have large, rose-purple centres and frilly petals of yellow, orange, crimson or copper scarlet.

Rough-stemmed Goldenrod *Solidago rugosa*
This a weed is found in abandoned fields, on woodland edges and roadsides. It is a tall plant, producing heads of small pale yellow flowers from July to October. It is mainly eastern in distribution.

Purple Coneflower *Echinacea purpurea*
The purple coneflower is a native of dry woods and prairies. It is also a popular garden plant and well known as a herb, being used for tea and extracts used medicinally, notably being thought to help prevent colds. The pretty purple (occasionally white) flowers have drooping petal-like ray florets.

Blazing Star

Spike gayfeather, *Liatris spicata*

This species occurs in the entire eastern half of the USA and Canada. The non-flowering plants resemble grass clumps until the flowers appear in midsummer. The bottlebrush flower spikes of fuchsia, rose and purple, which attract bees and butterflies, are unusual in opening from the top of the spike downward, continuing until late summer or early autumn.

Identification: A clump-forming, upright, hairless (or very sparsely hairy) herbaceous perennial with single or multiple stems arising from the base. The almost grass-like, mid-green basal leaves grow up to 30cm/1ft long; on the tall stems the leaves are narrow and arranged in whorls, emphasizing the plant's vertical, feathery effect. The inflorescence is a terminal spike to 60cm/2ft tall, of crowded, rose-purple, fuzzy flowerheads up to 12mm/½in broad. The lowest flowerheads are subtended by small leafy bracts.

Left: The plant resembles a grass clump when it is not in flower.

Distribution: Eastern USA and Canada.
Height and spread: 60 x 80cm/24 x 32in.
Habit and form: Herbaceous perennial.
Leaf shape: Linear.
Pollinated: Insect.

Below: The fuzzy bottlebrush-like flowers open from the top downward.

Yarrow

Milfoil *Achillea millefolium*

This very widespread species, also familiar in Europe and Asia, has a long history of medicinal use, as a treatment for fever and as a poultice. Native Americans used it for treating stomach disorders. The flat clusters of small whitish flowers top out the greyish green feathery foliage. A wide range of cultivated forms are available, with different flower colours – for example red, yellow and purple.

Identification: The long, finely divided leaves are 5–20cm/2–8 in long, bi or tripinnate, almost feathery, and arranged spirally on the stems. They are somewhat aromatic. The tiny flowers form clusters of heads each about 6mm/¼in wide.

Distribution: Throughout the region.
Height and spread: 30–90cm/1–3ft.
Habit and form: Perennial herb.
Pollinated: Insect.
Leaf shape: Finely dissected.

Left and above: Flowers can be white or pinkish in colour.

Left: The feathery leaves are arranged spirally along the stem.

Right: The plant produces one to several stems.

Orange Agoseris

Agoseris aurantiaca

This is the only member of the genus with orange flowers; all the others have yellow blooms. However, even in this species the flower colour can vary from rusty orange to lavender, and very rarely to pink, as the flower matures and dries out. The flowerheads have spreading rays and develop at the top of leafless stalks from June to August. Orange Agoseris is found growing in forest clearings and meadows in mountain areas, and will grow in nutritionally poor soil. It occurs scattered rather than in large colonies.

Above and Below: Single-stemmed flowers grow from a basal cluster of leaves.

Distribution: West Canada south to California and New Mexico.
Height and spread: 10–60cm/4–24in.
Habit and form: Perennial herb.
Pollinated: Insect.
Leaf shape: Long, narrow.

Left: Leaves look dandelion-like and can be cooked and eaten in the same way as spinach. The leaves may be smooth or covered in fine hair. They generally measure about 5–35cm/2–14in long, and taper to a point at the tip.

Identification: The flowerheads are about 2.5cm/1in across, and the leaves long and narrow. The fruit has a tip of silvery bristles. The stems are between 10–60cm /3in–2ft long. The leaves may be smooth-edged or marginally lobed, and are long and narrow.

Pale Agoseris

Mountain Dandelion *Agoseris glauca*

This yellow-flowered and rather dandelion-like species, also known as Mountain Dandelion, grows in open coniferous forests and sagebrush. It is also often referred to as false dandelion. The flowerheads are bright light yellow, on leafless stalks, which rise from a rosette of fleshy bluish-green leaves. Like other members of the genus, the plant has milky sap.

Right: The flowerhead grows singly on the thick stem.

Distribution: West Canada south to California, east to Minnesota.
Height and spread: 10-70cm/4-28in.
Habit and form: Perennial herb.
Pollinated: Insect.
Leaf shape: Narrow to lanceolate.

Identification: Flowerheads are about 2.5cm/1in across, made up totally of ray florets. The leaves are up to 35cm/14in long, broader above the middle, and sometimes divided. The seed-like fruit is tipped by fine white hairs.

Left: Leaves are a waxy, bluish-green to dark green.

OTHER SPECIES OF NOTE

Desert Marigold *Baileya multiradiata*
Often, large patches of desert are coloured a brilliant yellow with this plant's massed flowerings. It also grows at roadsides and is popular in gardens. A western species, it is mainly found in California and Texas. Stems are a soft, greyish green, as are the leaves, and the plant grows to about 60cm/2ft in height.

Arrowleaf Balsam Root *Balsamorhiza sagittata*
This has bright yellow flowerheads set against large grey-green leaves. It grows in grassland and open pinewoods, mainly in western hills and mountains. The roots were once used for medicine.

Philadelphia Fleabane *Erigeron philadelphicus*
This very pretty flower is widespread in damp sites. The flowerheads, which appear from April to June, are pink and white and daisy-like, the rays making a rather lacy fringe around the disc. The stems are hairy and can be tinged with purple.

Greeneyes
Chocolate Flower, *Berlandiera lyrata*
Not only does this have a rather chocolate coloured central disc, but it also smells of chocolate when the ray florets are plucked. It is a western species, common on roadsides and in grassy sites. The backs of the petals are strikingly streaked with brilliant red.

Heartleaf Arnica

Arnica cordifolia

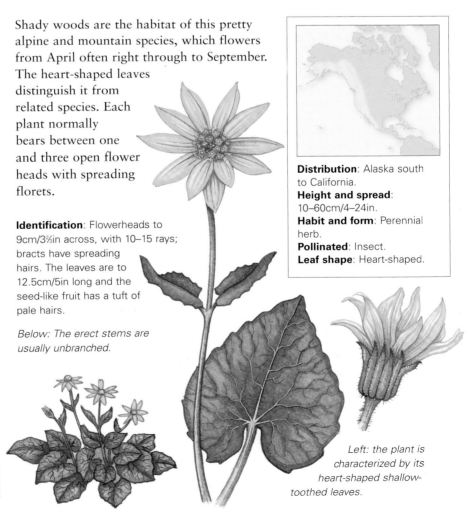

Shady woods are the habitat of this pretty alpine and mountain species, which flowers from April often right through to September. The heart-shaped leaves distinguish it from related species. Each plant normally bears between one and three open flower heads with spreading florets.

Identification: Flowerheads to 9cm/3⅝in across, with 10–15 rays; bracts have spreading hairs. The leaves are to 12.5cm/5in long and the seed-like fruit has a tuft of pale hairs.

Below: The erect stems are usually unbranched.

Distribution: Alaska south to California.
Height and spread: 10–60cm/4–24in.
Habit and form: Perennial herb.
Pollinated: Insect.
Leaf shape: Heart-shaped.

Left: the plant is characterized by its heart-shaped shallow-toothed leaves.

Brittlebrush

Incienso *Encelia farinosa*

At its flowering peak, from March to June, this attractive plant sometimes seems to be covered in a ring of bright yellow as the large flowerheads merge into one another. Its common name comes from the brittleness of its stems, which were chewed by Native Americans for the flavoursome resin they contain. Its fragrant dried stems were also used as church incense, hence another of its common names, Incienso. This shrub grows in deserts and dry slopes and does well in cultivation.

Below: Flowers are borne along the main stem with the oldest flowers at the base.

Identification: The flowerheads grow well above the grey leafy foliage, and each is about 7.5cm/3in across with long yellow rays. The plant grows to a height of about 150cm/5ft, and has a woody base and many branches.

Distribution: Mexico, California, Arizona, Utah.
Height and spread: 90–150cm/3–5ft.
Habit and form: Perennial shrub or sub-shrub.
Pollinated: Insect.
Leaf shape: Long, ovate.

Above: The oval-shaped leaves are silver-grey or whitish, and fragrant. The dried leaves may be burnt as incense.

Above: The capitula are about 3.5cm/1½in in diameter. Brownish disc florets develop, while the ray florets are bright yellow.

Common Sunflower

Helianthus annuus

The famous sunflower is one the best known of all members of the daisy family. A common wild flower of fields and plains, it is also widely grown in gardens, in a range of cultivated varieties. It has a long history of cultivation and many traditional uses. Yellow, blue and black dyes were extracted and used by Native Americans, and the seeds yield valuable oil, still widely used today. It requires full sun to do well and at the bud stage, cultivated varieties exhibit heliotropism, where the face tracks the sun from east to west throughout the day. This is not exhibited by the wild sunflower, however.

Identification: Tall and leafy, with coarse stems, branching into several flowering stalks. Each flowerhead is 7.5–12.5cm/3–5in across. The edible fruits are seed-like and flat.

Above: The head of the sunflower is made up of numerous small florets. The inner disc florets mature into the fruit that contain the seeds.

Right: The plant can reach up to 3.7m/12ft in height, and is a familiar sight as it is widely cultivated.

Distribution: Throughout.
Height and spread: 60–370cm/1–12ft.
Habit and form: Annual herb.
Pollinated: Insect.
Leaf shape: Ovate or heart-shaped.

Below: The familiar, nutritious seeds are encased in an edible husk.

Jerusalem Artichoke

Sunroot, Sunchoke *Helianthus tuberosus*

Distribution: Mainly eastern, but also in the north west.
Height and spread: 1.5–3m/5–10ft.
Habit and form: Perennial herb.
Pollinated: Insect.
Leaf shape: Ovate to lanceolate.

This sunflower relative was also cultivated by Native Americans for its nutritious potato-like tubers, and these are still eaten today. Note that the name 'Jerusalem' is actually a corruption of the Italian 'girasole' meaning turning to the sun. It is also known as Sunroot or Sunchoke, names that are derived from the original Native American word for the plant. It has rough branching stems and large golden flowerheads from August to October and grows naturally in fields and roadsides. It is tall and rangy and its branches can break under their own weight.

Identification: The flowerheads are about 7.5cm/3in across with 10–20 spreading rays, and narrow spreading bracts.

Left: The plant can grow up to 3m/10ft tall.

Left: The knobbly brown tubers have crisp white flesh.

OTHER SPECIES OF NOTE

Pearly Everlasting *Anaphalis margaritacea*
The tightly clustered white flowerheads can be dried and then last a long time – hence the common name. It is widespread in fields and roadsides and forest clearings and flowers from June to September.

Chinchweed *Pectis papposa*
This western plant is found in west Texas, Mexico and southern California, mainly in deserts and sandy roadsides. The branching stems bear clusters of small yellow flowerheads, that when massed have a strange lemony smell.

Plantainleaf Pussytoes
Antennaria plantaginifolia
Dense, compact clusters of fluffy white flowerheads tinged with pink bear a fanciful resemblance to cats' paws, hence the common name. It grows in open woods and meadows, mainly in the east. The plant forms a dense mat of dark green or greyish leaves that are hairy underneath.

Tall Ironweed *Vernonia gigantea*
This has tough, hairy, tall stems, generally unbranched except near the flowers. It bears loose clusters of blue-purple flowerheads that are pleasantly scented. The leaves are alternate, large and oblong or lanceolate. Another mainly eastern species of woods and meadows, it flowers from August to October.

Black-eyed Susan

Rudbeckia hirta

This is a widespread native of prairies, fields and open woodland. The stems are coarse and rather rough and the large daisy flowers are distinctive, with bright yellow spreading rays and a dark brown centre – hence the common name. The flowers appear from June to October. It is usually a biennial, flowering in the second year. *Rudbeckia* are quite popular as garden plants.

Identification: Flowerheads are to 7.5cm/3in across, the rays spreading out from the cone-shaped central disc. The leaves are to 17.5cm/7in long with coarse hairs.

Distribution: Throughout most of the region except the far north.
Height and spread: 30–90cm/1–3ft.
Habit and form: Biennial or short-lived perennial herb.
Pollinated: Insect.
Leaf shape: Lanceolate to ovate.

Below: The basal rosette of leaves will send forth flower stems in its second year.

Left: The diamond-shaped leaves have a rough texture.

HONEYSUCKLE FAMILY

Plants of the family Caprifoliaceae are mostly woody, including vines, shrubs, and small trees with a cosmopolitan distribution. There are about 16 genera and 420 species. The best known is the climbing garden honeysuckle, although it is a varied family with many ornamental shrubs, vines and occasional herbs in its ranks. The fruit is usually a berry.

Hobblebush

Viburnum alnifolium

Hobblebush is a common understorey shrub from north-eastern North America. It is usually found in high elevations, and is easily seen in the early part of the year when its leaves expand earlier than those of the canopy trees, allowing them to start photosynthesizing. These very large leaves are the plant's distinguishing characteristic. The bush produces white flowers in flat-topped clusters in late spring; the large, sterile outer flowers serve to attract insects and provide a landing area for them.

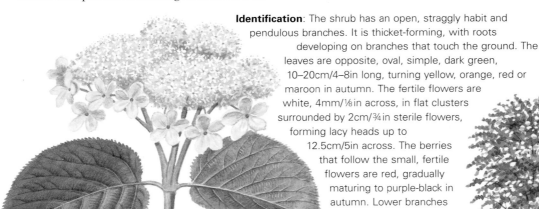

Identification: The shrub has an open, straggly habit and pendulous branches. It is thicket-forming, with roots developing on branches that touch the ground. The leaves are opposite, oval, simple, dark green, 10–20cm/4–8in long, turning yellow, orange, red or maroon in autumn. The fertile flowers are white, 4mm/⅛in across, in flat clusters surrounded by 2cm/¾in sterile flowers, forming lacy heads up to 12.5cm/5in across. The berries that follow the small, fertile flowers are red, gradually maturing to purple-black in autumn. Lower branches often lie prostrate along the ground making it easy to trip over – hence the name.

Distribution: North-eastern North America.
Height and spread: 1–3m/3–10ft.
Habit and form: Deciduous shrub.
Pollinated: Insect.
Leaf shape: Ovate.

Above: The fruits darken as they age.

Bush Honeysuckle

Diervilla sessilifolia

The bush honeysuckle is a small, low-growing, deciduous, suckering shrub from the south-eastern United States, from North Carolina to Georgia. It is covered with slender, pointed leaves that have a coppery tinge when young. Its two-lipped, yellow flowers are produced in clusters from early to late summer. It often forms thickets in light woodland due to its densely suckering habit.

Identification: The stems are brown and round, with striped bark. The leaves are opposite, simple and lance-shaped, up to 15cm/6in long, with a sharply serrated margin, smooth and dark green; the new growth is bronze-tinted. The tubular pale yellow flowers, 12mm/½in across, are borne in crowded 5–7.5cm/2–3in cymes. They form terminal panicles on the new growth in early to late summer, followed by fruiting capsules.

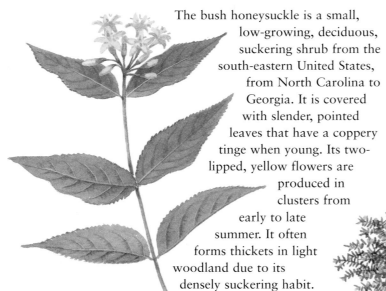

Left: The freely suckering habit means that it forms dense thickets among other shrubs.

Distribution: South-eastern USA.
Height and spread: 60–150cm/2–5ft.
Habit and form: Deciduous shrub.
Pollinated: Insect.
Leaf shape: Lanceolate.

OTHER SPECIES OF NOTE

Amur Honeysuckle *Lonicera maackii*
A native to east Asia, but now one of the commonest shrubs in the east of North America. It is a large, upright shrub that keeps its small opposite leaves for most of the year. It has pale pink to bright red tubular flowers and bright red berries, the latter much beloved of birds and squirrels in the autumn.

Twinflower *Linnaea borealis*
This creeping, broadleaf, evergreen shrub, with rounded, opposite leaves, is actually circumpolar, occurring in northern Europe and Asia. It inhabits dry or moist sites in pinewoods. It bears fragrant, pink, bell-like flowers in pairs, from early summer to autumn.

Fly Honeysuckle *Lonicera canadensis*
This erect, straggly shrub of open woodland in the north of the USA and Canada, has smooth, red branches and oval, slightly hairy leaves. The drooping, tubular, pale orange-red flowers, which appear in spring, are followed by characteristic double berries later in the season.

American elder
Sambucus nigra ssp. *canadensis*
This bushy, widely-spreading shrub forms dense thickets that bear sprays of attractive star-shaped, white flowers in spring and summer, followed by bunches of small, shiny blue-black, edible fruits. Leaves are divided into five to nine serrated leaflets.

Ledebour's Honeysuckle

Lonicera ledebourii

This shrub is found throughout the coastal ranges of western North America, occurring from northern Mexico and California in the south to British Columbia and northward into Alaska. It forms an erect shrub that is notable for its paired orange flowers, which are surrounded by two broad bracts. The flowers are later replaced by two purple-black fruits; as they ripen, the deep red bracts enlarge around them. The plant is chiefly found in moist places below 2,900m/9,500ft.

Identification: A sturdy, erect, deciduous shrub with stout, usually smooth young shoots. The leaves, up to 12.5cm/5in long, are oval to oblong, with a pointed or rounded base, dull dark green above, lighter and downy beneath. The leaf margins are hairy and leathery and the midribs are often somewhat arched. Funnel-shaped, paired flowers appear in summer from the leaf axils, heavily tinged orange or red with yellow tips and slightly protruding stigmas; behind them are two to four, purple-tinged heart-shaped bracts, which persist after the flowers drop and enlarge and spread around the fruits as they ripen to black.

Distribution: Western North America, from northern Mexico to Alaska.
Height and spread: 1.5–3.5m/5–12ft.
Habit and form: Deciduous shrub.
Leaf shape: Ovate-oblong.
Pollinated: Insect.

Above: The bracts are tinged purple, making a pretty contrast.

Snowberry

Symphoricarpos albus

Distribution: Alberta and Nova Scotia south to North Carolina and scattered elsewhere.
Height and spread: 30-120cm/1–4ft.
Habit and form: Deciduous shrub.
Pollinated: Insect.
Leaf shape: Oval.

The pure white waxy fruits give this plant its common name. The flowers are small, bell-shaped and pinkish white and appear from May to July. In the wild it is found at roadsides and on banks. Snowberry is quite a popular garden shrub and looks very pretty, as its fruits remain well into the winter. Coralberry *(S. orbiculatus)* and Wolfberry *(S. occidentalis)* have pink and greenish fruits respectively.

Left: The branching stems are dense and twiggy.

Right: The pinkish tubular blossoms and long-lasting white berries make this a favourite ornamental shrub.

Identification: Each flower has a five-lobed corolla and is about 6mm/¼in long. The oval leaves are about 5cm/2in long, dull grey-green with hairy undersides.

DUCKWEED AND ARUM FAMILIES

The duckweed family (Lemnaceae) contains four genera and about 25 species of mostly perennial, aquatic, floating or submersed herbs. The arum family (Araceae) are rhizomatous or tuberous herbs comprising about 105 genera and more than 2,550 species. They are characterized by a flower that is a fleshy spadix partially enveloped by a bract or spathe, which is sometimes brightly coloured.

Giant Duckweed

Spirodela polyrrhiza

This is the largest of all North American duckweeds, with a large (compared with other duckweed species), rounded plant body. Its reddish-purple lower surface and multiple roots make it easy to distinguish from all *Lemna* species. New plants are produced in a budding pouch at the base or along the margin of the plant body; these may overwinter in the sediment as dense, rootless, starch-filled daughter plants (winter buds). Giant duckweed is found throughout the USA from sea level to 2,500m/8,200ft in freshwater ponds, marshes and quiet streams. It is also widespread in Central America, Europe, Africa, Asia and northern Australia. It is largely absent from South America, where it is mostly replaced by *S. intermedia*.

Right: The flowers are microscopic and rarely seen.

Identification: This small, floating aquatic generally occurs in clusters of two to five, in dense populations. Clusters of slender fibrous roots hang down from the lower surface. The plant body is 2–10mm/¹⁄₁₆–½in long, oblong to round, flat; the upper surface is shiny dark green, the lower surface generally red-purple, with three to twelve veins visible in backlight; the flowers, rarely seen, are tiny, appearing in two lateral budding pouches, sheathed by minute membranes. The fruit is balloon-like, sometimes winged, containing a ribbed seed.

Right: The rounded plant bodies form dense colonies.

Distribution: USA, Central America, Europe, Africa, Asia and northern Australia.
Height and spread: Unlimited spread.
Habit and form: Floating aquatic.
Leaf shape: Leaves absent.
Pollinated: Water.

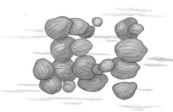

Skunk Cabbage

Symplocarpus foetidus

This North American plant of wet woodland, marshes and stream banks is one of the first to bloom in spring, although its flowers are often partly or wholly hidden beneath the previous year's fallen leaves. Like many other dark-coloured flowers, skunk cabbage is pollinated mostly by flies. The flowers actually produce heat, which is, of course, a benefit to any early flies out in cold weather. The leaves emerge after the flowers and smell unpleasant when they are crushed.

Identification: The large leaves, 30cm/12in or more across, are oval, heart-shaped at the base, bright waxy green, appearing after the flowers have bloomed; they are highly malodorous when crushed. The flowers appear from late winter to mid-spring: the actual flowers are tiny, located on the ball-like spadix inside the hooded, purplish-brown and green spathe, which is 7.5–15cm/3–6in tall.

Above: The flowers often appear as soon as the winter snows melt.

Distribution: North America.
Height and spread: 30–60cm/1–2ft.
Habit and form: Herbaceous perennial.
Leaf shape: Ovate.
Pollinated: Insect.

Below: The unpleasant-smelling leaves give this plant its common name.

Jack in the Pulpit

Indian turnip, *Arisaema triphyllum*

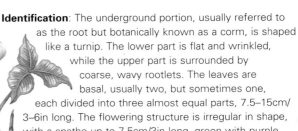

This common perennial has a wide distribution, stretching from Canada to Florida and westward to Kansas and Minnesota, where it can almost always be found near waterfalls or where water is running or splashing. Its large leaves, divided into three, radiate out from the top of the stalk and are usually the most noticeable feature, with the flowers mostly hidden beneath them. The flowers are enclosed in a green-and-purplish spathe and appear through the spring and into the summer. Later in the summer, the flowers are replaced by a black seed cluster that ripens to red.

Distribution: Eastern North America, Canada to Florida and westward to Kansas and Minnesota.
Height and spread: 65cm/26in.
Habit and form: Herbaceous perennial.
Leaf shape: Trifoliate.
Pollinated: Insect.

Right: The leaves are prominent.

Far right: A cluster of bright red, shiny berries appears from late summer.

Identification: The underground portion, usually referred to as the root but botanically known as a corm, is shaped like a turnip. The lower part is flat and wrinkled, while the upper part is surrounded by coarse, wavy rootlets. The leaves are basal, usually two, but sometimes one, each divided into three almost equal parts, 7.5–15cm/ 3–6in long. The flowering structure is irregular in shape, with a spathe up to 7.5cm/3in long, green with purple or brownish stripes, and a spadix covered with tiny male and female flowers.

OTHER SPECIES OF NOTE

Green Dragon *Arisaema dracontium*
A herbaceous perennial reaching 90cm/3ft, with one basal leaf, which is divided into seven to fifteen leaflets. The yellowish-green flowers are irregular in shape, first appearing in late spring and continuing into early summer. A very long, slender spadix extends far above the top of the sheathed spathe.

Flamingo Flower *Anthurium scherzerianum*
Extremely well known in cultivation, the wild plant is restricted to moist forest areas of Costa Rica. Spotted green foliage gives rise to orange-red flower spikes, held out above the highly ornamental, bright red, waxy spathes. The plant may grow terrestrially in open areas or as an epiphyte in thick forest.

Arrow Arum *Peltandra virginica*
An immersed plant that is found in swamps and marshes, most commonly along the Atlantic coastal plain. Its range appears to be actively expanding. Its leaves are arrow-shaped, clustered on long, succulent stems. Small, light yellow flowers, surrounded by a yellowish-green spathe, appear in spring and early summer.

Golden Club *Orontium aquaticum*
A herbaceous perennial found in swamp areas on the Atlantic coast of North America. It has bluish-green leaves covered in a powdery bloom that causes the water to bead. In spring, tiny yellow flowers are borne on a spadix at the end of a white cylindrical stalk It is threatened in some areas of North America.

Swamp Lantern

Yellow skunk cabbage, *Lysichiton americanus*

This common perennial plant is ubiquitous in the wetlands of the Pacific north-west. The large yellow spathes emerge very early in spring from a thick dormant bud and are extremely noticeable. The plants grow to 40cm/16in tall or more, with enormous, net-veined leaves. The pungent, skunk-like odour attracts various insect pollinators and is responsible for the plant's other common name, skunk cabbage.

Distribution: Pacific north-west.
Height and spread: 40cm/16in or more.
Habit and form: Herbaceous perennial.
Leaf shape: Ovate-oblong.
Pollinated: Insect.

Identification: The leaves are bold, oval to oblong, heart-shaped or straight at the base with wavy margins, smooth, green, soft-textured and prominently veined below. They are produced in loose rosettes, three to six per head, shortly after the flowers, ultimately appearing rather wilted, with a musky smell when bruised. The leaf stalks are short, pale, grooved above and winged. The bright yellow spathe is oval to lance-shaped, arising in late winter or early spring. The cylindrical spadix is short at first, lengthening in the fruiting stage. The fruits are green.

Left, right and above right: The yellow flowers of the swamp lantern are soon obscured by the large, cabbage-like leaves.

GRASSES, RUSHES AND SEDGES

Poaceae (Gramineae) is one of the largest families of flowering plants, with over 665 genera and 9,500 species. The Juncaceae, or rush family, is much smaller, with some 10 genera and about 400 species. Many of these slow-growing plants superficially resemble grasses, but are actually herbs or woody shrubs. There are about 100 genera and 4,350 species of sedge (Cyperaceae).

Giant Bamboo

Canebrake, rivercane, *Arundinaria gigantea*

Occurring widely along rivers and streams in the southern USA, in well-drained floodplain forests, this bamboo has a broad tolerance for weather and soil. It grows from sea level to 600m/2,000ft and can withstand extreme temperatures of -20 to 40°C/-4 to 104°F. It spreads by large fast-growing rhizomes to make extensive colonies, and once formed large dense stands called canebrakes in the floodplains of south-eastern rivers.

Above: Giant bamboo's tree-like stems are a familiar sight in flood plain areas of the southern USA.

Distribution: Southern USA.
Height and spread: 60cm–4m/2–13ft or more.
Habit and form: Woody grass (bamboo).
Pollinated: Wind.
Leaf shape: Linear.

Identification: Woody perennial and semi-evergreen smooth stems, 3cm/1¼in in diameter, emerge from the axils of strong, rapidly spreading rhizomes, forming dense stands. The leaves, borne on two-year old stems, are 7.5–20cm/3–8in long and 2.5cm/1in wide, with parallel venation, crowded at the tips. The flowers appear in early spring at irregular intervals of several years; panicles form on the branches on older portions of stem or directly from the rhizomes, consisting of a few racemes of large many-flowered spikelets. The fruit is a grain enclosed in the flattened spikelets.

Left: Despite its giant proportions, the flower spikes reveal that this is a grass.

Right: The spreading rhizomes enable the development of dense, extensive colonies of giant bamboo.

Oreobolus pectinatus

This grass-like herbaceous perennial is common in the Pacific coastal regions of temperate America, with a wide distribution from the coast up to montane meadows at altitudes of 3,700m/12,000ft or more. It ranges from Washington State, east to Colorado and south to Texas in the USA, and grows widely in South America. It forms a tight, hummocky mass, flowering between late spring and late summer depending on latitude and altitude and in cooler climates it is more likely to be an annual.

Identification: This annual or herbaceous perennial grows with or without rhizomes, which are generally heavy with scale-like leaves where present. The slender stems are cylindrical or flat, erect or generally spirally twisted. The leaves are basal in loose sheaths, the upper sheaths generally bearing 5–20cm/2–8in blades that resemble the stem, well developed, cylindrical or flat, or reduced to a small point; short, firm appendages are often present at the blade-sheath junction. The flowers are generally terminal, although often appearing lateral, with three or six stamens and one pistil; the seeds are numerous.

Distribution: Washington State, Colorado and Texas, USA, and South America.
Height and spread: 10–60cm/4in–2ft.
Habit and form: Grass-like herbaceous perennial.
Pollinated: Wind.
Leaf shape: Linear.

OTHER SPECIES OF NOTE

Abrupt-beaked Sedge *Carex abrupta*

A grass-like herb found in coastal prairie, forests, meadows, slopes and wetlands of the USA to elevations of 3,500m/11,500ft. The separate male and female plants have sharply three-angled, solid stems, with spikelets generally arrayed in a raceme, panicle, or head-like cluster.

Globe Flatsedge *Cyperus echinatus*
Occurring chiefly in upland prairies, sand prairies, glades, dry upland forests, pastures and disturbed sites, in the east and south USA, this species can be identified by its spherical flower clusters, red base, and short, knotty rhizomes, and by the long bracts that subtend the inflorescence, which appears in summer.

Fragrant Flatsedge *Cyperus odoratus*
An annual sedge with oval flower spikes and elliptic to oval, light brown flower bracts, six–twenty-four per spikelet, which are splotched reddish with a conspicuous mid-vein, appearing from midsummer to autumn. It is found in wet, disturbed soils in tropical and warm temperate parts of south-west North America.

Shore Rush *Juncus biflorus*
The shore rush is unusual in possessing leaf blades. It is usually found along sandy shores and ditches as single clumpy plants. The stiff, dark brown inflorescences occur at the stem tips in summer.

Big-leaf Sedge

Ample-leaved sedge, *Carex amplifolia*

This grass-like perennial has one or more sharply triangular stems, which arise from long, stout, creeping rhizomes. The smooth, flat leaves are distributed evenly along the stems. A single spike of male flowers appears at the tip of the stem, and several female spikes appear on short stalks below, in summer. It is found in swamps, bogs and other wet places, from lowlands to moderate elevations in the mountains, from British Columbia to California, being frequent and locally plentiful in the western portion of its range.

Identification: The stems are coarse and stout, sharply triangular, usually tinged dark red toward the base, with some bladeless leaf sheaths, and with the dry leaves of the previous year present. The leaves are light to blue-green, 8–20mm/⅜–¾in wide. The leafy bracts are slightly sheathing, the lowest usually surpassing the inflorescence of several elongated, well-separated, greenish-brown flower spikes, of which the male is narrow and terminal, and the females lateral, narrowly cylindrical, closely flowered, short-stemmed or stalkless.

Distribution: British Columbia to California.
Height and spread: 50–100cm/20–39in.
Habit and form: Grass-like herbaceous perennial.
Pollinated: Wind.
Leaf shape: Linear.

Below: The tall flowering stems often form dense stands in marshy areas along its range.

Saltmarsh Bulrush

Bolboschoenus maritimus syn. *Schoenoplectus robustus*

Distribution: Cosmopolitan in Northern Hemisphere, South America and Africa.
Height and spread: Variable to 50cm/20in or more.
Habit and form: Grass-like herbaceous perennial.
Pollinated: Wind.
Leaf shape: Linear.

This grass-like perennial is one of the most widely distributed plants of the Northern Hemisphere, being more or less circumpolar in boreal and temperate regions. It occupies a wide range of habitats up to at least 3,000m/10,000ft and from just inside the Arctic Circle to Mediterranean regions. It has a scattered occurrence in South America and Africa and is encountered in various other warm parts of Eurasia. It is remarkable in its range of tolerances, from coastal marsh to dry rangeland, and is quite variable as a consequence, leading to its having been classified and re-classified by botanists under several synonyms.

Identification: A grass-like herb with creeping, branching, scaly rhizomes. The stems are solitary, tuberous, and swollen at the base, arising from rhizomes, three-angled, leafy below. The tapered leaves, to 35cm/14in long, exceed the stems; the sheaths are often membranous, the lower ones often lacking blades. A terminal inflorescence appears in summer, subtended by leaf-like, rough bracts, twice its length; it bears between one and ten pointed brown spikelets, up to 3cm/1¼in long, stalkless or on arching stalks.

Right: The grass-like flowering stems of this herbaceous perennial are a common sight across much of the world, especially on brackish or saline shorelines.

IRIS FAMILY

The Iridaceae are perennial herbs growing from rhizomes, bulbs or corms. There are over 90 genera and 1,800 species in this family, occurring in tropical and temperate regions, but particularly around the Mediterranean, in South Africa and in Central America. The flowers of most new world Iridaceae occur as spikes at the top of branched or unbranched stems, each with six petals in two rings of three.

Tough-leaf Iris

Oregon iris, *Iris tenax*

This herbaceous perennial from north-western USA is found in pastures, fields and open oak woodlands, although it is unusual in coniferous forests unless they have been logged. It has a wide colour range from purple and lavender to white, cream and yellow. Where they occur, the handsome flowers provide brilliant colour displays along highways. The species name *tenax* is from the Latin for "tenacious", referring to the tough leaves, which were once used by Native Americans to make strong, pliable rope and cord.

Identification: The leaves are green and linear, tinged pink at the base, growing as tall as or taller than the numerous flower stalks. The flowers, 7.5–10cm/3–4in across, appear in early summer, one to two at the top of short stalks 30cm/12in tall; they are palest yellow to lavender or red purple, with lance-shaped falls 2.5cm/1in wide, reflexed, with a white or yellow central patch, suffused with purple veins, and lance-shaped standards 1cm/½in wide.

Distribution: North-western North America.
Height and spread: 30cm/12in.
Habit and form: Herbaceous perennial.
Pollinated: Insect.
Leaf shape: Linear.

Left: Tough-leaf iris is an attractive plant that is often cultivated in gardens for its showy blooms.

Prairie Blue-eyed Grass

Sisyrinchium campestre

This herbaceous perennial is found throughout the tall-grass prairie regions of North America, on the sandy soils of open areas. It is especially attractive after a controlled burn, when it is more noticeable. When not in bloom, it easily can be mistaken for a grass because of its grass-like leaves. It sports lavender to violet blossoms in early summer: as with many small prairie plants, it blooms relatively early in the year to take better advantage of the sun. The seedheads are small and pea-like.

Identification: This fibrous-rooted, often tufted, herbaceous perennial is covered with a fine bloom. It is sometimes purplish at the base with mostly basal, linear, grass-like leaves up to 3mm/⅛in wide. The flower stems are narrowly to broadly winged, with one or several flowers borne terminally, subtended by a two-bracted spathe: the outer bract is up to three times longer than the inner bract, and its margins are united above the base. The flower is blue-violet with a yellow centre and six regular petals with broadly pointed or rounded tips, 15mm/⅝in long. The three stamens are united by their filaments around the three-branched style. The fruit is a rounded, straw-coloured capsule containing numerous black seeds.

Distribution: North America.
Height and spread: 10–45cm/4–18in.
Habit and form: Herbaceous perennial.
Pollinated: Insect.
Leaf shape: Linear.

Tiger Flower

Tigridia pringlei

Distribution: Mexico.
Height and spread:
80–125cm/32–50in.
Habit and form: Herbaceous
perennial.
Pollinated: Insect.
Leaf shape: Lanceolate.

This bulbous perennial plant is native to Mexico and is most noteworthy for its large and brilliantly coloured iris-like flowers. The flowers are short-lived but flower in succession, one at a time on each inflorescence. The flower colours are quite variable and the ease of producing cultivars has led to this plant being widely cultivated both in the tropics and temperate regions. Consequently, it occasionally occurs outside its natural range as a garden escapee.

Identification: The basal leaves of this bulbous plant, which precede the flowers, are up to 50cm/20in long, lance-shaped, pleated and ranked alternately in a fan shape; the stem leaves are reduced to leaf-like bracts. On the flowering stem a few flowers are borne per spathe; they are large, showy, and shallowly cupped, with three outer, broadly oval, pointed, spreading segments 5–10cm/2–4in long, with broad stalk-like bases, orange, bright pink, red, yellow or white, variously spotted red, brown or maroon at the base; the three inner segments, alternating with the outer ones, are one-third as long, of similar ground colour but more distinctly marked. The staminal tube, 5–7.5cm/2–3in long, is erect and protrudes far beyond the flower cup; the anthers are erect and incurved.

OTHER IRIS FAMILY SPECIES

Copper Iris *Iris fulva*

From the south-eastern USA, this iris grows in moist areas in wetlands and along bayous. The beardless, crestless, deep copper flowers bloom in late spring, and the bright green, sword-shaped leaves remain attractive all through the growing season. The flowers attract hummingbirds.

Yellow Star Grass *Hypoxis curtissii*
A herbaceous perennial growing in glades and open woods throughout the eastern and mid-western USA, mainly on the coastal plain in alluvial soil or wooded swamps. The yellow blooms, with six parts, first appear in mid-spring and continue into mid-autumn. There may be two to nine flowers, usually there are three.

Western Blue Flag *Iris missouriensis*

The western blue flag or Rocky Mountain iris is indigenous from south Dakota to southern California, reaching north to British Columbia. It is a perennial with pale lavender flowers that often emerges through snow in spring. It grows in sunny, open, moist areas such as meadows surrounded by forests, and is most often found in extensive, dense patches in moist meadows from the foothills to the mountains.

Pinewood Lily

Propeller flower, *Alophia drummondii*

This lovely and interesting member of the iris family is native to the southern USA and Mexico. The plants grow from small, shallow bulbs and form loose colonies in sandy soils in lightly wooded areas. The velvety purple to red-purple flowers resemble those of *Tigridia* but they face to one side, unlike *Tigridia* flowers, which face upward. Each flower lasts only one day but the blooms open in succession. The plants are dormant in winter and flower from late spring until autumn.

Identification: The leaves, rising from the oval truncated corm, are 15–30cm/6–12in long, narrowly to broadly lance-shaped and strongly pleated. The flowering stem, simple or forked, appears in spring, bearing a few-flowered terminal raceme subtended by two spathes. Each flower has three rounded outer segments, up to 2.5cm/1in long, and three narrow inner ones, 15mm/⅝in long; they are red-purple to indigo or violet, fading to white, spotted brown at the centre and on the claws, with margins inrolled to a central band of hairs.

Distribution: Southern USA and Mexico.
Height and spread:
15–40cm/6–16in.
Habit and form: Herbaceous
perennial.
Pollinated: Insect.
Leaf shape: Narrowly to
broadly lanceolate.

Left: The narrow stem may be simple or branched. Leaves are lanceolate.

LILY FAMILY

The Liliaceae is a large and complex family, mostly consisting of perennial herbs that grow from starchy rhizomes, corms, or bulbs. It comprises about 290 genera and 4,950 species, including a great number of ornamental flowers as well as several important agricultural crops. Plants in this family have linear leaves, mostly with parallel veins, and flower parts in threes.

Rain Lily

Copper Zephyrlily *Zephyranthes longifolia*

Like many desert plants, this species flowers quickly after heavy rains bring life to its sandy desert habitat, hence its common name. The usual flowering period is from April to July. Each stem bears a single yellow, funnel-shaped crocus-like flower. It requires full sun and is grown in gardens in warm regions; in cooler areas it is generally potted and enjoyed as a house plant. In cultivation, it will flower throughout the year if kept alternately wet and dry.

Right: The solitary flowerheads face upward, much like crocuses.

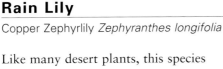

Identification: The individual flowers are each about 2.5cm/1in long with six segments. Outside the flowers have a coppery hue, but inside they are a brighter, clearer yellow. The leaves are few in number, rather long and narrow, and may be absent at flowering time. The fruit is an almost spherical three-chambered capsule containing black seeds.

Left: The basal leaves are narrow and grass-like, and grow independently from the stalk.

Distribution: Northern Mexico, north to west Texas and southern Arizona.
Height and spread: To 22.5cm/9in.
Habit and form: Perennial herb.
Pollinated: Insect.
Leaf shape: Very narrow.

Swamp Lily

Crinum americanum

Swamp lily is a wetland plant found in marshes and alongside streams, mainly in the south east of the region. It grows from an onion-like bulb and has erect, spreading, strap-like leaves. The clusters of fragrant, delicate, rather ragged-looking white flowers grow on leafless flower stalks, opening at any season, but usually from late spring through summer. It can be grown in the garden and propagated by division.

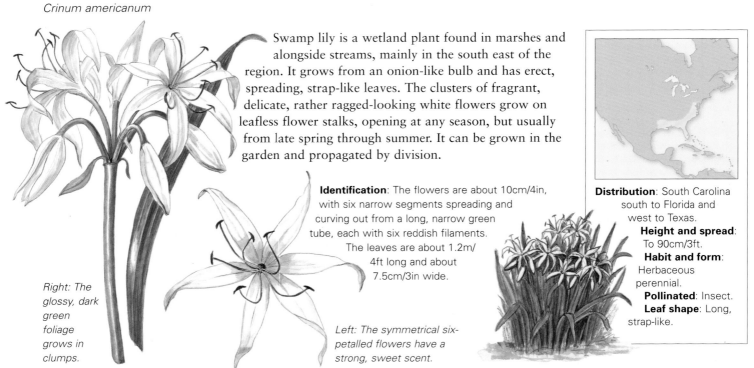

Right: The glossy, dark green foliage grows in clumps.

Identification: The flowers are about 10cm/4in, with six narrow segments spreading and curving out from a long, narrow green tube, each with six reddish filaments. The leaves are about 1.2m/4ft long and about 7.5cm/3in wide.

Left: The symmetrical six-petalled flowers have a strong, sweet scent.

Distribution: South Carolina south to Florida and west to Texas.
Height and spread: To 90cm/3ft.
Habit and form: Herbaceous perennial.
Pollinated: Insect.
Leaf shape: Long, strap-like.

Easter Lily

Atamasco Lily, Zephyr Lily *Zephyranthes atamasco*

Distribution: Maryland south to Louisiana and Florida.
Height and spread:
To 30cm/1ft.
Habit and form: Perennial herb.
Pollinated: Insect.
Leaf shape: Long and narrow.

Growing upright from an onion-like bulb, this lily grows to about 38cm/15in tall and has several long, narrow basal leaves. The flower stalk is fleshy and topped by a single, upward-facing, lily-like flower, which is white at first, then ages to a pale pink. It grows mainly in the southeast, flowering quite early, in March and April, usually around Easter. Both the leaves and bulbs of this plant are poisonous. It grows mainly in wet ditches and damp woods. It is an attractive species for the garden, especially for partly shaded sites. It should be transplanted when beginning to go dormant, into humus-rich soil, and kept moist in the growing season.

Below: The smooth single-flowered stem springs from an onion-like bulb.

Identification: Each flower is about 9cm/3¼in wide, with six lobes that curve gracefully outwards. The long leaves are narrow and rather sharp-edged.

Left: The leaves are flat and grass-like, and just shorter than the stalk.

OTHER SPECIES OF NOTE

Spider Lily *Hymenocallis liriosme*
The lily has unusual flowers with spidery white narrow segments spreading out from a membranous centre. It flowers in March to May and grows in marshes and ditches from Alabama, west to Texas and Oklahoma.

Redmargin Zephyrlily *Zephyranthes simpsonii*
This relatively rare species is native to the southeastern states – mainly Florida. It flowers from February to April, producing white flowers, tinged red or purple outside. In the wild it is found in pinewoods, savannas and wet pastures.

Small Camas
Camassia quamash
The pale blue to deep blue flowers grow in a raceme at the end of the stem. Each star-shaped flower has six petals. The stems are between 30–90cm/1–3ft long. The leaves are basal and have a grass-like appearance. The bulbs were boiled by women of the Nez Perce, Cree, and Blackfoot tribes.

Pinebarren Deathcamas
Zigadenus leimanthoides
A poisonous plant that, like others in the deathcamas (or star lily) genus, grows from a bulb and has long, slender leaves. The attractive, star-shaped flowers are yellowish-white, with six petals, and form clusters at the top of the stem.

Yellow Star Grass

Common Goldstar *Hypoxis hirsuta*

Very grass-like in its foliage, and easily overlooked amongst grasses, until it flowers. The star-shaped yellow flowers are often in groups of three at the tip of a hairy stalk. They open from March to September. Yellow star grass grows mainly in dry meadows, glades and open woods. In the garden this species is a good choice for a sunny border. It is very hardy and will also set seed and reproduce, and once established requires very little attention.

Distribution: New England, south to Florida, west to New Mexico, north to North Dakota and Saskatchewan.
Height and spread:
7.5–15cm/3–6in.
Habit and form:
Perennial herb.
Pollinated: Insect.
Leaf shape: Long, narrow.

Identification: Flowers are about 2cm/⅜in wide, with six perianth segments and six stamens. The fruit is a pod containing several black seeds.

Left: The narrow leaves are covered in soft, straight hairs.

Right: The slender flowering stems are usually shorter than the leaves.

Large-flowered Bellwort

Fairy Bells, *Uvularia grandiflora*

This clump-forming, erect herbaceous plant likes moist woods in mountain regions, and is found throughout most of eastern North America except the extreme north. It is usually confined to calcareous or limestone soils, although it is relatively common where it does occur. The yellow, bell-shaped flowers, with six partially twisted sepals, are held singly at the end of branched stems that appear to pass through the somewhat twisted, bright green leaves. It has the peculiar habit of drooping limply while in flower, only to stand upright once fertilization has taken place.

Identification: The bright green leaves are alternate and perfoliate, up to 12.5cm/5in long, smooth above and hairy below. There are seldom more than two leaves below the first fork in the stem, often none. The flowers have six lance-shaped to oval petals up to 5cm/2in long, slightly twisted, free, pale yellow, sometimes yellow-green; the stamens are longer than the style. The flowers first appear in late spring, continuing into early summer, drooping limply until fertilized. The fruit is a bluntly three-lobed capsule.

Left: The drooping flowers are the most significant feature.

Distribution: Eastern North America (except extreme north).
Height and spread: 75cm/30in.
Habit and form: Herbaceous perennial.
Pollinated: Insect.
Leaf shape: Perfoliate.

Left: The drooping flower stems can form large clumps, or even drifts.

Yellow Adder's Tongue

Trout Lily, *Erythronium americanum*

This distinctive plant is one of the earliest spring wild flowers in the eastern USA, ranging from New Brunswick to Florida and westward to Ontario and Arkansas, where it sometimes forms large colonies in damp, open woodlands. The leaves are distinctively mottled, with flowering plants always having two basal leaves. The solitary yellow flowers are often marked purple or brown, with six reflexed, petal-like segments.

Below: Yellow adder's tongue forms dense eye-catching colonies in damp woodlands.

Identification: The membranous, yellow-white bulb is tooth-like in appearance. The shiny leaves are basal, up to 20cm/8in long, in pairs, mottled brown and white, minutely wrinkled, with parallel, longitudinal veins. Yellow, nodding, bell-shaped flowers, up to 2.5cm/1in across, are borne singly, terminally, on a naked stem, from mid- to late spring. The six perianth segments, consisting of three petals and three sepals, are strongly reflexed, often brushed with purple on the outside and finely dotted within at the base; they have six stamens, shorter than the petals, yellow to brown anthers and a short-lobed stigma. The fruit is capsular, with a rounded or flat tip.

Distribution: Eastern USA.
Height and spread: 25cm/10in.
Habit and form: Herbaceous perennial.
Pollinated: Insect.
Leaf shape: Lanceolate.

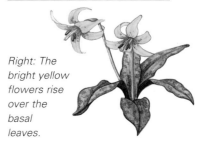

Right: The bright yellow flowers rise over the basal leaves.

Narrow-leaved Onion

Allium amplectens

Below: The bulb, with its papery skin.

Distribution: British Columbia to southern California.
Height and spread: 20–50cm/8–20in.
Habit and form: Herbaceous, bulbous perennial.
Pollinated: Insect
Leaf shape: Linear.

This perennial North American onion is found in yellow pine forest, foothill woodlands, grassy summits or slopes and more occasionally fields, streamsides or creek beds up to 1,850m/6,000ft, ranging from British Columbia to southern California. It thrives in clay soils and is common where it occurs. The four narrow leaves are grass-like and easily missed until the open umbels of peach, rose or white florets appear in late spring or early summer. These become papery once they have opened and persist in this state until the seedpod develops. It has a strong onion smell.

Identification: The bulbs, up to 2cm/¾in across, are solitary or on rhizomes, reforming each year, dividing at the base into daughter bulbs. Two to four narrow, flat, basal leaves, shorter than the stem, become twisted with age. The numerous flowers are borne in a spherical umbel on slender stalks up to 15mm/⅝in long; they have pointed, white to pink tepals, which become papery after opening, with shorter stamens, filaments broad at the base and yellow or purple anthers.

Above: The plant is attractive when in bloom.

Erythronium multiscapoideum
A native of shady wooded slopes in the foothills of the Sierra Nevada of California, this plant has become a popular garden plant and is one of the first western species to bloom, possessing white flowers with a yellow centre.

Beavertail Grass
Calochortus coeruleus
A common sight in gravelly openings in woodlands between 600–2,500m/ 2,000–8,200ft, from Oregon to north-western California, especially in the Cascade Range and High Sierra Nevada. It has one long, persistent basal leaf and white or cream, blue-tinged flowers, held on an unbranched stem.

Sego Lily *Calochortus nuttali*
The state flower of Utah has white bell-shaped flowers in umbels, and grows in dry country and across plains. The bulbs were once eaten in times of scarcity. The species name refers to Thomans Nuttal, the famous 19th century Harvard professor and naturalist.

Clubhair Mariposa Lily
Calochortus clavatus
Three large, butter–yellow petals form a cup-shaped bloom, which has an attractively marked centre characterized by the golden ring of 'hairs' around the dark brown stamen. The stalk is slender, smooth and branched. It is found in the foothills and chaparral of California.

Mount Diablo

Fairy Lantern *Calochortus pulchellus*

This plant from the western USA is found on wooded slopes and chaparral at altitudes of 200–800m/650–2,600ft, and is almost entirely restricted to the San Francisco Bay area. It grows in woodland and thicket vegetation, and the beautiful, nodding, conspicuously fringed, yellow flowers appear in late spring. The plant has one large basal leaf, longer than the stem, which withers around flowering time.

Identification: The erect stem is rather stout and usually branched. The basal leaf, 20–50cm/8–20in long, usually exceeds the stem. The two or three green leaves on the stem are up to 20cm/8in long, gradually smaller upwards, lance-shaped to narrow. The inflorescence is umbel-like, with one to many, nodding, globular to bell-shaped, deep yellow flowers. The sepals, not exceeding the petals, are oval to lance-shaped and pointed; the petals, up to 2cm/¾in long, are triangular, narrow at the base and sharply rounded at the tip, fringed, almost hairless outside, hairy within. The gland is deeply depressed, arched, bordered above by slender hairs; the filaments are flat, the anthers generally attached at the base. The fruit is an oblong, three-winged, nodding capsule.

Distribution: San Francisco Bay Area, California.
Height and spread: 10–30cm/4–12in.
Habit and form: Herbaceous perennial.
Pollinated: Insect.
Leaf shape: Lanceolate to linear.

Above: The showy yellow flowers are conspicuously fringed and are borne singly or in bunches.

Left: Restricted to woody thickets near San Francisco, the beautiful, globe-shaped, yellow flowers are very distinctive when they appear in the springtime.

ORCHID FAMILY

The Orchidaceae are terrestrial, epiphytic, or saprophytic herbs comprising one of the two largest families of flowering plants (second only to the Asteraceae) with about 1,000 genera and 15–20,000 species. The epiphytic types all depend upon the support of another plant and are generally forest-dwellers. They include some of the showiest of all flowers.

Pink Lady's Slipper

Cypripedium acaule

This beautiful, showy orchid is one of the largest-flowered of native orchid species. It sometimes grows in profusion, when the mass flowering is an impressive sight indeed. It is mainly a woodland species, especially in pinewoods, but also grows on rocky outcrops. Like others of this genus, it is much admired by gardeners and is threatened in the wild. However, it is difficult to grow so should be left in the wild. It flowers from April to July.

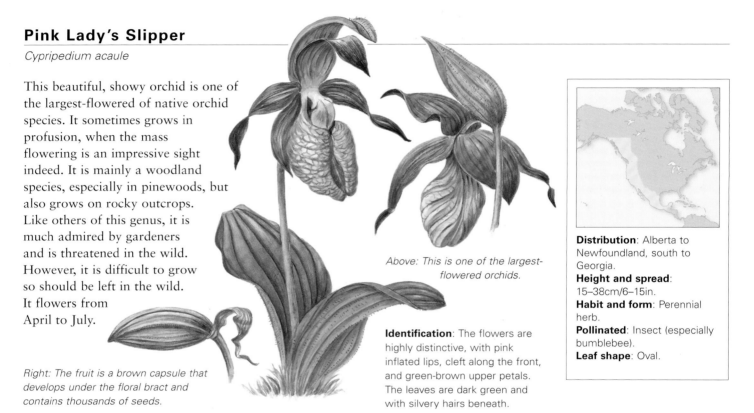

Above: This is one of the largest-flowered orchids.

Right: The fruit is a brown capsule that develops under the floral bract and contains thousands of seeds.

Identification: The flowers are highly distinctive, with pink inflated lips, cleft along the front, and green-brown upper petals. The leaves are dark green and with silvery hairs beneath.

Distribution: Alberta to Newfoundland, south to Georgia.
Height and spread: 15–38cm/6–15in.
Habit and form: Perennial herb.
Pollinated: Insect (especially bumblebee).
Leaf shape: Oval.

Large Yellow Lady's Slipper

Cypridium calceolus

This lady's slipper is also well known in Europe and also has a wide distribution in North America. It is mainly found inhabiting bogs, swamps and rich woods. Native Americans reportedly used the roots in a medicine to treat parasitic worms. The similar small yellow lady's slipper *(var. parviflorum)* has smaller, even more fragrant flowers, and is found mostly in wet limestone sites.

Identification: It has a leafy stalk with one or two fragrant flowers at the top. Each flower has an inflated yellow lip petal and two twisted greenish or brownish upper petals. The greenish-yellow sepals lie above (one) and below (two joined).

Right: A cross section of the yellow 'lip' petal, which is highly distinctive.

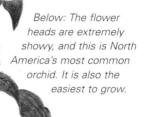

Below: The flower heads are extremely showy, and this is North America's most common orchid. It is also the easiest to grow.

Distribution: Alberta to Newfoundland, south to Georgia and in much of west.
Height and spread: 20–70cm/8–28in.
Habit and form: Perennial herb.
Pollinated: Insect (especially hawkmoth).
Leaf shape: Oval to elliptical.

California Lady's Slipper

Cypripedium californicum

This species is one of the most attractive of the lady's slippers, and unusual in often producing several flowers on each plant, all facing the same direction. The flowers open between May and July and the plant is typically found along streams and in moist soil, in cool sites, often among ferns. It is a native of the western United States, and only found in Oregon and California's mountainous regions.

Distribution: Northern California and southwest Oregon.
Height and spread: 30–120cm/1–4ft.
Habit and form: Perennial herb.
Pollinated: Insect (especially bumblebee).
Leaf shape: Lanceolate, broad.

Identification: The lip petal is about 2cm/¾in long, white with a pink flush or purple spots. The upper petals are like the sepals and yellow-green in colour. The flowers are produced in the upper leaf axils.

Left: The stem and alternate, plicate leaves.

Right: The plant may be found growing in large clumps. Often there are about 12 blooms per stem.

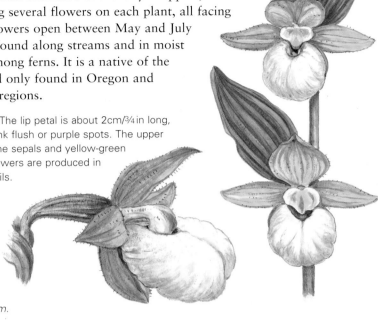

OTHER SPECIES OF NOTE

Clustered Lady's Slipper
Cypripedium fasciculatum
This lady's slipper is found in mountain forests from British Columbia south to California and Colorado. Each stem has up to four drooping brown or green flowers and two broad leaves. When the flower goes to seed a capsule forms and the stem becomes erect. The sepals are purple-green, while and the lip is yellow-green streaked with purple. The small flower is pollinated by a tiny wasp.

Rose Pogonia *Pogonia ophioglossoides*
This is an eastern species, of wet open woods, meadows and swamps. It has delicate rose-pink flowers that open between May and August and smell of raspberries. There is usually one flower per stem, although double flowers are known.

Dragon's Mouth
Arethusa bulbosa
The dragon's mouth or swamp pink is a terrestrial orchid found in peat bogs, swamps and wet meadows in the north-east of North America. There is one grass-like leaf, and the pink or white flowers, appearing in early summer, offer no nectar to pollinators, despite being attractively coloured and sweetly scented, apparently deceiving inexperienced queen bumblebees early in the season. The plant's beauty has led to over collection.

Showy Lady's Slipper

Cypripedium reginae

This, the tallest and one of the most impressive lady's slippers, has large flowers with a broad pink lip. The flowers seem to float above the hairy foliage. It is threatened by collection and picking, but is still fairly common in certain places, notably around the Great Lakes. The glandular hairs that produce a skin rash give it some protection. It grows in damp woods and in swamps, especially on limestone. It is available from nurseries and will grow well in gardens, in cool, shady sites.

Distribution: Saskatchewan east to Newfoundland south to North Carolina; Missouri; mainly eastern.
Height and spread: 30–90cm/1–3ft.
Habit and form: Perennial herb.
Pollinated: Insect (especially bumblebee).
Leaf shape: Elliptical.

Identification: The lip of each flower is up to 5cm/2in long and rather broad, contrasting with the waxy white upper petals and sepals.

Below: The orchids are found growing in clumps.

Below: The Showy Lady's Slipper became Missouri's state flower in the early 1900s.

Elegant Rein Orchid
Piperia elegans

This mainly western orchid has many fragrant white flowers clustered in a raceme along a sturdy stem, and opening from July to September. The flowers are quite closely packed and the spurs are almost interlocking, giving the plant an unusual appearance. It grows mostly in shrub and coniferous forests. There are several closely related species, and inland plants are more slender, with flowers less densely clustered.

Identification: The plant grows from a tuber-like root. It has a single flower spike up to 50cm/20in high, covered in flowers. The sepals and upper petals are white with a central green stripe. The lip petal has a long, slender, almost straight spur that extends horizontally out from the back of the flower. The leaves are up to 25cm/10in long and about 5cm/2in wide. There are two–five leaves per plant. The slender stalk is leafless.

Left: The flowers are densely packed together.

Right: The plant has two to five fleshy leaves around 25cm/10in long and up to 5cm/2in wide.

Distribution: British Columbia south to central California and east to Montana.
Height and spread: 20–40cm/8–16in.
Habit and form: Perennial herb.
Pollinated: Insect.
Leaf shape: Oblong.

Above: The flowers are rather hyacinth-like, creamy white and sweetly fragrant.

White Fringed Orchid
Platanthera blephariglottis

The White Fringed Orchid grows in damp and wet meadows, bogs and marshes, mainly in the east of the region. The classic habitat is on sphagnum-covered, sedge-rich sites with few or no shrubs. The name refers to the deeply cut fringe to the lip petal which gives the flowers a delicate appearance. It flowers from June to September, and the flowers have a faintly spicy fragrance. This attractive orchid is endangered over much of its range.

Identification: Flowers are about 4cm/1½in long, the upper sepal and two petals forming a hood arching over the lip. A long narrow spur projects behind each flower. The lower leaves are up to 35cm/14in long; the upper leaves are reduced bracts.

Right: Lower leaves are long and slender, while the higher leaves are bracts.

Distribution: Ontario east to Newfoundland, south to Florida and west to Texas.
Height and spread: 30–60cm/1–2ft.
Habit and form: Perennial herb.
Pollinated: Insect (moth).
Leaf shape: Ovate-lanceolate.

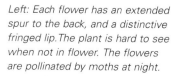

Left: Each flower has an extended spur to the back, and a distinctive fringed lip. The plant is hard to see when not in flower. The flowers are pollinated by moths at night.

Yellow Fringed Orchid

Platanthera ciliaris

Distribution: Rhode Island and New York south to Florida and west to Texas.
Height and spread: 30–75cm/1–2½ft.
Habit and form: Perennial herb.
Pollinated: Insect (especially butterfly).
Leaf shape: Lanceolate.

The flowers of this showy species are a deep orange or yellow, borne in clusters and opening from July to September. Each flower has a fringed lip that droops downwards. It grows in peaty and sandy wet woods, but also in meadows and on slopes. It often forms hybrids with white fringed orchids and others of the genus, making identification confusing where the species occur at the same sites.

Identification: The lip is 2cm/¾in long, and has a 4cm/1¼in long slender spur that projects backwards. There are two broad side sepals. The lower leaves sheath the stem and are up to 25cm/10in long.

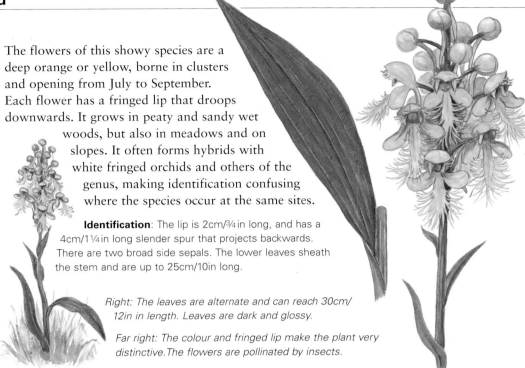

Right: The leaves are alternate and can reach 30cm/ 12in in length. Leaves are dark and glossy.

Far right: The colour and fringed lip make the plant very distinctive. The flowers are pollinated by insects.

OTHER SPECIES OF NOTE
Bog Rein Orchid Bog Candles
Platanthera leucostachys
This fragrant orchid of bogs and wetlands is a western species found from British Columbia southwards. It a pale green stem with many small white that seem to twine around it. The blooming period is June to September.

Round-leaved Rein Orchid
Platanthera orbiculata
This large-flowered species is also from the north west. Each tall, erect flowering stalk carries up to 25 white or greenish-white flowers, between June and August. The large (up to 15cm/6in diameter), round leaves tend to lie rather flat on the ground.

Ragged Fringed Orchid *Platanthera lacera*
This is one of the more common fringed orchids. It is found from Manitoba to Newfoundland, south to Georgia, and west to Texas. Its whitish-green or cream flowers are arrayed in narrow spikes, from June to September.

Alaska Rein Orchid *Piperia unalascensis*
Found scattered south from Alaska, in dry woods and streamsides, this plant has pale green rather unobtrusive flowers in open slender racemes. The stalks are up to 70cm/1½ft in height. Each plant has two to four narrow leaves, which fade as the flowers open. The blooming period is April to August.

Large Purple Fringed Orchid

Platanthera grandiflora

A beautiful specimen, the large purple fringed orchid has many-flowered clusters of fragrant, deep lavender flowers, opening from June to August. It grows at the edges of swamps, on wet meadows and in cool, moist woods. Fringed orchids are pollinated by insects, especially (as in this species) by moths. As the moth feeds on the nectar in the spur it brushes against the anthers which release sticky masses of pollen that adhere to the moth's body. Some of this pollen may then be transferred to another flower.

Identification: Flowers are 2.5cm/1in long, and the lip has three fringed lobes and a spur. The sepals and petals are all coloured a similar deep lavender. The lower leaves are long and sheath the stem; the upper leaves are small.

Right: The large purple fringed orchid depends upon fungi in forest soil to help it absorb nutrients.

Distribution: Ontario east to Newfoundland and south to Georgia.
Height and spread: 60–120cm/2–4ft.
Habit and form: Perennial herb.
Pollinated: Insect (especially moth).
Leaf shape: Ovate-lanceolate.

Left: The leaves partly sheathe the stem.

Stream Orchid

Chatterbox, Giant Helleborine, Epipactis gigantea

This orchid takes one of its names from the fact that the 'lip' and 'tongue' of the flower move when disturbed. Because each flower looks a little like an open mouth this adds to the effect! The green-brown and pink flowers appear from March to August. The favoured habitats are in damp ground, such as wet flushes, near ponds and alongside streams. Once it has found a habitat it likes, it can be abundant there, although in many areas it is rare. The orchid normally grows in dense patches. It can be grown in the garden, where it needs regular watering, and can be propagated by division. The plant lies dormant in the winter.

Distribution: British Columbia south to Mexico.
Height and spread: 30–90cm/1–3ft.
Habit and form: Perennial herb.
Pollinated: Insect (especially bee and wasp).
Leaf shape: Lanceolate.

Left: The leaves are alternate and clasp the stem.

Far left: The stream orchid will form dense patches, usually near water.

Identification: Flowers are 2.5–4cm/1–1½in wide with greenish sepals, two pink or purple upper petals and a two-lobed lip, the latter to 2cm/¾in long.

Showy Orchis

Galearis spectabilis

Identification: Each flower is 2.5cm/1in long and has three sepals fused with two upper petals to form a pink or purple hood over the white, spurred lip. The leaves are up to 20cm/8in long and sheath the stem at their bases.

Below: The plant favours the woodland floor.

Showy orchis is well-named as it has up to 15 beautiful pink and white (and, rarely, all white or all pink) flowers, borne from April to June on a short stalk from between two large, glossy leaves. Flowers appear before the leaves have fully developed. The flowers are also fragrant and contain rich supplies of nectar in their spurs. It grows around swamps and in rich moist woodland, especially beech and maple, usually in thick humus, and often with trilliums. It is one of the earliest of orchids to flower in the spring, and colonies have been known to persist for decades at one site.

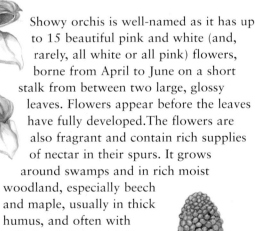

Distribution: Ontario to New Brunswick and south to Georgia.
Height and spread: 12.5–30cm/5–12in.
Habit and form: Perennial herb.
Pollinated: Insect.
Leaf shape: Ovate or elliptical.

Left: The seed head is also distinctive.

Left: The name Galearis is derived from the Greek 'galea' which means 'helmet' and refers to the shape of the sepals and petals.

Downy Rattlesnake Plantain

Rattlesnake Orchid *Goodyera pubescens*

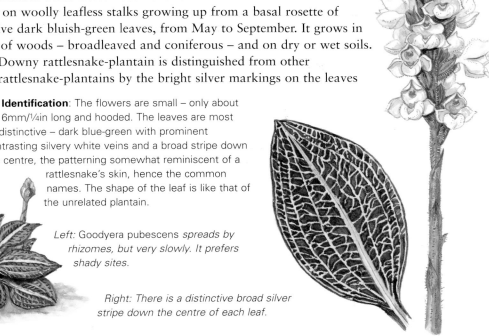

The cylindrical white flowerheads of this eastern woodland orchid develop on woolly leafless stalks growing up from a basal rosette of decorative dark bluish-green leaves, from May to September. It grows in a range of woods – broadleaved and coniferous – and on dry or wet soils. Downy rattlesnake-plantain is distinguished from other rattlesnake-plantains by the bright silver markings on the leaves

Identification: The flowers are small – only about 6mm/¼in long and hooded. The leaves are most distinctive – dark blue-green with prominent contrasting silvery white veins and a broad stripe down the centre, the patterning somewhat reminiscent of a rattlesnake's skin, hence the common names. The shape of the leaf is like that of the unrelated plantain.

Left: Goodyera pubescens *spreads by rhizomes, but very slowly. It prefers shady sites.*

Right: There is a distinctive broad silver stripe down the centre of each leaf.

Distribution: Ontario to New Brunswick and south to Florida.
Height and spread: To 45cm/18in.
Habit and form: Perennial herb.
Pollinated: Insect.
Leaf shape: Ovate.

OTHER SPECIES OF NOTE
Nodding Ladies' Tresses *Spiranthes cernua*
This is one of several species found in the east, this one from Ontario to Nova Scotia, south to Georgia and west to Texas. It has creamy white fragrant flowers and grows in damp meadows.

Hooded Ladies' Tresses
Spiranthes romanzoffiana
With its flowers arranged in spiral rows and the individual flowers hooded, this attractive plant grows scattered over most of northern North America, in damp, open habitats.

Small Whorled Pogonia
Isotria medeoloides
This rare orchid has the unusual habit of becoming dormant for ten years or more between flowering. An eastern species of dry woodland, it has one or two yellow-green flowers on a greenish stem. The whorled leaves can reach 8cm/3in in length, and 4cm/1⅜in wide. There are usually five leaves.

Broad-leaved Twayblade *Listera convallarioides*
With a range from Alaska south to southern California and east to Newfoundland, and scattered further south, this is a rather unobtrusive, woodland orchid with small green flowers, open from June to August.

Greenfly Orchid

Epidendrum conopseum

This is an epiphytic orchid, one that lives rooted onto other plants rather than in the soil (although epiphytes may root in pockets of soil on trees). It has grey-green flowers that are sometimes tinged purple, borne in a terminal cluster. It flowers throughout the year, but mainly January to August. The usual host trees are magnolias, live oaks and cypresses. This orchid is often found together with the epiphytic, resurrection fern (*Polypodium polypodioides*).

Identification: The flowers are only about 8mm/⅓in wide with a three-lobed spreading lip and the leaves are smooth and sometimes purplish.

Distribution: Louisiana and Florida north to North Carolina.
Height and spread: To 40cm/16in.
Habit and form: Perennial herb.
Pollinated: Insect.
Leaf shape: Long, elliptical.

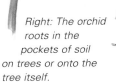

Left: The leaves are generaly green, but sometimes a purplish colour. They are elegant and elliptical.

Right: The orchid roots in the pockets of soil on trees or onto the tree itself.

WILD FLOWERS OF SOUTH AND CENTRAL AMERICA

Unlike North America, which separated from Asia relatively recently in geological terms, South America was an isolated continent for millions of years, having originally been part of the ancient super-continent Gondwanaland. South America's plants are closely allied to those of Africa and Australasia. When North and South America became linked, their combined flora formed some of the most diverse and spectacular plant communities on the planet, and it is, botanically, the world's richest continent. The tropical and subtropical region covered in this chapter has an extraordinary range of habitats, including chapparal, rain and evergreen forests, arid deserts and grassy savannas. Of course, the flora of the region is particularly affected by the temperatures throughout the seasons, the intensity of sunlight, and day length, all of which differ markedly over the wide range of latitudes.

Above from left: Passion Flower (Passiflora quadrangularis), *Royal Water Lily* (Victoria amazonica) *and White Frangipani* (Plumeria alba).

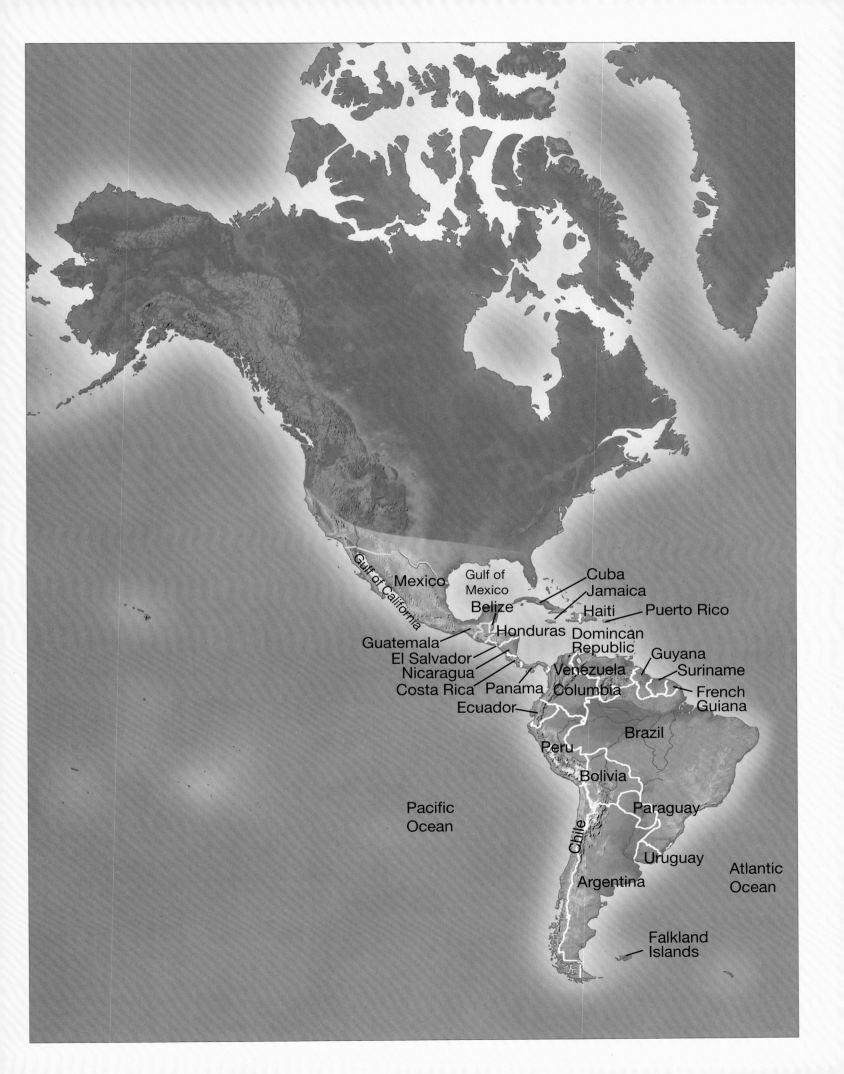

Gulf of California

Mexico

Gulf of Mexico

Cuba

Jamaica

Belize

Haiti

Puerto Rico

Honduras

Domincan Republic

Guatemala

Guyana

El Salvador

Suriname

Nicaragua

Venezuela

Costa Rica

Panama

Columbia

French Guiana

Ecuador

Brazil

Peru

Bolivia

Pacific Ocean

Paraguay

Chile

Uruguay

Atlantic Ocean

Argentina

Falkland Islands

BIRTHWORT, POPPY AND BOUGAINVILLEA FAMILIES

The birthwort family (Aristolochiaceae) contains about 500 species of woody vines or herbs. The poppy family (Papaveraceae) comprises of 25 genera and 200 species that usually have milky or coloured sap. The Bougainvillea family (Nyctaginaceae) has about 390 species, mainly in the tropics and subtropics.

Giant Dutchman's Pipe

Giant Pelican Flower, *Aristolochia gigantea*

This impressive vine was discovered by the explorer Carl Friedrich Philipp von Martius around 1820. It is a vigorous climber, grows tall and produces huge, fragrant, fleshy and rather lemon-scented flowers. It is easy to grow in cultivation, and can even stand the occasional frost, though it does best under glass. It can be grown in a large pot and moved to shelter in cold weather. In subtropical or tropical regions it thrives outdoors and flowers from spring to autumn, attracting many insects, including butterflies.

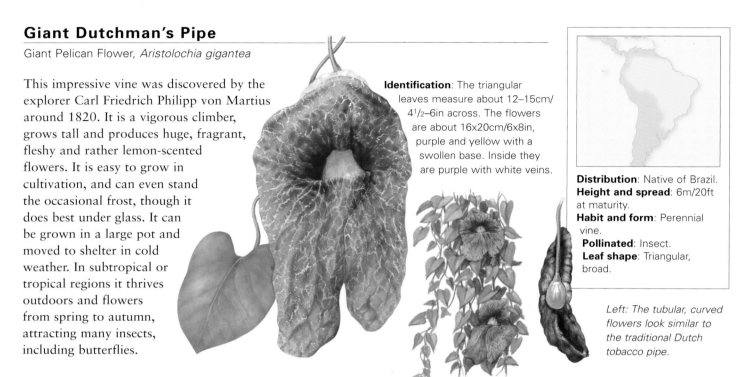

Identification: The triangular leaves measure about 12–15cm/4¹/₂–6in across. The flowers are about 16x20cm/6x8in, purple and yellow with a swollen base. Inside they are purple with white veins.

Distribution: Native of Brazil.
Height and spread: 6m/20ft at maturity.
Habit and form: Perennial vine.
Pollinated: Insect.
Leaf shape: Triangular, broad.

Left: The tubular, curved flowers look similar to the traditional Dutch tobacco pipe.

Mexican Prickly Poppy

Goatweed, *Argemone mexicana*

This showy annual relative of the poppies can commonly be found in its native West Indies and Central America, and flowers throughout the summer. It has been introduced into many countries and is now a common weed in many tropical areas worldwide. It is usually found on rocky open ground, waste ground, and more occasionally on roadsides and by railways. Although it originates in a semi-tropical climate, it is remarkably well adapted to colder and drier conditions. All parts of the plant are poisonous but it is widely used as a medicinal herb.

Distribution: West Indies and Central America.
Height and spread: 25–100cm/10–40in.
Habit and form: Annual.
Leaf shape: Oblong.
Pollinated: Insect.

Identification: A coarse, erect annual herb, sparsely to moderately branched and covered with prickles. The stems, 25–100cm/10–39in tall, exude a milky sap that turns yellow on exposure. The blue-green leaves are oblong to lance-shaped, irregularly pinnately lobed and serrated, the edges crisply wavy and spiny. The upper leaves are alternate, stalkless, usually clasping the stem, with thorns along the major veins, which are white and prominent. The flower buds open to solitary, bright yellow or white, showy flowers up to 6cm/2¼in across, with numerous yellow stamens.

Above: The buds are rounded and sparsely prickly.

Right: Yellow flowers appear at the stem tips.

Pelican Flower

Aristolochia grandiflora

Distribution: Mexico, Central America and Caribbean, including Jamaica and Trinidad.
Height and spread: To 4.5–5m/10–15ft.
Habit and form: Perennial vine.
Pollinated: Insect.
Leaf shape: Triangular, cordate.

Pelican flower is not hard to grow, requiring only partial sun, and it flowers from spring right through to autumn. It can even be grown in a hanging basket, when it looks most impressive. In the wild it often grows alongside rivers and streams. The structure of this imposing flower is complex, with a fleshy lobe leading to a bent tube and finally into an inflated chamber at the base.

Identification: The solitary, fleshy flower is 20cm/8in across, as large as that of *A. gigantea*, and has a long thin, dangling appendage on the lower lobe. It is blotched purple, white, yellow, green and red, with an inflated pouch. It emits a rather unpleasant odour that attracts insects including butterflies. The leaves are large – about 20x15cm/ 8x6in and deep green in colour.

Above and left: The 30cm/1ft-long, heart-shaped flower is adorned with an elegant, tapering tail. At the centre of the flower is a deep purple bull's-eye .

OTHER SPECIES OF NOTE

Bougainvillea peruviana
A native of Peru, Colombia and Ecuador. This plant has smallish flowers, usually pale magenta and wrinkled, and several varieties are available. It is unusual in having green-coloured bark.

Jarrinha
Aristolochia cymbifera
This native of Brazil is a climber that can reach up to 7m/23ft. It has grey-green leaves and rather unusual ivory white flowers that are mottled and veined maroon, with a beak-like lower lip. The plant's root is sometimes used in traditional medicine to treat digestive complaints and as a sedative, as well as for common skin problems such as eczema.

Rooster Flower *Aristolochia labiata*
This South American climber is also a native of Brazil. It has broad heart-shaped leaves and huge 2.5cm/1in wide flowers which are mottled red, green, yellow and purple. This species is also commonly cultivated and can reach 6m/20ft. The flowers bloom from midsummer to autumn.

Calico Flower *Aristolochia littoralis*
The calico flower of South and Central America has greenish-yellow to white flowers, with maroon veins and marbling and a darker throat. It is a vigorous climber, up to 3m/10ft and is ideal for greenhouse cultivation, flowering from June to August and doing best in partial shade.

Paper Flower

Bougainvillea glabra

This native of Brazil is widely naturalised in tropical and subtropical regions, and is also commonly grown in conservatories. The common name refers to the papery flowers (actually thin bracts associated with the small flowers). The genus name celebrates the French sailor Louis Antoine de Bougainville (1729–1811). Each apparent flower has purple bracts with three small yellow true flowers in the centre. Several cultivated varieties exist, such as those with bracts of deep pink, purple, bright red, dark violet, coral, or pure white.

Distribution: Native of Brazil.
Height and spread: To 7m/22ft.
Habit and form: Perennial climber.
Pollinated: Insect.
Leaf shape: Elliptic.

Identification: The elliptic leaves are a paler green beneath, and pointed. The purple or magenta bracts (sometimes white) fade with age and sometimes persist after flowering.

Right: The richly hued bracts make a vivid splash of colour.

Far right: The small true flowers are found among the coloured bracts.

WATER LILY AND PICKEREL WEED FAMILIES

The water lilies (Nymphaeaceae) are aquatic plants of six genera and some 60 species. They have showy flowers on long stalks, and are often considered the most primitive of flowering plants. In the New World there are some truly remarkable examples. The pickerel weeds and relatives (Pontederiaceae) are erect or floating aquatics. There are about 30 species, in nine genera, in the warmer parts of the world.

Pickerel Weed

Wampee, *Pontederia cordata*

Pickerel weed typically grows in shallow fresh water, rooted in the mud, but with its tapering, heart-shaped leaves and flowers opening above the surface. It spreads by means of a creeping rhizome and has long flower stalks with 15–20cm/6–8in spikes of violet-blue flowers opening from June to November. It is usually found at the margins of ponds, streams and in marshes. The seeds and young leaves are edible.

Right: The individual flowers resemble tiny orchids.

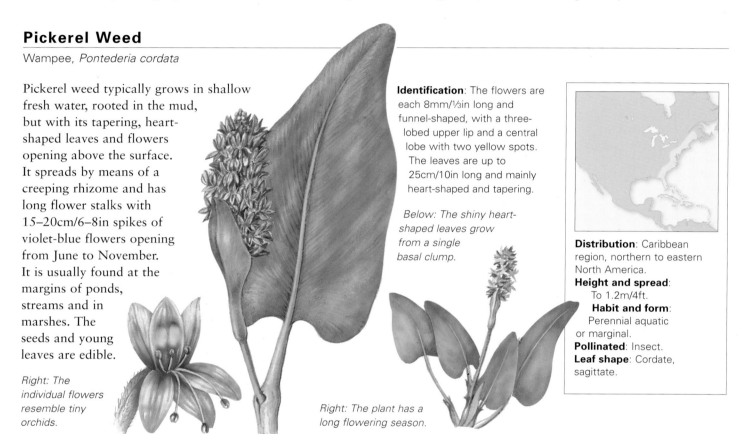

Identification: The flowers are each 8mm/⅓in long and funnel-shaped, with a three-lobed upper lip and a central lobe with two yellow spots. The leaves are up to 25cm/10in long and mainly heart-shaped and tapering.

Below: The shiny heart-shaped leaves grow from a single basal clump.

Right: The plant has a long flowering season.

Distribution: Caribbean region, northern to eastern North America.
Height and spread: To 1.2m/4ft.
Habit and form: Perennial aquatic or marginal.
Pollinated: Insect.
Leaf shape: Cordate, sagittate.

Water Hyacinth

Eichhornia crassipes

This notorious aquatic plant has a bad reputation because it is responsible for clogging waterways in many tropical regions, notably in areas to which it has been introduced, such as Africa and in the southern United States. However, it is also useful for removing pollutants from the water, such as excess nitrates and heavy metals, and with regular harvesting, the water quality will gradually improve. In its native South America it is generally less of a problem. It is a fascinating floating plant with beautiful spikes of lavender, funnel-shaped flowers and inflated leaf stalks to aid buoyancy. It grows in lakes, slow rivers, ditches and marshes and flowers from June to September.

Identification: Each flower is 5cm/2in across and has six lobes, the upper lobe with an obvious yellow spot. The leaves are bright shiny green to 12.5cm/5in wide, with spongy bulbs at the base.

Distribution: South America.
Height and spread: Stalks to 40cm/16in above the water.
Habit and form: Floating aquatic.
Pollinated: Insect.
Leaf shape: Round or kidney-shaped.

Left: The showy lavender-coloured flowers form beautiful rafts of colour on lakes and waterways.

Royal Water Lily

Amazonian giant water lily, *Victoria amazonica*

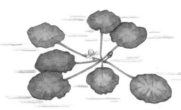

Distribution: Equatorial Brazil.
Height and spread: Stalks are 7–8m/22–26ft tall.
Habit and form: Aquatic perennial.
Pollinated: Beetle.
Leaf shape: Orbicular, extremely large.

This giant water lily was "discovered" in 1801 and caused a stir when it was introduced to Europe in the mid-1800s. It is native to equatorial Brazil, where it grows from large, tuberous rhizomes in the calm waters of oxbow lakes and flooded grasslands along the Amazon River. Its gargantuan, glossy green leaves grow to 2.1m/7ft in diameter, with a pronounced maroon lip around the circumference. The lush, 30cm/12in flowers are variously white or pink on the same plant. They open at night, and have a pineapple fragrance.

Identification: The floating leaves, on long stalks, are 1.2–1.8m/4–6ft across, oval with a deep narrow cleft at one end, becoming almost circular when full grown, with the margin turned up all round, green above, deep purple below, with prominent flattened, spiny ribs, united by cross ribs. Round, prickly stalks bear solitary flowers 25–38cm/10–15in across, pear-shaped in bud, fragrant, with numerous petals; they open white on the first night, becoming pink later.

Left: The night blooming flowers are spectacular.

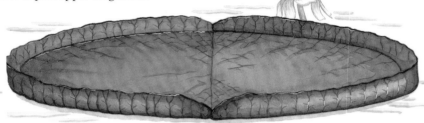

Santa Cruz Water Lily

Victoria cruziana

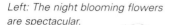

This giant water lily, only slightly smaller than *V. amazonica*, is found in the cooler waterways of Argentina and Paraguay, as it is more cold-tolerant. It has smaller leaves with a higher lip, which are generally green. The buds lack thorns on the sepals and the flowers are creamy white the first night, becoming light pink the second night. In the autumn in cooler regions the leaves slowly disintegrate as the water cools down. Outside the tropics this species is best grown each season from seed.

Identification: The leaves are densely, softly hairy beneath. The rim measures up to 20cm/8in and is the tallest rim of all floating aquatics.

Distribution: Northern Argentina, Paraguay, Bolivia and Brazil.
Height and spread: Stalks are 1.8m/6ft long.
Habit and form: Aquatic perennial.
Pollinated: Insect.
Leaf shape: Round.

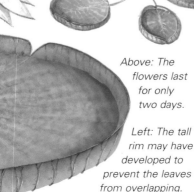

Above: The flowers last for only two days.

Left: The tall rim may have developed to prevent the leaves from overlapping.

OTHER SPECIES OF NOTE

Amazon Water Lily
Nymphaea amazonum
Widely distributed throughout South and Central America, this water lily has creamy lemon-white, night-blooming flowers. The sepals are an attractive purplish-black, mottled with green-and-white stripes. The leaves are green, spotted purple-brown above, with purple-brown below.

Tropical Blue Water Lily *Nymphaea elegans*
Found in ponds, ditches and cypress swamps in Florida, the West Indies and Central America, this water lily is a day-blooming aquatic perennial with immensely showy, fragrant flowers in hues of blue or violet, with intense yellow centres.

Nymphaea flavovirens
This is a vigorous water lily with ovate leaves that measure up to 45cm/18in across. Native to Mexico and South America it has white, strongly fragrant flowers. There are more than 20 cultivars and hybrids of this species, with blue, yellow, pink and red flowers.

Night Lily *Nymphaea gardneriana*
Another South American water lily, this species has rusty brown leaves that are mottled underneath. The flowers, measuring up to 15cm/6in across, are creamy white with whorled petals. This is one of a number of species that flower mainly at night, and uses odour, rather than colour, to attract pollinators.

CACTUS FAMILY

The members of the cactus family (Cactaceae) are mostly spiny succulents with photosynthetic stems, comprising about 130 genera and 1,650 species. Their leaves are generally extremely reduced and ephemeral or absent altogether. Most members of the family are native to the Americas, being found as far north as Canada and as far south as Patagonia.

Golden Stars

Lady fingers, lace cactus, *Mammillaria elongata*

The name *Mammillaria* is derived from the Latin word *mamilla*, which means "nipple", and refers to the small tubercles (fleshy lumps or "warts") on each cactus. This cactus from Mexico, where it generally occurs at altitudes of 1,350–2,400m/4,400–8,000ft, forms long finger-like branches that grow both erect and prostrate, creating club-like clusters. The many tiny, recurved spines are gold, and the small white to pale yellow 12mm/½in flowers are produced in spring.

Identification: A succulent plant forming many stemmed clusters. The stems are elongated, cylindrical and finger-like, 12–30mm/½–1¼in in diameter. The tubercles are slender and conical and the axils naked, or nearly so. The slender, needle-like radial spines are variable in number from 14–25, and are white to golden-yellow to brown, the degree of colouring varying from plant to plant. Pale yellow to pinkish 12mm/½in flowers, sometimes flushed pink or with pink midstripes, are borne in spring, followed by pink fruits, becoming red.

Right: The long finger-like stems are studded with white flowers in the early spring.

Distribution: Central Mexico.
Height and spread: 15cm/6in.
Habit and form: Spiny succulent.
Leaf shape: Absent.
Pollinated: Insect.

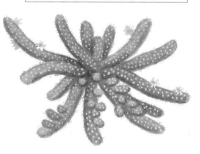

Texas Prickly Pear

Nopal, *Opuntia lindheimeri*

This North American cactus is a succulent shrub or subshrub that usually grows up to 1m/3ft high, although it can sometimes reach higher than this, with a spread of up to 3m/10ft. In the wild it is found on rocky hills and mountain slopes in Texas, New Mexico and Mexico, up to 1,400m/4,600ft. It grows only two or three "pads" high, with the pads covered with cushions of golden-brown barbed spines. In the summer, bright yellow, orange or dark red flowers are produced at the edges of the pads, and these are later followed by edible, purple fruits.

Identification: The jointed stems are flattened into green or blue-green, oval to rounded or (rarely) elongated pads, 15–25cm/6–10in long; the leaves are reduced to translucent yellow spines in all but the lower areoles, one to six per areole. The flowers are yellow, orange or red and showy, 5–7.5cm/2–3in across, and the fruit is purple with a white top, fleshy, egg-shaped or elongated, 2.5–7.5cm/1–3in long.

Distribution: Texas, New Mexico and Mexico.
Height and spread: 1x3m/3x10ft.
Habit and form: Spiny succulent.
Leaf shape: Absent.
Pollinated: Insect.

Left: The strange jointed stems form a low spreading shrub.

Far left: The showy flowers appear in summer and are followed by purple, edible fruit.

Crab Cactus

Thanksgiving cactus, *Schlumbergera truncata*

This epiphytic cactus is native to a small region north of Rio de Janeiro in South America, confined to dense virgin forest between 1,000–1,500m/3,300–4,900ft. It usually grows on forest trees, by rooting into plant debris trapped among branches, or more occasionally on decaying humus in stony, shady places. The forests where it grows have distinct wet and dry seasons, although temperatures are fairly constant all year round.

Distribution: North of Rio de Janeiro, Brazil.
Height and spread: Up to 30cm/12in.
Habit and form: Epiphytic, occasionally lithophytic, succulent subshrub.
Pollinated: Insect.
Leaf shape: Absent.

Far right: The fleshy stems form a dense mass with flowers appearing at the tips.

Identification: Erect, then pendent, flattened, jointed stems have oblong, bright green segments, 4–6cm/1½–2¼in long, with four to eight prominent, forward-projecting, tooth-like marginal notches and small areoles with a few very fine bristles. Deep pink, red or white, two-tiered, short-tubed flowers with yellowish anthers, up to 7.5cm/3in long, are borne on terminal segments, appearing at the start of the wetter season.

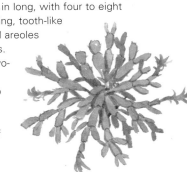

Leaf Cactus

Barbados gooseberry, gooseberry shrub, *Pereskia aculeata*

This climbing, leafy cactus is now seldom found truly wild. It is frequently grown as an ornamental or occasionally for its fruit in some tropical countries. In many areas it has escaped from cultivation and become thoroughly naturalized. In 1979, its cultivation was banned in South Africa because it was invading and overwhelming natural vegetation.

Identification: An erect woody shrub when young, it becomes scrambling, climbing or vine-like with age, with branches up to 10m/33ft long. The spines on the trunk are long and slender, in groups; those on the branches are short, recurved, usually in pairs, borne in the leaf axils. The deciduous, alternate, short-stemmed, waxy leaves are elliptic, oblong or oval, with a short point at the tip, 3.5–10cm/1¼–4in long, sometimes fleshy. White, yellowish or pink-tinted flowers, 2.5–4.5cm/1–1¾in long, lemon-scented, with a prickly calyx, are borne profusely in panicles or corymbs. The fruit is round, oval or pear-shaped, 12–20mm/½–¾in across, lemon- or orange-yellow or reddish, with thin, smooth, rather leathery skin. It retains the sepals and a few spines until it is fully ripe.

Distribution: West Indies, coastal northern South America and Panama.
Height and spread: 10m/33ft.
Habit and form: Woody shrub.
Pollinated: Insect.
Leaf shape: Elliptic.

Above: The curious fruits are initially leafy as they develop.

Glaziou's Arthrocereus

Arthrocereus glaziovii

Identification: The stems are short, cylindrical and ribbed, and densely covered in fine spines. The spreading white, scented flowers open at night. Each flower measures up to 6cm/2in long.

Right: The beautiful flowers perch on short, thick stems. They are very fragrant, and open at night to attract pollinating moths.

This genus has only four species, all endemic to Brazil. This species is only found in the wild in certain southern mountains of Brazil, although it is grown in cultivation and is sometimes available through specialist outlets. It is named for Auguste François Marie Glaziou, a 20th century French plant collector in Brazil. Its habitat is on thin iron-rich soils and it is threatened by mining activities, although a few sites seem safe. It began to be grown soon after it was discovered in the 1880s and is not hard to cultivate, being propagated by cuttings. Like most cacti it needs to be kept out of frosts and watered only sparingly, in this case using only soft rainwater.

Right: The short finger-like stems grow in spreading clumps. They are extremely spiny.

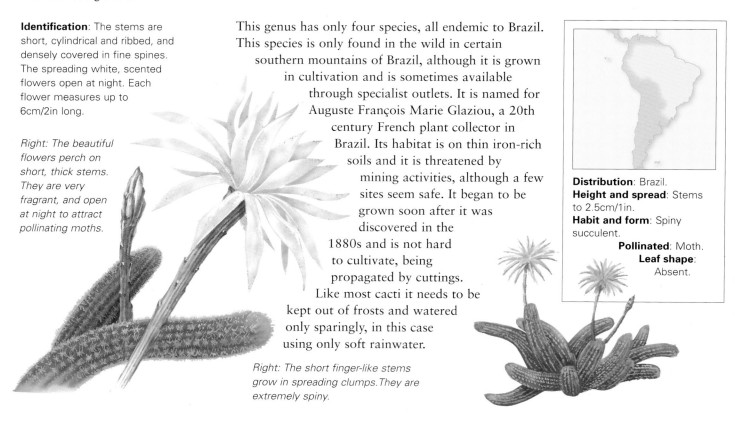

Distribution: Brazil.
Height and spread: Stems to 2.5cm/1in.
Habit and form: Spiny succulent.
Pollinated: Moth.
Leaf shape: Absent.

Roseta do diabo

Discocactus horstii

Roseta do diabo grows wild in rocky savanna and thorny scrub. It is one of Brazil's most remarkable cacti with a squat habit, growing as if pressed into the ground. The ridged surface is covered in curved spines that act as wicks channelling dew towards the plant's tissues. The low growing habit may have evolved as an adaptation to fire, which often occurs in the dry habitats. Over collection of this pretty cactus has caused it to be rare in the wild, but it is now partly protected in reserves.

Identification: This dwarf genus has a characteristic rounded, broad, flat stem with up to 20 prominent ridges. It grows close to the soil. The white flowers form at the woolly centre of the plant and are fragrant.

Distribution: Brazil, north-east Paraguay and east Bolivia.
Height and spread: 8cm/3in.
Habit and form: Spiny succulent.
Pollinated: Moth.
Leaf shape: Absent.

Far left: The flower is spectacular, and grows atop a rounded, ridged stem. Flowers may develop fully in just one day.

Left: The sweet-smelling white flowers bloom only at night. Their scent attracts moths which pollinate the cacti.

Golden Ball Cactus

Golden Barrel Cactus, *Echinocactus grusonii*

Distribution: Mexico.
Height and spread:
To 1.5m/5ft.
Habit and form: Spiny
succulent.
Pollinated: Insect.
Leaf shape: Absent.

This must be one of the most impressive of all cacti with its rotund, almost cushion-like growth. Well-grown specimens look like stools but on close inspection are not to be sat upon, protected as they are by rows of sharply-pointed golden spines, in clusters of up to fifteen. In the wild it grows only in a river canyon in Mexico, where it is critically endangered, partly by construction of a dam. But it is widely cultivated and therefore familiar to lovers of cacti the world over. It requires warm sunny conditions on well-drained soil.

Identification: Young plants are almost spherical, but gradually become barrel-shaped as they age. The flowers are rather modest – yellowish, toothed cups, produced only when the cactus has grown quite large.

Right: The ball-like cacti grow in tight clusters.

Left: The small yellow flowers are hidden in the wool at the top of the cactus.

Espostoopsis dybowskii
This plant is remarkable in being the only member of its genus, and is also unique in its shape – tall and tree-like with woolly cylindrical stems. It grows in north-east Brazil on hills and thorny outcrops. The flowers, which may be pollinated by bats, form among woolly outgrowths.

Melocactus pachyacanthus
This native of eastern Brazil grows happily on limestone outcrops. The small, white or magenta tubular flowers develop at the top of the stems on a raised cushion-like base. The plant grows to about 30cm/1ft tall and may be 20cm/8in across.

Arthrocereus melanurus
This shrubby cactus from eastern Brazil grows to 1m/3ft or more tall, branching at the base. Its stems are about 2.5cm/1in in diameter with 10–17 ribs and yellow-brown spines. The flowers are greenish-brown. Mining and urbanization have threatened the plant's habitat.

Arthrocereus rondonianus
Also from eastern Brazil, this species of cactus has a slender, ascending stem to 75cm/29½in tall, up to 18 ribs and green or golden yellow spines. The fragrant pale lilac-pink flowers have hairy spines.

Schwartz's Mammillaria

Mammillaria schwarzii

This species was discovered by Fritz Schwartz, lost, and then re-found in 1987 on a rock face in Mexico, where it is now critically endangered, mainly because of illegal collecting. As with many cacti it is widely grown by enthusiasts and is rather a beautiful species, producing many pale, yellow-centred flowers around the margins of the rounded, spiny plant. It needs good drainage and careful watering, and high light intensity. The genus contains about 175 species, the majority native to Mexico. Many are grown, mainly for their impressive, often colourful flowers.

Distribution: Mexico.
Height and spread:
To 3cm/1in tall and
3.5cm/1¼in across.
Habit and form: Spiny
succulent.
Pollinated: Insect.
Leaf shape: Absent.

Identification: Cylindrical in shape and covered in spines. The central spines are white, with darker tips. The flower is white with red midveins, up to 5mm/⅜in long and 12mm/½in in diameter. The fruit is red, and the seeds are black.

Right: In bloom, the cactus is studded with delicate flowers.

ELAEOCARPUS AND MALLOW FAMILIES

The Elaeocarpaceae are mainly tropical and subtropical shrubs and trees, with around 12 genera and 350 species. They include a few useful timber trees and some ornamental plants, with a few species producing edible fruit. The Malvaceae are herbs, shrubs or trees of about 75 genera and as many as 1,500 species. Members of the family are used as sources of fibre, food and as ornamental plants.

Chile Lantern Tree

Crinodendron hookerianum

In spring and early summer distinctive, long, lantern-shaped flowers are produced. They hang from shoots clothed with narrow, dark green leaves. In its native southern Andean-Patagonic region of Chile, it grows in open areas or under forest canopy, chiefly in regions with medium or high rainfall. The exact timing of flowering depends upon its location and altitude.

Identification: Straight, ascending branches, downy when young, become rather sparsely furnished and rangy with age. The leaves are opposite, 5–10cm/2–4in long, short-stalked, narrowly elliptic to oblong or lance-shaped, with pointed tips and serrated margins, usually curved downwards, glossy dark green above with sparse bristly veins and pinnately veined, paler and more downy beneath. The lantern-like scarlet flowers hang below the branchlets on red-tinted, downy flower stalks.

Left: The fruits are pear-shaped, three-winged and 12mm/½in long.

Distribution: Chile and Argentina.
Height and spread: Up to 9m/30ft.
Habit and form: Small tree.
Pollinated: Insect.
Leaf shape: Narrowly elliptic.

Left: This is a popular tree for gardens with acidic soil.

Trailing Abutilon

Abutilon megapotamicum

There are about 150 species in this tropical and subtropical genus, known as flowering maples or parlour maples due to the shape of the leaves. This species is a trailing shrub and grows wild in Brazil. The pendulous red and yellow flowers resemble miniature Chinese lanterns and produce a lot of nectar, making this shrub very attractive to insects. Cultivars include 'Variegatum', with leaves mottled yellow, and 'Wisley Red', with deep red flowers.

Left: The stamens extend beyond the corolla in a 'bottle-brush' effect.

Identification: A hairless trailing shrub, growing to 2.5m/8ft long, with heart-shaped, sometimes lobed or toothed leaves to 8cm/3in. The drooping flowers grow singly in the leaf axils and have a tubular red calyx to 2.5cm/1in long and yellow petals to 4cm/1½in.

Distribution: Brazil.
Height and spread: To 2.5m/8ft.
Habit and form: Perennial shrub.
Pollinated: Insect.
Leaf shape: Cordate-lanceolate.

Left: The climbing habit of this slender-stemmed shrub is ideal for gardens.

OTHER SPECIES OF NOTE

White Lily Tree
Crinodendron patagua
This large shrub or small tree, with evergreen, dark green leaves, is from southern Chile. In late summer, it bears numerous white, fringed, open, bell-shaped blossoms that are lightly scented and hang below the branches. These are followed by creamy seedpods, tinted with red.

Abutilon insigne
Often grown as a house plant, this shrubby species is wild in Colombia and Venezuela and was introduced to cultivation in 1851 by Lucien Linden. In temperate climates it must be grown in a greenhouse. The drooping flowers are whitish or pink, with crimson veins and edges.

Pavonia multiflora
One of about 150 species of tropical and subtropical species, this shrub, grows to 2m/6¹/2ft tall, with solitary bright red flowers with blue anthers. It is a native of Brazil where it grows in forests near Rio de Janeiro.

Abutilon (Corynabutilon) *vitifolium*
This soft-wooded shrub comes from Chile. It is a soft-wooded shrub with downy foliage and pretty pale lilac flowers. Cultivars exist with white or larger flowers and it is quite a popular garden plant, but requires protection from frosts.

Nototriche compacta

This unusual species is one of the most extraordinary of South America's wild flowers, occupying one of the most inhospitable of habitats in the world, 3,100–4,200m/10,200–13,800ft high in the Andes of the south-west. To survive in this harsh environment it grows low as dense cushions, clinging tightly to the rocks to avoid desiccation from the cold dry winds. Gardeners keen on alpines find this a challenging species to cultivate. The seeds germinate quite well but the plant often becomes 'leggy' and less attractive. To thrive, it needs a sunny spot and protection from moisture. There are about 100 species, confined to the Andes.

Distribution: High Andes of South America.
Height and spread: 5–10cm/2–4in.
Habit and form: Perennial, cushion-plant.
Pollinated: Insect.
Leaf shape: Lobed.

Identification: The small lobed leaves are silvery-white and softly hairy. The flowers are white or pale lilac and open in summer.

Below: Nototriche compacta *grows in woolly mounds close to the ground.*

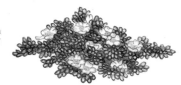

Macqui

Aristotelia chilensis

This weedy shrub grows in damp, humus-rich soils on lower mountainsides by rivers in southern Chile. It is a colonizer that quickly invades cleared forests and waste ground and forms extensive stands. It is very abundant in areas of high rainfall, with distribution between Illapel and Chilé, in mountain ranges, the Central Valley and the Archipelago of Juan Fernandez. The young reddish shoots bear small, white flowers in spring and early summer, followed by shiny, black, edible fruits in the autumn.

Distribution: Southern Chile.
Height and spread: Up to 5m/16ft.
Habit and form: Shrub or small tree.
Pollinated: Bee and other insects.
Leaf shape: Ovate.

Identification: On this evergreen shrub or small tree the young shoots are reddish and the bark of older branches is smooth, peeling off in long fibrous strips. The oval leaves are 5–10cm/2–4in long, shallowly toothed, opposite and alternate, glossy dark green above, paler beneath and sparsely downy on the veins, smooth when mature; the leaf stalk is reddish. Greenish-white, star-shaped flowers, usually in three-flowered axillary and terminal clusters, appear in late spring and early summer, followed by spherical black fruits, 6mm/¼in in diameter.

Far left: Macqui often forms extensive stands on land cleared through logging.

Right: The black, edible fruits appear in autumn.

PASSION FLOWER, BEGONIA AND COCOA FAMILIES

Passifloraceae has some 575 species, mainly climbing lianes with tendrils. The begonia family (Begoniaceae) has about 1,000 species, also warm temperate and tropical. Members of both families are grown for their fruit and flowers. Cocoa is the most famous of some 1,500 species of Sterculiaceae.

Granadilla

Passiflora quadrangularis

This is a familiar climber, with beautiful, complex flowers. Spanish missionaries are said to have seen symbols of the crucifixion in the flowers of members of this genus: the five anthers are the five wounds of Christ, the three-parted style represents the three nails and the central receptacle is the pillar of the cross, while the filaments of the flower suggest the crown of thorns. The fleshy roots and fruits are edible; the latter is often made into jam or used as flavouring for ice-cream. The species name refers to the square stems.

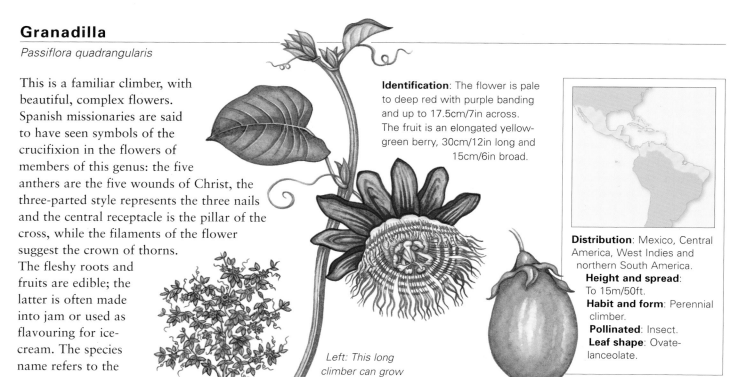

Left: This long climber can grow to over 15m/50ft.

Identification: The flower is pale to deep red with purple banding and up to 17.5cm/7in across. The fruit is an elongated yellow-green berry, 30cm/12in long and 15cm/6in broad.

Distribution: Mexico, Central America, West Indies and northern South America.
Height and spread: To 15m/50ft.
Habit and form: Perennial climber.
Pollinated: Insect.
Leaf shape: Ovate-lanceolate.

Lachay Begonia

Begonia octopetala

This begonia grows wild only in Peru, where it is found on steep hills north of Lima that are affected by winter mist and fog. The wild stocks are endangered by habitat loss. This rather unusual begonia was first cultivated in 1805, and flowered in the Glasgow Botanic Garden in 1836. It is one of only a few frost-hardy begonias, but is rarely seen in cultivation.

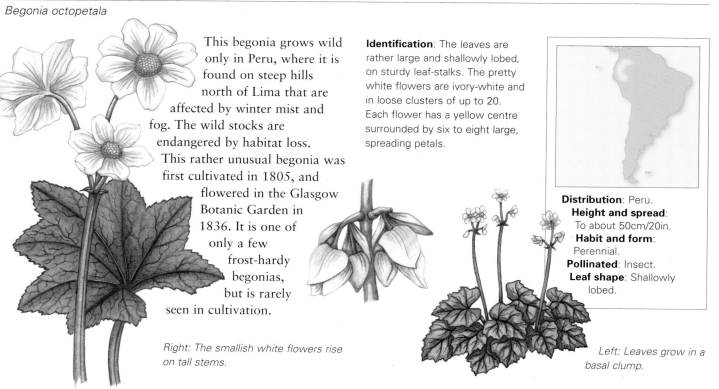

Identification: The leaves are rather large and shallowly lobed, on sturdy leaf-stalks. The pretty white flowers are ivory-white and in loose clusters of up to 20. Each flower has a yellow centre surrounded by six to eight large, spreading petals.

Distribution: Peru.
Height and spread: To about 50cm/20in.
Habit and form: Perennial.
Pollinated: Insect.
Leaf shape: Shallowly lobed.

Right: The smallish white flowers rise on tall stems.

Left: Leaves grow in a basal clump.

Cacao

Chocolate Nut Tree, *Theobroma cacao*

Distribution: Central and South America.
Height and spread: 5.5–12m/18–40ft.
Habit and form: Evergreen tree.
Pollinated: Insect.
Leaf shape: Oblong.

Right: Cacao is a small, understorey evergreen tree.

One of the world's most famous useful plants, cacoa yields medicines as well as cocao itself, used to make chocolate. Native to the Andean foothills it is now widely cultivated in the tropics for chocolate. The stimulating chemicals include theobromine and caffeine and hundreds of others, including some that slow the build-up of fatty deposits in arteries. Native South Americans used this plant long before Europeans arrived, and the seeds were valued and even used as currency. It was introduced to the West Indies in about 1525 by the Spanish, and reached Ghana (now the main producer) in 1879.

Above: The fruit contains five rows of seeds – the cocoa 'beans'.

Identification: The leaves are red-brown or green and 10–40cm/ 4–16in long. The small flowers are whitish-pink and sprout in clusters direct from the trunk. The large ribbed fruit is yellow, brown or purple and up to 30cm/1ft long.

OTHER SPECIES OF NOTE

Meloncillo *Passiflora suberosa*

This is a rather variable passion flower with small, green, inconspicuous flowers that lack petals. It ranges from Paraguay and Argentina, north through the West Indies and into Mexico and Texas. The fruit is purple or black when ripe and about 1.5cm/⅝in across.

Crato Passion Fruit *Passiflora cincinnata*
A tender perennial native to Paraguay, Argentina and Brazil, though widely introduced further north, this vine grows to 4.5m/15ft long. Its leaves are variable in shape, and the flowers are to 12cm/5in across and blue with yellow centres. The fruit is yellow-orange when ripe.

Lemon Passion Flower *Passiflora citrina*
Sadly, this is a rare species in the wild. It is a small, elegant vine from moist pine woods in the hills of Honduras and Guatemala. Its yellow flowers are pollinated mainly by hummingbirds. It can be grown in a conservatory or greenhouse and reaches about 6m/20ft. The flowering season is from April to August.

Begonia scharfii (haageana)
This woody-stemmed begonia has clusters of pretty pink flowers, up to 5cm/1½in across, and the stems and leaves are covered in red hairs. The deep green leaves, to 25cm/10in long are a reddish-bronze colour on the undersides.

Handflower Tree

Monkey's Hand, *Chiranthodendron pentadactylon*

This remarkable plant takes its name from the unusual flowers, whose stamens look a bit like a hand. It is the only species in its genus. The flowers were regarded with awe by native people who gave the tree religious significance. It was also used in medicine, to treat eye disorders and haemorrhoids. The species became more well known after it had been introduced to Mexico towards the end of the 18th century.

Identification: The large solitary flowers grow opposite the leaves. There are no petals and the bell-shaped calyx consists of reddish leathery sepals. The 5cm/2in-long stamens are fused into a long tube, opening into five red anthers which resemble a hand. The leaves have brown hairs on the underside.

Right: This fast-growing evergreen tree can reach 14m/46ft.

Distribution: Mexico and Guatemala.
Height and spread: To 14m/46ft.
Habit and form: Evergreen tree.
Pollinated: Bird and bat.
Leaf shape: Lobed.

Below: The fruit is long, brown and woody, splitting into five lobes.

NETTLE, DEADNETTLE, SPURGE, MARCGRAVIA, BRAZIL NUT AND MANGOSTEEN FAMILIES

The nettle family (Urticaceae) contains about 1,050 species, often armed with stinging hairs. Deadnettle (Labiatae) has about 6700 species, including herbs such as mints, while Euphorbiaceae has 240 genera and 6,000 species, including herbs, shrubs and trees. The Marcgraviaceae are about 110 species of tropical lianes or epiphytes. The Brazil nut family (Lecythidaceae) consists of 285 species of trees and shrubs. Mangosteen is one of the most famous fruits of the 1,370-strong Guttiferae.

Cannon-ball Tree

Couroupita guianensis

Identification: The leaves grow to 30cm/12in, and the flowers have petals about 5cm/2in long, yellowish on the outside and red inside, with hundreds of closely-packed stamens.

It is the large, round fruits of this remarkable plant that give it its common name. This tropical American genus contains about four species, of which the cannon-ball tree is the best known. Racemes of yellow and red, waxy, sweet-scented flowers grow from the trunk and attract many different insect pollinators. A proportion of these flowers then develop into the large, characteristic fruits. Before ripening, the fruit pulp can be used as a drink, but later on the ripe fruits smell unpleasant (at least to humans). The tree also produces useful timber.

Right: The cannon-ball-like fruit can measure up to 24cm/9½in in diameter.

Distribution: Brazil to Panama; widely cultivated.
Height and spread: To 35m/115ft.
Habit and form: Tree.
Pollinated: Insect.
Leaf shape: Lanceolate to ovate.

Pineapple Sage

Salvia elegans

Pineapple sage grows naturally in oak and pine scrub forests at elevations from 2,400–3,100m/8,000–10,000ft in Mexico and Guatemala. It is a semi-woody, sometimes almost herbaceous, subshrub, with soft, fuzzy leaves and bright red, two-lipped flowers arranged in whorls of four at the ends of the stems. It flowers in late summer and autumn, and can occasionally be found in warmer climates as a garden escapee, due to its popularity in cultivation. The bruised foliage smells like fresh pineapple, hence its common name. It is bird-pollinated and is especially popular with ruby-throated hummingbirds.

Identification: The plant has an open-branched, airy habit, with square stems on which the leaves are opposite; the branches also originate on opposite sides of the main stem. The leaves are softly fuzzy, light green and 5–10cm/2–4in long, oval to triangular, straight or heart-shaped at the base, with serrated margins. Ruby-red, two-lipped flowers, 2.5–5cm/1–2in long, are tubular with a hood-like upper lip and spreading lower lip. They are arranged in four-flowered, terminal whorls, on 20cm/8in spikes. It rarely sets seed outside its native range, due to a lack of pollinators.

Distribution: Mexico and Guatemala.
Height and spread: 1–1.5m x 60–90cm/3–5 x 2–3ft.
Habit and form: Herbaceous perennial or subshrub.
Pollinated: Hummingbird.
Leaf shape: Ovate to deltoid.

Left: The felt-like leaves and bright red flowers make this a handsome specimen in late summer.

OTHER SPECIES OF NOTE

Peregrina Spicy Jatropha
Jatropha integerrima
This spurge is an evergreen shrub or small tree with groups of bright red, star-shaped flowers and glossy foliage. Native to the West Indies, it is often grown in tropical gardens. It has also become established in south Florida. It attracts insects and hummingbirds.

Buddha Belly Plant Bottleplant Shrub,
Jatropha podagrica
The common name is derived from the swollen stem. Native to Central America, it is a common tropical weed and is also easily cultivated. It needs a sunny spot and not much watering.

Purple Dove Vine
Dalechampia roezliana
A South American perennial that is found from Argentina to Mexico. Unlike other *Dalechampia* species, this small shrub has erect stems. It grows to 45cm/1½ft and has simple evergreen leaves. Its small, unshowy flowers are unusual in that each apparent flower is a cluster of small flowers, set between pink bracts.

Marcgravia brownei
One of several species in this genus of epiphytic climbers, this has shiny leathery leaves and clusters of upturned yellow flowers that attract hummingbirds, which pollinate the flowers as they feed. It produces ball-shaped red fruit.

Clusia grandiflora

This genus contains about 145 species of tropical American trees and shrubs. This species has large white flowers (male and female flowers separate), usually three or four at the end of a shoot. It is a shrub, with leathery leaves. The related balsam apple *(Clusia major)* is rather similar and often grown in cultivation. Bees visit the flowers and gather resin from them. They then use this resin to help them build their nests, and it has been discovered that the resin has anti-microbial properties and so helps keep the bees' nests free of disease.

Identification: The male flowers have a dense ring of stamens at the centre, surrounding a resinous mass of reduced stamens. The female flowers ripen into a round, woody fruit, about 12.5cm/5in long, opening to reveal the seeds, which have fleshy orange arils.

Distribution: Guyana.
Height and spread:
To 6m/20ft.
Habit and form: Shrub.
Pollinated: Insect.
Leaf shape: Obovate.

Below: The hard round fruit is pale green to whitish.

Left: The opened fruit is star-shaped.

Artillery Plant

Pilea microphylla

This small, brittle succulent is usually a prostrate herb. It grows from Mexico south as far as Brazil, in moist tropical forest edges and glades. It has very small leaves, tiny greenish female flowers and larger, pinkish, male flowers. It gets its common name by virtue of its "catapult mechanism" for dispersing pollen. Its minute, lime-green leaves on short, arching stems give it a fine textured, fern-like appearance, and it quickly spreads to form quite large colonies.

Identification: The stems are succulent and densely branched, sometimes slightly woody at the base, spreading or tufted, 5–50cm/2–20in long. The leaves, crowded all along the stem on short leaf stalks, are oval to elliptic, 2–12mm/1/16–½in long, those of a pair very unequal in size; the upper leaf surface is crowded with elliptic hard cysts, the lower surface finely netted with veins, the margins smooth. Tiny green flowers appear all year round, in stemless clusters, followed by tiny brown fruits.

Distribution: Mexico to Brazil.
Height and spread:
15–45cm/6–18in.
Habit and form: Annual or short-lived herbaceous perennial.
Leaf shape: Obovate.
Pollinated: Insect.

Right: The brittle, arching stems quickly form a large, spreading colony of fern-like growth.

PRIMULA AND DOGBANE FAMILIES

The Primulaceae include 22 genera and around 1,000 species, occurring mainly in temperate and mountainous regions of the northern hemisphere. Only one species of Primula naturally occurs south of the equator, in South America. The 155 genera and 2,000 species of the dogbane family (Apocynaceae) are distributed primarily in the tropics and subtropics with a good representation in the neotropics.

Mandevilla campanulata

This is a rare plant from Panama, from a genus of about 120 species of tuberous perennials from Central and South America. Several, such as Chilean jasmine *(M. laxa)* are grown in cultivation, and a number of hybrids and cultivars also exist and are commonly grown in the tropics. Most have pink or white flowers but this one has attractive pale yellow blooms. This species is endangered in the wild, where its range is restricted to a small region of central Panama. It is therefore rarely seen. However, it has great potential as a garden plant or houseplant and this may save it from extinction.

Above: The pretty cultivar Mandevilla x amoena Alice du Pont is a better-known relative of Mandevilla campanulata.

Identification: Twining liana with milky sap and ovate leaves. The flowers are pale yellow and tubular, with a five-parted corolla.

Distribution: Panama.
Height and spread: To 4m/13ft.
Habit and form: Perennial twining vine.
Pollinated: Insect.
Leaf shape: Ovate.

Left: The flowers are sweetly scented.

Violet Allamanda

Allamanda violacea

This evergreen vine or climbing shrub from Brazil has large, rich purple, funnel-shaped blooms, which appear throughout the year and fade to pink with age, giving a two-toned effect. The light green leaves are arranged in whorls on weak, sprawling stems. The plants exude a white, milky sap when cut, and all parts are poisonous. They are naturally found growing along riverbanks and in other open, sunny areas with adequate rainfall and perpetually moist soil.

Right: The seed is released throughout the year from a spiny capsule.

Far right: Allamanda climbs rapidly, smothering nearby vegetation.

Identification: An erect or weakly climbing, evergreen shrub with woody stems and green, hairy leaves, 10–20cm/4–8in, in whorls, usually of four. The leaves are oblong to oval, abruptly pointed, with the secondary veins joined in a series of arches inside the margins, downy above, more densely so beneath. The funnel-shaped flowers, 7.5cm/3in long, have a narrow tube and five flared, rounded lobes; they are rose purple with a darker throat. The fruit is a round, spiny capsule.

Distribution: Brazil.
Height and spread: Up to 3–6m/10–20ft in height.
Habit and form: Evergreen scrambling shrub.
Pollinated: Insect.
Leaf shape: Oblong.

White Frangipani

Plumeria alba

Distribution: Puerto Rico and Lesser Antilles.
Height and spread: 6 x 4m/ 20 x 13ft.
Habit and form: Small tree.
Pollinated: Insect.
Leaf shape: Lanceolate.

Frangipani is well known throughout the tropics and has long been cultivated for its intensely fragrant, lovely, spiral-shaped blooms, which appear at the branch tips from early summer to late autumn. Originating from Puerto Rico and the Lesser Antilles, the tree is unusual in appearance, with long, coarse, deciduous leaves clustered only at the tips of the rough, thick, sausage-like, grey-green branches. The branches are upright and crowded on the trunk, forming a vase or umbrella shape with age. They are brittle although usually sturdy, exuding a milky sap when they are bruised or punctured.

Identification: The glossy, dark green leaves, 30cm/12in or more long, are alternate and lance-shaped, often blistered, with prominent feathered veining, usually finely hairy beneath. The fragrant, showy flowers are white with yellow centres, usually borne on bare branches in terminal clusters, with five spreading petals, up to 6cm/2¼in across, and a tubular base up to 2.5cm/1in long. They are followed by hard brown fruits up to 15cm/6in long.

Above: The five-petalled flower head.

Far left: The tree has a uniform round crown.

OTHER SPECIES OF NOTE

West Indian Jasmine *Plumeria rubra*
This small tree is native to dry, rocky habitats in southern Mexico and grows as far south as Costa Rica. Its thick, succulent stems, clusters of leathery leaves and abundant, fragrant blooms in red, pink, yellow or white have led to it being widely planted across the tropics.

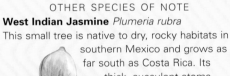

Primula magellanica
This is the only *Primula* species found south of the equator, in southern South America. It spends the winter as a resting bud; the white flowers, with a yellow eye, appear in spring, in a cluster of flowers atop an erect stem. The plant prefers damp woodland.

Golden Trumpet *Allamanda cathartica*
The golden-yellow, white-throated tubular flowers are very large in some cultivated forms of this plant. It climbs and clambers to 6m/20ft. It has become naturalized in many tropical areas, but can sometimes be a troublesome (though attractive) weed.

Chilean Jasmine *Mandevilla laxa*
This Argentinian climber grows to about 4m/13ft tall and has glossy heart-shaped leaves with a purplish underside. Its abundant trumpet-shaped flowers are white or ivory-coloured, and highly fragrant. Its long seed pods contain fluffy seeds that readily self-sow.

Brazilian Jasmine

Pink Allamanda, *Mandevilla splendens*

This attractive, evergreen vine chiefly occurs in the wild at altitudes of around 900m/2,950ft in the Organ mountains near Rio de Janeiro. It is endowed with beautiful, large, deep pink, funnel-shaped blooms, which are highly visible against the large, downy, dark green, evergreen leaves. Pink allamanda has become popular as a garden plant in many countries and is sometimes found as a garden escapee in warmer climates.

Identification: The stems of this evergreen, twining shrub or liana are initially downy and green, later woody, and exude a milky sap when broken. The fine-textured, downy leaves, up to 20cm/8in long, are opposite, broadly elliptic with a pointed tip and heart-shaped base, with feathered veining and a wavy margin. Fragrant, trumpet-shaped, yellow-centred, rose-pink flowers, 7.5–10cm/3–4in across, appear all year round in lateral racemes of three to five; they have five spreading, abruptly pointed petals. The fruits are paired, brown, cylindrical follicles, which are inconspicuous.

Distribution: South-eastern Brazil.
Height and spread: 6m/20ft.
Habit and form: Twining, evergreen shrub.
Pollinated: Insect.
Leaf shape: Broadly elliptic.

Left and right: The pink, showy flowers are produced almost every month of the year.

CAPER, NASTURTIUM AND PEA FAMILIES

The caper family (Capparidaceae) has about 650 species of shrubs, herbs and trees, mainly from warm or arid areas. The nasturtium family (Tropaeolaceae) consists of about 90 species of more or less succulent herbs. The pea family (Fabaceae or Leguminosae) is found in both temperate and tropical areas. It comprises about 640 genera and 18,000 species, mostly herbs, but also shrubs and trees.

Spider Flower

Spider Plant, *Cleome hassleriana*

One of about 150 species in this genus, the spider flower is quite popular as a garden plant, even in temperate areas where it can be planted out in summer beds. It is quite tender and needs protection from wind and rain as well as frost. Seeds can be germinated under glass. Various cultivars exist, notably 'Violet Queen' with purple flowers and 'Helen Campbell' with white flowers. The wild species usually has white, pink or purplish flowers.

Identification: The stems and leaves are covered in soft, sticky hairs. Leaves have between five and seven leaflets. Flowers are borne in a dense terminal cluster, and the filaments of each flower extend beyond the petals. The fruits are held on thin stalks, giving a spidery effect.

Distribution: Paraguay, Argentina and southern Brazil.
Height and spread: To 150cm/5ft.
Habit and form: Annual herb.
Pollinated: Insect.
Leaf shape: Lanceolate.

Right: Delicate flowers are borne on long, slender stems.

Canary Creeper

Tropaeolum peregrinum

This annual creeper is well known as a garden plant. It grows quickly, and clambers up fences and trellises, producing pretty yellow flowers. Its common name probably comes from the fact that it was first introduced into Europe via the Canary Islands, rather than from the canary yellow colour of its flowers. It is also known as Canarybird Vine.

Identification: The leaves of this creeper are usually five-lobed and it clings by means of twisted petioles. The long-stalked flowers have a hooked spur, are about 2cm/³⁄₄in across and yellow, the upper petal dissected at the edge and with a red-spotted base.

Above: The two large upper petals have attractive fringed edges.

Distribution: Peru and Ecuador.
Height and spread: To 2.5m/8ft.
Habit and form: Annual or perennial climber.
Pollinated: Insect.
Leaf shape: Lobed.

Left: This bushy climber grows well on supports or up through tall host plants.

Scarlet Flame Bean

Rose of Venezuela, *Brownea ariza* (=grandiceps)

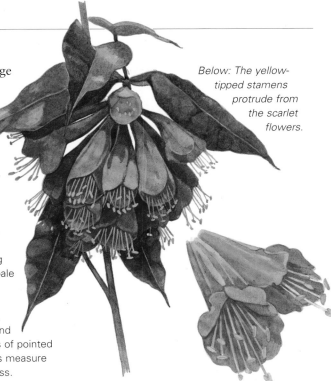

Below: The yellow-tipped stamens protrude from the scarlet flowers.

This small tree produces beautiful large heads of bright red flowers which dangle down beneath the foliage. The flowers are a little like those of rhododendrons. The fruit pods are velvety and droop in clusters. The generic name honours the author and botanist Patrick Browne (1720–1790).

Distribution: Colombia and Venezuela.
Height and spread: 9–12m/30–40ft.
Habit and form: Tree.
Pollinated: Bird and insect.
Leaf shape: Pinnate.

Right: Brownea ariza is a slow-growing tree that does not exceed 12m/40ft.

Identification: Young leaves are mottled pale pink and greenish, turning brown and green as they mature. Mature leaves are long and pinnate, with 12–18 pairs of pointed leaflets. Flower clusters measure up to 20cm/8in across.

OTHER SPECIES OF NOTE

Steriphoma elliptica
This native of Trinidad and Venezuela has yellow flowers with a slight reddish tinge, and the leaves are hairy on the undersides. It grows to a height of about 3.7m/12ft.

Steriphoma paradoxa
This is a beautiful native of the forests of Colombia, Venezuela and Guatemala, between 762–1,220m/2,500–4,000ft above sea level. The yellow flowers have long graceful stamens.

Peruvian Nasturtium
Tropaeolum tuberosum
This is is a close relative of Canary Creeper but has red-orange rather than yellow flowers. It is native to Peru and Bolivia – where it is called 'anu' – and grows on mountain slopes and in valleys around 3,000m/1,000ft. A climber, it wraps its leaf stalks around other plants, and flowers from June to October. In gardens, it will thrive in sheltered, sunny locations in well-drained soil. The potato-like root tubers are edible after boiling and have a peppery taste.

Mountain Immortelle *Erythrina poeppigiana*
Spiky clusters of reddish-orange pea-flowers that open before the leaves appear, make a most impressive display on this plant. Originally from the Andes of Peru, it is now found in many parts of South America and in the West Indies. The bright flowers attract birds and insects.

Red Powder Puff

Calliandra haematocephala

This small tree or shrub is a fast-growing species that produces unusual red 'powder-puff' flowers from November through April. These are often visited by butterflies and hummingbirds. It can be grown indoors in a pot if kept trimmed, and outside in warm climates. They can even be pruned and maintained as a hedge. The leaves display 'sleep' movements, folding together at night.

Below: The evergreen leaves are smooth and silky.

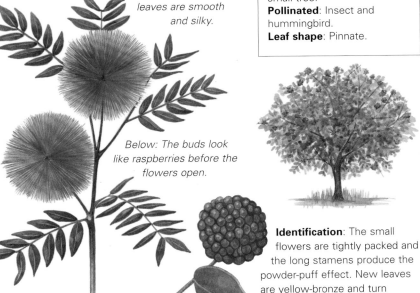

Below: The buds look like raspberries before the flowers open.

Distribution: Peru, Bolivia and Brazil.
Height and spread: To 6m/20ft.
Habit and form: Shrub or small tree.
Pollinated: Insect and hummingbird.
Leaf shape: Pinnate.

Identification: The small flowers are tightly packed and the long stamens produce the powder-puff effect. New leaves are yellow-bronze and turn metallic green as they mature.

AGAVE, CRASSULA AND PROTEA FAMILIES

The Agavaceae include 550–600 species in around 18 genera, and are widespread in tropical, subtropical and warm temperate regions. The Crassulaceae are mostly succulents, with flowers similar to those of the rose and saxifrage families. The Proteaceae are a large family of about 80 genera and 1,500 species.

Echeveria subrigida

This plant from Mexico is extremely restricted in its range, occurring only in San Luis Potosi and Tultenango Canyon. It was originally classified as a *Cotyledon* species but was later included in *Echeveria*. This plant has been confused with *E. cante*, mainly as a result of the trade in cultivated plants, but the true species is a robust plant with smooth leaves, whose flowers have unique scarlet nectaries.

Far left: Up to fifteen yellow-red flowers with greyish sepals appear on a tall spike in summer.

Above: The flower attracts insect pollinators.

Identification: A large, solitary, evergreen, succulent rosette, 30cm/12in in diameter, with a stem up to 10cm/4in long. The oval to lance-shaped leaves, 15–20cm/6–8in long, are held closely in the rosette. They are pointed, pale blue-green with red margins, upturned and very finely toothed. The flower spike, which appears in summer, is 60–90cm/2–3ft high, bearing six–fifteen flowered branches with a few bracts, 3–5cm/1¼–2in long, triangular to lance-shaped, ascending, grey-purple sepals, and flowers to 2.5cm/1in across, five-sided, not very constricted at the mouth, red, bloomed white outside, yellow-red inside.

Right: The red-edged leaves form a handsome rosette.

Distribution: San Luis Potosi and Tultenango Canyon, Mexico.
Height and spread: 60–90cm/2–3ft.
Habit and form: Evergreen succulent.
Pollinated: Insect.
Leaf shape: Obovate to oblanceolate.

Donkey's Tail

Burro's tail, *Sedum morganianum*

This plant, widely cultivated for its highly ornamental stems and leaves, is almost certainly a native of Mexico, although to date it has never been found in the wild. It sometimes appears as a garden escapee, although even the history of its cultivation remains a mystery. It is an attractive succulent, with spindle-shaped leaves with a silver-blue cast and pendulous branches. The deep pink flowers appear in spring but are rarely seen.

Identification: This pendulous to horizontal, trailing evergreen perennial has numerous prostrate or pendulous stems, sparsely branched and woody at the base. The leaves, to 2cm/¾in long, are very succulent, blue-green, alternate, spirally arranged, overlapping, oblong to lance-shaped, pointed, incurved and flattened. Pendent flowers, 12mm/½in across, borne terminally on long stalks, deep pink with five long-pointed, oval petals, may appear from spring onward.

Left: The dense pendulous stems have made this a favourite feature plant with gardeners.

Distribution: Mexico.
Height and spread: Trailing to 60cm/2ft.
Habit and form: Succulent evergreen.
Pollinated: Not known, probably insects.
Leaf shape: Rounded, oblong-lanceolate.

Left: The flowers appear at the stem tips.

Chilean Flameflower

Chilean Firebush, *Embothrium coccineum*

Distribution: Southern Argentina and Chile.
Height and spread: Up to 10m/33ft.
Habit and form: Shrub or small tree.
Pollinated: Bird.
Leaf shape: Elliptic or oblong.

Far right: The Chilean firebush is an evergreen and, rarely, a deciduous tree.

This variable shrub or small tree is the sole representative of its genus, and is endemic to southern South American forests. The flameflower grows over a wide geographic range in the temperate forests of southern Argentina and Chile, and is frequently found along the edges of forest fragments as well as in open, agricultural landscapes. Its main pollinators are birds, with two species in particular – a flycatcher, the white-crested elaenia, *Elaenia albiceps*, and a hummingbird, the green-backed firecrown, *Sephanoides sephanoides* – thought to be the principal pollinating species.

Identification: A variable shrub or tree, with ascending stems, suckering at the base in some forms, clumped and sparsely branched. The leaves, up to 12.5cm/5in long, are undivided and very variable in shape: elliptic or oblong to narrowly lance-shaped, hairless, pea-green with olive veins or dark green. The long-lasting flowers, on red-green stalks, are borne in terminal or axillary crowded racemes up to 10cm/4in long, usually appearing in spring but variable according to location. They are tubular, red or vivid scarlet, although yellow and white forms have occasionally been recorded, up to 5cm/2in long, splitting into four narrow lobes that reflex and coil; each flower carries one stamen. The style is long, slender, protruding and persistent in the fruit.

OTHER SPECIES OF NOTE

Pachyphytum bracteosum
This succulent from Mexico is found on rock escarpments on limestone cliffs, between 1,200–1,850m/4,000–6,000ft. It has upright flowering stems of 30cm/1ft or more, with white succulent bracts surrounding pink-red, five-lobed flowers with prominent yellow stamens.

Mexican Firecracker *Echeveria setosa*
A variable species, endemic to small areas of Mexico, and in danger of extinction in the wild. The stemless rosettes of densely packed, glaucous or green, hairy leaves, give rise to flower spikes of pentagonal, red-and-yellow flowers in spring and early summer.

Fox Tail Agave *Agave attenuata*
This species from central Mexico has very wide, fleshy, soft, pale blue-green leaves with a felt-like texture, and forms a leaning or creeping trunk with age. The curving flower spike grows up to 3m/10ft, and is densely covered in green-white drooping flowers, producing fruit at the base and new plantlets at the tip.

Adam's Needle *Yucca filamentosa*
Looks a little like a small palm, with evergreen, strap-like leaves up to 90cm/3ft long, taking the form of a rosette. The leaf margins are decorated with long, curly threads or "filaments" that peel back as the leaf grows. Erect flower spikes of large white flowers may reach 3.5m/12ft in summer.

Century Plant

American aloe, *Agave americana*

This is probably the *Agave* most commonly grown as an ornamental plant, and as a result, it has spread throughout the temperate and tropical areas of the world. Because it has been extensively propagated its exact origin is uncertain, although it probably originates in eastern Mexico. The flowers appear at any time after the plant has reached ten years old, so it does not live up to its common name.

Identification: A rosette-forming, short-stemmed, evergreen perennial, with leaves up to 2m/6½ft long, curved or reflexed, lance-shaped, pointed, light green to grey, wavy-edged to toothed, with rounded teeth 12mm/½in long and irregularly spaced, brown to grey; the leaves have a terminal spine up to 5cm/2in long, awl-shaped to conical, brown to grey. The inflorescence grows to 9m/30ft. The large, asparagus-like stalk grows from the centre, bearing 15–35 spreading horizontal branches, with pale yellow flowers.

Distribution: Uncertain, probably eastern Mexico.
Height and spread: Up to 9m/30ft when flowering.
Habit and form: Evergreen succulent.
Pollinated: Insect.
Leaf shape: Lanceolate.

Above: The small, individual flowers are held in dense "brush-like" umbels.

Right: The huge flower spikes appear only on plants of ten or more years.

WOOD SORREL, PHLOX AND VERBENA FAMILIES

There are only six genera but 775 species in the Oxalidaceae, which is mainly tropical, consisting of small trees, shrubs and herbs. The 20 genera and 290 species of the phlox family (Polemoniaceae) include herbs, lianas, shrubs and small trees. The verbena family (Verbenaceae) has 950 tropical species.

Tree Oxalis

Oxalis ortgiesii

This species is native to the Andean foothills of Peru and Ecuador. It is an upright perennial with a tree-like stem and hairy, greenish-purple foliage. This shrub is sometimes known as Fishtail oxalis due to the shape of its leaves. The many-flowered inflorescence is about 30cm/1ft long.

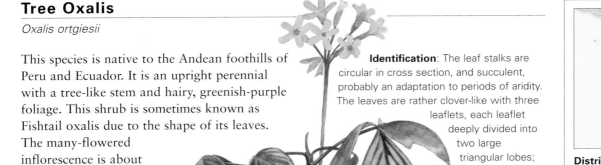

Identification: The leaf stalks are circular in cross section, and succulent, probably an adaptation to periods of aridity. The leaves are rather clover-like with three leaflets, each leaflet deeply divided into two large triangular lobes; olive green to purple above and reddish-purple and hairy beneath. The flowers are lemon yellow with dark veins.

Left: Slim stems support the delicate yellow flowers.

Left: The flowers measure about 2.5cm/1in across.

Distribution: Ecuador and Peru.
Height and spread: To 45cm/18in.
Habit and form: Perennial shrub.
Pollinated: Insect.
Leaf shape: Divided, lobed.

Lucky Clover

Good Luck Plant, *Oxalis tetraphylla*

Bearing a superficial resemblance to a clover, this species produces brick-red, pink or white flowers in the summer. It dies back to form a bulb over the winter but re-grows very rapidly the following spring. Lucky Clover is cultivated as much for its attractive variegated purple and green leaves as for its pretty flowers. In one popular cultivar, 'Iron Cross', the inner sections of the leaflets are entirely purple.

Identification: This bulbous, stemless perennial has long hairy leaf stalks and clover-like leaves with four (sometimes three) leaflets, hence the common names. The leaflets usually have a V-shaped purple marking above and are hairy beneath.

Left: The umbrella-shaped flowers open into green-centred funnels.

Distribution: Mexico.
Height and spread: To about 40cm/16in.
Habit and form: Perennial.
Pollinated: Insect.
Leaf shape: Four-lobed.

Left: This plant's spreading habit means it creates good ground cover in gardens.

Mexican Ivy

Monastery Bells, Cup and Saucer Vine, *Cobaea scandens*

Distribution: Mexico.
Height and spread: To 6m/20ft.
Habit and form: Perennial climber.
Pollinated: Insect, bird and bat.
Leaf shape: Pinnate.

This familiar garden and greenhouse climber is a native of Mexico, and widely naturalised in the tropics. The bell-shaped flowers are green and smell musky at first, but mature to a pretty purple shade and then smell pleasantly of honey. They attract insects, and possibly also hummingbirds and bats. It grows rapidly, clambering on other plants, fences or trellises, securing itself by means of coiling tendrils. In temperate climates it is usually grown from seed and treated as an annual, although it can be kept indoors in the winter, as a perennial. A white-flowered form is quite popular.

Identification: The leaves have large leafy stipules and the leaflets (four to six) grow to about 10cm/4in. The corolla has a saucer-shaped calyx, and usually matures to a rich purple colour.

Left: In gardens, this vigorous vine requires regular cutting back to prevent it from choking other plants.

OTHER SPECIES OF NOTE

Oxalis dispar
This native of Guyana has long-stalked leaves with three long leaflets, and bright yellow, scented flowers from spring to winter. It has slender branches and few leaves and grows to about 60cm/2ft.

Oca *Oxalis tuberosa* is native to Colombia. This succulent-stemmed yellow-flowered perennial has a greenish-purple stem and scaly edible tubers. These are traditionally eaten roasted or boiled, like potatoes, and taste like sweet potato or chestnuts. Oca root has been used as a food source since before the Incas. The leaves should not be eaten in quantity as they contain oxalic acid, which can be harmful.

Cobaea hookerana
This is found growing wild in the mountain forests of Venezuela. It has strange dangling flowers with long stamens that open during the night, and these attract moths (especially hawkmoths), which transfer the pollen that brushes on to their wings.

Verbena peruviana
A tender perennial, often grown as an annual and pot plant. Despite its name, it comes from Argentina and Brazil. It has a profusion of striking brilliant scarlet flowers and blooms from late spring through summer. Cultivars vary, with white, lavender and white, and pink flowers.

Fleur de Dieu

Queen's Wreath, Sandpaper Vine *Petrea kohautiana*

The French common name means 'flower of God', a suitable label for this impressive vine with its long clusters of beautiful blue and violet flowers. The species name celebrates Franz Kohaut who collected it on Martinique between 1819 and 1821. It grows by twining and clinging and develops rough leaves from which dangle the long inflorescences. When in full bloom, and covered in flowers, it can look rather like a wisteria from a distance.

Distribution: West Indies, Antilles.
Height and spread: To 10.5m/34½ft.
Habit and form: Evergreen perennial vine.
Pollinated: Insect.
Leaf shape: Elliptic.

Identification: The flower clusters grow to about 3m/10ft as racemes from the leaf axils, consisting of individual pale lilac to purple flowers, blooming from late winter to late summer. The flowers only last about two days but the bluish sepals persist, and slowly go grey.

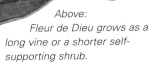

Above: Fleur de Dieu grows as a long vine or a shorter self-supporting shrub.

NIGHTSHADE AND BINDWEED FAMILIES

The nightshade family (Solanaceae) are herbs, shrubs, or trees of about 85 genera and 2,800 species.
They are frequently vines or creepers and while a few are edible, others are poisonous, some deadly.
Bindweeds (Convolvulaceae) are mostly twining herbs or shrubs, sometimes with milky sap, comprising
about 55 genera and 1,700 species. Many have heart-shaped leaves and funnel-shaped flowers.

Blue Dawn Flower

Morning Glory, *Ipomoea learii* syn. *I. acuminata, I. indica*

This fast-growing, tropical American climbing vine has large, saucer-shaped flowers borne in clusters of up to five. The flowers open bright blue-violet and fade to rose or soft red-violet, which creates an overall two-tone effect when the vine is in heavy bloom. Each flower lasts for only one day, but the plant is extremely floriferous.

It occurs widely outside its native range, as it has long been admired as a garden plant and has escaped from cultivation. It usually prefers coastal habitats and moist forests. Originally native to tropical America, it is now pan-tropical and is often a troublesome weed where introduced.

Identification: A herbaceous, perennial climber, to 6m/20ft tall, often forming a woody base. The stems, which often have a woody base, are almost hairless and much branched. The leaves are oval to rounded with a tapering, pointed tip and a heart-shaped base, sometimes three-lobed, from 5–18cm/2–7in long on long stalks. The inflorescences are single to few-flowered, appearing densely on 5–20cm/2–8in stalks. The short-lived, funnel-shaped flowers are intense blue or purple, rarely white, 5–7.5cm/2–3in long and across. The rounded fruits, up to 12mm/½in in diameter, contain one to four brown seeds.

Distribution: Tropical America.
Height and spread: 6m/20ft.
Habit and form: Herbaceous perennial climber.
Pollinated: Insect.
Leaf shape: Ovate to orbicular.

Left: A fully open flower.

Left: The seeds are held in small fruits.

Right: The plant is a fast-growing twining vine.

Yesterday, Today and Tomorrow

Brunfelsia calycina

This bushy, evergreen or semi-deciduous shrub has fragrant, deep indigo-blue flowers that age to white over three days. It is rather slow-growing, with foliage that is normally dense and medium green, although young leaves may turn purplish in cool weather. The flowers appear in spring with indigo, lavender-blue and white flowers all present on the bush at the same time, leading to its common name. Originally a native of Brazil, it has been widely planted throughout the tropics and may sometimes be encountered as a garden escapee.

Identification: Though it may grow to 3m/10ft, this shrub is often much smaller and freely branched. The leaves, 7.5–15cm/3–6in long, are oblong to lance-shaped, pointed, glossy deep green above and paler beneath, on short stalks. The flowers appear in clusters of one to ten at the ends of shoots or from the leaf axils; they are 2.5–7.5cm/1–3in across, with five spreading, rounded, overlapping lobes and a tube up to 4cm/1½in long, purple with a conspicuous white eye at the mouth, ringed with blue.

Distribution: Brazil.
Height and spread: 3m/10ft.
Habit and form: Shrub.
Pollinated: Insect.
Leaf shape: Oblong to oblong-lanceolate.

Far left and left: The flowers emerge a deep indigo blue and fade to white over three days.

Red Angel's Trumpet

Brugmansia sanguinea syn. *Datura sanguinea*

Distribution: North and central Colombia to northern Chile.
Height and spread: 11m/36ft.
Habit and form: Arborescent shrub.
Pollinated: Hummingbird.
Leaf shape: Ovate to oblong.

This small, shrubby tree, native to the Andes, is most noted for its large drooping flowers, which are brilliant orange-red at the mouth with yellow veins, fading to yellow at the base. They are produced in great profusion during the growing season. The velvety, grey-green leaves further enhance the look of this striking plant. It prefers cool, moist areas in mountains, where it is pollinated by hummingbirds. It was originally restricted to north and central Colombia to northern Chile, but it has been widely cultivated, with many cultivars now in existence, and is often encountered as a garden escapee outside its original range.

Identification: The young growth of this tree-like shrub is softly downy, and the branches are leafy near the tips. The broadly lance-shaped, wavy-edged leaves are alternate, up to 18cm/7in long. The pendent flowers are up to 25cm/10in long, emerging from a tubular, hairy, toothed calyx; the corolla is narrowly tubular, bright orange-red, yellow-green at the base, veined yellow, with backward-curving 2.5cm/1in lobes. The fruits, which are enclosed within the persistent calyx, are egg-shaped, downy and pale green to yellow.

Above: The flowerhead is greenish before it opens fully.

Far left: Brugmansia is a tree-like shrub.

Juanulloa mexicana
This rare species has a scattered distribution in semi-deciduous and wet forest habitats from Mexico to Colombia, Ecuador and Peru. It is pollinated by hummingbirds, and occurs as a hemi-epiphyte or liana climbing tree trunks, with the tubular orange flowers often going unnoticed among the tree canopy.

Chilean Jessamine *Cestrum parqui*
This small- to medium-sized, upright shrub, native to seasonally wet forests in southern South America, bears dense panicles of greenish-yellow flowers at the branch tips. The flowers are fragrant nocturnally and are pollinated by moths. After the flowering period come the glossy black or purplish fruits, which are favoured by various birds. The seed is spread by birds and floodwater.

Beach Morning Glory
Calystegia soldanella
This common but attractive seaside plant has an extremely wide global distribution, commonly found on many coastlines in both temperate and tropical regions.
It is usually prostrate, unlike its climbing relations, and has distinctive, kidney-shaped leaves. The bright pink flowers, with five white stripes and a yellowish centre, fade quickly through the day.

Painted Tongue

Salpiglossis sinuata

This branching annual or occasionally biennial plant is from the southern Andes. Its velvety funnel-shaped flowers, which resemble those of a petunia, are often veined and overlaid in contrasting colours. The leaves are mostly basal, and the flowers are borne on long stems above them. The plant has been widely cultivated, with many varieties raised in gardens. It may occasionally be encountered as an escapee from cultivation where conditions are suited for its growth.

Identification: The plant has sticky, branching stems and leaves up to 10cm/4in long, alternate, elliptic to narrow oblong, wavy-edged, toothed or deeply divided, on long stalks. The flowers, which appear in summer, are solitary, long-stalked, with a tubular calyx and funnel-shaped corolla with five notched, pleated lobes, up to 7.5cm/3in long and 5cm/2in across. They are yellow to ochre, mauve-scarlet or violet-blue with darker purple veins or markings.

Distribution: Southern Andes, South America.
Height and spread: 60cm/2ft.
Habit and form: Annual.
Pollinated: Insect.
Leaf shape: Elliptic to narrow oblong.

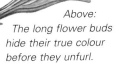

Above: The long flower buds hide their true colour before they unfurl.

Below: The sticky, branched flower stems arise from a mass of basal leaves.

FIGWORT AND COFFEE FAMILIES

The figwort family (Scrophulariaceae) comprises mostly herbs but also a few small shrubs, with about 190 genera and 4,000 species, the majority of which are found in temperate areas, including tropical mountains. The coffee family (Rubiaceae) is very large with about 630 genera and 10,200 species. It is diverse, including trees, shrubs, lianas and herbs, centred mainly in the tropics and subtropics.

Sand Lady's Slipper

Calceolaria uniflora

This remarkable flower is native to the extreme south of South America, in Argentina and Tierra del Fuego. It has become a favourite among specialist alpine gardeners, not least because of its showy and unusual flowers. The common name is confusing – although it likes sandy soil, the name 'lady's slipper' is normally applied to orchids of the genus *Cypripedium*. The British genus common name is Slipper Flower or Slipperwort. In the wild it grows in exposed, windy sites on well-drained soils. In cultivation it is challenging to grow, requiring free-draining compost and grit. Birds may be involved in pollination and apparently peck at the white patch on the flower's lip.

Identification: The leaves grow in flat rosettes and are about 3cm/1¼in long, slightly hairy, with tiny teeth. Each plant produces one or two flowers. These are yellow, with a long oblong lower lip, dotted red and with a large white blob at the tip.

Left: The striking flowers appear almost oversized in comparison to the plant's height.

Distribution: Patagonia and Tierra del Fuego.
Height and spread: To about 10cm/4in.
Habit and form: Perennial herb.
Pollinated: Bird, insect.
Leaf shape: Spoon-shaped.

Panama Rose

Rondeletia odorata

In Cuba this evergreen shrub grows in coastal rocky sites. It produces strongly scented clusters of orange and red flowers. There are about 150 species in this genus, mostly from South or Central America. The genus is named for Guillaume Rondelet (1507-1566) who was an influential botany teacher and professor at Montpellier in France. It should be grown in moist, slightly acid soil and is best propagated by cuttings or from seed.

Identification: The short-stalked leathery leaves are about 5cm/2in long, the largest to 10cm/4in, and have a rough margin. The flowers have striking yellow throats with a corolla tube that is about 15mm/½in long.

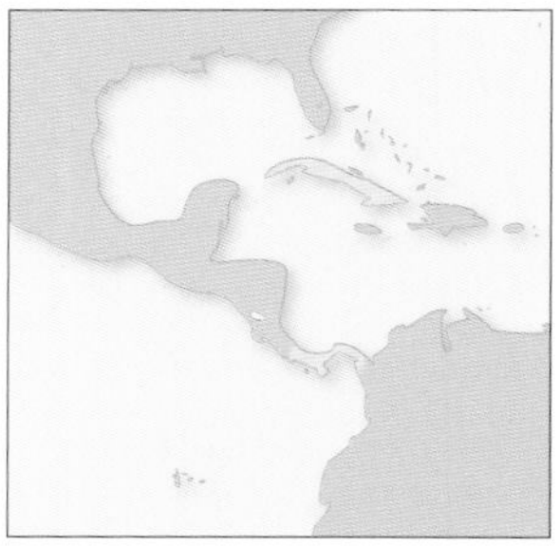

Distribution: Panama and Cuba.
Height and spread: To 3m/10ft.
Habit and form: Perennial shrub.
Pollinated: Probably moth.
Leaf shape: Ovate to oblong.

Left: The vivid flowers are highly fragrant.

Calceolaria purpurea

Distribution: Santiago region of Chile.
Height and spread: 60–80cm/24–32in.
Habit and form: Herbaceous perennial.
Pollinated: Insect.
Leaf shape: Ovate.

This striking herbaceous or occasionally woody perennial is a native of Chile, originating in the Santiago region. Its purple flowers have the balloon or sac-shaped lower lip that is characteristic of all of the species in this genus. The flowers are held on long, freely branching, leafy spikes above the foliage over a long period between summer and early autumn.

Identification: A herbaceous perennial, woody at the base, sticky to glandular, with tall, robust, branched stems. The wrinkled oval leaves, narrowing toward the leaf stalk and irregularly serrated, up to 12.5cm/5in long, form rosettes at the base. On the stem they are stalkless and opposite. The many-flowered inflorescences, freely branching, are held above the basal rosettes. The flowers are a bright purple-pink and look a little like two cushions or balloons.

OTHER SPECIES OF NOTE

Ourisia coccinea
This alpine species from the southern Andes of Chile is found in rocky soils, usually close by streams or near to running water. Its broadly elliptic or oblong leaves are held basally, with the 30cm/1ft flower panicles crowded at the top with scarlet, drooping flowers.

Calceolaria darwinii
This tiny alpine or sub-alpine herbaceous perennial originates from Tierra del Fuego and southern Patagonia, often in very exposed, well-drained sites from sea level to 1,200m/4,000ft. It flowers in the brief southern summer, revealing intricate, slipper-shaped large yellow flowers with ochre and blood-red streaks. It is thought to be bird-pollinated.

Mimulus naiandinus
A half-hardy perennial native to the Andes of Chile, which grows in damp, marshy sites and alongside streams. It was discovered in 1973, and has since become quite a popular garden plant, being easy to raise from seed. It produces pretty pale pink, yellow-throated flowers.

Ferdinandusa speciosa
This little tree produces spectacular terminal clusters of vivid red flowers. It is native to marshy habitats in Brazil, and is also grown, being well suited to glasshouse cultivation. In the wild it is pollinated mainly by two species of hummingbird.

Creeping Gloxinia

Mexican Twist, *Lophospermum erubescens*

This vigorous climbing plant is a native of the mountainous areas of Mexico, Jamaica, Venezuela and Columbia, occurring at altitudes of around 1,000m/3,300ft, but it is frequently found far outside this range as a garden escapee. It is sometimes classified with *Asarina*, but differs from this exclusively European genus in having five lobes on the flower, compared with the two lobes of the other genus. It has soft, hairy stems and leaves that give it the appearance of a creeping foxglove.

Distribution: Mexico, Jamaica, Venezuela and Colombia.
Height and spread: 3m/10ft.
Habit and form: Trailing vine.
Pollinated: Insect.
Leaf shape: Deltoid.

Identification: The plant is densely, softly downy and grey-green throughout, with stems that are woody at the base, softer and hairy above. The leaves, up to 7.5cm/3in long and 15cm/6in across, are more or less triangular, toothed, with twining leaf stalks. The flowers also have twining stalks, and leaf-like calyces with lobes 2.5cm/1in broad. The downy, trumpet-shaped, rose pink flowers are 7.5cm/3in long with five blunt or notched lobes and a tube swollen on one side, white, and marbled within. They appear in summer and autumn, followed by spherical capsules containing many winged seeds.

Left: The downy, rose-pink flowers have foxglove-like markings.

GENTIAN AND BELLFLOWER FAMILIES

Worldwide, the gentian family (Gentianaceae) comprises around 74 genera and 1,200 species, mainly herbs, and a few shrubs or small trees. The bellflower family (Campanulaceae) are herbs, shrubs or rarely small trees, usually with milky sap, comprising about 70 genera and 2,000 species. Many of the species of both families are highly ornamental and have become familiar plants in cultivation.

Star of Bethlehem

Hippobroma longiflora

This native of southern USA, southward to Brazil, Peru and the West Indies, is a perennial herb with poisonous milky sap. Its generic name, *Hippobroma*, translated from the Greek, means horse poison, indicating how potent it is. The plant has almost symmetrical star-shaped flowers with long tubes, which appear at various times of the year depending upon location.

Identification: The non-woody stem is green and smooth, with a rosette of narrow, stalkless, oval to lance-shaped, coarsely lobed leaves, with feathery veination and doubly toothed margins, mostly 10–15cm/4–6in long. The panicle usually comprises two to three white flowers on short, hairy stalks. The calyx is 2.5cm/1in long; the flowers are star-shaped with five pointed, spreading lobes, 2.5cm/1in long, on a narrow tube, usually 7.5–12cm/3–4in long. The twin-celled capsule is bell-shaped and downy, with numerous small seeds.

Left: The star-like flowers are held high on hairy stalks.

Distribution: Southern USA, Brazil, Peru and the West Indies.
Height and spread: 20–60cm/8–24in.
Habit and form: Herbaceous perennial.
Pollinated: Insect.
Leaf shape: Oblanceolate.

Hypsela reniformis

This unusual South American creeping plant is mainly found in Chile, but its range stretches from Ecuador to Tierra del Fuego, in mountainous regions along the Andes. It grows in moist open places, especially at the southern end of its range. The dense mats of small, rounded, shiny leaves are topped with upturned, pale pink, crimson-lipped flowers that make an eye-catching display during summer. It is a vigorous plant, spreading 30–60cm/1–2ft in a year.

Right: The pink flowers have a long tube and stamens. The flowering period lasts from June to September, making this a popular choice for gardeners. It is also known as Pixie Carpet.

Identification: This small, prostrate, creeping herb forms a dense mat of cover, with hairless stems up to 5cm/2in long. The often crowded leaves, up to 12mm/½in long, are elliptic to round or kidney-shaped. The solitary flowers, with two ascending and three descending petals, are white suffused with pink, veined carmine, yellow at the centre, and are borne throughout the summer months. They are followed in autumn by erect green berries.

Distribution: Western South America from Ecuador to Tierra del Fuego.
Height and spread: 5cm/2in; indefinite spread.
Habit and form: Prostrate, perennial herb.
Pollinated: Insect.
Leaf shape: Reniform.

Deer Meat

Centropogon cornutus

Distribution: South and Central America to the Antilles.
Height and spread: 3m/10ft if freestanding, but may reach 9m/30ft with support.
Habit and form: Shrub.
Pollinated: Probably hummingbird.
Leaf shape: Ovate.

This brightly coloured shrub is widespread from South and Central America to the Antilles. Its long tubular red flowers are designed to be pollinated by hummingbirds. Deer meat is water-tolerant and is often found growing along riverbanks, in low-lying wetland areas or in clearings in wet forest areas, particularly those where inundation is seasonal and there is a noticeable dry season. It is capable of forming a freestanding shrub but more often than not will scramble upward through other bushes and small trees to make a sizeable specimen.

Identification: An upright shrub with milky sap and oval, alternate, toothed leaves. The flowers are asymmetrical on long stalks, usually arising singly from the leaf axils near the top of the stems. Each flower is two-lipped, five-lobed, bright red or deep carmine to pale purple; the five-bearded anthers are united into a tube around the style. The corolla tube opens along the upper side, with two lobes above and three below. The fruit is a five-chambered fleshy berry, with the remains of the style persisting, giving a beaked appearance, with the five thin, pointed green sepals also persisting, giving a dome-like appearance.

OTHER SPECIES OF NOTE

Siphocampylus orbiginianus
A native of Bolivia, this is an impressive shrub reaching 2m/6½ft in height. It has mid-green leaves arranged in threes around the green stems, which are topped with long, tubular flowers. The blooms are red with yellow-green stripes down the tube and pointed, greenish or yellow lobes.

Lisianthus umbellatus
This shrub can reach 3.5m/12ft. It has leaves clustered at the ends of its branches, and it bears numerous dense umbels of sweetly scented yellow-and-green flowers. The species occurs only in Jamaica, where it and several closely related species are found across the mountainous areas.

Centropogon coccineus
This striking plant is one of about 230 species in the tropical bellflower genus. This species, from Brazil, is a hairless shrub growing to about 90cm/3ft. It has pendulous, deep crimson flowers that are attractive to the hummingbirds that pollinate the plant.

Lisianthus capitatus
This plant resembles *L. umbellatus* except that it has almost stalkless flowers. Also like *L. umbellatus*, it hails from Jamaica, but is rather more widespread, and locally common at the edges of woodland on limestone between 305–915m/1000–3000ft above sea level.

Flor de Muerto

Lisianthus nigrescens

The flor de muerto, so named because it was a favoured decoration for graves in southern Mexico, is native only to the states of Veracruz, Oaxaca and Chiapas. It is an intriguing plant and one of the rarities of the plant world, as it bears a true black flower. It has been collected since it was first described in 1831, although documented collections number less than two dozen. Despite its unusual character it is virtually unknown in cultivation or for that matter outside its native range.

Identification: A large-stalked shrub, rather open and much branched, with smooth stems. The stalkless leaves are oblong to lance-shaped with pointed tips and three to five veins, nearly united at the base. The stems are crowned with tall, flower spikes, to 1m/39in long, covered with nodding flowers 5cm/2in across, with spreading lobes, recurved at the tips; the stamens do not protrude beyond the mouth of the flower. Depending on the angle at which they are viewed the flowers appear blackish-purple or inky-black, with a satiny texture.

Distribution: Veracruz, Oaxaca, and Chiapas, southern Mexico.
Height and spread: 2m/6½ft.
Habit and form: Shrub.
Pollinated: Insect.
Leaf shape: Oblong-lanceolate.

Left: The flowers are inky black and have a satiny texture.

PINEAPPLE FAMILY

*Almost entirely restricted to tropical and subtropical America, the pineapple family (Bromeliaceae)
consists of 2,400 species in about 60 genera. As well as the familiar pineapple, it includes many epiphytic
species (some called 'air plants') and also the strange dangling Spanish moss (Tillandsia usneoides).*

Friendship Plant

Queen's Tears, *Billbergia nutans*

There are some 54 species in
the genus found from
Mexico southwards. This
fine bromeliad grows
epiphytically (attached to
another plant) in its natural
environment, forming clumps,
but adapts well to being grown
terrestrially. It should be kept in
partial shade in a slightly acid soil.
Curiously, it can be
persuaded to flower by enclosing the plant in
a plastic bag with a ripe apple for about a
week. It should then come into flower in
one or two months. This is triggered by
the ethylene given off by the apple. The
flowers are purple-edged with green
centred petals that roll up to expose long
light green filaments, heavy with pollen.
The leaves are long and slender.

Identification: The leaves are
narrow and scaly beneath, often
with toothed margins. The
inflorescence is tall and arching
with slender pink overlapping
bracts, contrasting
with pale yellow-
green flowers,
each with a pale
pink calyx.

Distribution: Northern
Argentina, Paraguay, Uruguay
and southern Brazil.
Height and spread:
To 40cm/16in.
Habit and form: Perennial
epiphyte.
Pollinated: Insect.
Leaf shape: Narrow, toothed.

*Left: The plant has an
elegant, arching habit,
with vivid flowers that dangle
from the slender pink and
green stems.*

Pitcairnia corrallina

This unusual bromeliad has brilliant red
flower clusters that seem to creep along the
forest floor. It grows in swamps and near
streams in a limited area of Colombia.
There are about 260 species of these
pineapple relatives, nearly all found in South
and Central America. The garden hybrid
P. x *darblayana* is the result of crossing this
species with *P. paniculata*; it has brick-red
sepals and vivid red petals.

Identification: The
long, red, arched
inflorescence
contrasts with the
green leaves.
The latter are
strap-like with
toothed margins.
The red petals do
not open far and
their lobes are
edged white.

Distribution: Colombia.
Height and spread: 1m/3ft.
Habit and form:
Perennial herb.
Pollinated: Hummingbird,
insect.
Leaf shape: Linear-
lanceolate.

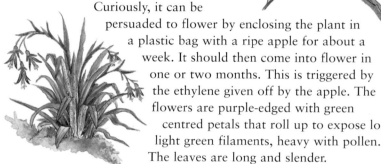

*Above:The vividly-coloured flower spikes fall to the
ground. Like many pitcairnias, this plant prefers
shady woodland areas.*

*Centre: The narrow, tube-like
flowers are ideally suited to
pollination by hummingbirds.*

Left: The leaves are lanceolate.

Pink Quill

Tillandsia cyanea

Distribution: Ecuador and Peru.
Height and spread: To 25cm/10in.
Habit and form: Perennial epiphyte.
Pollinated: Insect, bird.
Leaf shape: Linear to triangular.

Pink quill is well named; its flattened spike of overlapping pink bracts is unusual and decorative. It has become very popular as a houseplant and is not hard to grow. The foliage is impressive through the year and the flower spike, which lasts for several months, produces large purple flowers set against the bright pink bracts. It was once common in the rainforests of western Ecuador but is now much rarer, having been over-collected. Luckily it thrives in cultivation, being raised from seed and also using tissue culture techniques.

Identification: Epiphytic (grows upon another plant) with arched, lanceolate leaves with pointed, thick apex. The inflorescence, which appears in the winter, is a spike of overlapping pink bracts with blue-violet blooms.

Right: Blue-violet flowers appear one by one from the tips of the bracts.

Right: The plant forms a rosette of slender, arching leaves.

OTHER SPECIES OF NOTE

Rainbow Plant *Billbergia chlorosticta*
A colourful epiphytic species from Brazil, which grows to about 50cm/20in and has toothed leaves that are red-brown below and mottled creamy-white. The arching inflorescence has large red bracts and greenish-yellow, blue-tipped flowers. It thrives in a warm, damp atmosphere.

Billbergia zebrina
In the wild this grows on trees in temperate and subtropical forests in central and southern Brazil. It has very attractive leaves that are up to 90cm/3ft long and purple-bronze with silver bands, in a vase-shaped cluster. The greenish-yellow petals contrast with the pink bracts.

Pitcairnia nigra
Another weird and wonderful species that grows wild in Ecuador, and is often grown in cultivation. Its leaves are up to 15cm/6in across. The flower spike is about 50cm/20in long, arising from a stalk of some 20cm/8in. The flowers are pale at the base and blackish-purple at the tip.

Spanish Moss
Tillandsia usneoides
This member of the family couldn't look much less like a pineapple! It resembles a moss or lichen and dangles from trees, as long as 7m/23ft. It was once used for stuffing mattresses. It grows from Argentina and Chile, north to the south-eastern USA.

Tillandsia lindeniana

There are about 400 members of this fascinating genus, many of them epiphytes, ranging from the southern US through Central and South America. Their leaves are usually tightly packed and in most species covered in absorbent hairs, enabling them to take in moisture from damp air and mist. This species has a large rosette of long thin leaves. It is native to the Andes of Ecuador and Peru and was introduced into cultivation in the 1860s. It has rather large deep blue flowers. Garden forms include one with red bracts and white flowers.

Identification: The long narrow leaves grow to about 40cm/16in, arching decoratively. The flattened inflorescence is about 20cm/8in long with waxy overlapping pinkish and green bracts, and the blue flowers have spreading petals.

Distribution: Ecuador and Peru.
Height and spread: To 80cm/31½in.
Habit and form: Perennial epiphyte.
Pollinated: Insect.
Leaf shape: Linear.

Above: The plant takes root in a tree.

Left and centre: The inflorescence is vivid pink, with blue flowers.

Queen Mary Bromeliad

Aechmea mariae-reginae

This genus contains about 170 perennial herbs with strap-like leaves, often with spiny margins and forming a funnel- or tank-like base. They are native to South and Central America, and most grow as epiphytes anchored to the branches of forest trees. The locals of the Caribbean coast of Costa Rica revere the flower and use the plants to decorate their churches. This is a rather rare species growing in the tops of tall trees. The flowerhead is remarkable: a woolly white cone-shaped structure over 50cm/20in long with pink bracts dangling from its base. It is grown in botanic gardens and can be propagated by cuttings.

Distribution: Costa Rica.
Height and spread: 1.2m/4ft across.
Habit and form: Perennial herb.
Pollinated: Hummingbird.
Leaf shape: Strap-shaped.

Identification: A large plant over 1m/3ft tall when in flower. The flowers are white with a tinge of blue at the tips of the petals, turning red later. Male and female flowers are on separate plants (the plant is dioecious). The bright pink bracts form a skirt-like base to the inflorescence.

Left: The bright pink bracts fold right back to expose the unusual flower head.

Right: The flowers turn from blue to red at the tip as they mature.

Puya raimondii

This, one of about 170 species, is the largest known bromeliad, and one of the world's most impressive plants. The rosette of spiky leaves alone reaches 3m/10ft, but when it flowers, the inflorescence can reach a truly staggering 12m/40ft! In its natural habitat in the Andes of Peru and Bolivia it takes 80-100 years to flower. Then it grows the huge mass of over 8,000 individual flowers that last for about three months. The spiky rosettes of pointed waxy leaves are inhabited by many animals, including nesting birds, and the flowers are pollinated by several species of hummingbird. It is grown in several botanic gardens, and when it flowers it becomes a magnet for visitors and a major tourist attraction.

Identification: The tough leaves form a dense rosette up to 2m/6½ft long, scaly beneath and with hooked spines along the margins. The inflorescence is up to 12m/ 40ft tall and 2.4m/8ft broad with thousands of white flowers.

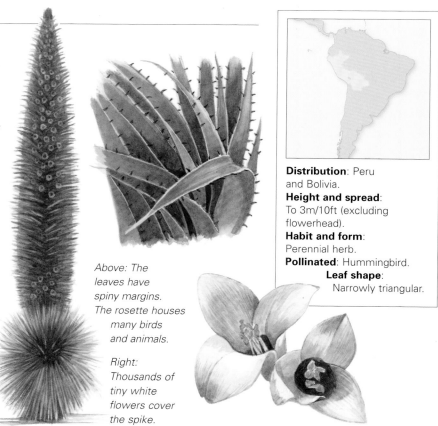

Above: The leaves have spiny margins. The rosette houses many birds and animals.

Right: Thousands of tiny white flowers cover the spike.

Distribution: Peru and Bolivia.
Height and spread: To 3m/10ft (excluding flowerhead).
Habit and form: Perennial herb.
Pollinated: Hummingbird.
Leaf shape: Narrowly triangular.

Canistropsis billbergioides

Distribution: Brazil.
Height and spread: 45cm/18in.
Habit and form: Perennial herb.
Pollinated: Insect.
Leaf shape: Strap-shaped.

Right: The plant puts on its most colourful display from May to September.

A popular houseplant, this species is an epiphyte that has become rather rare in the wild through collection. It grows in the lower forest canopy in the rainforests of south-eastern Brazil. Being rainforest species they are used to shade and so make good houseplants. They are also surprisingly hardy for tropical species. Several varieties exist, such as 'Citron', 'Persimmon', 'Blood Orange' and 'Tutti Frutti'.

Identification: Large green leaves surround a colourful cluster of overlapping bracts that may be orange, pink, red or yellow. The actual flowers are inside the cup-like bracts and are white or greenish-white, opening from May to September. The leaves vary from green to lavender.

Left: The small, white flowers have four petals. They nestle at the centre of the bright, showy bracts.

OTHER SPECIES OF NOTE

Nidularium fulgens
This popular houseplant comes from Brazil. It is protected in a National Park as it has been severely over-collected in the past. It has lime-green leaves with darker spots and an orange, pink or red floral rosette of brightly coloured bracts. The actual flowers are blue and white.

Vriesea heiroglyphica
An epiphytic bromeliad from the Brazilian Atlantic rainforests, this grows large – to 2m/6½ft tall – and has beautifully marked green and white leaves, and cream flowers on a tall stalk. The flowers stay open at night, when bats are the main visitors.

Sapphire Tower
Puya alpestris
This native of Chile has arching white-scaled hooked leaves. When flowering it grows to 1.5m/5ft tall, producing a branching pyramidal electric blue-green inflorescence with contrasting orange stamens. It may be grown in full sun or partial shade and can stand quite high temperatures.

Ochagavia carnea (=*lindleyana*)
Originating from Chile, this plant is now well known in cultivation. It has a rosette of up to 50 stiff, toothed leaves and a many-flowered, rounded inflorescence with bright rose-pink bracts and petals.

Guzmania wittmackii

There are about 125 species in this genus of evergreen epiphytes, named after the Spanish naturalist Anastasio Guzman who died in 1802. Their colourful stems and bracts have made them popular in cultivation, but several species are threatened in the wild. Hummingbirds and bats are some of the major pollinators. The long primary bracts range from pink to orange and red, and the flowers are white or yellow. This species is a parent of many bromeliad cultivars including the famous 'Orangeade'.

Identification: The leaves reach 85cm/33in long and are slightly scaly. The inflorescence is bright red and rather leaf-like with red floral bracts and a creamy white stalk.

Distribution: Colombia and Ecuador.
Height and spread: 50cm/20in.
Habit and form: Perennial herb.
Pollinated: Hummingbird.
Leaf shape: Strap-like.

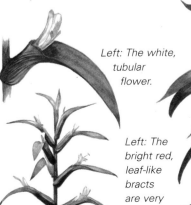

Left: The white, tubular flower.

Left: The bright red, leaf-like bracts are very striking.

BANANA AND GINGER FAMILIES

The banana family (Musaceae) are tropical perennial herbs, with six genera and about 200 species.
As well as bananas, they contain strelitzias and heliconias, the latter genus with about 100 species.
Gingers, the Zingiberaceae, are perennial herbs, mostly with creeping horizontal or tuberous rhizomes,
comprising about 50 genera and about 1,100 species with a wide distribution, mainly in the tropics.

Parrot's Beak

Popokaytongo, *Heliconia psittacorum*

This herbaceous, upright, small *Heliconia*, native to Central and South America, is highly variable. It is found in forests, although it is also common in meadows and some savannas, like buttercups in cooler regions, usually forming dense clonal colonies with erect, leafy shoots in groups of 50 or more. It generally grows to no more than 60cm/2ft tall. Parrot's beaks are exotic flowers, consisting of orange-red bracts with a dark spot at the end, arising from a central point on the stem. They are abundantly produced all year round.

Distribution: Central and northern South America.
Height and spread: 60cm/2ft.
Habit and form: Herbaceous perennial.
Pollinated: Hummingbird.
Leaf shape: Obovate.

Identification: A rhizomatous herbaceous plant with pseudostems composed of overlapping, sheathing leaf bases. The large leaves, in two vertical ranks with smooth margins, resemble those of bananas. The flowers, in erect or pendent inflorescences, consist of brightly coloured, leaf-like bracts, arranged on two sides or spirally, each subtending a coiled cyme of flowers, each flower in turn subtended by a membranous floral bract; the true flower consists of two whorls joined at the base with varying degrees of fusion within and between the whorls. The fruit is a one to three-seeded drupe, blue or red to orange at maturity.

Right: The bright orange flowers are produced abundantly throughout the year.

Wild Plantain

Balisier, *Heliconia caribaea*

The tree-like *Heliconia caribaea* is actually a herbaceous plant, the stems being made up of leaf bases. It is native to Jamaica, east Cuba and St Vincent, although it has been widely planted outside this range and, along with its numerous cultivars, has become naturalized across tropical America and beyond. The flowers can be held high on tall stems with the red spathes contrasting vividly with the white flowers. The blue fruit that follows is also eye-catching.

Distribution: Jamaica, East Cuba and St Vincent, West Indies.
Height and spread: 2.5–5m/8–16ft.
Habit and form: Tree-like herbaceous plant.
Pollinated: Hummingbird.
Leaf shape: Oblong.

Identification: Large pseudostems arise from a thick underground rhizome. The leaves are up to 1.2m/4ft long, oblong, with an abruptly pointed tip and rounded base, on leaf stalks up to 60cm/2ft long, often glaucous or thickly waxy. The inflorescence is 20–40cm/ 8–16in long, erect and straight, with 6–15 bracts up to 25cm/10in long arranged in two overlapping rows; they are broadly triangular, red or yellow, sometimes with green or yellow keels and tips. Each bract bears 9–22 flowers with straight or slightly curved sepals up to 6cm/2½in long, white with green tips; the upper sepals curve upward, the lower sepals are spreading. The fruits are up to 15mm/⅝in long.

Left: The tree-like growth resembles a banana plant and gives rise to the common name.

Expanded Lobster Claw

Heliconia latispatha

This tree-like herbaceous plant is native to Mexico, and Central and South America, although it is very widely cultivated and has become naturalized far outside this range. It is frequently found along forest edges growing in full sun to half shade. There is some colour variation in the bracts, ranging from orange to red. The erect inflorescences of spirally arranged bracts appear all year round, but more abundantly from late spring through summer, with each inflorescence lasting for several weeks on the plant.

Distribution: Mexico, Central and South America.
Height and spread: 3m/10ft.
Habit and form: Tree-like herbaceous plant.
Pollinated: Hummingbird.
Leaf shape: Broadly oblong to ovate.

Right: The inflorescence stem curls in alternating arcs between each of the claw-shaped flower bracts.

Identification: Pseudostems arise from a thick underground rhizome. The leaves are up to 1.5m/5ft long, broadly oblong oval, sometimes edged red. The inflorescence is 30–50cm/12–20in long, erect, held above the leaves; it consists of 20–30 slender, spreading keeled bracts, spirally arranged, not overlapping, dark red or orange to green-yellow; the flowers are yellow, edged and tipped with green.

OTHER SPECIES OF NOTE

Spiral Ginger *Costus malortieanus*
A familiar sight in the rainforests of Costa Rica down as far as Brazil. Spiral ginger is most noteworthy for its spiralling stems, which are thought to be an adaptation to make the best of available light. The pyramidal flower spikes are held at the end of leafy stems, with one small, tubular, yellow flower arising from each bract.

Shining Bird of Paradise *Heliconia metallica*
Native from Honduras to Bolivia, this *Heliconia* is more noteworthy for its handsome foliage than its pretty but comparatively less significant inflorescences. The leaves are a satiny dark green with a light midrib and often a wine-purple underside. The pink or red flowers and greenish bracts are held on long stalks away from the leaves.

Hanging Heliconia
Heliconia rostrata
This native of Colombia, Venezuela, Ecuador, Peru and Bolivia is frequently found at relatively low elevations, along seasonally flooded Amazon tributaries. Its popularity in cultivation has led to its spread throughout the tropical world. Pendent inflorescences of red and yellow bracts last for several weeks on the plant. It is also known as Lobster Claw.

Monkada

Renealmia cernua

Monkada is a tall and showy ginger plant, with hard and waxy orange and yellow bracts held terminally and reminiscent of a pineapple. The light green foliage is wavy on the edges and notable for its "ginger" scent when crushed. It is most commonly encountered in humid areas and on slopes beneath trees, being widely distributed in forested tropical regions from Mexico to South America.

Distribution: Central and South America.
Height and spread: 90cm–5m/3–16ft tall.
Habit and form: Herbaceous.
Pollinated: Birds and probably insects.
Leaf shape: Elliptic.

Below: The waxy orange and yellow bracts are somewhat pineapple-like.

Identification: An aromatic perennial herb, 90cm–5m/3–16ft tall with leafy stems, leaves two ranked. The leaves are 10–45cm/4–18in long, narrowly elliptic, acuminate, glabrous. Inflorescence racemose, terminal on long stems, to 25cm/10in long, ovoid, bracts red to yellow, sometimes tinged green, triangular, acute. Calyx to 12mm/½in long, tubular, three-lobed, same colour as bracts; corolla to 2.5cm/1in long, yellow to white; petals to 8mm/⅜in long, lip erect, not spreading, three lobed, to 8mm/⅜in long, yellow to white, ovate, base and margin pubescent. The fruit is a fleshy capsule.

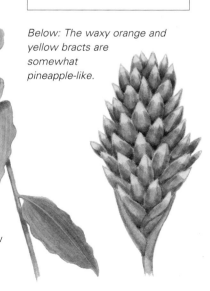

LILY FAMILY

The lily family (Liliaceae) is a large and complex family, mostly consisting of perennial herbs that grow from starchy rhizomes, corms or bulbs. It comprises about 290 genera and 4,950 species, including many ornamental flowers as well as several important agricultural crops. They are found throughout the world, especially in dry areas, in warm and temperate regions.

Barbados Lily

Hippeastrum puniceum

Hippeastrum means horse star, and probably refers to the large size of the star-like blooms. Barbados Lily is the most widespread species in its genus, common in open situations and common across Barbados as well as Central America, the West Indies and much of tropical South America. Its tall stems bear between two and four large, elegant, bright red, orange or pink flowers, which have a beautiful fragrance and attract bees, hummingbirds and butterflies. A mature plant may bloom for 10 months of the year. In some areas, such as Hawaii, it is considered to be invasive.

Identification: There are four–six bright green leaves at 30–60cm/1–2ft long and about 3cm/1in wide, tapering to a tip. Two–four tubular flowers per plant top a simple stem. The tepals are usually orange, but may rarely be pink or even white. They are about 7cm/3in in length. The tube is either the same colour as the tepals or green. The style is long, exceeding the stamens by about 1cm/½in. The bulb is ovoid and about 4–5cm/1½–2in in diameter.

Above: The flower heads dangle above the 60cm/2ft long leaves.

Distribution: West Indies, Central and northern South America.
Height and spread: 40–60cm/1½–2ft tall.
Habit and form: Bulbous perennial.
Pollinated: Insect and bird.
Leaf shape: Strap-shaped.

Left: The plant is often found alongside irrigation ditches, and favours disturbed sites.

Urceolina urceolata

Confined to the Peruvian Andes, this bulbous perennial has curiously shaped flowers that hang down on slender stalks. The lower part of the stalk-like flower tube swells abruptly into an urn-like upper part, giving rise to the generic name, which means "little pitcher". The stalked leaves usually develop later than the flowers, which are normally yellow with green-and-white tips.

Left: The yellow flowers with green tips appear in spring and are up to 8cm/2¾in long.

Identification: Four hairless, oval to oblong, pointed leaves, up to 50cm/20in long and 15cm/6in wide, bright green above, paler below, on 10cm/4in stalks, appear at the same times as the flowers. In spring and summer, a leafless, solitary stem bears a small umbel of four to six nodding, tubular flowers up to 10cm/4in long, the upper two thirds urn-shaped, usually yellow, more rarely cinnabar-red, orange or white, with green tips and sometimes with white margins. The fruit that follows is a capsule.

Distribution: Peruvian Andes.
Height and spread: 30cm/12in.
Habit and form: Herbaceous, bulbous perennial.
Pollinated: Insect.
Leaf shape: Ovate to oblong.

Distribution: Colombia to Chile.
Height and spread: 45cm/18in.
Habit and form: Herbaceous bulbous perennial.
Pollinated: Insect.
Leaf shape: Linear.

Right: The plant looks similar to wild onion at first sight.

Glory of the Sun

Leucocoryne ixioides

This South American bulbous plant is distantly related to the onions, *Allium* species, differing in having three fertile stamens instead of six. The plant's name is derived from the Greek words *leukos* meaning "white" and *koryne* meaning "club" referring to the prominent, infertile anthers. The flowers appear in spring and can be white, pink or pale lilac, with the plant being very variable in its wild setting. Ranging from Colombia to Valparaiso, it is especially abundant between the region of Coquimbo and the river Bío Bío in Chile.

Identification: The leaves are basal, slender and grass-like, withering before the flowers appear. Six to nine fragrant flowers in a loose umbel appear in spring on stalks up to 6.5cm/2½in long; they have six tepals, with the lower parts fused into a white basal tube and the upper parts free and spreading, white or more usually deeply edged lilac to violet blue. Three slender, cylindrical yellow-white staminodes, sometimes with dark tips, are joined to the perianth at the mouth of the basal tube.

OTHER SPECIES OF NOTE

Golden Lily-of-the-Incas
Alstroemeria aurea
This spreading, tuberous perennial, native to Chile and Brazil, has become a very popular garden plant. The stems carry lance-shaped, twisted leaves, which are topped during the summer by loose heads of yellow or orange flowers, tipped with green and usually streaked with dark red, usually in clusters at the end of thin leafy stems.

Coicopihue *Philesia magellanica*
This small, low-growing shrub has deep rose, waxy flowers. It is a fairly common evergreen plant in the cold, wet, swampy rainforests of southern Chile. It has a "box-like" habit of growth, spreading by subterranean stolons that can grow up to 1.2m/4ft. The leaves are small, leathery and glossy green.

Green Amaryllis *Hippeastrum calyptratum*
From the Brazillian coastal rainforests, this epiphyte has shapely greenish-yellow flowers that emit a rather sour odour, and this attracts bats as pollinators. It is a vulnerable species in the wild, having been over-collected.

Leucocoryne purpurea
One of the most beautiful species in this genus of 12 from Chile, where it grows in Mediterranean scrub. Its grass-like leaves dry and wither and are then followed by an impressive display of purple flowers, between three and eight to each stem. In some areas it flowers in colonies along the roadsides. It can be propagated from corms or from seed and grown under glass in cooler climates.

Inca Lily

Peruvian Lily *Alstroemeria pelegrina*

Distribution: Chile.
Height and spread: To 60cm/2ft.
Habit and form: Perennial herb.
Pollinated: Insect.
Leaf shape: Lanceolate.

One of 50 species of South American lilies, the Inca Lily is important as a wild ancestor of many hybrids that are now cultivated throughout the world, partly for the cut flower industry. Yet in the wild it has a very restricted range, being found only in a certain part of the Mediterranean region of Chile, where it grows in dry scrub habitats, often among rocks close to the Pacific shore. Many of these sites are threatened by property development.

Identification: The flowers are mainly pink, with white and yellow markings towards the centre; they open in summer and autumn. They are either solitary or in groups of two or three. The stems grow from a network of underground fleshy roots and rhizomes.

Right: The flowers have six tepals with striking markings.

Far right: The seedpod opening.

Amazon Lily

Eucharis amazonica

This is one of the best-known members of this genus of South American lilies, which contains some 17 species. In the wild it grows in north-eastern Peru, where it is known from only a few populations in the rainforests of the lower slopes of the eastern Andes. It has large dark green leaves and large white flowers that are sweetly-scented. As many as six flowers develop on leafless stalks in the early summer. The Amazon Lily has become a much-prized species among keen gardeners and is not difficult to grow. It thrives outdoors in tropical and subtropical climates, and can also be grown in containers, either outside or as a houseplant. Although its natural habitat is damp, flowering may be induced by subjecting the plants to short dry spells.

Identification: The long, elliptic leaves are rather wavy, with a sharp tip. The flowers have a long, curved tube, and open, spreading ovate lobes, to 9cm/3½in across. At the centre of each flower is a toothed cup-shaped structure formed from the fused stamens.

Above and right: The flowers are white and daffodil-like in shape. The leaves are dark and highly glossy.

Distribution: Peru.
Height and spread: To 60cm/2ft.
Habit and form: Perennial herb.
Pollinated: Insect.
Leaf shape: Elliptic.

Cojomaria

Paramongaia weberbaueri

This magnificent flower, the only member of its genus, is a rare endemic from the western foothills of the Andes of Peru and Bolivia. Only three wild populations are known, and sadly it is often picked by locals for sale in markets. Its bright daffodil-like, yellow fragrant flowers have made it a great favourite. Cojomaria has the largest flowers of any member of the amaryllis section of the lily family. In cultivation it is best grown in containers, and can be propagated from seed, although it does demand carefully controlled growing conditions.

Identification: The individual flowers can reach 20cm/8in across, with a tube 10cm/4in long, and six spreading lobes. From the centre extends the trumpet-like corona with the stalks of the stamens attached below the rim.

Above: The flowers resemble daffodils but are very large and have a wonderful scent.

Right: The plant is rarely found in the wild and over-collection threatens existing colonies.

Distribution: Bolivia and Peru.
Height and spread: To 60cm/2ft.
Habit and form: Bulbous herb.
Pollinated: Insect.
Leaf shape: Linear, narrow.

Blue Amaryllis

Worsleya rayneri

Blue amaryllis is another species in a genus all of its own. With its spectacular clusters of lilac or pale blue flowers, it has gained an almost legendary status among gardeners. It has a perilous existence in the wild, being found in just two sites in the mountains north of Rio de Janeiro. As these habitats are rather inaccessible, it is not easily collected, but fires pose a problem in the dry season. It is a challenge to cultivate it, partly because its roots have a moisture-collecting outer layer and must be undisturbed to function efficiently.

Distribution: Organ Mountains, Brazil.
Height and spread: 2m/6½ft.
Habit and form: Evergreen bulbous perennial.
Pollinated: Insect.
Leaf shape: Strap-shaped.

Identification: An evergreen bulbous perennial with narrow strap-shaped curving leaves to 1m/3ft long. The flowers develop in terminal umbels of four to six flowers. The blue or mauve funnel-shaped perianth has curving lobes spreading from a tubular base.

OTHER SPECIES OF NOTE

Peruvian Lily Vine
Bomarea caldasii
In the Andes of Colombia and Ecuador this lily is quite common at altitudes of 1,830–3,660m/ 6,000–12,000 ft. The flowers, growing in dangling clusters, are either orange-red or yellow. It is a half-hardy climber suited to a sunny border or greenhouse in cooler regions.

Griffinia liboniana
This species is endemic to the Atlantic rainforests of Brazil, where it is endangered by habitat loss. It has pretty flowers with lilac and white spreading lobes. It is best grown in shady moist conditions, either outside in tropical or subtropical regions, or as a container plant in temperate climates.

Chilean Bellflower Copihue, *Lapageria rosea*
Plant enthusiasts regard this plant highly, as one of the finest of temperate climbers. It is a woody, twining vine producing large numbers of red, waxy bell-like flowers, contrasting well with the lush, deep green evergreen leaves. If frost protected, it does well in temperate regions.

Pamianthe peruviana
An epiphyte from the mountain rainforests of the western Andes of Bolivia and Peru, this species has large, fragrant white flowers. The segments surrounding the central corona have a central green stripe.

Chilean Blue Crocus

Tecophilaea cyanocrocus

Sometimes placed in a separate family (Tecophilaeaceae), this pretty flower was saved from extinction by re-introduction from cultivated stock. The wild distribution is very limited – high alpine meadows near Santiago in Chile, at altitudes of about 3,000m/10,000ft, where it was reduced to apparent eradication by grazing and over-collection. Luckily, two wild populations were then found, in 2001. It is rather tricky to grow, requiring cool conditions and gritty soil, but rewards with displays of deep blue or blue and white flowers.

Identification: The narrow leaves grow to about 12.5cm/5in. The flowers are about 3.5cm/1½in across, gentian blue and veined, sometimes with a white margin, or white in the neck.

Left: The plants grow to about 10cm/4in tall.

Distribution: Chile.
Height and spread: 10cm/4in.
Habit and form: Perennial herb.
Pollinated: Insect.
Leaf shape: Linear-lanceolate.

Below: The flowers are a deep, unusual blue with white centres.

ORCHID FAMILY

The orchid family (Orchidaceae) is widespread and spectacular with respect to its diversity in the Americas. The northern continent shares many genera with Eurasia, and even where species have been separated by geographic isolation for long periods, such as those found in South America, they often show a striking similarity to species found in similar habitats elsewhere on the planet.

Masdevallia tricallosa

This orchid occurs in Peru, in wet montane forests at altitudes of around 2,000m/6,500ft. It may grow as an epiphyte, terrestrial or lithophyte. It often goes unnoticed in the canopy, partly because it is out of view, but also because the small rhizomatous growth is easily overlooked when not in bloom. It is distinguished by its distinctive white flower, which appears in the rainy season, singly on a short stalk. The actual petals are deep inside the flower, but the three sepals are very showy, with long tails.

Identification: Spreading epiphyte, growing from a short, creeping rhizome from which (unusually for the genus) appear minute pseudobulbs. The blackish, erect, slender ramicauls, are enveloped basally by two to three tubular sheaths, carrying a single, apical, erect, leathery, yet pliable, ovate to elliptical or lanceolate leaf. The inflorescence is erect and slender, 5cm/2in long; single flowered, arising from low on the ramicaul, with a bract below the middle and a tubular floral bract carrying the flower at or just below leaf height. The flowers are triangular, white, with a small labellum partly hidden deep inside the flower and three large sepals fused along their edges each with a long tail. It is distinguished by three conspicuous, dark purple calli at the apex of the lip in the centre.

Distribution: Peru.
Height and spread: Low creeper.
Habit and form: Epiphyte.
Pollinated: Insect.
Leaf shape: Ovate to elliptical.

Left: The plant may grow on trees, rocks or in the ground.

Scarlet Maxillaria

Ornithidium coccineum syn. *Maxillaria coccinea*

This epiphytic orchid species is found in montane forests in the Greater and Lesser Antilles. The flowers, which are usually red, are held in dense clusters, often tucked under the foliage, and are characterized by three fleshy sepals arranged in a triangular fashion. The style and stamens are fused together and curved over in jaw-like fashion over the lip.

Identification: The rhizome is covered in overlapping, papery sheaths. The pseudobulbs are up to 4cm/1½in long; oval, compressed and one-leaved. The leaves, up to 35cm/14in long and 2.5cm/1in wide, are narrow, oblong, pointed or blunt-tipped, and folded at the base. The flowers, in clusters on wiry 5cm/2in stalks, are bright fuchsia-pink. Their sepals are about 12mm/½in in length, spreading, fleshy, oval to lance-shaped, tapering and concave. The petals, up to 8mm/⅜in long, are oval to lance-shaped, tapering or pointed. The lip, to 8mm/⅜in long, is fleshy and three-lobed. The capsule is beaked.

Distribution: Greater and Lesser Antilles.
Height and spread: 50cm/20in.
Habit and form: Epiphyte.
Pollinated: Insect.
Leaf shape: Linear oblong.

Left: Scarlet maxillaria may be found growing on trees in tropical regions. The small flowers dangle in bright clusters.

Left: The flowers of scarlet maxillaria can be seen from quite a distance, thanks to the bright red colour of the sepals.

Fringed Star Orchid

Epidendrum ciliare

This is a very widespread species of epiphytic orchid, ranging from the southern part of North America, Mexico, throughout the Caribbean and parts of South America. The pseudobulbs are oblong and compressed, with one or two leathery leaves. The erect clusters of waxy flowers, which can be extremely variable in size, are strongly fragrant at night. They appear all year round, with the best flowers in spring and early summer.

Distribution: Southern North America, Mexico, Caribbean and South America.
Height and spread: Creeping, not exceeding 15cm/6in.
Habit and form: Epiphyte.
Pollinated: Insect.
Leaf shape: Oblong-ligulate.

Identification: The pseudobulbs are tufted, cylindrical, up to 15cm/6in long, with one to three leaves at the tip of each. The leaves are up to 28cm/11in long, lance-shaped, leathery and glossy. The erect raceme, up to 30cm/1ft tall, bears a few or several flowers, with their stalks concealed by large, overlapping, purple-spotted sheaths. The flowers are large and very fragrant, with thin, tapering tepals up to 7.5cm/3in long, white to green or pale yellow. The white lip, joined to the basal half of the column and up to 5cm/2in long, is deeply three-lobed: the lateral lobes are flared and fringed and the mid-lobe is long and straight.

OTHER SPECIES OF NOTE

Laelia anceps
This native of Mexico and possibly Honduras grows on rocks and trees at the fringes of dense forests, and is extremely popular in cultivation. The large, 10cm/4in flowers are generally light lavender with a darker lip and throat and are borne in a cluster of between two and six blooms on the end of a long spike.

Zygopetalum intermedium

Found in the states of Santa Catarina to Espiritu Santo, Brazil, at elevations of 600–1,200m/2,000–4,000ft, this medium-sized, terrestrial or epiphytic orchid has long, erect, racemes with three to ten showy, fragrant, waxy, long-lived flowers, with a pale blue lip and maroon-spotted green sepals.

Epidendrum medusae
These flowers are most unusual in having a fleshy maroon lip with its margin deeply divided into a mass of filaments – hence the specific name, referring to the Greek Medusa with a head of writhing snakes.

Masdevallia stumpflei
This species grows among rocks in the Peruvian Andes. It produces bright red flowers with a characteristic three-lobed appearance. Many species and hybrids are now available and they are not difficult to grow.

Spider Orchid

Brassia longissima

This epiphytic orchid is found in the rainforests of Costa Rica and is considered to be a variety of *B. lawrenciana* by some authorities. However, it differs from that species principally in its longer, tail-like sepals. The flowers are very striking and strangely scented, and appear on pendent racemes of six or more, borne at the start of the rainy season.

Identification: The pseudobulbs, up to 10cm/4in long, are oblong, laterally compressed and glossy pale green, usually with two leaves growing from the tip. The leaves are up to 40cm/16in long, narrowly oblong to lance-shaped, pointed or tapering. The raceme is arching to pendent, often surpassing the leaves, with thin textured flowers with very long, twisting, pale green or yellow tepals, striped red-purple at the base, often with inrolled margins; the lip is up to 4.5cm/1¾in long, white to pale green or pale yellow, fiddle-shaped with a long, tapering tip.

Distribution: Costa Rica.
Height and spread: Creeping, not exceeding 10cm/4in.
Habit and form: Epiphyte.
Pollinated: Insect.
Leaf shape: Narrowly oblong.

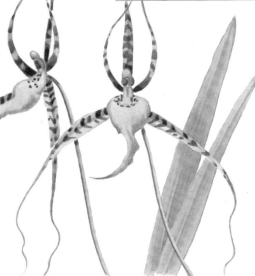

Dracula Orchid

Dracula vampira

This rather sinister-named orchid is one of over 60 species in the genus. The name actually translates as 'little dragon' and refers to the spurs on the sepals. It has unusual flowers, bat-like in some species and in this case very dark; almost black. The background colour to the flowers is actually green, but this is overlain by very dark purple-black stripes and smudges. In the wild this orchid is restricted to the forests of a single mountain (Mount Pichincha) in Ecuador at altitudes up to 2,000m/6,550ft. It grows as an epiphyte on the branches of trees. It can be grown in moist shady conditions, ideally in a basket with bark and compost and may flower throughout the year.

Above and right: The white lip petal is surrounded by dramatic, dark and tapering sepals.

Identification: The leaves are up to about 28cm/11½in long, and each inflorescence stalk has several flowers, each of which up to 30cm/12in long and 15cm/6in wide. The strange flowers have rounded sepals, each ending in a thin tail, up to 11cm/4½in long. The much smaller petals and lip are white with purple or pink veins. The flowers dangle down below the main plant, which is usually found growing on tree branches.

Distribution: Ecuador
Height and spread: 30cm/12in.
Habit and form: Pendulous epiphyte.
Pollinated: Insect.
Leaf shape: Fleshy.

Left: The flowers extend some distance from the rosette of leaves, on elegant, slender stalks.

Lindley's Barkeria

Barkeria lindleyana

Most of the approximately fifteen species of these fine rainforest orchids are threatened in the wild. This species is one of the most beautiful, with its large pink, purple or white flowers opening on arching stems, each carrying up to twenty flowers. It grows in montane forests, where there is a dry season in the winter. It also appears sometimes in nearby gardens. It requires bright sunny conditions with good air circulation, but also high humidity, regular feeding, and a resting dry period. The name commemorates two people: George Barker (1880–1965), an Edwardian orchid collector, and John Lindley (1799–1865), a famous botanist.

Distribution: Mexico and Costa Rica.
Height and spread: Stems to 60cm/2ft.
Habit and form: Epiphyte.
Pollinated: Insect.
Leaf shape: Linear-lanceolate.

Left: There are up to 20 flowers on each stem.

Identification: Each flower can be 8cm/3in across and remain open for several months. 'Bulbs' (technically pseudobulbs) grow to about 15cm/6in, cane-like. The leaves are sometimes tinted rosy pink. The flowers range from white to pink or deep purple, with the lip a darker shade.

Broughtonia sanguinea

This genus contains just five species from the West Indies. This Jamaican species is a small, compact orchid treasured for its bright red flowers, borne on long arching stems. It grows in low-altitude rainforest. A healthy plant will produce flowering spikes through much of the year. It grows best in a well-drained pot or on an epiphyte slab, in bright sun and should be well fed and watered when actively growing. Older plants can be rejuvenated by removing the roots. It needs warm conditions (minimum 20°C/68°F), high light and high humidity. It has been used to produce hybrids with species of Cattleya, the products being known as cattleytonias.

Distribution: Jamaica.
Height and spread: Leaves to 18cm/7in.
Habit and form: Epiphytic orchid.
Pollinated: Insect.
Leaf shape: Narrow-oblong.

Right: The flower has a prominent, rounded lip.

Identification: It has a compact cluster of small, flat pseudobulbs, each with two or three small leathery leaves. The flowerheads reach about 30cm/12in long and grow from the tips of the 'bulbs'.

Above: The psuedobulbs are covered in a papery skin. The petals are deep scarlet.

OTHER SPECIES OF NOTE

Christmas Cattleya *Cattleya trianae*
A winter-flowering species that is now rare in its Colombian rainforest home, but very popular in cultivation, both as the species and in various hybrid forms. The genus contains about 70 species, many of them epiphytes. The flowers are pinkish or white with a crimson central lobe and yellow disc.

Cattleya bowringiana
A popular species from Guatemala and Belize, this grows in soil, on rocks and also as an epiphyte on branches. It produces up to 25 flowers per spike. These are usually rose–lavender, but there are varieties with flowers almost white, and nearly blue.

Lepanthes calodictyon
A diminutive orchid from Peru that is unusual in being valued for its decorative leaves rather than its flowers. The flowers are tiny and bright red and yellow, contrasting with the emerald green leaves, which have brown veins. In its northern Andean home, it is an epiphyte on trees at elevations of 750–1,300m/2,450–4,250ft.

Nun's Orchid *Lycaste skinneri*
One of a genus named after plant hunter George Ure Skinner (1804–1867). The flowers may be white, pink or lavender. The white sepals look like a nun's veil, hence the common name. It is the national flower of Guatemala.

Ondoglossum crispum

This species, one of about 100 in the genus, is one of the most highly prized of all orchids and was at the centre of the orchid-mania in Victorian times. It was discovered by Karl Theodor Hartweg in 1841, and grows in cloud forest in Colombia. It was savagely over-collected and specimens fetched huge prices in Europe. As a result of this and of forest clearance it is now much rarer in the wild, though still popular and abundant in collections. The species name refers to the crinkly edges of the flower parts.

Identification: The flowering stems are arched with three or four large sparkling white flowers. The petals and sepals have toothed or uneven margins and the lip is usually blotched red with a yellow centre.

Distribution: Colombia.
Height and spread: 1m/3ft.
Habit and form: Epiphytic orchid.
Pollinated: Insect.
Leaf shape: Linear-lanceolate.

Above: The lip has distinctive yellow and red markings.

Far left and centre: The bud, and the arching raceme of stunning flowers, which grow from pseudobulbs.

Holy Ghost Orchid

Dove Orchid *Peristeria elata*

This fine large orchid is the national flower of Panama, where it was previously much commoner than it is now. A combination of local picking, collection for the overseas orchid trade, and habitat destruction has resulted in its decline in the wild. The flowers are often used to decorate churches at Easter. It grows mainly on the ground in leaf litter, from sea level to about 600m/2,000ft. The inner parts of the strongly-scented flowers resemble a white dove with its wings raised. The Dove Orchid is best grown in shallow clay pots with a well-draining leafy substrate, and kept moist in the growing season.

Identification: The slender flower-stalks each carry 10-15 fragrant flowers, each with five overlapping white, waxy petals surrounding a dove-shaped central structure.

Distribution: Costa Rica, Panama, Venezuela and Colombia.
Height and spread: Flower stalk to 1.5m/5ft.
Habit and form: Terrestrial orchid.
Pollinated: Insect.
Leaf shape: Elliptic-lanceolate.

Left: The pseudobulbs can get large with maturity, about the size of tennis balls.

Left: The white flowers bloom sequentially on the tall spike. It usually flowers in late spring.

Phragmipedium besseae

Identification: The vivid scarlet (sometimes orange or yellow) flowers are the main feature of this orchid. The dark green foliage produces a stalk with one to six flowers that open in sequence. Each flower is about 5cm/2in across.

The 20 species in this genus are often called tropical slipper orchids, because of the shape of the flower. This species was first found in Peru but may now be extinct there, although it still grows in Ecuador. Its natural habitat is close to running water, such as along the banks of streams, among mosses and humus. It was over collected after its discovery in 1981 and then fetched very high prices. Now it has been produced from seed in large numbers so pressure on the wild stocks has been reduced. In cultivation it should be watered with pure mineral-free water, or rainwater; tap water may cause damage. It has been used to produce many hybrids with a range of varied flower colours.

Distribution: Colombia, Ecuador, (Peru).
Height and spread: 25cm/10in.
Habit and form: Terrestrial orchid.
Pollinated: Insect.
Leaf shape: Narrow.

Right: The bud, drooping from the elegant stem.

Left and right: Flower spikes are sent forth from the rosette of lush, tapering leaves. The flowers are vivid in colour and have a slipper-shaped lip. Over collection due to its beauty, as well as loss of habitat have devastated this species, and it is now endangered.

Sophronitis lobata

Distribution: Brazil.
Height and spread: Flower spikes to 35cm/14in.
Habit and form: Epiphytic or terrestrial orchid.
Pollinated: Insect.
Leaf shape: Ovate-oblong.

This fine orchid has large, rather elaborate and ornate flowers and is therefore very popular among enthusiast growers. As with many orchids, this trade has led to its decline in its native wild sites near Rio de Janeiro in Brazil, in this case rock outcrops and as an epiphyte on the branches of trees. Artificial propagation has meant that this splendid orchid is now widely available from specialist orchid nurseries in many countries. Fortunately it is relatively trouble-free to grow, although not always easy to bring into flower.

Identification: A small orchid with fleshy leaves. Each club-shaped 'bulb' is 10–20cm/4–8in tall and produces a single leaf. The flower spikes grow from spring to early summer and each has six or more flowers. The individual flowers are as large as 15cm/6in across and pure white with spreading outer lobes.

Right and below:
The flowers are large and have an attractive spreading shape, but the overall plant is fairly small, with a single leaf.

Right: The smooth and club-shaped bulb.

OTHER SPECIES OF NOTE

Phragmipedium caudatum
This plant is normally an epiphyte. Its flowers have ribbon-like red-tinted spiralling petals that may be as long as 60cm/24in. The rest of the flower is greenish, with a pink and yellow slipper-shaped lip. It grows from Mexico to Peru.

Pleurothallis tuerkheimii
This grows from Mexico to Panama. It belongs to one of the largest of all orchid genera, with over 1100 species. It is one of the more widespread species and usually grows as an epiphyte. It is also fairly easy to grow and produces a many-flowered inflorescence with maroon and white flowers.

Sophronitis jongheana
Discovered in 1854, this species hails from Brazil. It grows as an epiphyte in rainforests, at altitudes of 1,300–1,600m/4,250–5,250ft. The magnificent flowers are to 15cm/6in across, and a delicate pale pink. Plants can easily be grown from seed, and many hybrid forms have been bred from this species.

Vanilla *Vanilla planifolia*
Familiar from the flavouring prepared from the dried fruit pods, vanilla is native to South and Central America and the West Indies, although it is now widely cultivated as a crop. It is a scrambling vine, clambering up tree trunks. The flowers are large and yellow or green and last only a short time, often less than a day.

Stanhopea tigrina

The elaborate flowers of this epiphyte look more like a tropical coral reef fish than a rainforest orchid. They produce a sweet fragrance, attractive to pollinating insects. Although each flower lasts only a few days, large plants produce many flowers in succession. The major pollinators are bees, and the complex structure of the flower carefully guides each bee, ensuring pollen sticks to its body. In cultivation it grows best in a slatted basket lined with tree bark or coconut fibre. The flowering shoots appear from under the basket.

Identification: The egg-shaped 'bulbs' are up to 6cm/2½in tall and the single ribbed leaf measures about 35x12cm/14x4in. The flowers are large and complex, creamy-yellow with purple-brown tiger-stripes and blotches.

Below: Large plants may produce several flowers in succession.

Distribution: Mexico.
Height and spread: Leaf to 35cm/14in.
Habit and form: Epiphytic orchid.
Pollinated: Insect
Leaf shape: Elliptic-lanceolate.

Left and below:
The buds open to reveal showy flowers.

GLOSSARY

Annual a plant which completes its entire life-cycle within a year.

Anther the pollen-bearing portion of the stamen.

Areole elevation on a cactus stem, bearing a spine.

Axil the upper angle between an axis and any off-shoot or lateral organ arising from it, especially a leaf.

Axillary situated in, or arising from, or pertaining to, an axil.

Basal leaf arising from the rootstock or a very short or buried stem.

Beak a long, pointed, horn-like projection; particularly applied to the terminal points of fruits and pistils.

Beaked furnished with a beak (above).

Beard (on flower) a tuft or zone of hair as on the falls of bearded irises.

Berry indehiscent (non-drying) fruit, one- to many-seeded; the product of a single pistil. Frequently misapplied to any pulpy or fleshy fruit regardless of its constitution.

Biennial lasting for two seasons from germination to death, generally blooming in the second season.

Boss-like (of the standard) Taking on the appearance of a boss (round metal stud in the centre of a shield or ornamental work).

Bract a modified protective leaf associated with the inflorescence (clothing the stalk and subtending the flowers), with buds and with newly emerging shoots.

Branched rootstock a branching underground stem.

Bromeliad a member of the pineapple family (Bromeliaceae). Most bromeliads

Below: *Shepherd's Purse* (Capsella bursa-pastoris) *in bloom.*

are native to South America, and many of them grow as epiphytes on tree branches.

Calcicole a plant dwelling on and favouring calcareous (lime-rich) soils.

Calcifuge a plant avoiding and damaged by calcareous soils.

Callus ridge (calli) superficial protuberances on the lip of many orchid flowers.

Capsule (of fruit) a dry (dehiscent) seed vessel.

Carpet-forming with a dense, ground-hugging habit; hence "carpet-like".

Cauline (of leaves) attached to or arising from the stem.

Chlorophyll green pigment that facilitates food production and is present in most plants.

Cleistogamous with self-pollination occurring in the closed flower.

Climbing habit any plant that climbs or has a tendency to do so, usually by means of various adaptations of stems, leaves or roots.

Clubbed spur a tubular or sac-like basal extension of a flower, generally projecting backward and containing nectar, gradually thickening upward from a slender base.

Clump-forming forming a tight mass of close-growing stems or leaves at or near ground level.

Column (of the flower) a feature of orchids, where the style and stamens are fused together in a single structure.

Composite (of flowers and leaves) a single leaf or petal divided in such a way as to resemble many.

Compound (of flowers and leaves) divided into two or more subsidiary parts.

Contractile roots roots which contract in length and pull parts of a plant further into the soil.

Convex petal with an outline or shape like that of the exterior of a sphere.

Cordate heart-shaped.

Cormous perennial a plant or stem base living for two or more years with a solid, swollen, subterranean, bulb-like stem.

Corolla a floral envelope composed of free or fused petals.

Corona a crown or cup-like appendage

Above: The blooms of the Cannon-ball Tree (Couroupita guianensis).

or ring of appendages.

Corymb an indeterminate flat-topped or convex inflorescence, where the outer flowers open first.

Creeping habit trailing on or under the surface, and sometimes rooting.

Culms the stems of grasses.

Cupped (flowers) shaped like a cup.

Curving spur a tubular or sac-like basal extension of a flower, generally projecting backward and containing nectar, being curved in shape.

Cyathia flower form, shaped like a cup.

Cylindrical follicle cylindrical elongated fruit, virtually circular in cross-section.

Cyme (flowers) a more or less flat-topped and determinate flowerhead, with the central or terminal flower opening first.

Decumbent base (of the stem) lying horizontally along the ground but with the apex ascending and almost erect.

Decurrent where the base of a leaf extends down to the petiole (if any) and the stem.

Deeply cut petals or leaves with deeply incised lobes.

Deeply segmented petals or leaves that are sharply divided into several segments.

Dehiscent the opening of a plant structure at maturity, such as a ripe fruit to release its seeds, or an anther to release its pollen.

Deltoid an equilateral triangle attached by the broad end rather than the point; shaped like the Greek letter delta.

Dilated concavity dilating, broadened, expanded, in the manner of the outer

Below: Sweet Fennel (foeniculum vulgare) *has a delicate aniseed fragrance.*

surface of a sphere.

Dioecious with male and female flowers on different plants.

Disc floret part of the central flowerhead in the Asteraceae. Short tubular florets as opposed to the peripheral ray florets.

Dissected leaf shape cut in any way; a term applicable to leaf blades or other flattened organs that are incised.

Domed flowerhead Compound flowerhead arranged in a dome shape.

Drupe a one- to several-seeded fruit, contained within a soft, fleshy, pericarp, as in stone fruits.

Ellipsoid resembling an ellipse shape.

Epidermis the outer layer of plant tissue; skin.

Epiphytic growing on plants without being parasitic.

Ericaceous in broad terms, resembling *Erica* spp. In habit, plants preferring acidic soil conditions.

Evergreen plant with foliage that remains green for at least a year, through more than one growing season.

Farinose having a mealy, granular texture on the surface.

Filament stalk that bears the anther at its tip, together forming a stamen.

Floret a very small flower, generally part of a congested inflorescence.

Genus the first name of a plant described under the binomial system of botanical naming.

Glandular bearing glands, or hairs with gland-like prominence at the tip.

Glandular inflorescence a compound flowerhead with a glandular surface.

Glycoside a compound related to sugar that plays many important roles in living organisms, with numerous plant-produced glycosides used as medications.

Hastate arrow-shaped, triangular, with two equal and approximately triangular basal lobes, pointing laterally outward rather than toward the stalk.

Haustorium a sucker in parasitic plants that penetrates the host.

Hemi-parasite only parasitic for part of its life cycle; not entirely dependent upon the host for nutrition.

Hemispheric a half sphere shape.

Herb abbreviation for herbaceous. Not the culinary herb.

Herbaceous pertaining to herbs, i.e. lacking persistent aerial parts or lacking woody parts.

Herbaceous perennial herbaceous plant living for three or more years. Referred to as herb.

Hip the fleshy, developed floral cup and the enclosed seeds of a rose.

Hooded flowers one or more petals, fused and forming a hood over the sexual reproductive parts of the flower.

Hooked spurs a tubular or sac-like basal extension of a flower, generally projecting backwards and containing nectar; being hooked in shape.

Inflorescences the arrangement of flowers and their accessory parts in multiple heads, on a central axis or stem.

Keeled (leaves) a prominent ridge, like the keel of a boat, running longitudinally down the centre of the undersurface of a leaf.

Labellum a lip, especially the enlarged or otherwise distinctive third petal of an orchid.

Layering stems rooting on contact with the earth and forming colonies of cloned plants.

Leaf
   Lobed divided into (usually rounded) segments, lobes, separated from adjacent segments.
   Toothed possessing teeth, often qualified, as saw-toothed or bluntly toothed.

Uneven margins with one margin exceeding the one opposite.

Wavy margin having a wavy edge.

Leaf axil the point immediately above the point of leaf attachment, often containing a bud.

Leaf tip
   pointed ending in a distinct point.
   rounded with no visible point.

Leaflet units of a compound leaf.

Lenticel elliptical and raised cellular pore on the surface of bark or the surface tissue of fruit, through which gases can penetrate.

Liana a woody climbing vine.

Lignotuber a starchy swelling on underground stems or roots, often used to survive fire or browsing animals.

Lip petal, or part thereof, which is either modified or differentiated from the others, on which insects can alight.

Lithophytic growing on rocks or stony soil, deriving nourishment from the atmosphere rather than the soil.

Low-growing plants that do not reach any significant height; ground hugging.

Membranous capsule seedpod with thin walls.

Mesic a type of habitat with a moderate or well-balanced supply of moisture, e.g. a mesic forest.

Midrib the primary vein of a leaf or leaflet, usually running down its centre as a continuation of the leaf stem.

Monocarpic dying after flowering and bearing fruit only once.

Monopedal a stem or rhizome in which growth continues indefinitely from the apical or terminal bud, and generally exhibits no secondary branching.

Below: The pretty bloom of Herb Robert (Geranium robertianum).

Above: Purple Morning Glory (Ipomoea purpurea) *is a South American native.*

Monoecious A plant with both male and female flowers/flower parts on the same plant (Syn. Hermaphrodite).

Morphologically pertaining to the study of the form of plants.

Mucilage viscous substance obtained from plant seeds exposed to water.

Nectary a gland, often in the form of a protuberance or depression, which secretes and sometimes absorbs nectar.

Node the point on a stem where one or more leaves, shoots, whorls, branches or flowers are attached.

Open habit growing loosely with space between the branches.

Panicle indeterminate branched inflorescence, the branches generally resemble racemes or corymbs.

Pea-like flowers that are like those of the pea (*Pisum* spp.).

Pendent hanging downward, more markedly than arching or nodding but not as a result of the weight of the part in question or the weakness of its attachment or support.

Pendent raceme raceme inflorescence with a pendent habit.

Pendulous branch branch with a pendent habit.

Perennial a plant lasting for three seasons or more.

Perfoliate a sessile leaf of which the basal lobes are united, the stem seems to pass through the blade.

Perianth the collective term for the floral envelopes, the corolla and calyx, especially when the two are not clearly differentiated.

Perianth tube the effect of fused petals resulting in a tubular flower shape.

Petaloid sepal segment that encloses the flower when in bud that resembles a true petal.

Petaloid tepal tepal that resembles a petal.

Photosynthesis the synthesis of sugar and oxygen from carbon dioxide and water, carried out by all green plants.

Pinnate feather-like; an arrangement of more than three leaflets in two rows.

Pinnatifid pinnately cleft nearly to the midrib in broad divisions, but without separating into distinct leaflets or pinnae.

Pistil the female reproductive organs of a flower with one or more carpel.

Pod appendage containing seeds:

  Inflated pod fruits that are inflated and balloon like.

  Cylindrical pod elongated fruits, virtually circular in cross-section.

  Flattened distinctly flattened along one plane.

Pinnatisect shape deeply and pinnately cut to, or near to, the midrib; the divisions, narrower than in pinnatifid, are not truly distinct segments.

Pouched bracts a modified protective leaf associated with the inflorescence and possessing a pouched shape.

Primary rays The outer petaloid rays, usually associated with a composite flower such as those in Asteraceae.

Procumbent trailing loosely or lying flat along the surface of the ground, without rooting.

Prostrate lying flat on the ground.

Pseudobulb the water-storing thickened "bulb-like" stem found in many sympodial orchids.

Pseudostem not a true stem but made up of leaf sheaths.

Quadrangular stem four-angled, as in

Below: Plumeria rubra *is a red variety of Frangipani, better known for its white blooms.*

the stems of some *Passiflora*.

Raceme an indeterminate, un-branched and elongate inflorescence composed of flowers in stalks.

Ramicaul thin leaf stem usually associated with orchids.

Rambling habit an unruly spreading or partially climbing growth habit.

Ray floret a small flower with a tubular corolla and the limb expanded and flattened in a strap-like blade, usually occupying the outer rings of a capitulum (daisy flower).

Reflexed abruptly flexed at more than a 90 degree angle.

Reniform kidney shaped.

Reniform scale kidney-shaped leaf scale.

Rhizome underground stem.

Rhizomatous producing or possessing rhizomes; rhizome-like.

Rhombic ovate oval to diamond-shaped; angularly oval, the base and apex forming acute angles.

Root sucker stem arising directly from the roots of a parent plant.

Rootstock the roots and stem base of a plant.

Rosette forming leaves arranged in a basal rosette or rosettes.

Runcinate a leaf, petal or petal-like structure, usually oblanceolate in outline and with sharp, prominent teeth or broad, incised lobes pointing backward toward the base, away from a generally acute apex, as in *Taraxacum* (dandelion).

Runner prostrate or recumbent stem, taking root and giving rise to a plantlet at its apex and sometimes at nodes.

Sagittate arrow- or spear-shaped, where the equal and approximately triangular basal lobes of leaves point downward or toward the stalk.

Saprophytic deriving its nutrition from dissolved or decayed organic matter.

Scalloped rounded in outline in the manner of a scallop shell.

Scape an erect, leafless stalk, supporting an inflorescence or flower.

Scrambling habit not strictly climbing but vigorous with a tendency to grow over surrounding vegetation.

Seed ripened, fertilized ovule; an embryonic plant.

Seedhead describes the fruiting bodies of a plant.

Seedpod describes the enclosing body around developing seeds.

Semipendent flowerhead only partially pendent in nature.

Sepal modified leaf-like structure, enclosing and protecting the inner floral parts prior to its opening.

Serrated toothed margin, with teeth resembling those of a saw.

Shrub a loose descriptive term for a woody plant which produces multiple stems, shoots or branches from its base, but does not have a single trunk.

Shrublet a small shrub or a dwarf, woody-based and closely branched plant.

Sickle-shaped crescent-shaped.

Single flowers with one set of petals.

Solitary flowers borne singly (i.e. not in an inflorescence).

Spadix (Spadisces pl.) a fleshy, columnar flower, often enclosed in a spathe and typical of plants in the family Araceae.

Spathe a conspicuous leaf or bract subtending a spadix or other inflorescence.

Spathulate spatula-shaped, essentially oblong, but attenuated at the base and rounded at the apex.

Species name the second name used to identify a plant with particular characteristics under the binomial system of botanical naming.

Spike an indeterminate inflorescence bearing sessile flowers on an un-branched axis.

Sprawling spreading untidily.

Spreading stems or branches extending horizontally outward.

Spur a tubular or sac-like basal extension of the flower, projecting backward and often containing nectar.

Stalked a general term for the stem-like

Below: The distinctive foliage of Agrimony (Agrimonia gryposepela).

support of any organ.

Stamen the male floral organ, bearing an anther, generally on a filament, and producing pollen.

Staminode sterile stamen or stamen-like structure, often rudimentary or modified, sometimes petal-like and frequently antherless.

Standard (1) in pea flowers, the large, uppermost petal; (2) an erect or ascending unit of the inner whorl of an *Iris* flower.

Stigma the end of a pistil that receives the pollen and normally differs in texture from the rest of the style.

Stipule leafy or bract-like appendage at the base of a leaf stem, usually occurring in pairs and soon shed.

Stolon a prostrate or recumbent stem, taking root and giving rise to plantlets at its apex and sometimes at nodes.

Stoloniferous possessing stolons.

Straggly untidy, rather stretched in appearance.

Subopposite more or less opposite, but with one leaf or leaflet of a pair slightly above or below its partner.

Suborbicular more or less circular.

Subshrub a perennial with a woody base and soft shoots.

Subspecies a species further divided into distinct populations.

Succulent thickly cellular and fleshy.

Suckering shrub shrub with a tendency to produce root suckers as part of its normal growth.

Tendril a modified branch, leaf or axis, filiform, scandent, and capable of attaching itself to a support either by twining or adhesion.

Tepal perianth segment that cannot be defined as either petal or sepal.

Terminal at the tip or apex of a stem.

Terrestrial living on land; growing in the soil.

Tessellated chequered, composed of small squares as in the flower of *Fritillaria meleagris* or the intersecting vein pattern of some leaves.

Thorn sharp hard outgrowth from the stem wood.

Throat the central opening of tubular or bell-shaped flowers.

Toothed margin leaf edge possessing teeth, often qualified, as saw-toothed or bluntly toothed.

Trailing prostrate but not rooting.

Above: The delicate blooms of Soapwort, or Bouncing Bet (Saponaria officinalis).

Trefoil leaf divided into three leaflets.

Trifoliate three-leaved.

Tuberoid in the manner of a tuber.

Tuberous bearing tubers, tuberous-bearing tubers, or resembling a tuber.

Tulip-shaped similar shape to the flower of a tulip.

Tussock-forming forming a tight mass of close growing stems or leaves at or near ground level, with grass-like leaves.

Twining vine a climbing plant that twines around a support.

Two-lipped (flower) with two lips.

Umbellate resembling an umbel.

Umbel a flat-topped inflorescence like a corymb, but with all the flowered pedicels (rays) arising from the same point at the apex of the main axis.

Unisexual a flower that is either male or female.

Upright a flowerhead that is held vertically or nearly so.

Upright habit Growth that is vertical or nearly so.

Variety a distinct population that does not merit the status of species or sub-species in its own right.

Vein/veinlets an externally visible strand of vascular tissue.

Vestigial a leaf that was functional and fully developed in ancestral forms, but is now smaller and less developed.

Vine a general term to describe some climbing plants.

Whorl when three or more organs are arranged in a circle at one node or, loosely, around the same axis.

Woody ligneous (containing the plant protein lignin), approaching the nature of wood.

INDEX

Below: A phragmipedium orchid, with showy sepals.

Above: Mountain Avens (*Dryas octopetala*).

Below: Tiger Lily (Lilium columbianum) in full bloom.